'A blockbuster . . . a roller-coaster read' – *Daily Express*

'An exciting, well-told tale . . . Inspirational stuff' – *ME Magazine*

'An accomplished debut' – *Publishing News*

'Look to your laurels, Jilly Cooper, Barbara Taylor Bradford et al . . .' – *What's On*

'Lucinda Edmonds is Britain's most exciting young new novelist' – *Girl About Town*

Other books by Lucinda Edmonds

Hidden Beauty
Enchanted
Not Quite an Angel

Lucinda Edmonds trained as an actress. She made a sensational debut with her first novel, *Lover & Players*, which was followed by *Hidden Beauty*, *Enchanted* and, most recently, *Not Quite an Angel*. She lives in the Leicestershire countryside, and is currently working on her fifth novel.

Lovers & Players

LUCINDA EDMONDS

POCKET BOOKS

New York   London   Toronto   Sydney   Tokyo   Singapore

This book is a work of fiction. Names, characters,
places and incidents are either the product of the author's
imagination or are used fictitiously.
Any resemblance to actual events or locales
or persons, living or dead, is entirely coincidental.

First published in Great Britain by
Simon & Schuster in 1992
First published by Pocket Books,
an imprint of Simon & Schuster Ltd, in 1993
A Paramount Communications Company

Copyright © Lucinda Edmonds, 1992

This book is copyright under the Berne Convention.
No reproduction without permission.
All rights reserved.

The right of Lucinda Edmonds to be identified as author of this
work has been asserted in accordance with sections 77 and 78 of the
Copyright Designs and Patents Act 1988.

Simon & Schuster Ltd
West Garden Place
Kendal Street
London W2 2AQ

Simon & Schuster of Australia Pty Ltd
Sydney

Excerpts from 'Love Changes Everything' from
Aspects of Love; music: Andrew Lloyd Webber
lyrics: Don Black and Charles Hart
© Copyright 1988, The Really Useful Group Ltd, London.
Reproduced by kind permission of copyright owners.

Excerpts from 'Not While I'm Around' (Sondheim)
© Copyright Warner Chappell Music Ltd.
Reproduced by kind permission.

A CIP catalogue record for this book is
available from the British Library.

ISBN 0-671-85525-5

Typeset in Baskerville 10/13
by The Electronic Book Factory Ltd, Fife, Scotland

Printed in Great Britain by
HarperCollins Manufacturing, Glasgow

For Owen

September 1977

Overture and Beginners

> 'Love,
> Love changes everything:
> Hands and faces,
> Earth and sky,
> Love,
> Love changes everything:
> How you live and
> How you die.'

DON BLACK AND CHARLES HART,
Aspects of Love

1

SHE SLOWLY MADE HER WAY up the crowded London Underground escalator. Her ill-fitting dress could not conceal the small but perfectly proportioned body beneath. As she stepped out on to the pavement, the autumn breeze caught her long blonde hair. Her pale porcelain skin was flushed in anticipation. Others stared, but she did not notice.

She stopped in front of the nondescript building, then joined the crowd of young people pushing up the steps. Once inside, she stood in the crowded lobby, unsure of what to do next.

'All new students please go through the blue doors and wait in the theatre for Mr Holmes.' A man was trying to make himself heard above the noisy throng.

She followed others through the doors. The small auditorium was filling up, with most of the seats nearest the stage already occupied. She slipped into the back row and sat down next to a girl who seemed to be asleep. Her presence disturbed the girl, who rubbed her eyes and started rummaging through her pockets.

'Excuse me, but have you got a light?' The American drawl was unmistakable.

'No, I'm sorry, I don't smoke.'

'It's okay, I found them.' The girl lifted a tattered book of matches triumphantly from her pocket and, despite the 'No Smoking' signs, proceeded to light up.

'Hi, Frankie Duvall.' The girl stretched out her hand.

'Jenna Short, nice to meet you. Which year are you in? You look as though you've been here a while.'

'Oh no, first day today. My pop used to grace these hallowed portals a few centuries ago. I'm on the two-year drama course, Group B.'

'I'm in Group B, too.'

'Good to meet a fellow classmate.' Frankie stretched and sighed. 'Boy, am I wrecked! I drank so much on the plane coming over yesterday that I knew if I didn't get up at six this morning, shower and have ten cups of coffee and twenty cigarettes, I'd never make it to this joint on time.'

Jenna watched her in fascination. She was beautiful, with chestnut eyes and raven hair that curled effortlessly around her heart-shaped face. 'You're an American then?'

'You mean I have an accent? Jesus, that'll never do in a building where Laurence Olivier used to go to the john!' She laughed. 'As a matter of fact I'm one hundred per cent pure English, but I was born in the States and seem to have picked up their accent. Christ! I haven't been up this early since Pops had his last divorce hearing!'

'Excuse me, is that seat taken?'

Jenna turned to her left. A girl with a freckled face and ginger hair, who was wearing a dress that did nothing to hide her short rotund figure, was pointing to the seat next to her.

'No, it isn't,' Jenna replied.

'Come and join the sleepy-time gang at the back,' said Frankie.

'Thanks awfully'. The girl smiled, showing a large set of white teeth, and sat down in the chair next to Jenna. 'Bettina Langdale, super to meet you both. I'm on the two-year drama course, how about you two?'

'The same,' Frankie answered.

A bell rang.

'I'm jolly nervous about this, aren't you?' whispered Bettina.

Before Jenna had time to reply, the doors behind them opened and a tall, elegant man dressed in a tweed jacket and paisley bow tie made his way to the front and mounted the steps to the stage. A hush fell over the now full auditorium. Frankie ground out her cigarette on the floor.

Theodore Holmes surveyed the new intake with interest from his position on the stage. A couple of beauties in the back row, one dark and the other fair, like the Gypsy and the Rose. Of course, women were not his preference, but that had never stopped him appreciating beauty. He remembered each from their audition, and the girl with the ginger hair sitting next to them. Her father was Lord Langdale, a patron, and a generous one at that, of the school.

Theodore Holmes had run the British School of Drama for twenty-five years. He had nurtured the prestigious reputation that attracted the foreign students whose substantial fees made possible the generous scholarships available to British students. In the past few years the profession had changed a lot, and not for the better in his opinion. Newfangled approaches to teaching, less emphasis on the classics and people rising to stardom in a fifteen-second commercial.

Looking down at the eager faces, he wondered if even one of them had any idea what kind of a profession they were entering. He doubted it. He knew that only one or two – if they were lucky – would make it through the next few years to rise to the very top of the hardest profession there was.

But that was the reason he stayed. The discovery of new talent was the most exciting feeling in the world, and the one thing that kept him going, year after year. For among this bunch of youngsters, there was always the possibility . . .

Theodore Holmes cleared his throat. 'Good morning, ladies and gentlemen. It's a pleasure to welcome you all to the British School of Drama. I hope that your time with us will be both happy and productive. I do not need to tell you that all of you have been chosen for the promise you showed at your auditions. This school is regarded as the best. That does not necessarily mean we produce Oliviers and Bernhardts every year, but that the actors who leave this school are professionals. Acting is ninety per cent discipline, five per cent talent and the rest, unfortunately beyond this school's control, is luck. We can provide the tools you will need to do your future job to the best of your ability, but how much you actually learn while you are here is down to you.

'Now, as to classes. There is a large and complicated timetable in the lobby. You are all members of a specific group which has been given an individual colour. Each class has been colour-coded to show when you should be where. Lastly, may I just say that I hope our faith in you is justified, not just by us who will help you, but by the hard work you will put in while you are here. I wish all of you success, both now and in the future.'

'Jesus! That improvisation lesson was a nightmare.' Frankie stood naked in the middle of the changing room, skin glowing from the hot shower she had just taken.

Jenna could not help but stare at her. Frankie had long supple legs, a slim waist and firm, full breasts that led to an elegant neck. Her height and poise made her eligible to grace any catwalk.

Jenna was staring because she had never before seen another girl naked. In the flat she shared with her mother, and at the small Catholic girls' school she had attended, nakedness was a sin. She hurried to put on her bra and knickers.

Frankie, meanwhile, still in the nude, and with a Lucky Strike hanging out of her mouth, was parading around the room, entertaining everyone with impressions of the tutors they had had that day.

'Hey, and get a load of Theo! That guy needs a good screw, but it isn't us girls that can satisfy him.'

'What on earth do you mean, Frankie?' asked Bettina.

'Don't you know? Theo's a faggot, a queer. He's gay, and I don't mean he's happy. Get my drift?'

She looked round at the uncomprehending faces and realized that none of them had any idea of what she was talking about.

'Okay, to spell it out in black and white, Theodore Holmes, principal of the most revered academy for dramatic art in Great Britain, is a homosexual. In other words, he prefers men! So, my sweet innocents, your first lesson in this oh so rotten profession: never think your female attributes will cut any ice with our principal – 'cos they won't!'

Jenna was dreading the thought of catching the tube back to the tiny, dismal flat where her mother would be waiting for her. So when Frankie asked if anyone wanted to join her for a coffee, she agreed immediately.

'Okay,' said Bettina.

They didn't have to walk far before Jenna noticed a small café on the other side of the road.

'A cappuccino for me with extra chocolate on top, and what do you guys want?'

'I'll have the same.'

'Me too,' said Jenna.

'Right, three cappuccinos with extra chocolate.' Frankie lit up a cigarette. 'So, how come you two wound up in the same class as me? You don't look like theatrical types.'

'I just want to be an actress,' said Jenna.

Frankie smiled. 'I suppose that's as good a reason as any to go to drama school.' She shrugged. 'Me, well, I've gone into the family business, the only daughter of a famed English actor who sold his soul to Hollywood and never returned to tread the boards again. My pop is Daniel Duvall, heard of him?'

'Heard of him?' Bettina exploded, nearly knocking over her cappuccino. 'He's my favourite actor. I've been to see most of his films at least five times. I'm in love with Daniel Duvall and I've wanted to marry him since I was six! Is he coming to see you soon?'

'Bettina, you really wouldn't want to marry him. He's been through three wives already, including my mother. I've had more "aunties" than you've had hot dinners! And dear old Pops is so busy being such a big famous movie star and stud that if I see him in the next year I'll be lucky. I never saw him when I lived in the same house as he did, so I doubt if he'll be flying over here to take his daughter to dinner.' Frankie lit up another cigarette. 'So,' she said, 'you guys don't smoke? No? I've been puffing away ever since I stole Auntie Cindy's pack when I was twelve. Anyway, we still haven't found out why you're here, Miss Langpot, or whatever your wacky English name is.'

'Langdale, actually,' said Bettina good-naturedly. 'Well, I suppose it was the more exciting option. I mean, better than secretarial college. And my pa is a patron of the school, so I thought, why not? Both my parents think it's a stage I'm going through and when it passes, I'll marry the right sort of chap. Personally, I don't think any of them would want me. I was definitely the ugliest deb of the season!' Bettina laughed and looked at her watch. 'I'd better be moving, actually, otherwise Gerry will be ringing my parents to say I've fallen into the hands of rogues and vagabonds.'

'Who's Gerry?' asked Frankie.

'Oh, my brother, the heir to the title, the family seat up in Yorkshire and an awful lot of cows and sheep! He works for a merchant bank and has been entrusted with keeping his baby sister out of trouble. I'm staying at his flat in Knightsbridge. Anyone want to share a cab in that direction?'

'No, I'm staying in an awful converted warehouse place my pop bought a couple of years back. It's not exactly what I'd call cosy but it does have a great view of the Thames. Are you going my way, Jenna?'

Jenna was feeling horribly out of place. The only time she had ever been to Knightsbridge was when her mother had taken her on a bus to see the Christmas lights that decorated the front of Harrods and that had been years ago. As for the Thames . . . she thought of the murky canal down the alleyway from her flat where she had been told by her mother never to venture.

'No thanks, Frankie, I live the other way.'

'Okay. Well, let's get the show on the road.' Frankie produced a five-pound note to pay for the coffees.

They walked outside and Frankie hailed a cab.

'See you both tomorrow. I'm going to get some shut-eye.'

The taxi disappeared off down the street.

'Come on, Jenna, I'll walk with you to the tube. What do you think of our American cousin?'

'I think she's, well, she's certainly different.'

'That's for sure,' Bettina smiled as they reached the entrance to the tube station. 'Good night, Jenna, see you tomorrow.'

2

JENNA TURNED THE KEY in the lock, opened the door and stepped into the tiny hall. She hung her coat on a peg before walking into the kitchen where her mother was sitting at the table, reading a paper.

Joyce Short was a small woman with greying hair and eyes that, although faded, were once the same striking blue as her daughter's. Her face still showed a hint of the pretty girl she had once been. Joyce looked up as Jenna entered.

'Well?'

'I'm sorry I'm late. I had a coffee with two of the girls in my class.'

'Your tea is in the oven, probably spoiled by now. When you've finished, wash up your plate, please. I'm going to watch television.'

The voice was flat and unemotional.

'Mother, I had a lovely day at school. I met this girl called Bettina whose father's a lord and someone called Frankie whose father is a famous –'

'Very nice, I'm sure, but next time, please let me know

if you intend to be in late so I don't waste my time cooking food that will be ruined.' With that, she picked up the paper and walked out of the kitchen.

Jenna sighed, went to the oven and took out the plate of mince and potatoes. Her mother was right, it was ruined. She had no appetite anyway, so she tipped it into the bin and rinsed her plate. She took an apple and a glass of milk and went into her bedroom. She switched on the light, shut the door, sank on to the bed and closed her eyes. This was her space, the only part of the world she could really call her own. She opened her eyes and gazed at the carefully framed pictures of her favourite actors and actresses. She thought of them as old friends, as the people she could trust and talk to when, once again, her mother didn't want to listen.

There had been many times since she had first decided that she must go to drama school when she was sure it would never happen. She had no idea why she felt that she wanted to be an actress; no bolt of lightning or particular incident to make her feel the way she did. Until her audition, the only people who had known about her dream were those now staring back at her from the walls.

There was only one drama school she had wanted to go to: the British School of Drama, where almost every great British actor had trained. In the biographies she had borrowed from her local library, all the actors talked about their time at the school with great fondness and respect.

So she had saved the ten-pound audition fee from her Saturday job at the shoe shop and sent off her application form, not daring to tell her mother. Shortly thereafter a letter arrived telling her of the date of her audition.

She'd had no idea what speeches she should do for an audition. The information provided on the form told her that she needed to perform something from Shakespeare and a modern speech. She had taken an excerpt from *Romeo and Juliet*, which she was working on for her English A level. Unsure of her modern speech, she had visited French's Theatrical Bookshop in Covent Garden and bought *Selected Audition Speeches for Actresses*. In that she had found a speech from a play called *The Diary of Anne Frank*.

Jenna worked on the speeches in her bedroom, keeping her voice down if she heard her mother in the hallway. She managed to take a day off school in early February, feigning illness, which had given her plenty of time to arrive for the audition at two that afternoon.

When she nervously entered the small studio, there were three people, two men and one woman, sitting at a long trestle table. She was asked to perform her Shakespeare speech first. As she took her opening position, her heart was banging so loudly that she was sure they could hear it. She took a deep breath and began.

The panel watched her. Theodore Holmes, sitting in the middle, felt that special tingle making its way up his spine. Her performance as the small Jewish girl trapped in an attic confirmed what he had already seen and he could hardly contain himself as Jenna had walked from the room.

'God, she's good! Raw, but completely natural. I've seen

that speech from *Romeo and Juliet* countless times and I'd almost forgotten how beautiful it could be.'

The others on the panel nodded in agreement.

Jenna, meanwhile, was sitting in the small anteroom with six other candidates. They waited anxiously for the telephone to ring to let them know if they would be re-called.

It rang and everyone in the room jumped, then giggled nervously. The young boy sitting nearest to the instrument bravely picked it up, listened and announced that everyone except Jenna should go downstairs to the registrar's office.

Jenna was left alone. She wanted to cry. They had all been chosen and she hadn't. She thought miserably of the business college that the nuns and her mother were so keen on her attending after she left school in the summer.

Ten minutes later, the telephone rang again. She looked around and realized that no one was going to pick it up except her, so she lifted the receiver.

'Hello,' she said despondently.

'Jenna,' said a warm voice, 'can you pop down to the registrar's office just near the front entrance?'

'Okay,' said Jenna, and walked down the stairs, steeling herself for the inevitable.

The registrar was an old gentleman with a pair of half-moon glasses perched on the end of his nose.

'Sit down, my dear.'

Jenna sat and swallowed the lump in her throat.

'Now, the principal, Mr Holmes, would like to see you again.'

'Yes,' said Jenna miserably.

The registrar looked concerned. 'Do you want to come back for a re-call, Jenna?'

She looked at him. 'I'm sorry, did you say re-call?'

'Yes. Mr Holmes would like to see you next Wednesday at three o'clock. Can you make it?'

'Of course.'

'Good. Can you prepare another Shakespeare speech so Mr Holmes can work with you on that as well?'

Jenna nodded, and he showed her to the front door. 'Goodbye, Jenna, see you next Wednesday.'

Jenna danced all the way to the tube. She felt ecstatic. When she arrived home she got out her *Complete Works of Shakespeare* and flicked through the pages. She decided to learn a speech by Titania from *A Midsummer Night's Dream*. It began, 'These are the forgeries of jealousy.' Jenna had no idea, in her innocence, that it was one of the most famous speeches for women that Shakespeare had written.

She spent the following evenings in her room, learning and perfecting the speech. The next Wednesday, she walked through the doors of the drama school with a little more confidence than the last time she had been here.

The registrar greeted her in the lobby and took her up to the same studio. Mr Holmes was waiting for her.

'Hello again, Jenna. How are you?' He shook her hand and realized that not only did this slender girl have a great gift for acting, but she was very beautiful as well.

What a combination, he thought to himself, and asked Jenna to repeat her performance of Juliet. He had worried that her last rendition might have been a fluke, or that he had exaggerated her talent. But as he watched her again, he knew that he had not. They spent time working on both Shakespeare speeches. Theodore watched as Jenna grew in confidence and responded to his direction.

For Jenna, it was like a dream come true.

'Right, Jenna, I think that's enough for today. Come and sit down. Now, you've mentioned on your application form that you're going to need some kind of financial assistance if you win a place here. I must warn you that your particular local council does not have a good track record for giving grants to drama students. Last year they did not award any and I don't think this year will be very different.'

Jenna struggled to come back from the forest full of birds and trees to mundane matters such as money.

'You're sure your parents can't assist you?'

'I don't have a father and my mother doesn't even know I've come to audition.'

Theodore smiled. 'Well, I think you may have to tell her. Are you aware that the school grants scholarships to certain pupils that can't afford the fees?'

Jenna had not thought about the financial side. 'No, Mr Holmes, I didn't know.'

'The scholarship only provides for the fees, so you would have to find money to support yourself while you're at the school.'

'I have a Saturday job.'

'Good. Right, well, obviously we have more boys and girls to see and we have a short list of ten for the three scholarships. We'll be letting you know if you've gained a place and a scholarship in a couple of weeks' time. Goodbye, Jenna.'

She solemnly shook his hand and said goodbye and thank you, then walked down the stairs and out of the building.

The next two weeks were a nightmare. Jenna jumped between remembering the wonderful parts of the audition when Mr Holmes had said things like 'very good' and 'that was just right', and remembering what he had said about all the others that were in line for places and scholarships.

When she had rushed to greet the postman on the seventeenth day after the audition and there was no letter, she started to lose hope. And by the time it arrived, a week after that, she had given up meeting the postman. So the letter was waiting by the side of her cereal bowl in the kitchen. She opened it as casually as possible, for her mother was eyeing her suspiciously from the other side of the table. As she read that she had won not only a place but a scholarship, too, not even her mother's stern expression could stop the euphoria welling up and bursting out.

'Yippee!' she shouted and went to kiss her mother on the cheek. 'Read this, Mother, and please don't be angry with me because I've done it.'

Jenna watched her mother's face turn ashen as she read the letter. She put it down and stared hard at her daughter. Joyce said nothing for a long time as she watched the eager face in front of her. She couldn't believe it. She'd had no idea that Jenna had any interest in becoming an actress.

At last she spoke. 'Why didn't you tell me about this, Jenna?'

Jenna swallowed. 'I, well, I wanted to see if I could get in and keep it as a surprise.'

Joyce wondered if she was dreaming. 'Jenna, I don't think you realize what you would be getting into if you took this place.'

'Mother, I know exactly what I'm doing. I've wanted to be an actress for as long as I can remember.'

'Well, you've never mentioned it before. Jenna, this is a whim that you will regret for the rest of your life. How can a child of your age know what she wants?'

'Mother, I'm not a child. I was eighteen five months ago.'

Joyce struggled to find the words she needed. 'Do you realize that these schools take people in, give them false hope of success and then turn them out two years later into a world that already has the majority of actors unemployed? What makes you think you'd be any different?'

'I just know I will be.'

'Oh, really? And to think that I've spent the last eighteen years struggling so that you can have a good education and find a secure job at the end of it. What do you do to repay me? Fill your head with ridiculous dreams of a life that you have absolutely no conception of. I'm sorry, Jenna, but I forbid you to go!'

Jenna stared open-mouthed at her mother. She had not expected such vehemence. However, this was the fulfilment of a dream that not even she could destroy. So for the first time in her life, she took a deep breath and fought back.

'I'm sorry if you don't approve, Mother, but I am eighteen now and you can't forbid me to do anything. I'm going to take that place in September. I'm grateful for all you've given me, but I *have* to do this. I had hoped that you might be pleased.'

The tears welled in her eyes.

'I'm going to school.' Jenna left the kitchen, picked up her bag and slammed the front door behind her.

She walked determinedly down the street, trying to shake off the misery that engulfed her.

Joyce sat alone in the kitchen. She knew she could not stop her daughter. She put her head in her hands and let the tears flow.

3

JENNA COULD NOT REMEMBER a time when her mother had hugged and kissed her. Joyce fed her well and she was always warmly clothed. But deprived of love and attention, Jenna had become a reserved little girl who spent much of her time alone in her room.

The other children at her junior school eyed her suspiciously, as children always do when they feel someone is different. She was never allowed to have friends round to play and therefore was never invited to their homes in return. So she watched with envy as the children in her class went to stay with each other, planned trips to the cinema and started clubs in the playground that she was never asked to join.

Jenna was not sure why her mother did not want her to invite anyone back to the flat, but as she grew older she wondered whether Joyce was ashamed of their tiny home, which was in a shabby block on the fringes of Hornsey in North London. Whatever the reason, it inhibited Jenna to the extent that, on the few occasions a friendship was tentatively offered, she would shy away.

Her mother was always waiting at the school gate. They walked home to the flat just five minutes away and Jenna would go straight to her room to do her homework while Joyce busied herself in the kitchen. At six o'clock Jenna would go into the kitchen to eat her tea.

After Joyce had washed the dishes and Jenna had dried them and put them back into the cupboard, her mother would disappear into the sitting room and the television would be switched on. Jenna, once again left to her own devices, would go to her room to read or dream. At ten thirty, the television in the sitting room would be turned off and Jenna would hear her mother close the door to her bedroom.

Her mother never went out in the evening and no one except the milkman rang the doorbell.

As Jenna grew up, she realized that most of the children at her school had not only a mother, but a father, too. One day, when she was seven years old, she had asked her mother why she didn't have a daddy like the others. Joyce's face had turned pale and her thin lips had set in a hard line.

'Your father is dead, Jenna. He died before you were born. Now eat your tea.'

And that had been that. She had never dared to mention it again. She knew her mother would get cross and she hated that.

She wondered if she had any other relatives, but there were no family photographs in the flat and no cards arrived for either of them at Christmas or on their birthdays.

Jenna began to dream. Her favourite dream was the one

where there was a knock at the door, and a tall handsome man opened it and swept her up in his arms. He would kiss her and hold her and say, 'Jenna, my daughter, I've been looking for you everywhere!' And he would put her in a big car and take her off to live with him.

Jenna would often try to talk to her mother about her day at school, but she didn't seem interested in listening. She never came to see her daughter in the nativity or singing in the choir on speech day.

Jenna asked her why she couldn't come and Joyce told her that she could not afford to take an afternoon off from the office she worked in as a typist if Jenna wanted to have nice things for tea. Jenna knew this wasn't true. She knew it was because her mother didn't love her.

By the time she moved to the convent school at the age of eleven, she had stopped trying. Her mother was pleased when Jenna had passed the entrance exam. She had smiled.

She knew her mother was very keen on God because she took Jenna to Mass every Sunday. But Jenna wasn't so sure. She couldn't understand, if God was love, why her mother didn't love her.

She grew into adolescence slowly, not understanding the subtle changes that were taking place in her body, and the whispered comments and giggles that passed round the changing room full of fourteen-year-old girls. They started talking of boys and parties, but it was a world Jenna didn't know. She did well in her exams and the nuns suggested she stay on to take her A levels. They said that she had an

LOVERS & PLAYERS

aptitude for figures and should apply to go on a course at a business college.

Jenna had other plans. She knew exactly where she wanted to go.

She managed to find a Saturday job at a shoe shop on the parade close to the flat. She knew she would need some money to put her plan into action.

Her dreams were not going to be in vain.

She was going to escape.

4

'SO, BOYS AND GIRLS, you haff come to this school to learn how to be actors. Well, let me introduce myself to you. My name is Rudi Gregorov and I haff been an acting tutor here since 1951.'

The Russian opened his arms as if to embrace the whole class in front of him. 'We will do Shakespeare togezer, Chekhov and Brecht. You will grow to loff them all. Now, I haff introduced myself. I want to know who you are and if there is any talent among you. We shall do a little acting each, to see what we haff got. Right, we start with you, Mr . . .'

Jenna was sitting next to Frankie, who was making strange facial movements that were uncannily like Rudi Gregorov's. Jenna wanted to giggle but she was petrified. She was convinced she would be the least talented in the class and dreaded standing up in front of her fellow classmates and performing.

She waited nervously as other students stood up, said their name and walked to the centre of the studio to begin their speech. Most people were doing Shakespeare, she realized, calming a little. Rudi sat and watched silently from behind his desk at the front of the studio, with his glasses perched on his nose and his arms folded. She thought he was a very odd-looking man, small and almost pixielike, with his bald head and only a few wisps of hair sprouting from just above his ears.

Jenna had heard of his reputation for reducing students to tears. She was thankful that he seemed to be saving his acid tongue for a later date. Suddenly, Frankie was next. She went to stand in the centre of the studio and said her name.

'Frankie Duvall,' said Rudi, clapping his hands together. 'Danny Duvall's child. I taught your farzer when he was here. Perhaps one day you can explain to me why he left a splendid classical career here to make Hollywood pictures. He had such talent. Let's see if you haff inherited any of it.'

Frankie smiled and launched into a rousing version of Katherine from *The Taming of the Shrew*. She finished and stood there waiting for a comment from the maestro. None was forthcoming. She walked back to her seat and sat down. It was Jenna's turn.

'I see we haff an angel in our class,' said Rudi. 'Well, my angel, let us see if you can make us all fly. Begin.'

As always when Jenna was acting, she forgot where she was and only when she had finished did she hear Rudi's voice saying, '. . . don't do Juliet again until you really understand how she feels, my angel. Next.'

Jenna sat down, her cheeks burning. Insecurity gripped her. She didn't have any talent. She shouldn't be here.

She hardly noticed Bettina, who was giving a lively performance as Maria from *Twelfth Night*. She did not know how many performances she had missed, when through her thoughts drifted a rich, male voice. She looked up. He was slim, very tall with dark-brown hair and bright-blue eyes.

Jenna sat transfixed, as did every other female in the room. He gave a brilliant rendition of one of Hamlet's major speeches. Jenna could hardly drag her eyes away from him, even as he sat down.

She leaned over to Frankie. 'What did he say his name was?'

'Matthew Valmont. He's gorgeous and he knows it.'

'Okay, ladies and gentlemen, thank you for trying to act for me. I enjoyed watching you, even if you were all dreadful. I see I haff a lot of work to do if the public are going to pay good money to watch you on a stage. The public is not foolish, they know an actor who is performing for their own pleasure, and that, my little ones, is what you haff just done. There will be no absence from classes, ozerwise you can go and work in an office where they may tolerate indiscipline. I don't. Is that clear? Good. I see you tomorrow, bright and early, and zen we really begin to work.'

Rudi strode out of the studio, leaving behind a silent class.

People slowly began to drift out. Jenna watched as Matthew Valmont disappeared out of the door with a small cluster of women around him.

'Anyone for coffee?' asked Frankie.

It was the end of the first week and Jenna, Bettina and Frankie had got into the habit of mulling over the day's events in the café across the road.

All three of them were exhausted. Their day began at eight thirty with a general warm-up. Frankie would arrive in her tracksuit seconds before the class was due to start and growl all the way through the body and voice exercises, complaining that it was still the middle of the night.

The rest of the morning would be taken up with dialect, text or improvisation classes. Even though the school was famous for producing classical actors, it aimed to give students a comprehensive package of skills. These included ballet lessons, tap and historical – or hysterical, as Frankie called it – dance. They also had twenty minutes a week of private singing tuition.

'I'll be auditioning for *A Chorus Line* at this rate,' Bettina had joked.

There were fourteen students in Group B, nine girls and five boys. Jenna was just able to put names to faces by the end of the week.

'Oh, I can't come for coffee tonight,' said Bettina. 'I'm off to catch the train to Yorkshire to see Ma and Pa. We've got a huge house party this weekend and the loyal daughter has to be there just in case some noble young bloodhound has a fancy for ginger hair and freckles! Have a good weekend and I'll see you on Monday.' She dashed off.

Frankie and Jenna went across to the café and sat in their favourite booth.

'God, I've never been so glad to get to the end of a

week before. I'm really beat! I'm going to spend all day tomorrow in bed, then catch a show in the evening. Do you want to come?'

Jenna knew that she had to be up at seven so she could be at the shoe shop by eight. She would spend the whole day serving customers and would not arrive home until after six. She would just have enough energy to eat the shepherd's pie that her mother always cooked on Saturdays, before falling into an exhausted sleep.

The thought of spending the whole day in bed and just getting up in time to go to the theatre seemed blissful.

'No thanks, Frankie,' she sighed. 'I work on Saturdays and I need the money.'

'Look, Jenna, Pops is loaded and he's given me this useful little gadget called a credit card that he pays for. So you just say the word and we'll be off to see whichever show you want.'

Jenna nodded.

'Hey!' Frankie nudged Jenna across the table. 'Look who's just walked in.' She watched Jenna's face light up. Matthew Valmont was making his way to an empty table with a tall, willowy blonde who was also in their group at school.

Jenna knew that she was staring but she couldn't help herself.

'Boy, is that one gonna go far! He oozes sex appeal, but he isn't my type. I've seen them all before, cruising down Sunset and working in bars, hoping to get a break into films.'

'Paula Franklyn's very glamorous, isn't she?' Jenna said, watching the girl with Matthew.

'Yes, not bad, I suppose. She certainly wasted no time sinking her claws into the best-looking guy in the school.'

Jenna watched as Matthew put his arm round Paula and she kissed him full on the mouth.

'Did you say you were eighteen?' asked Frankie, lighting a cigarette.

'Yes. Actually, it's my nineteenth birthday next Saturday.'

'Hey, you're ten months older than me. I only turned eighteen two months ago. Boy, that was one hell of a party. You got anything planned?'

'No, not really. To be honest, I haven't even thought about it.'

'Jenna, birthdays are a damn good excuse for a blow-out and not an opportunity that should be passed by. So we'll have to organize something.' Frankie thought for a moment. 'I think you should come and stay at my place for the weekend. Then we can go shopping, have dinner and maybe go for brunch at the Savoy. That's where Pops always goes when he's in town. What do you say?'

Jenna wanted to say it sounded perfect. But she had to work at the shop on Saturdays to pay her fares to school the following week. Also, her wardrobe looked like something out of *Hard Times*.

'Thanks for the offer, Frankie, but I have to work on Saturdays and I –'

'For Christ's sake, Jenna! One Saturday isn't going to make any difference and no one should have to work on their birthday. Look, it won't cost you a penny, promise. And don't get uptight and start any of that silly English pride business. Pops really is loaded and I'm lonely in this town by myself. So do it as a favour to me. Please.'

It was tempting. She supposed she could take a few pounds out of her meagre savings account to see her through the following week. After all, it was a special occasion and she knew what saying no to offers of friendship could do.

'Oh, all right. I'll ask my boss if I can have the day off.'

'Great. That's settled then. You just tell your nice Mr Boss-man that Auntie Frankie is coming over from the States to take you out for your birthday. Deal?'

'Deal.' Jenna laughed.

She felt a tap on her shoulder and turned round to see Matthew Valmont standing behind her.

'Hello, I'm Matthew Valmont. And you are?'

Jenna's mouth went dry and she couldn't speak.

'That's Jenna, who's been dumbstruck all of a sudden, and I'm Frankie.'

'I believe we'll be seeing quite a lot of each other, so I thought I'd come and introduce myself. Also,' he leaned towards Jenna, 'I just wanted to say that I enjoyed your Juliet. See you around.'

'Hey,' Frankie said when he had gone. 'That wasn't Larry Olivier who just gave you a compliment, you know.' She studied Jenna's face. 'Boy, do you have it bad or what?'

Jenna blushed. She did.

5

THE FOLLOWING FRIDAY, Jenna sat on her bed with the entire contents of her wardrobe spread around her small room. She had nothing suitable for all the places that Frankie had promised to take her. She put her only decent dress, which was more than four years old and looked it, into her case and threw in the best of the rest. She wondered if spending the weekend with Frankie was such a good idea.

She sighed, shut the suitcase and walked next door to the kitchen where her mother was sitting, eating her usual two pieces of toast and marmalade.

There was a parcel and a card by the side of her plate.

'As you'll be away tomorrow I thought I'd give you those now.'

'Thank you, Mother. Can I open it?'

'If you want.'

Jenna undid the package and found a woolly hat, gloves and scarf in a dull brown colour.

'To keep you warm on your journeys to *that* school.'

An uneasy truce had developed between them. Joyce

knew she couldn't stop her daughter going to the school, and Jenna knew to keep quiet about what she did there.

'Thank you, Mother, they'll be very useful.'

She hastily ate a piece of toast, eager to be on her way to school. She knew that Joyce didn't approve of her going away for the weekend, but she had chosen to ignore her comments and had only told her she was staying with a friend in her class.

Jenna got up from the table and went to her room to pick up her case.

'Will you be back for Mass?' asked Joyce from the kitchen.

'I don't know, but I doubt it. Goodbye, Mother.'

As she walked down the road, Jenna's spirits rose. She started looking forward to the weekend ahead of her.

'Right, let me give you the plan,' said Frankie, sipping her cappuccino. 'Tonight we're going to stop off for a drink on the way home, then we'll maybe pick up a pizza so we can both get an early night. You're going to need all your strength for tomorrow, kiddo. I've got a hair appointment booked for you in the morning, then we'll have some lunch and go shopping. As for the evening . . . well!' Frankie grinned. 'We'll just have to wait and see.'

'Did you say you booked me a hair appointment, Frankie?' asked Jenna, anxiously touching her hair.

'Jenna, that mane of yours hasn't seen a pair of scissors since you were a babe in arms. Just remember, you're in my hands this weekend so you'd better start trusting me. Now drink up and we're out of here.'

The taxi that Frankie hailed headed up the Strand and turned off towards Covent Garden.

'Okay, here will do fine.' They clambered out of the taxi and Jenna followed Frankie down some steps and through an unmarked door.

'This place has only recently opened. Christ! It seems half the size of the one in New York.'

They were in a restaurant which was virtually empty. Frankie led Jenna to the long bar, pulled out a couple of stools and ordered a bottle of champagne.

'Of course, Jenna, you're not seeing it at its best. People don't really start coming in until after the shows.'

'Where are we?'

'This, my dear child, is Joe Allen. The most famous theatrical restaurant in New York and now London. This is where you'll come to dine when you're a superstar.'

The barman filled two glasses with champagne.

'Cheers! Here's to the first weekend of the rest of your life.' Frankie downed her glass in one.

Jenna was not going to let Frankie know she had never tried alcohol, let alone champagne, before. She put the glass to her lips and felt the bubbles tickle her nose. She took a deep breath and swallowed, feeling the golden liquid swim easily down her throat.

Frankie polished off most of the bottle. Jenna just enjoyed the fact that she was out on a Friday night, drinking champagne in a famous restaurant.

'Right. Time to go back to the bat cave.'

As the taxi took them over Tower Bridge, Jenna looked at the lights flickering on the Thames and realized that although she had always lived in London, she'd never seen it as a place of beauty before.

'This is it, madam,' Frankie said as they entered a huge lobby.

The porter behind the desk tipped his hat at them.

'Evening, Robert,' said Frankie, and pressed the lift button. They stepped inside and Jenna watched the numbers ascend on the panel in front of her. The lift drew to a smooth halt and the doors opened on to a deeply carpeted lobby with only one door. Frankie rummaged in her bag for keys and unlocked the door. Jenna followed her.

'This is what they call the penthouse flat.'

In front of Jenna were full-length windows giving a fabulous panoramic view of London. As her eyes adjusted, Jenna could make out the landmarks on the skyline. Just to the east was Tower Bridge, bedecked in white lights, while to the west was the dome of St Paul's Cathedral.

Jenna was amazed by the size of the room she was standing in. It had a high, vaulted ceiling and was decorated in soft pastel colours. There were large, comfortable sofas set near a fireplace. Frankie lit the ornate gas fire. The flames brought cosiness and a focus to the room. She pressed a button on the wall and heavy silk curtains glided soundlessly together, shutting out the dancing lights of the city.

'I'll show you your bedroom. I've put you in the one next to mine.'

They walked down a long corridor and Frankie led Jenna into the prettiest room she had ever seen. Everything was upholstered in a Sanderson print of soft pink flowers. In the centre stood a small four-poster bed with matching drapes.

Frankie dumped Jenna's case on the bed. 'Pops fitted this out for me when he had the interior designer do the place over. He still thinks I'm ten. It's so kitsch, I hate it.'

Jenna saw her own small room with its threadbare candlewick bedspread and yellowing wallpaper. She decided she liked 'kitsch', whatever that was.

'Come and see Pops's room, where I stay. Now that's got real imagination.'

The room was enormous, carpeted in a heavy cream shag pile. It was dominated by a circular bed covered in a tiger-skin bedspread and set on a plinth.

'Hop on for the ride,' said Frankie, pulling Jenna on to the bed. She turned a knob and the bed slowly started to turn around and around.

'One of Pops's little gadgets. I'm amazed it doesn't have a trap door through which he can dispose of any "auntie" who doesn't come up to scratch.'

She turned the knob off and Jenna lay there feeling sick.

'Right, you go and wash up and I'll send out for a nice juicy pizza. Then I want your attention for at least an hour while I try to do something about your completely hopeless dress sense.'

They ate the pizza by the fire. Jenna was beginning to feel a little like Alice having passed through the looking-glass and was loving every second of it.

'Okay, follow me.' Frankie took Jenna into what she called a dressing room.

'Now, there's gotta be something here that suits you.' Frankie started throwing open the mirror-clad doors of the cupboards that lined the room.

Jenna looked on in wonder, as the cupboards revealed rail upon rail of clothes.

'Whose are all these?'

'Well, some are mine and then some are Auntie Liz's, with a little number or two from Auntie Debs. Ah, here we have something that should fit you.'

Jenna tried on designer dress after suit as Frankie rummaged through the clothes, picking things out.

They both agreed that their favourite was a blue Chanel suit with traditional gold buttons down the front. It showed off Jenna's slim legs and made her feel very sophisticated.

'My, my, Cinderella, doesn't that turn you into a princess? Well, you can wear that tomorrow when we go shopping and at least tonight has given me an idea of what I'm going to buy you for your birthday. Right, time for bed. Room service, namely me with a mug of coffee, will arrive in your room at nine o'clock so we can be ready to leave by ten.'

Jenna reluctantly gathered together the clothes she had taken off. They looked so cheap and nasty compared to the wonderful garments she had been wearing for the past hour.

'Night, Frankie.'

'Night. Sleep tight in your flowery bower.' She winked at Jenna, who on impulse flung her arms around her friend and hugged her tight.

When Frankie had gone she opened the door to a cupboard, only to find that it was a bathroom. She cleaned her teeth, then climbed into the soft, cosy bed.

She thought of her mother, fast asleep on the other side of London.

She snuggled under the covers and hoped the weekend would last for ever.

6

'WELL, WHAT DOES MADAM THINK?' asked the dark, Italian hairdresser.

For the past hour Jenna had been sitting in a state of trepidation as she watched her golden locks falling like feathers around her. The hairdresser held a mirror up to show her the back.

'You see, you are not bald. I have only layered and shaped your hair to make it more beautiful.'

'Thank you very much. It does look better.'

Jenna glanced at her nails, which had been painted a subtle pink by the manicurist, and decided she liked being pampered. She could see in the mirror that Frankie was walking towards her.

Frankie smiled knowingly. 'Told you it would be an improvement.' She went to the desk and handed over a credit card. She signed and turned to see Jenna's watchful eyes.

'Listen, this is all on Pops, 'cos he pays the bill, so don't worry about it. Come on, we're going on a hunt to find your birthday present.'

For the next two hours Jenna followed Frankie into and out of nearly every boutique along the Kings Road. She tried on outfit after outfit. Frankie kept shaking her head and dragging her off to the next shop. At last, just as Frankie was talking about her stomach needing to be filled, she stopped in front of a window.

'That is perfect,' she pronounced, and once again Jenna found herself in front of another mirror in another dress. This time, even she had to admit it looked good. The dress was made of black taffeta, with puffed sleeves sitting just beyond her shoulders, a V neckline and a tight bodice that tapered to her tiny waist, hugged her hips and showed off her legs.

'We'll take it,' said Frankie immediately, 'and while we're at it, I'm going to try this.'

'This' was a red creation in shot silk, with a top and matching pantaloons. A huge sash in black and gold finished off the ensemble. Frankie emerged looking like a reject from a harem, but stunning into the bargain.

Jenna had glanced at the price tag on her dress as she was changing. It was reduced in the sale from three hundred and fifty pounds to two hundred pounds. She gulped when the entire bill, along with shoes that Frankie had bought to match her outfit, came to over four hundred pounds.

It was no wonder that she could not eat the pasta in front of her. She was thinking that she and her mother could probably live on that amount of money for at least two months. Frankie, meanwhile, was tucking in hungrily and between mouthfuls she talked nonstop.

'That dress was made for you, and it was even reduced so you don't need to feel guilty about it. Anyway, happy birthday!' She raised her glass of Frascati. 'Now, the next job is to find you a couple of casual outfits that you can wear to school to stop you looking like Little Orphan Annie. I want to buy a couple of sweat suits, too, for those evil morning warm-ups.'

They went to Harrods, where Frankie's credit card worked overtime. Two hours later they emerged, laden down with bags and parcels. Frankie was sporting a huge fedora that she had insisted on buying in the hat department.

'Anything else before we go?'

Jenna laughed and shook her head. 'No, Frankie, I really think that if I don't sit down in a minute my arms are going to drop off.'

'Fine, let's hail a cab and go home. We've got a long night in front of us.'

As Frankie opened the door to the flat, the telephone was ringing.

'Why don't you go and lay out your dress and have a bath? Then I'll come and do your face.'

An hour and a half later, Jenna stood in front of a mirror in the dressing room and stared at the sophisticated woman in the black dress. Her newly styled hair was shining and the subtle make-up which Frankie had expertly applied had accentuated her huge eyes and shaped her lips.

'You know, Rudi was right, you do look like an angel,' Frankie remarked softly, having amazed herself at the change she had wrought in her friend.

'You don't look half bad yourself!' Jenna laughed at the tall, striking figure dressed in her new red outfit.

'Well, no one could miss me, that's for sure! Oh yes, just one last thing. Here we are. Happy birthday!' And she handed Jenna a small giftwrapped box.

'Frankie, I thought that the dress was –'

'My darling Jenna, you're my friend and I feel sure that we're going to know each other for the rest of our lives. Now, if you had a father that was stinking rich and I had nothing, you'd want to buy me presents, wouldn't you?'

Jenna nodded. 'Of course, but . . .'

'So, open that box and shut up! What's mine is yours, and one day, I just have a feeling that you'll be able to pay me back a hundred times over, okay?'

Inside the box was a small string of pearls with a pair of matching drop earrings.

'To go with the dress.'

'Oh, Frankie, I don't know what to say! I . . .'

'Then say nothing. Just promise to stick by me always?'

Suddenly a sadness came into Frankie's eyes. She looked like a little girl lost. Jenna went over and hugged her. 'Of course I will, Frankie. I've never had a real friend before and I certainly don't intend to lose her now I've found her.'

'Good, 'cos neither do I.'

'I'm going to, what was that phrase you used the other day? Stick like . . . ?'

'Stick like shit!' Frankie laughed. 'Now, I'll call down to Robert to get us a cab, and we'll go to the new hotel just over the river for a drink.'

Frankie left the room. Jenna couldn't understand how she, who had nothing, could feel sorry for a girl who lived like a princess and had everything money could buy. There was something vulnerable about Frankie underneath the tough act that she put on for the rest of the world.

The two of them had something in common.

Loneliness.

7

'JENNA, YOU'RE NOT GOING to sit there with a rod up your arse all night, are you?' Frankie giggled. 'Relax and enjoy yourself. This is your night.'

Jenna nodded and sipped her drink. They were sitting in an extremely plush bar at the top of the newly opened Tower Hotel. She wasn't quite sure how to react to the way the men had stared at her as she had walked into the bar.

'So, what's the score with your love life?' Frankie enquired, eating an olive.

'Oh, no one really,' said Jenna.

'Are you still intact, as they say?'

'Pardon?'

Frankie leaned nearer and whispered, 'I mean, my dear, what I am trying to ask, as subtly as I can, is whether you have been deflowered yet, made it in the back seat, lost your cherry? Okay, Miss Innocence, are you still a virgin?'

Jenna's shocked 'Of course!' gave Frankie the giggles.

'Fine. I suppose you're going to wait until you marry, are you?'

'Well, yes, I suppose so.'

Frankie laughed cynically. 'Well, I won't hold you to that, but good luck anyway.'

'Do you miss your father?' Jenna asked quietly.

Frankie's eyes clouded. 'No. I very rarely saw him when I lived with him. I mean, our house makes that flat across the river look like a broom cupboard. He was always away on location somewhere when I was a child. He's never been the paternal type. Of course, he's spoiled me rotten moneywise. I think it's because my mother died when I was one, and he's always felt guilty for being away so much.' She shrugged, and it was obvious that she had had enough of this particular line of conversation. 'Anyway, I'm a big girl now, and I don't need Pops to wipe my nose any more. Come on, it's time to make a move, otherwise we'll be late.'

Frankie signalled for the waiter and opened her handbag. 'Shit!' she said, throwing the contents out on the table.

'What's wrong?'

'Damn it! I've left my wallet with all my credit cards at home. We'll have to go back for it. Thank God I've just got enough money to pay for the drinks and a cab to the apartment.'

The taxi drew to a halt and Frankie held out the keys to Jenna. 'Be an angel and run up and get the wallet. I'm sure it's on the table in the sitting room. I'll stay here and hold on to the cab.'

Jenna got out of the lift on the top floor, unlocked the door and opened it. She groped around for the light switch.

Suddenly the lights went on without her touching the switch and a sea of faces appeared in front of her. The faces started shouting and laughing. She made out cries of 'Surprise!' and 'Happy birthday!'

Someone she recognized was walking towards her. The girl held out her arms and gave her a huge hug.

'Wake up, Jenna! You'll start catching flies if you don't shut your mouth. It's me, Bettina, and these are all our friends from school. This is your surprise birthday party, courtesy of Miss Frankie Duvall and Miss Bettina Langdale.'

'Speech, speech!' someone cried.

'Yes, for goodness' sake, say something before we all get too drunk to understand,' said Bettina.

The room fell silent and Jenna felt someone propel her forwards. She turned round to see Frankie grinning.

'I told you birthdays were just a good excuse for a blow-out,' she whispered. 'Now, go on, say something. Actresses are meant to have half a dozen thank you speeches prepared for this sort of occasion.'

'Well,' said Jenna shyly, clearing her throat, 'I'm, well, I'm very surprised, as you may have noticed. Thank you all for coming. And also, a special thank you to Frankie and Bettina who I will never trust again for as long as I live. Now, could I please have a drink?'

A champagne flute was thrust into her hand by Bettina.

'Turn those lights down and the music up. Let's have a party,' shouted Frankie, who was immediately pulled off to the other side of the room. The throb of the music started to bring the room to life and people began to dance. Jenna stood there, feeling totally disoriented. She took a leaf out of Frankie's book and downed the champagne in one. She quickly felt better. 'This is all for me,' she kept saying to herself as she tried to make her way towards Frankie and Bettina.

'So, are you happy? Auntie Frankie said it would be a good night, didn't she? Some surprise, eh?' Frankie turned to Bettina and they started giggling like naughty schoolkids. 'Sorry about the forgotten wallet, but we had to get you out of the flat so that Bettina here could set up the booze and let everyone in. I think even the waiter believed me!'

'We both thought that it was too good an opportunity to be missed and that it would give us all a chance to get to know everyone better out of school,' Bettina added. 'And I must say, Jenna, you really do look absolutely beautiful. I know Frankie said that she was going to do you over, but the difference is amazing!' She turned to Frankie. 'I wonder, could you do the same for me?'

The three girls giggled and stood in the kitchen talking and drinking. Jenna thought she had never felt so happy.

A while later, Jenna felt a hand on her shoulder. She turned to see Matthew Valmont standing behind her.

'Happy birthday, Jenna!' He leaned forward and kissed her on the cheek. 'You look absolutely stunning tonight. May I have the next dance?'

She nodded. He took her hand and led her into the sitting room.

A slow song was playing on the stereo and she felt her heart lurch as Matthew's strong arms encircled her.

They swayed slowly to the music. He pulled her closer and she rested her head on his shoulder. A tingling sensation started at the base of her stomach and made its way down to the part of her that was slowly awakening for the first time. The feeling of his body so close to hers was turning her legs to jelly. When he reached down to kiss her gently on the lips, it seemed the most natural thing in the world to kiss him back. She closed her eyes as their lips met. Then suddenly he pulled away.

'Thanks for the dance, Jenna. See you around.' Matthew took Paula's outstretched hand and was led away, leaving Jenna standing alone in the middle of a swaying mass of people.

Jenna felt her face turning red. She was sure that everyone had noticed what had happened. She pushed her way towards the patio doors, which had been opened to let some air into the smoky room, and stepped out on to the balcony into the privacy of darkness.

Jenna shivered in the chill night air. Tears welled up and she let them fall. She felt completely humiliated. The night which had been so magical had been ruined. She longed to be in her own tiny bedroom with the faint sound of the television emanating from the sitting room. Maybe it wasn't as glamorous as all this but at least it was safe.

She wiped her nose noisily on her hand, longing for a tissue.

'Beautiful night, isn't it?' A deep resonant voice came out of the darkness.

Jenna, who thought that she had been alone in her

misery, nearly jumped out of her skin. She turned apprehensively to see where the voice was coming from and made out a shadowy figure smoking a cigarette, not ten feet away from her.

The figure spoke again. 'It's not often you can see the Seven Sisters and the Belt of Orion. It must be a very clear night.'

'Excuse me?'

'The stars, my dear, the stars. Follow my hand and you'll see the Sisters huddling very close together, like fireflies taking shelter from the rain. And then just over there is the Belt of Orion. My mother used to tell me a story about the Great Bear when I was a babe in arms. It's the one shaped as such, hanging down below. Can you see it?'

'Yes, I think I can. What was the story your mother used to tell you?'

'Ah, well, my dear, the story goes that if you look out of your window late at night when you should be tucked up in your little truckle bed like a good child, the Great Bear will see you, take shape and come out of the sky. Then he'll pluck you out of your room with one of his great paws, take you back to his lair in the sky and have you on toast for breakfast the next morning.'

Jenna laughed in spite of herself and felt a little better.

The man moved towards her and pulled a large white handkerchief out of his pocket. He offered it to her.

'Clean yourself up before they think a panda has escaped from London Zoo.' He gently wiped a finger under her eye and showed it to her with raised eyebrows. It was black.

'Pity to spoil your image, although you do make a very touching picture. So long, Miss Jenna Short.'

He moved towards the open door, then stopped and turned round. 'Name's Charlie Devereaux, by the way. See you.' And with that he disappeared inside.

Jenna decided she needed to make a dash for the bathroom.

She laughed as she saw her dishevelled reflection in the mirror and tried to mop herself up as best she could. She really didn't feel in a party mood any more, but Frankie and Bettina had laid all this on for her and she owed it to them to put on a brave face and go back out.

She came out of the bathroom to see Bettina draped around a man who was half her size and went into the kitchen to find Frankie holding court. Jenna poured herself a large drink and half-heartedly joined in the conversation. She looked around to see if the boy on the balcony was anywhere to be seen, but he had vanished. She downed her drink and poured herself another. She wandered into the sitting room, where the party was still in full swing. She sat on a chair opposite a sofa which was awash with writhing bodies. She polished off her glass and found another half-full glass of something sitting on the table beside her chair, so she drank that as well.

'Want to dance?' asked a boy she knew from her group at school.

'Why not?' She closed her eyes as she leaned on his shoulder. Her head was beginning to spin and she felt sick. She opened her eyes and saw Matthew next to her, totally involved in a passionate kiss with Paula.

'Excuse me,' she said to the boy, staggered down the corridor and found the door that led to her room. She breathed a sigh of relief at the sight of the cosy bed. She just needed to lie down for a moment, then she would feel better. She slipped off her shoes and sank gratefully on to the mattress. She closed her eyes and slept.

8

JENNA AWOKE TO a buzzing sound that she realized was coming from inside her head. She opened her eyes and knew if she moved, she would be very sick all over the beautiful coverlet.

'I'm dying,' she moaned, as her head pulsated. She wondered how she could make it to the bathroom, then realized she would have to make a dash for it when she felt her insides heave. She hung over the toilet as most of yesterday's intake was unleashed into the bowl. She knelt there hugging the toilet until she was pretty certain that it was safe to leave. She stood up unsteadily, washed her face and collapsed back on the bed. She closed her eyes, waiting for the end to come.

Voices were drifting to her from other rooms and she thought she could hear Bettina's high-pitched giggle.

The black dress that she was still wearing was terribly crumpled. She sat up, unzipped the dress and walked gingerly over to the cupboard to hang it up.

'It looks like I feel,' she mumbled to herself, and went into the bathroom to take a shower. The hot jet of water cleared her brain a little. She emerged, wrapped in a luxurious white towel, and went to sit on the bed again.

She put her head in her hands as the previous night came back with painful clarity. She was aghast that she still felt the gnawing sensation in the pit of her stomach which she knew now had nothing to do with the alcohol she had consumed. She wished she could empty her heart the way she had emptied her stomach but knew that was impossible. The feeling was embedded deep inside.

'Oh dear,' she said, and laughed wryly at the way the phrase did nothing to describe the way she really felt.

She dressed and took her throbbing head down the hallway to the kitchen, where Frankie and Bettina were sitting eating breakfast.

Frankie looked at Jenna, her eyes twinkling. 'Aha, 'tis Sleeping Beauty! Well, as you've conveniently missed most of the cleaning-up, I suggest you sit yourself down and have some breakfast.'

Jenna shook her head vehemently.

'Does Auntie Frankie think that little Jenna might have a teensy-weensy hangover?'

She nodded.

Frankie smirked. Bettina got up and steered Jenna towards a chair at the table and sat her down.

'My pa, who drinks like a fish, always has a jolly good breakfast when he has a hangover, and I suggest you do the same.' She buttered some toast, poured a cup of tea and put it in front of Jenna. 'Come on, tuck in, it'll make you feel heaps better. Anyway, we can't wait for you to spill the beans on Mr Valmont. Don't think you weren't noticed.

Paula's face was a picture when she saw you together. You were lucky to get out alive last night, my girl!'

Jenna put her head in her hands and groaned.

'Come on, dish the dirt! We're desperate to know what Mr Hunko said to you before he was so cruelly dragged away. Is he leaving Paula, or what?'

Jenna shook her head miserably. 'No, he's not. And we were only dancing.'

'And kissing,' Bettina cut in.

'And gazing into each other's eyes,' Frankie interjected.

'And . . .'

'Oh, shut up, you two! Anyway, Bettina, I saw you draped around some man at least four foot shorter than you. Who was he?'

Bettina blushed. '*Touché*. Did I make a real fool of myself?'

'Nooo,' Frankie drawled. 'Not really. I mean, apart from the fact that he really was four foot shorter than you and not exactly what could be described as the stud of the western world. I think the fact that you kept pressing him to your bosom and telling him that he brought out your mothering instinct was disturbing him somewhat.'

Even Jenna had to laugh as she watched Bettina's face.

'Oh dear, I think I arranged to see him on Tuesday to discuss his Oedipus complex! Anyway, it was a jolly good party, wasn't it? Good way to break the ice with our fellow classmates and all that.'

Frankie yawned. 'Sure was. Did you enjoy it, Jenna?'

'Apart from this dreadful hangover.'

'I'm not surprised. I saw you pouring yourself a straight glass of tequila at one point.' She checked her watch. 'I was going to take us all to the Savoy Grill, but as it's ten to two, I don't think that —'

'Ten to two!' Jenna gasped.

'Yes, my little lush. I hope you've learned how alcohol can turn nice girls into drunken monsters who stay in bed all day and kiss other people's boyfriends at parties.'

'Don't, please, Frankie!'

'Leave her alone, she's sensitive,' Bettina chastised. 'Anyway, I must be getting back because Gerry will probably have called the police by now. I suggest you have an early night tonight, Miss Short, and I'll see you both bright and early tomorrow morning to face the Russian pixie.'

'Okay, hon, I'll take care of Miss Hangover of the Year. You go home.'

'Thanks for everything, Bettina. I really appreciate it.'

'Yes, you look as though last night did you the world of good, Jenna, my dear!' Bettina laughed as she went to collect her coat and bag.

When Bettina had gone home, they went into the sitting room with two cups of steaming tea.

'Listen, Jenna, I've got an idea.'

'What is it?' asked Jenna suspiciously, eyeing Frankie's thoughtful face.

'Well, I was just wondering. I mean, since I live in this huge place all alone, I end up getting bored out of my brains most nights. And as I'm sure we're going to have a lot of work to do for school and could use each other's help, I was wondering if you'd like to come and live here with me?'

'Oh, Frankie, it's so lovely of you to ask, but you know how broke I am. I couldn't come here and live off you and –'

'I've thought about that. Pops gives me fifteen pounds a week to pay a cleaner. I'm sure that between us, we could manage to keep the flat tidy. That would save hiring someone and would cover your keep here.'

'Frankie, it's a lovely thought but –'

'Do you cook?'

'Well, yes,' said Jenna. 'I mean, I got my exam in domestic science . . .'

'That's settled, then. You come and stay here with me rent-free, help me do the cleaning and do all the cooking. I usually end up going out to eat, spending oodles of money and staying up late when I should be sitting at home like a good girl studying. So you see, you'll be doing me a favour by keeping me in at night and saving me money into the bargain. You can even come in the cabs I get to and from school so you won't have to worry about fares. Now, Jenna, please say yes!'

Jenna thought of the beautiful bedroom down the hallway that was hers for the taking. Then of her mother who would be left all alone.

'Look, I'll even write out a contract if you want. I mean, I'll expect cordon bleu every night and the apartment spotless, so don't think it's that great a deal.' The brown eyes beseeched Jenna. 'Just think of the fun we could have – I mean, in between you slaving in the kitchen, that is.'

A plan was formulating in Jenna's mind. She would still have to keep her Saturday job to give her some money to live on. Maybe she could go home afterwards to stay with her mother and accompany her to Mass on Sunday morning. She knew her mother would not approve. But she was nineteen now and she wanted very badly to come and live here with Frankie.

'Well,' she said cautiously, and explained her plan, pointing out that her mother deserved to see her at least one night of the week.

'It's just a pity it has to be Saturday. I mean, that's the fun night of the week. But I suppose it's better than nothing. So you'll move in tomorrow?'

Jenna smiled at Frankie's need for everything to be immediate. 'No, not tomorrow. I'll have to discuss it with Mother. But yes, I'll move in next week if you're really sure you want me to.'

Frankie did a jig round the sitting room. 'Of course I really want you to! Now shut up and start planning the first week's menu!'

Jenna returned home from the party that night still feeling too hung over to face what was going to be a difficult conversation with her mother. So she waited until Tuesday, by which time she knew exactly what she was going to say, and had a list of what she hoped were practical reasons for going to stay with Frankie. She had decided to leave out the fact that Frankie's father was a famous film star, since she knew her mother would certainly not approve of that.

Jenna talked for ten minutes, mentioning every reason why it would be a good idea to stay with Frankie. She emphasized that she would not be moving out because she would be home for the Christmas holidays.

Joyce sat there listening, her face as expressionless as always.

'Well, Jenna, you know I can't stop you, and if that's what you want, then you'd better do it. Clear the table, will you? There's a film starting in five minutes that I want to watch.'

And she disappeared into the sitting room.

Jenna felt more guilty then than if her mother had ranted and raved and forbidden her to go. She also felt hurt that her mother didn't seem to care that her only daughter was moving out.

The following Sunday she packed her small case full of enough clothes to take her through the week and went into the kitchen to say goodbye.

'I'll see you next Saturday.'

'Right.'

She moved to the front door.

'Take care, Mother.'

'Yes.'

'Goodbye then.'

'Goodbye, Jenna.'

Jenna wanted to cry. She walked off down the road to the tube trying to swallow the lump in her throat. Then she thought of Frankie and the pretty room that was waiting for her and decided she wouldn't think any more about why her mother hated her so much.

That night, Joyce sat in front of the television, unable to see the screen for the tears that were pouring from her eyes.

9

JENNA QUICKLY SETTLED DOWN to living with Frankie. The two of them found that they got on extremely well. They became inseparable inside as well as out of school. Bettina often came to stay at the flat and the three of them enjoyed many nights of pasta, wine and shared dreams.

The only dark spot on Jenna's horizon was the Saturday night when she went home to see her mother. She started to dread the short walk from the shoe shop back to the tiny flat where her mother would be sitting as usual in the kitchen reading the paper.

She behaved as though Jenna hadn't gone away and the routine was exactly the same. She never asked what kind of week Jenna had had, although at first Jenna had tried to make an effort to talk to her mother. The response had been so monosyllabic that she had eventually given up, and just counted the hours until she was back with Frankie.

'I don't know why you don't say to hell with her and move in here permanently.'

'No. She is my mother and I do owe her something.'

'A raised middle finger, if you ask me. Anyway, it's none of my business, but I just hate to see you looking so miserable every Friday night, when we should be looking forward to a fun-filled weekend.'

Jenna decided to drop the subject since it seemed impossible to explain, and resigned herself to the fact that at least it was only one night of the week; a small price to pay for the happiness she had on the other six days.

They would often dash straight to a theatre after school and buy a student standby ticket, Frankie loyally sitting in the gods with Jenna when they both knew she could afford a box.

Time after time Frankie would insist she was so starving she couldn't wait until she got home to eat, and drag Jenna into a hamburger joint. Then she would pay for both of them because, she said, it hadn't been Jenna's idea.

Jenna would sometimes climb into her four-poster and pinch herself hard to make sure she really wasn't dreaming.

She was enjoying the course immensely. The only dark spot at school was that Matthew had hardly talked to her since her birthday party and Jenna felt that he was making a deliberate effort to ignore her.

While deep inside she knew that the way she felt about Matthew was pointless, it didn't mean she could prevent herself from thinking about him night and day.

At first Frankie had thought it was all very funny, but as she saw the way Jenna felt, it started to irritate her.

'Honestly, Jenna, you've got boys swooning over you, in case you hadn't noticed, and you go and pick the only man who is one hundred per cent taken. Anyway, he's too good-looking and his type are always trouble. Steer clear and stop wasting your time. Trust me, he's a rat. I can smell them a mile off.'

Jenna nodded her head obediently and then went off to bed and dreamed about Matthew as usual. Frankie was right, she had a line of men who were always offering to take her for coffee or to the theatre, but they weren't Matthew, so she said no.

She had looked around the school often for the man called Charlie Devereaux, her knight errant on the balcony. She discovered he was on the director's course and had kept his handkerchief in her bag to return to him with thanks if she saw him, but she didn't.

Bettina had fallen head over heels for one of the young tutors who took them for improvisation, but at present, despite her incredible performances as an iron filing and a cabbage, she was getting nowhere.

'He never even notices me,' she wailed one night as the three of them sat eating pizza in front of the fire.

'Honestly, you two!' said Frankie, shaking her head. 'I've got a flatmate who drools over a man who is about to walk down the aisle with another woman and a friend who has fallen for a man who is not allowed to go out with her, even if he wanted to. God give me strength!'

'I know that,' said Bettina. 'The trouble is, that makes it seem even more romantic. I mean, he could be desperately, desperately in love with me, and unable to say anything for fear of getting me expelled and himself unemployed.'

Frankie just nodded her head patiently and said, 'Yes, Bettina.'

Bettina threw a cushion at her. 'Oh, Frankie, you're dreadful! Don't you have one romantic bone in your body? Haven't you ever been madly in love with anyone?'

'Nope.' Frankie shook her head and folded her arms.

Bettina and Jenna sighed and raised their eyebrows at each other. Frankie's attitude towards men was a mystery to them both. She, like Jenna, had a string of men who adored her and yet she never, to the knowledge of either of them, went out with anyone. They had questioned her to find out why, but she was always evasive and would quickly change the subject, as she did now.

'So, what's happening at Christmas, you guys?'

Jenna shuddered. The weeks had flown by so quickly that she could hardly believe they had only two weeks of term left. And she for one did not want to think about returning to share a lonely turkey with her mother.

'Well, I'm going home to Langdale Hall for a round of nonstop dinner parties and brisk walks to the village church knee-deep in mud. Yuk! I'd much rather stay here and plot my campaign of action on how to get my favourite tutor into the sack, as you would say, Frankie. Unfortunately, that's the way things are when you're a daughter of the aristocracy.' Bettina sighed. 'Never mind. What are you doing, Frankie?'

'Oh, going back to see dear old Pops because I know he's been pining away alone for his darling daughter.'

'I'll swop you.' Bettina giggled. 'I wouldn't mind being in his Christmas stocking when he wakes up!'

'You can have him, Bettina. The house'll be full of people I don't know all giving me Barbie dolls and patting me on the head because they still think I'm six. Pops'll get drunk as a skunk and disappear off on location two days later.' She stared into the fire morosely. Then her face lit up. 'Jen, why don't you come with me?'

'Frankie, you know I have to go home for Christmas. My mother has only got me.'

'Oh, just tell the miserable old bag to get lost and find herself a chimney to get stuck in and come with me to LA.'

Jenna tried to look horrified, but Frankie was so outrageous that she had to laugh.

'God, you're coarse!' said Bettina.

'Yep, that's me, just a li'l old Yankee girl strugglin' with the finer ways of English etiquette. Oh, please, please, please come with me, Jenna! I'll hate to be all by my lonesome.'

'No, Frankie,' Jenna said, as firmly as she could. There was no way, however much she'd like to, that her conscience would let her leave her mother alone at Christmas.

'I see. Well, if that's the way it is, and you couldn't stand to spend Christmas with your best pal, I understand.'

'Shut up, Frankie!' Jenna and Bettina chorused together. They both knew her when she was determined to get her own way.

'Oh, well, it was worth a shot.' Frankie shrugged.

'Of course, you'd both be very welcome up at Langdale Hall with me, but seeing as though you both have other plans, maybe we can arrange a weekend for the three of us to visit the homestead in the spring. Now, I suppose we'd better get down to that essay for Rudi.'

'By the way, has either of you given any thought to what you're going to use as a stage name? We have to fill in that form for *Spotlight* and hand it in next week,' said Frankie.

Every year, a special section in the actors' casting directory was reserved for students. They had to provide a photo and other details, such as their height, weight and the colour of their hair.

'I'm going to stick to my own name,' said Bettina.

'What about you, Jenna?'

'I haven't even thought about it, to be honest.'

Frankie looked serious. 'Well, you really should do something about that terrible name of yours.'

'What do you mean?' Jenna looked hurt.

'Well, the Jenna part's okay, but the Short part is dreadful. You need a name that conjures up a picture of elegance, sexiness and mystery. Now, let me see.' Frankie thought for a while. 'I've got it. What about Shaw? It's similar to your own name and it sounds just great. Jenna Shaw. Yep, that's it.' Frankie looked pleased with herself. 'What do you think?'

Jenna repeated it a few times out loud. She had to admit that it sounded better than her real name. 'I like it.'

'Good. So, from now on, that's your name. And that's

what I'll call you so you can get used to it. This calls for a toast. To Miss Jenna Shaw, star of the future!'

The three girls raised their glasses.

10

ON THE LAST DAY of the first term, the students crowded excitedly into Rudi's final class. He was looking as implacable as ever.

'Well, my little ones, the end of your first term in my hands. So, how do you feel?' He looked around the room. 'Exactly the same, perhaps, or different? Well, I can tell you that some who haff learned what I haff taught are feeling different and those of you who haff not will feel the same. I do not need to tell you who is who, because you all know. So I say congratulations to those who deserve it and nothing to those who don't. I hope you all haff a good Yuletide and I don't want one of you coming back with a fat belly due to too much Christmas pudding. Next term we will work even harder, yes? Okay, you go away now and giff your poor old teacher a good rest. Class dismissed!'

A half-hearted cheer went up as Rudi left, and people started drifting out. Jenna sat there feeling depressed. All she had to look forward to was working at the shoe shop for four weeks.

She tried to cheer herself with the thought that, if she could earn enough, it would mean that she could give up the job altogether next term.

Jenna followed Frankie and Bettina down to the changing room and helped carry their suitcases to the front door of the school.

'Happy Christmas! Have a good one and think of me tomorrow, stomping through the woods in my wellies, trying to find a tree that Ma approves of.' Bettina climbed into a taxi and waved frantically as it moved off along the street.

'I'm afraid I've got to dash, too. Don't look so forlorn, Jenna. I told you you should be getting on that plane to Tinsel Town with me tonight. Now, you've got the keys to our place so you can water Herbie?'

Jenna nodded. Herbie was a very large rubber plant that they had seen languishing in a flower shop one day and taken pity on.

'And you know you can stay there the whole time if you want, don't you?'

Jenna nodded again, feeling a lump in her throat. She didn't know how she could face the next four weeks without her friend. She noticed Frankie looked a little tearful as well.

She gave Jenna a hug. 'You've only got to pick up the telephone and you can be on a plane to see me. I'll miss you, kiddo. Take care of yourself.' Frankie flagged down a taxi and clambered in with her suitcases. 'Bye, Jenna.'

Jenna waved pathetically as Frankie's taxi disappeared from sight. She couldn't face going home just yet so she crossed the road, went into the coffee shop, sat down and ordered a cappuccino. The lump was growing in her throat once more and a large tear plopped into her coffee.

'You know, fair maid, I'm beginning to get a complex about this. Every time I see you, you're in tears. I don't have a never-ending supply of white handkerchiefs.'

He was looking quizzically at her. In the light of day, he was handsome. His hair had been cut shorter and Jenna thought how well it suited him. Eyes of an unusual grey-green were twinkling.

'Hello. I've got your hanky in my bag.'

'Well, then, I suggest you pull it out and use it again. And seeing as that is twice you've used it with no fee, I think you should buy me a coffee to show your gratitude.'

Jenna ordered another coffee and pulled the hanky out to blow her nose.

'It's been sitting there for two months so that if I saw you, I could give it back.' She giggled. 'Well, I can hardly give it to you like this so I'd better take it home and wash it again.'

'What a bizarre creature you are! Have you been crying nonstop since I last saw you, or do you take a breather occasionally to have some sustenance?' Charlie smiled at her. 'One would presume that you're following in the footsteps of the fair Miss Ellen Terry?'

'Yes, I'm on the two-year acting course.'

'Well, if you want a piece of advice . . .' He beckoned her nearer and whispered, 'I think you've perfected tragedy and it's time to move on to the next chapter.'

She laughed. 'You're on the director's course, aren't you?'

'That is where I tread my humble path through life, yes,' he replied.

'So you hope to direct when you leave?'

'Oh, good lord no,' he said, a look of dramatic horror on his face. 'Well, actually, yes and no. Although you may not realize it, you're probably looking at one of the greatest playwrights ever to hit the twentieth century. The written word, not the spoken one, is my master. I came here to learn the technical side so that I don't have to hire some mealy-mouthed ex-chorus-boy director to come in and ruin my masterpiece.'

'I see.'

'Trouble is,' he continued, 'living in Finsbury Park, with the underground shaking the house to its foundations, and neighbours who think that Marvin Gaye is the new Messiah and worship at the altar of the ghetto blaster until four in the morning, it's quite hard to believe that you're the next Oscar Wilde. Still, they fought tuberculosis and we fight ghetto blasters, both equally damaging in their own way.' He slurped his coffee moodily.

'Have you written much?' Jenna asked.

'Little sister, I burn the midnight oil, or should I say the meter, until after Marvin has been laid to rest and is having a jolly good kip. Many of the forests are now bare because of the amount of paper I toss into the wastepaper bin.'

'Do you live with your parents?' Jenna asked.

Charlie threw back his head and laughed loudly.

'Why is that so funny?'

He wiped his eyes. 'I do apologize. It's just the thought of Ma and Pa leaving their large house in the leafy suburbs of Surrey to live in Finsbury Park. No, the reason that I'm subjected to the indignity of sharing my bathroom with six other humans of indeterminate races is that my folks cut me off without a bean when I was sent down from Cambridge.'

'Sent down?'

'It means I was kicked out, sacked, smacked on the botty and sent home in disgrace.'

'What did you do that was so awful?'

'Well, there I was, quietly reading English and following in the footsteps of so many of our great playwrights at Trinity, when some son of a lord got stoned out of his mind, thought he was a fish and dived into the fountain, not bothering to come up for air. I happened to be around at the time and pulled him out. Ungrateful beast, I wish I'd left him there to die! I mean, I saved his life, but he went crying to the dean saying that some nasty second-year had tried to drown him, and out I went. Pretty rotten, really. I suspect it had something to do with the fact that his father was donating a library at the time, and having had the blame laid at my feet, me or the library had to go. Naturally the latter won. More coffee?'

'And was it your fault? Did you try and drown him by giving him drugs?'

'That, dear lady, is a very good question. Now let me see.' His eyes were twinkling. 'Put it this way, if it went to trial, I think the jury may just find me guilty. Anyway, that explains why I'm holed up in dear old Finsbury Park, shelf-stacking in Tesco's to pay my way through the director's course.'

'Do you ever take drugs?'

'In my wealthier days I did indeed indulge in a little weed, but the fact is, I'm so damned broke now I can't afford the paper to make the joint, let alone anything to put in it.'

'I live near Finsbury Park.'

'Wonderful!' He drained his coffee cup. 'Because, sweet maid, I must now depart and trek on down to my awaiting ton of baked beans. And therefore, as I must leave you so ungallantly alone, I shall expect you and my handkerchief to dinner next Thursday, the twenty-ninth. Sixty-one, Seven Sisters Road, eight thirty. I shall see you then?'

He looked questioningly at her.

'All right,' she said without thinking.

'Good.' He reached for her hand and kissed it. 'Farewell. Oh, Jenna?'

'Yes?'

'My place is a tear-free zone, so leave them on the mat before you come in. *Adieu*, until then.'

On the tube back home, Jenna didn't feel half so down as she had expected.

She liked Charlie. She liked him a lot. And she looked forward to seeing him again.

11

CHRISTMAS DAY ARRIVED and Jenna spent an unexciting day going to church in the morning with her mother, sharing a small turkey and watching television all evening.

There had been four presents under the tree; three for Jenna and one for Joyce. Bettina had bought her a print of Ellen Terry playing Juliet and Frankie had given her a beautiful cashmere sweater in a cornflower blue that matched her eyes. Her mother had unfortunately bought her a cheaper, similar sweater in a dull green.

Joyce had commented on the fact that her friends must be well off to be able to buy such expensive presents. Jenna had just nodded.

The highlight of the day was when a slightly drunken Frankie had called and made her laugh with tales of Tinsel Town.

'I'll be home in ten days so hold on to your hat. So long, kiddo.'

When she had put the telephone down, Jenna went to join her mother in the kitchen and began to dry the dishes.

'That was Frankie calling from LA.'

'Yes, dear. Can you put the remains of the turkey in a pan and I'll boil the bones tomorrow for some soup.'

Jenna was counting the hours until Frankie was back and she could return to the penthouse flat.

Her mother's continuing coldness upset her. She really doesn't seem to care, Jenna thought as she lay awake in bed that night. She switched on the light, found a pad and a pencil and wrote down some figures. She calculated that, if she worked every day until the end of the holiday helping Mr Jones, the manager of the shoe shop, with his January sale, it would mean that she would just about have enough money to get her through the next term without having to work on Saturdays. That would mean she need only come to see her mother for Sunday lunch. The thought cheered her enormously.

Charlie was hanging out of the window waiting for her when she arrived.

'Thank God you're here, otherwise I might have turned into a block of ice and you could have stuck me in your gin and tonic and drunk me,' he said as she entered his bedsit. It was miserable. Tiny, with a bed in the corner, a desk untidily piled with paper, a Baby Belling oven, a fridge, which rattled, and a small wash basin.

'Make yourself comfortable, my dear. It's not much but I like to call it hovel. Every great artist has to suffer, you know. I am at the bottom of an illustrious list of those who have sacrificed material possessions for their art. Mind you, I think there's a limit. I dream about having a hot bath, instead of the stone-cold jobs that are enough to freeze my . . . Anyway, dinner will be served in approximately ten minutes.'

They drank cheap wine out of chipped mugs and dined on what apparently was Charlie's speciality, pasta à la damaged tins, which was surprisingly good.

While Charlie did the washing up, Jenna sat on the bed and read his latest play, which he had just finished.

As an actress she knew she would be delighted to play one of his beautifully drawn characters. It took her a little under an hour to finish it. She looked up and saw Charlie sitting at his desk, arms crossed, staring at her.

'This really is good, Charlie.'

His face lit up. 'Do you think so?'

'Yes, I do.'

'Thank God for that. If you had said you didn't like it I would have been forced to chuck you out of the window, which would have made a horrible mess in the street below.' He looked seriously at her. 'I'm very glad you like it, Jenna. I haven't shown it to anyone else.'

'Well, you ought to, like people who could produce it.'

'I know. I intend to show it to Theo and see if he'll let me direct it in my final year.'

'You must, Charlie, it deserves an audience.'

They chatted for hours. Jenna relaxed and felt confident and comfortable in his company. Of course, he wasn't Matthew, but she liked him very much. When she said she must get the last tube back, he looked so crestfallen that she promised to come back for dinner again the following Thursday.

He insisted on escorting her to the tube and kissed her hand as she prepared to descend the steps.

'Thank you, fair maid, you have given much pleasure to an old man.'

'How old are you?'

'Twenty-three. Nearly in my coffin.'

She laughed, waved goodbye and ran down the steps.

Charlie walked slowly back to his room, deep in thought.

He drained what was left of his wine. Of course, he had fallen in love with her the first moment he had seen her on the balcony.

And now he knew, with startling clarity, that there would never be anyone else for him except Jenna. Ever.

12

THE DAY BEFORE Frankie flew back from Los Angeles in the middle of January for the start of the spring term, Jenna handed in her resignation at the shoe shop and told her mother that she would no longer be coming to stay on Saturday nights but would join her for Sunday Mass. This produced the usual non-reaction.

There was a reunion at the penthouse flat the night Frankie arrived back. The two girls chattered until the early hours. When Jenna climbed into her bed, she felt only relief that the holidays were over.

She was pleased to be back at school and grateful that she had given up her job, because the workload was much heavier than the term before.

'That guy is a sadist,' Frankie said one night, yawning. She looked at her watch. 'Come on, Jen, I've had it. How does Rudi expect us to give a command performance at nine tomorrow morning when we've been up studying the scene for him all night?'

It was half past two in the morning and they had spent the entire evening hearing each other through their respective speeches, acting as director, prompt and critic. Jenna shrugged and took herself wearily off to bed. Although she worked conscientiously, Rudi's reaction to her performance was always the same. He would just stare at her and say, 'Thank you, angel. Next.'

There was no doubt about the male star of the year. Matthew Valmont was getting a reputation on the school grapevine for being the 'man most likely to'. Jenna watched him in class as his performances grew in strength and stature. The fact that he had talent as well as charisma and good looks made the pedestal that Jenna had put him on even higher.

There was a rumour circulating around the school that his relationship with Paula was floundering, but whenever Jenna saw them they seemed inseparable.

Charlie and she had become firm friends, regularly spending Thursday nights together. Jenna had even managed to talk, for the first time in her life, about her lonely childhood and her mother.

When she had finished, he had sat there staring at her thoughtfully.

'I suppose you've never asked her why she resents you so much?'

'No. We very rarely talk, Charlie. It's amazing that two people could have lived under the same roof for all these years and hardly know each other. Do you think she does resent me?'

'Jenna, my dear, anyone who is as miserable and bitter as you say she is must have had something pretty nasty happen to her.'

Charlie had been very sympathetic about her mother, but quiet when Jenna talked to him about her feelings towards Matthew. She mentioned it to Frankie one night while she was cooking supper.

'Jen, you innocent, it's simple.' Frankie threw up her arms in despair. 'The guy goes funny when you talk about Matthew and your never-ending crush on him, because Charlie is in love with you.'

Jenna was startled. 'He's never tried to kiss me, Frankie.'

'That means he's a gentleman. Anyway, he knows that the only man you cream over at night is Mr M. Hunko, and that the poor starving playwright doesn't have a hope.'

'You're so disgusting, Frankie!'

'I know. But irresistible and gorgeous with it.'

'I give up.' Jenna laughed and checked that the spaghetti was cooked. The telephone rang and Frankie picked it up.

'Oh, hi, Bettina. He what?' Frankie yelled to Jenna, 'Guess who's just asked her duchessness out for coffee? Yep, you've got it, her very own baby Stanislavski.' She went back to the phone. 'Well, I hope you're going to the North Pole for this cup of coffee, because you know what will happen if anyone sees you. So long, babe, see you tomorrow.'

Jenna was serving up the supper. Frankie sat at the kitchen table, unusually quiet.

'Aren't you happy for her?'

'Yes and no, Jen. I'm just concerned that, because of the way Bettina feels about Mark, she won't be as careful as she should be. She could end up getting herself into lots of trouble.'

'They're only going for coffee.'

'Yes, but you know how strict the school is about tutors fraternizing with the students. Anyway, we'll both have to monitor the situation carefully, for the sake of our amorous ginger friend. I smell trouble, though I hope I'm wrong.'

The next few weeks proved Frankie right . . . and wrong. Right, because Bettina and Mark launched into a big affair, and wrong, because they took great pains to make sure that no one found out. Scared stiff of being discovered, they would often come round to the flat to have dinner and stay the night in one of the spare rooms.

Both girls liked Mark and were happy that he seemed to worship Bettina.

'I may have some good news that'll make all our lives a little easier,' Mark announced one night.

As usual, Bettina was wrapped round him on the sofa.

'What's that?'

'Well, I don't want you to get too excited just yet, but I've applied for a position at another drama school.'

'Really?'

'I would actually be director of drama if I got it.'

Bettina clapped her hands in delight. She knew that Mark wanted to be principal of a renowned drama school one day. And being director of drama was a step towards it.

'Which school is it?' asked Jenna.

'The Academy of Performing Arts.'

Frankie whistled. It was nearly on a par with their own school.

'I went for my first interview a week ago and this morning I got a letter saying they want to see me again next week.' Mark looked lovingly at Bettina. 'Then we might be able to step out of the closet and I would be able to keep you more in the style to which you are accustomed.' He kissed the top of her head.

'You know I don't care, Mark. I'd be quite happy living in a dog kennel in Zimbabwe as long as I was with you.'

Frankie made a retching sound. 'I think I shall retire before I throw up all over you both. 'Night, all.' And she disappeared off to bed.

Bettina sought out Jenna one lunchtime two weeks later at school. 'I need to talk to you, Jen.' They arranged to meet in the café while Frankie was having a fencing lesson.

'Mark has got the job. He starts in September.' Her eyes sparkled. 'And he's asked me to marry him.'

Jenna choked on her coffee. 'He's done what?'

Bettina looked disappointed. 'Jenna, I would have expected Frankie to say that, but not you.'

'I'm sorry, Bettina. I'm just surprised, that's all. You've known each other for less than three months. What are your parents going to say?'

'Oh, Jen, I know. But I love him so much and he loves

me and he's thirty-five. We want to have children before he gets much older.'

'What about your career?'

'Well, I'll have to leave school at the end of this year if I'm going to marry him, and we won't be able to tell anyone until he has officially left the school after the summer term ends. I intend to tell my parents then.'

'Won't they go mad? I mean, you're always telling me how they want you to marry some rich landowner from the right background.'

'I know, Jenna, believe me, I know. You've no idea how awful it is living up to the standards of generations of Langdales. How I wish I was you and could just announce my marriage, have a nice quiet wedding and go and live with the man I love and have his babies.'

For the second time in her life, Jenna found herself feeling sorry for a girl who had everything.

'They can't stop me, Jenna. I'm twenty next month and all they can do is never speak to me again. I may lose my family, but I really believe Mark is worth it.'

'Bettina, you know I'll support you in everything you do. I like Mark enormously, but please think very carefully before you make the final decision.'

'I will, Jenna, I promise. Please keep what I've told you a secret, won't you?'

Jenna nodded and the two girls went off to their respective classes, knowing that Bettina's mind was made up.

Bettina came round to the flat one evening during the Easter holidays to tell Frankie of her decision. Jenna was not there, having found herself a job selling ice creams five evenings a week at the Globe Theatre on Shaftesbury Avenue.

Frankie reacted as expected. She ranted and raved and told Bettina she was out of her mind.

'So, when are you going to tell your parents about all this? I tell you, my reaction to this news is tame compared to what they'll say.'

'We're both going to go up to Yorkshire at the end of the summer term.'

'I see. And what about your notice to the school? I'm sure Theo will be straight on the telephone to your father if you quit.'

'Yes, we've thought of that. I'm going to work during the summer holidays to get the money to pay the autumn term's fees, even if I won't be there. I'll hand my notice in after I've spoken to Ma and Pa.'

'It's not going to look too good for Mark, starting a new job as director of drama, at the same time as it becomes public knowledge that he's been screwing around with a student at his old school.'

'That's why we'll be getting married before he starts and then it's all respectable.'

'Well, Bettina, I can't say I approve, because I think you're crazy giving up your career for the sake of a man, but I hope you'll be very happy together.'

'Thanks, Frankie. Obviously you're sworn to secrecy

until the end of next term, but I just wanted you to know, even if you don't approve.'

Frankie didn't. But she knew that there wasn't a damn thing that she could do about it.

13

HALFWAY THROUGH the summer term the telephone rang at the flat and Jenna answered it. A deep male voice that she recognized but couldn't place asked if Frankie was home. She said yes, she was, and asked who wanted to talk to her.

'This is Daniel Duvall, Frankie's father.'

Jenna gulped and went to get Frankie out of the bath.

'Hi, Pops, how's tricks? You are? Next Wednesday's fine. Is it okay if I bring a couple of friends? Great. See you at the Hilton Rooftop Bar at eight. Bye, Pops.'

Frankie sauntered into the kitchen. 'Pops is flying into town next Wednesday. I'm taking you and Bettina to dinner with him. Maybe it'll make our smitten friend forget her darling acting tutor for a couple of hours or so.'

Daniel Duvall checked into the Hilton Hotel and took the lift to his suite on the twenty-second floor. The porter wheeled in his luggage and Daniel tipped him generously. He looked around at the usual bland luxury and wondered if he should have gone to stay in his apartment with his daughter.

The suite consisted of a large, plushly decorated sitting room with a well-stocked bar in the corner, two bedrooms and two bathrooms. He walked over to the floor-length windows and surveyed Park Lane beneath him. Coming back to London never ceased to fill him with a sense of disquiet.

Daniel disliked hotel rooms, forced as he was to spend a vast amount of time in them. He always marvelled at the way so many lives passed through them, yet somehow they managed to retain their air of indifference.

He sighed, went over to the bar and fixed himself a large scotch. He sat in a comfortable armchair and checked his watch. Two hours before he met Frankie. He settled back and closed his eyes.

Daniel Duvall had black hair that was greying very slightly at his temples, which gave him an air of elegant maturity that women found irresistible. His dark amber eyes were famed around the world for the way they could flash in anger or turn to limpid pools. He was forty-nine and looked forty. He kept his five-foot-nine frame in shape by working out regularly in his private gym. He dressed with a simple English elegance.

Daniel Duvall was a superstar. His face was probably known to more people around the world than the Pope's, his many films shown far and wide to an international audience. The deep, haunting tones that slipped like melted honey from his tongue and compelled the audience to listen were possibly even more famous than his face.

His prowess as a lover was also world-famous. A fact that Daniel himself found surprising, remembering, as he did, the gauche, undersized teenager he had been.

Other men looked on jealously as a string of beautiful women went into his bed and out of his life. He derived nothing but a fleeting moment of physical pleasure from these couplings and afterwards would feel only loathing for being so weak in his need for female comfort.

It had not always been like that, but when Blanche had died . . . well, he had not loved since, and eighteen years was a long time. It was almost as though his ability to love had died with her. All that he was able to give and receive was a physical manifestation of that purer force.

As his fame had grown, he had tried to end the pain of his terrible loneliness by taking advantage of bedding the many women who were only too delighted to come to his arms. He would turn the light off and imagine that the supple body below him was her.

He had tried marrying again – a peroxide, plastic imitation – but divorced three months later. Then there had been a wild Mexican actress, an animal in bed and a vixen out of it, who had caught and tamed him with her constant appetite for sex. After six months of marriage, he discovered that he alone was not enough to satisfy her and so followed another divorce.

That had been over twelve years ago. He had not tried again. He resigned himself to the fact that, for as long as he lived, there would never be another woman he could love like his first wife.

Daniel drained his glass and headed for the bathroom.

At eight o'clock precisely he was sitting in the Rooftop Bar sipping champagne.

He saw Frankie emerge from the lift and stood up to greet her.

'Hi, Pops, how are you?' Frankie kissed him and sat down.

He poured her a glass of champagne and realized once more that Frankie bore no resemblance to her mother.

'Good to see you, Pops. You look well.'

'You too, darling.'

'Though I'd like to flatter myself that you flew over especially to see me, I presume that isn't the case. What are you doing here?'

'I'm off to Wales tomorrow for two weeks to do some location on my new picture. I thought I'd spend a night in London to see my favourite daughter.' Daniel struggled to make the words sound less false than he knew them to be. He took a large gulp of champagne. 'How's my alma mater, then?'

'Fine. Rudi's the same as ever, by all accounts.'

'Good, good.'

Silence fell as they both tried to think of something to say. After a few awkward seconds, Frankie said, 'You'll meet two of my best buddies tonight. Jenna Shaw, who you spoke to on the telephone and who lives in the flat with me, and Bettina Langdale, whose father is a lord. She's in love with you so be gentle with her, okay?'

Daniel smiled and said he would.

They struggled through the next forty-five minutes, each of them feeling depressed about the fact that they were so uncomfortable with each other. Frankie was truly relieved when she saw the unmistakable head of red hair coming towards their table.

'Here they are, Pops. Bettina is the one with red hair, and Je –'

But Daniel wasn't listening. Blanche was walking towards him. She looked exactly the same as he remembered her. Slightly younger and thinner and perhaps her hair was a little longer, but it was his Blanche. He watched as she looked around the bar and physically had to stop himself from putting up his hand and waving to her. No matter, she seemed to recognize him as her gaze stopped at his table and her face lit up into the beautiful smile he cherished. As she moved closer, he realized that his memories had underestimated her radiance. He stood up as she arrived at his table. He longed to take her in his arms and smother her in the kisses he had saved for eighteen years . . .

'Jenna, this is my dad. Pops, wake up and say hello to Jenna.'

Daniel struggled to free himself from the illusion. Blanche, or Jenna, as Frankie called her, was extending her hand. She smiled at him and his heart beat against his chest.

'Hello, Mr Duvall. It's a pleasure to meet you.'

Even her voice was the same.

'Yes, er, hello, Jenna. It's, well, it's very nice to meet you too.'

'And this is Bettina Langdale.'

Frankie could see that her friend was tingling with excitement at meeting her hero. But her father was behaving very strangely, standing there staring at Jenna as though he'd seen a ghost.

Bettina put out her hand to Daniel. 'It's wonderful to meet you, Mr Duvall. I'm sure Frankie has told you what a big fan of yours I am.'

Daniel didn't seem to hear. Frankie coughed and he shook Bettina's outstretched hand.

Everyone sat down except Daniel. 'It's okay, Pops, I know this is England and the British like to stand on ceremony, but even they sit down to have a drink.' Frankie raised an eyebrow at him and he sat, desperately trying to regain control. He tried to stop himself staring at the exquisite figure in the black dress. He dragged his eyes away and signalled for the waiter.

'Another bottle of champagne, please. Do you like champagne, er, Jenna?'

The cornflower-blue eyes met his. 'Yes, very much.'

It was Bettina who saved Daniel and the evening from being a complete disaster. Once her confidence returned, she chattered nonstop, keeping his attention diverted from the beautiful girl who sat opposite him.

After dinner, Daniel escorted the three of them downstairs to a taxi.

'Pops, are you all right?' Frankie asked as she kissed him good night.

'Fine, Frankie. Sorry if I've not been my usual self. It's the combination of jet lag and alcohol, you know.' He kissed her. 'Take care and I'll call you from Wales.'

'Thank you, Mr Duvall, for one of the best evenings of my whole life!' said a slightly tipsy Bettina, throwing her arms round his neck and planting a big kiss on his cheek before clambering into the taxi alongside Frankie.

'It's been a pleasure to meet you,' said Jenna politely.

'And you, Jenna.'

He couldn't bear to say goodbye to her. He wanted to drag her back inside and ask her to explain what she was doing back in his life.

Pangs of pain gripped him as he watched her climb in to the cab. She was driving away into the night and he was powerless to stop her.

He stumbled up to his suite, tears blurring his eyes, and fixed himself a stiff scotch. He paced the room and had another drink, trying to fight the memories, but they were there and he was unable to stop them.

He remembered the softness of her body, the golden hair spread across the pillow as he made love to her and she cried, 'Daniel, I love you.'

He remembered the night she had told him, three months after their marriage, that she was going to bear him a child, and the way he had taken her tenderly in his arms and cried with joy.

Francesca Holly Duvall had been born seven months later and had further cemented their love.

He was blissfully happy, with his career in Hollywood beginning to take off, and his beautiful young wife who shunned publicity and was perfectly content to stay at home and take care of their baby daughter.

Then he remembered that last day. He shuddered involuntarily.

They had, as usual, spent Sunday in bed, playing with the laughing one-year-old and putting her gently into her cot when she finally fell asleep. They had made love and Blanche had made him promise that he would never leave her. He had sworn he wouldn't because he could not live without her.

She had asked if she could try out his new car on the short trip she needed to make to the store to buy milk for the baby. He had kissed her and handed her the keys. Blanche had said that she loved him and he was to stay exactly where he was until she got back.

When the telephone call came an hour later, he had driven Blanche's car down to the mortuary. He had been met by a policeman who had explained that his wife had been innocently waiting for a red light to turn green when her car was hit from behind. She had died painlessly and immediately of a broken neck. The policeman then asked him to identify his wife – a task made all the more painful by the fact that she appeared completely untouched.

That night he had drunk himself into oblivion. He repeated this for the next two months, refusing to believe that she wasn't coming back.

Francesca had been taken over by a nanny and Daniel rarely saw her. She was only a cruel reminder of the tragedy his love had suffered.

So Francesca, or Frankie, as she had decided to call

herself when she was ten, was someone who had shared his home, but not his love.

He avoided her. The pain and guilt were too much for him to bear. He knew how cross Blanche would have been with him for rejecting their only child. He hoped she'd understand that it was because of her, because of the way he loved her, that he found it impossible to be the father that his conscience told him he should be.

So they had drifted apart. Daniel had bought a succession of increasingly large houses until he realized that each time he moved, Blanche followed. All photographs of her had been packed into suitcases with the rest of her belongings and put in the attic.

He never spoke to his daughter about her mother. He supposed that she had been too young to remember her, for not once, even as she had grown older, had Frankie asked him about her. He felt guilty about removing all traces of Blanche from their lives, but looking at a photograph of her face every day had proved impossible.

He realized now that Frankie had no idea what a beauty Blanche had been, for surely she would have spotted the likeness between her friend and her dead mother?

Guilt surged once more inside him for what he had selfishly denied his daughter. He remembered when she had come to him and asked if she could audition for his old drama school in England. It was the first stirring of paternal pride he'd had since Blanche died.

When Frankie had been accepted he had opened a bottle of champagne and seen his daughter in a new light. She had grown into a beautiful woman – the pale delicate beauty of Blanche had been transmuted into the dark striking vivacity of his daughter.

Daniel stirred in his chair and reached for the bottle of scotch. He stood up, went to the window and looked out at London. There were so many memories here.

He wondered if tonight had been an illusion. The resemblance was unbelievable. It was Blanche. And after all those years of trying to forget, he had fallen in love with her all over again.

14

'I JUST CAN'T BELIEVE it's the final day of our first year,' said Frankie as the three of them clinked glasses.

Rather than the usual coffee, they had decided to treat themselves to a drink in a pub before they went home. One drink had turned to two. Then others from their group had arrived and they'd lost track of time. By eight o'clock, they were in the mood to continue.

'Come on everybody, let's go back to my place,' Frankie said rashly. 'They'll kick us out of here in a minute if we get any noisier. Everyone buy a bottle on the way and we'll see you there.'

News travelled fast and by ten o'clock, the flat was full of celebrating students.

Bettina had called Mark, since he had officially left that afternoon, and Matthew arrived without Paula. Jenna did her best to ignore his presence and concentrated on having a good time. The trouble was, wherever she went, he seemed to follow. She wondered if she was imagining it until she went out on to the balcony to get some fresh air. He followed and stood next to her.

'Hi, Jenna.'

'Hi, Matthew,' she said as casually as she could.

'Jenna, I, well, I wanted to wish you a good holiday.'

'Thanks. And you.' She was so startled that he was out here talking to her that she couldn't think of anything to say. She felt his arm slide slowly round her shoulder. The touch of his body so near hers turned her legs to jelly once more.

They stood like that for a long time.

'Jenna, I just want to say that –'

There was a noise behind them. Two students appeared on the balcony. Matthew quickly withdrew his arm.

'It doesn't matter. Have a good holiday and I'll see you next term.' He disappeared inside.

She spent the night going over and over the incident in her mind. She told Frankie the next day while she was packing her case in preparation for her journey back to the States.

Frankie shrugged. 'I don't know, Jenna. I did hear that he was having problems with Paula. But having said that, I know that they're going to spend the next two months travelling round Europe together. So I wouldn't lose sleep over him if I were you.' She carried on packing.

Jenna felt disappointed, but she decided that Frankie was right and she'd spent too long mooning around after Matthew.

Frankie flew off to stay at Palm Beach with some friends of her father's. She had begged Jenna to go with her. Jenna had to refuse, knowing she would have to work every day of the summer holiday that she could.

Frankie had asked her if she would stay in the flat while she was away to look after it. When Jenna told her mother she was not coming home for the holidays, Joyce had nodded. Jenna didn't think she cared.

She went back to her job at the Globe Theatre on Shaftesbury Avenue as an usherette. It was perfect for her. She didn't have to be at the theatre until six thirty and she was able to watch the play and study the actors free of charge every night.

Bettina came round to visit the day before she took Mark up to meet her parents and break the news of their engagement.

Jenna had bought some bread and pâté for lunch and they sat eating and talking.

'Actually, Jen, I've not told you everything.'

'What do you mean?'

Bettina swallowed. 'I'm two months pregnant.'

'Bloody hell!'

'I know. Pretty careless of me, really, but there we go.'

'Does Mark know?'

'Oh yes, he's thrilled. He's going up to Edinburgh as soon as we get back from Yorkshire to see the play he's directing performed at the festival. He wants me to come and stay with you. He says pregnant women should not be left by themselves. I think at two months he's being a little overprotective, but would that be okay?'

'Fine, I'll be glad of the company. As long as you don't go into labour on me!'

Bettina laughed and said, 'I'll do my best not to, I promise.'

A week later Jenna found a drunken, tear-stained Bettina waiting for her in the lobby of the block of flats when she arrived home from the theatre.

As soon as she saw Jenna, Bettina burst into tears. Jenna steered her up in the lift to the flat, sat her on the sofa and went to make her a large mug of steaming black coffee.

'I'm so sorry,' Bettina gulped, 'but I couldn't think of anywhere else to go.'

'Don't worry about that. Just tell me what's happened?'

Slowly, in between torrents of tears and mounds of tissues, Jenna managed to coax the story out of her.

'I couldn't possibly tell Mark. His job is his life and I can't ask him to give that up. I know he would and he'd just be miserable for the rest of his life. Oh, Jen, I've got to go and kill our baby tomorrow. I want to die, I want to die!'

Jenna fed her more coffee and she started to sober up.

'The worst thing was that Pa was so terribly sweet when we first told him about everything. He even opened a bottle of champagne.' She managed a little laugh. 'So when he asked me if I'd mind staying home a bit longer to sort out wedding plans, of course I said yes. I saw Mark off on the train to Edinburgh and we were both so happy, Jen.' She shook her head. 'When Pa told me what he was going to do a couple of days later, I thought he was joking, at least to begin with.' Bettina blew her nose. 'I had no idea he was on the board of governors at the Academy of Performing Arts as well as our school. He swore that he would make it his business to ensure that Mark would never work again as a tutor, let alone as a director of drama.'

'Why does he hate Mark so much?'

'Oh, he doesn't hate Mark. He hardly knows him. He just went on and on about the responsibility that's placed on your shoulders when you're a peer of the realm. Pa couldn't have his daughter running off to marry some penniless drama tutor and have his baby. The funny thing is, Jen, I don't hate him. I mean, I've been brought up with all this nobility rubbish and I'm afraid that's just my lot in life.'

Bettina's face was red and blotched from crying. Jenna wished there was something she could do to help.

'You can always run away with him.'

'No. That's one thing that I've managed to make up my mind about. I would be destroying Mark's dreams. I love him too much to ask him to go and work in some dreadful office.'

'But don't you think he ought to know about the abortion?'

'Absolutely not. If he knew I'm being forced into it he'd move heaven and earth to marry me and save the baby. Really, Jen, it's better all round if I just do as my father wants. Then Mark can call me all the names under the sun when he gets the letter I've sent him but at least he'll have a career.'

'What exactly have you said in this letter?'

'Oh, not much, just a pack of lies. Things like I made a mistake, that he couldn't give me what I wanted and I felt I was too young to be a wife and a mother.' The tears poured down her cheeks again.

'I don't think he'll believe you, Bettina.'

'To be honest, it doesn't matter. I'll be on a plane to the south of France in three days' time. I'm supposed to recuperate there before I start a History of Art course in Florence in September.'

'That sounds like fun. You might enjoy it, Bettina.'

'I didn't have a say in the decision. Pa wants to make sure that I'm as far away from Mark as possible.'

Eventually Bettina fell into an exhausted sleep on the sofa. Jenna covered her with a blanket and spent a sleepless night wondering why life was so cruel.

15

ONCE BACK AT SCHOOL in September, Frankie and Jenna grew closer to fill the gap left by Bettina.

They had both been cast in a production of *A Midsummer Night's Dream*, which would be performed in the school theatre just before Christmas.

Their graduating year would be spent working mainly on productions that enabled them to show their talent to agents and casting directors. There were three productions a term and the students had all been told that each one of them would get a chance to play a major role.

The story concerned a group of courtiers who had mischief made on them by fairies in a forest. They would love the first person they saw when they opened their eyes. This created a lot of confusion and there was a scene in which Helena and Hermia – Paula and Jenna – had to fight over Lysander, who was played by Matthew.

'As if to hold a mirror up to life', Frankie had quoted

poetically. She was delighted to be cast as Titania, the queen of the fairies.

Jenna shared most of her scenes with Paula and Matthew. She tried to ignore the fact that they seemed to have a row every day. Paula had even walked out of the rehearsal in tears on one occasion. Matthew was very polite to Jenna and had asked her if she wanted to spend time after school going through a couple of their scenes. She had refused, remembering her vow after the end-of-term party not to waste any more time thinking about him. But she trembled when he put his arms around her and stage-kissed her.

Two weeks before the production was due to open, she was sitting in the kitchen with her mother on Sunday, eating lunch.

'Mother, I was wondering if you would like to come and see me in the play I'm doing. It's *A Midsummer Night's Dream*. I can get you a free ticket.'

Joyce shook her head. 'No thank you, Jenna. I'm having to stay late at the office during the Christmas period so I won't be able to make it.'

At the party after the opening night, everyone seemed to have someone who had come to see them. Jenna had no one. She tried not to let it hurt but it did. She was just thinking of going home when someone lifted her off the floor and twirled her round. It was Charlie.

'Alas, my dear, you are once again looking sad and abandoned. Good grief, I can't let you out of my sight for a second before you've found yourself another catastrophe. Whatever is wrong?'

Jenna was delighted to see him. 'Oh, nothing, Charlie. Just that everyone seems to have someone telling them how good they were,' she answered truthfully.

'Oh, fishing for compliments, are we?'

'No, it's not that, I . . .'

He took her small hands in his and looked deep into her eyes.

'Jenna, my angel, be patient. Your time will come. Hell, I watched it and I thought you knocked them all off the stage.'

He had also seen the way she had looked at Matthew during their love scenes.

'Thanks, Charlie. I appreciate it. It's just been a bit of an anticlimax, that's all.'

'Give the poor old moguls a chance, sweet maid. They have only just seen the startling new talent that emerged on the stage tonight. By tomorrow morning I'm sure they'll be jamming the telephones to Theo to find out who you are. Seriously, Jenna, and you know I don't use that word often, I happen to believe that you're one of the most talented young ladies I have ever had the good fortune to witness on the stage. Now, as I have some very good news, I'm taking you out for a celebratory pizza this minute. Or as soon as I can find my coat, which I've left somewhere around here. Back in a minute.'

Matthew had left the crowd he was with and was walking towards her. He kissed her on the cheek.

'Congratulations! You were super. I think we make

a very good team, don't you?' His eyes searched her face.

'Yes.'

'Listen, Jenna, I was wondering if you'd like to come with me for a quick bite to eat.'

She saw Charlie walking back towards them.

'I'm afraid I can't, Matthew. I'm going with Charlie to –'

'Never mind. Perhaps some other time. Hello, Charlie. Bye, Jenna.'

Hello, Charlie; goodbye, Matthew, she sighed to herself as they made their way through the crowd and out into the night.

'I hope I didn't put paid to anything back there,' said Charlie, knowing he had and not feeling in the least bit sorry about it. They walked down the road to an Italian restaurant, sat down and ordered two pizzas.

'Well, do you want to hear my wonderful news or not, Miss Misery Guts?'

Jenna tried to forget about the romantic dinner for two that she could have been having with Matthew. 'Of course, Charlie. What is it?'

'Theo has read my play. He's said I can direct it and put it on in the school theatre during the final term.'

'That's fantastic, Charlie!'

'Yes, it is rather. It means that I can invite the whole of the profession to watch with wonder at my amazing talent and hopefully get a job out of it, too.'

'I really am thrilled for you.'

'Well, I'd love you to be in it, of course, but a little bird tells me you may be very busy in your last term, so I've been told I can't cast you.' He casually got on with his pizza. Jenna's heart leaped. If Theo had said that Charlie couldn't cast her in his play, that must mean that she had a leading role in one of the final-term plays. She knew one of them was *Romeo and Juliet*. She sent up a secret prayer.

When the cast lists for the final term productions went up on the big notice board, Jenna joined the throng of anxious students. But before she had time to see the list of names, Frankie emerged from the crowd of people.

'Jenna, you've got it! They've cast you as Juliet!'

They went out for a celebratory dinner at Joe Allen.

'Here's to the future.' Jenna lifted her glass.

'And here's to being so famous that when we book a table here again they don't stick us in the corner by the john! How are you going to handle the fact that your Romeo is being played by Mr Valmont?'

Jenna shrugged. Since she had turned down Matthew's offer of dinner that night over four months ago, he had hardly spoken to her.

'I'll cope.'

'Well, he's been single for nearly two months since he finally dumped Paula.'

'I know.'

'And someone's bound to pounce on him soon if you

don't. Especially as he is getting so much attention from agents and casting directors.'

What Frankie said was true. The buzz was that Matthew had already got himself an agent, apparently one of the best.

'You'd better start writing those letters,' said Frankie.

'I know. I need an agent and a job so that I can get my Equity card.'

'It's such a silly system. I mean, until you get your Equity card, you can't work. On the other hand, you can't get a job without it.'

'I'm going to try and get as many people as I can to come and see me as Juliet. I just hope I can get an agent and someone to employ me,' sighed Jenna. 'Anyway, are you pleased with your part in the final-term show, Frankie?'

'I'm thrilled. Me doing Noël Coward is going to be something special, I can tell you. I'll be the most outrageous Madame Arcati the London stage has ever seen.'

'Have you given any more thought to afterwards?'

'This is when it's really useful to have a famous film star for a father. He's bringing over his agent from the States to see *Blithe Spirit*, and the director of his new picture is going to be in London. Hopefully he'll come along as well. To be honest, Jen, if Mimi, Pops's agent, offers to take me on her books, I'm in no position to refuse. It'll be back to Hollywood for me. Anyway, let's not think about that yet.'

'I'd miss you dreadfully if you did go to LA.'

'And I'd miss you, Jenna. You'll just have to come over and visit me as often as you can.'

'I got a letter from Bettina today.'

'How is she?' asked Frankie.

When Jenna had told her what had happened to Bettina and Mark, Frankie had not been surprised. She'd had a bad feeling about it all along.

'She seems all right. At least her letter was a bit more cheerful than the others I've had. It's probably because she's coming back to live with her parents in June. She says she might be able to sneak along and see the end-of-term shows.'

'It'll be good to see her again.'

Jenna nodded in agreement.

Although rehearsals for *Romeo and Juliet* didn't start for another month, Jenna spent as much time as she could studying her part. By the time it came to the first read-through for the play, she was almost word-perfect.

Rudi was directing. This was a great honour since he chose only one production a year to turn his hand to.

Most of the cast were already assembled when Jenna entered the big studio.

'Hello, Jenna.' Matthew patted the chair next to his.

She sat down and nervously fumbled in her bag to find her script.

Rudi came in and sat down behind his desk.

'Good afternoon, ladies and gentlemen. I hope you are all well. We will be very busy in the next four weeks. The play we are going to perform is my favourite of the many great works that Shakespeare wrote so I will expect great things from each one of you. So kindly open your scripts and we will begin reading.'

Rudi sat with his eyes closed as he listened to the young students read the play. He recalled discussing the casting with Theo, when the latter had insisted on Jenna for Juliet. Although Rudi agreed that Jenna possessed remarkable talent, he had not been sure about her playing Juliet.

He listened closely to her reading. There was no doubt about the fact that she had been studying hard for the past month, for her lines were well rehearsed and read with a degree of understanding. But there was something missing that he could not pinpoint. Maybe she needed to fall in love. Although he was a genius as a teacher, he had little control over his students' emotions. He opened his eyes and looked up as they came to the end of the play.

'Okay. That was not bad, but not nearly good enough to be put on a stage. I shall expect you two,' – he pointed to Matthew and Jenna – 'to meet me here tomorrow at five o'clock to work on the love scenes. The rest of you I will see on Friday at nine o'clock sharp. Class dismissed.'

Matthew raised his eyebrows at Jenna. 'I think this is going to be tough. I'll see you tomorrow.'

The following day, Rudi sat with the two of them, discussing the characters and what he believed were their strengths and weaknesses. They worked on small pieces of the text, usually only getting as far as three or four words before he stopped them.

'You must remember, both of you, that although these

two loffers haff become famed the world over and been played by famous actors time and again, you haff to put your own stamp on the character. Forget what you haff seen before and create from inside yourself. Okay, we read that speech again . . .'

16

'No! No! *NO*! JENNA, do not say zese oh so beautiful words as though you are speaking to a cabbage! You loff this man, you are prepared to die for him. Let us try again.'

Jenna took a deep breath and started the speech for the fifth time.

> ''Tis but my name that is my enemy;
> Thou art thyself, though not a Montague.
> What's Montague? It is not hand, nor foot –'

'*Stop*!' Rudi put his head in his hands.

Jenna wanted to cry, scream or wring Rudi's neck; she wasn't sure which. It was a Saturday afternoon and there were two weeks to the opening night. Jenna had spent the last three weeks in hell, with Rudi constantly shouting at her. Today, he had called an extra rehearsal for Matthew and her to work on the balcony scene.

Jenna had considered dropping out and letting another

student take over Juliet. She just seemed unable to produce the performance that Rudi wanted.

She fought back the tears and decided that if he said another word, that was it. She would walk out of the classroom, out of the production and never return.

Rudi must have sensed that she was at the end of her tether. 'Okay, we leave it for today. You are tired. I will go home now and hope that on Monday morning you haff woken up.' Rudi closed his battered satchel and stalked from the room.

Jenna watched him go and then promptly burst into tears.

'Oh God, I'm awful, I'm so awful. I'm dreadful! I should stop trying to pretend I'm an actress.'

Matthew's arms came around her, timidly at first, as if he was scared she might force them away, then firmly as Jenna sobbed. When the crying had worn itself out and she was at the hiccuping and sniffing stage, Matthew pulled out a hanky and gently wiped her eyes.

'They'll have to recast me, that's all there is to it,' she said dejectedly.

'Oh, Jenna, really! You're being incredibly self-indulgent. You know what Rudi's like. Look, let's go through the scene again.'

'I couldn't.'

'I want to go through this scene again, so be a professional and do it for me, will you?'

The harshness in Matthew's voice brought her to her

senses. With an embarrassed 'sorry', she climbed back on the dais.

'But, soft! What light through yonder window breaks? It is the east, and Juliet is the sun.' He spoke the words to her. As he climbed up the balcony to hold her in his arms and kiss her, she felt the familiar churning in her stomach. This time, however, instead of the technical stage-kiss when their firmly closed lips met, she felt Matthew's tongue prising her mouth open. The shock that he was really kissing her disappeared as she responded and the world melted away.

They stood there, in the deserted studio, arms tightly wound round each other, kissing with all the fervour of the young lovers they were portraying.

'Oh Jenna, my Jenna, how long I've waited to do this,' he murmured.

After an eternity in which Jenna's body had turned to jelly and the stirring in her groin had become almost unbearable, their lips parted and they stood holding each other, neither sure of what to do or say next.

'I don't want to let you go,' said Matthew softly. 'Will you come home with me?'

She knew there was nothing she could do to stop herself.

'Yes.'

Jenna remembered little about the journey in a taxi to Matthew's small studio flat in Fulham. She held Matthew's hand as he led her quickly up the many stairs to the top of the old Victorian house.

Once inside, Matthew picked Jenna up in his arms

and carried her to the bed. He held her to him as though she was a tiny baby, something to be treasured and looked after at all costs. Jenna's body tingled with new responses as he kissed her once more. He put his hand gently to her breast. She sighed as he undid her blouse, grateful to him for removing the material that lay between his hands and her delicate pale skin.

Jolts of pleasure ran through her body as he put his mouth to first one breast, then the other. The nipples hardened beneath his kisses.

He tore at his shirt and the rest of his clothes until he stood in front of her, naked. She looked with fascination at the huge shaft that was standing upright between his legs.

He lay down beside her once more and kissed her again. She could hear his breathing coming in short, violent bursts as she felt his hardness press against her still covered thigh. Gentle hands roamed her body and travelled up under her skirt towards the part of her that was desperate to be touched. Fingers traced the line of the triangle of lace that was covering her most intimate part and she gasped as they found their way inside.

Matthew removed the rest of her clothes until she lay naked next to him.

'Jenna,' he whispered, 'you are perfect. Oh God, you're even more perfect than I imagined.'

His mouth locked over hers as his hand guided him inside her. He began to thrust into her, calling her name, telling her he loved her, that he had always loved her. The thrusts became frenzied, almost violent. The pain whipped through her and then was gone, as pleasure took its place.

Suddenly, Matthew arched, groaned and sank down on to Jenna and held her tight.

She wanted to cry. She was not sure why. She felt him slip out of her, felt the sensation of hot liquid travelling from inside her on to the sheets below.

Matthew saw the colour of the liquid trickling down her thighs.

'Jenna.' He pushed himself up on his elbow and looked down at her. 'Thank you for letting me be the first.' He traced the contours of her face with his fingers and his blue eyes fixed on hers.

'I love you, Jenna. You know that, don't you?'

'I love you, too.'

They lay entwined, alone together, until their passion rose again from the gentle kisses. Matthew took her hand in his and led it to his manhood. His fingers sought out the small button, sheathed in tiny curls, that would bring her pleasure. Her body jumped involuntarily as he touched her there. When he felt she was ready, he entered her again.

Jenna felt her breathing quicken at the same pace as his, and the tension in her body became unbearable. The throbbing coming from deep inside her built apace until the world exploded into a thousand stars. This time they cried out together as a feeling of utter contentment and peace replaced the urgency of before.

Later, Matthew went out to buy fresh bread, cheese, tomatoes and wine. While he was gone Jenna took a bath. Then they sat on the bed and ate hungrily.

'Are you happy, Jenna?'

'Very', she said, biting into a tomato.

'You know, I think I've loved you since the moment you stood up on that first day in Rudi's class. But by then I was already with Paula. When I eventually managed to escape, you had Charlie.'

Jenna stared at him in disbelief. 'Matthew, for starters, I've never "had" Charlie, as you put it. He's a very close friend but, well, he has never been more than that. And I find it hard to believe you spent a year and a half with a girl you didn't really like.'

'I know. In the beginning I did like her. I really thought I was in love with her.' Matthew shrugged. 'She's very attractive and was er, well, to be blunt, very good between the sheets.'

Jenna shuddered. He noticed and pulled her to him.

'Anyway, it's all over now. This is what feels right. It's you I want, my Juliet.' He kissed the tip of her nose.

'Mind you, I think there will be two pretty miserable faces at school when they realize what's happened.'

Jenna nodded. She hoped Charlie would be be happy for her.

Matthew noticed her frown and said, 'Jenna, please tell me you feel the same way. I couldn't bear it if you didn't.'

She took his hand and squeezed it.

'Yes, I do, Matthew, I really do.'

They fell back on to the bed, food forgotten, and made love for a third time.

17

'WELL, I KNOW I ASKED for a miracle, but I did not believe my prayer would be answered.' Rudi gazed thoughtfully at Jenna, who had just given the kind of performance that he'd been trying to drag out of her for weeks. 'That was like watching a different girl. You too, Matthew, you are much improved. What has happened?' He gazed at them both. 'No, don't answer that. I do not wish to know. Just make sure that it lasts anozer ten days, please. Then we will really have something to show to the public. Okay, I see you tomorrow. Good night.'

As he walked from the room, he noticed Matthew squeeze Jenna's hand and he smiled to himself. He knew exactly what had happened. He chuckled as he made his way downstairs to report to Theo that Romeo and Juliet had both made a remarkable improvement and there would be a play worth watching, after all.

Jenna, who had not been back to the flat since Saturday, having spent Sunday night with Matthew, opened the door to find a disgruntled Frankie lounging on the sofa.

'And where the hell have you been?'

She knew exactly where Jenna had been, along with most of the school, but she wasn't going to let her off the hook that easily.

'With Matthew.'

'Really?' Frankie drawled. 'Thanks for letting me know. I nearly had half of Scotland Yard out looking for you yesterday.' She tried to look stern but she couldn't quite manage it.

'Frankie, I'm sorry.'

Frankie thought she had never seen anyone look less sorry in her life. Jenna was positively glowing.

'I, well, time went so quickly and I ... .'

'... I was too busy screwing Matthew to stagger out of bed to call my best buddy.' She watched her friend go bright red.

Jenna managed a half-hearted 'Frankie!'

'So, what was he like?'

'If you mean what was our weekend like, well, it was wonderful.'

'Cut the crap, hon, you know exactly what I mean. Did the earth move, is he as well endowed as he looks in his jock strap? Is it lurve?' She drew out the last word but didn't need Jenna to answer as she looked at her sparkling eyes.

'Frankie! It was wonderful. I mean, he was wonderful.'

'Jesus, I think I'm going to puke. And what was all this about saving it until you were married?'

Jenna looked guiltily at her. 'I know. I feel bad about that, but it just felt so right. I'll probably be damned in hell for ever but I think it was worth it.'

'Did you use anything?'

Jenna looked guilty again. 'No, but it's okay. I ... I found out this morning that I'm not, well, I'm not pregnant.'

'Sounds as though you were very stupid and very lucky. Didn't you think about what happened to Bettina?'

'I know I should have done. But it all happened so fast I ...'

'That's how little accidents are brought into the world. I hope you're going to get yourself fixed up soon.'

'Frankie, would you mind coming with me to one of those places, you know, family-planning clinics? I don't think I could face going by myself. But an illegitimate baby would be ten times worse and I could never, never do what Bettina did.' The thought appalled her as she remembered the way the nuns had talked about the dreadful punishment that awaited anyone who took a life from inside themselves.

The previous night she'd slept fitfully. She had watched Matthew lying peacefully beside her, while she was fighting with her conscience over what she had done. She could not believe that anything as beautiful as what she had just shared with Matthew could possibly be wrong. Jenna had consoled herself with the thought that, if God was love, and she was in love with Matthew, he would understand.

'If I have to,' Frankie sighed.

'Sorry?' said Jenna, immersed in her thoughts.

'I said if I have to, I'll accompany you to the clinic. Wake up, honey!'

'Thanks, Frankie. I'd really appreciate it.'

Frankie phoned for an appointment and they went a couple of days later, when neither of them had to be at school for rehearsals until lunchtime.

The Margaret Pyke Clinic just off Soho Square catered solely for women. Although Jenna felt embarrassed by the personal nature of both the examination and the questions, the female doctor quickly put her at her ease.

The doctor told her about the different methods of contraception, and they both agreed that she should opt for the Pill.

Matthew and Jenna spent every spare moment they could together. As their trust grew, they talked to each other about their pasts.

Matthew had been born in Gateshead, where his father worked down the coalmines. He had married at eighteen and Matthew, having been the main reason for his premature union, was resented by his father from the start. Both Matthew and his mother suffered regularly from violent physical outbursts wreaked on them by his drunken father on returning from the local pub. Matthew, who adored his mother, would lie with his pillow over his head while his father took her as she screamed. When Matthew was thirteen his mother died and he started to fight back. As soon as he had finished school, he had earned the fare to London and arrived penniless in the big city.

He had immediately found himself a job washing up in the kitchen of a large restaurant and moved into a dingy flat in Clapham with one of the waiters.

'I was so determined, Jenna. My father accused me of

being a fairy because I was interested in the theatre. I gave myself five years to save up enough to go to drama school. I did anything I could to earn money.' He chuckled. 'You should have heard me when I arrived here. Reet broad Geordie I was, hinny! I took voice lessons before I auditioned for the school.'

'Nobody would guess now.'

'I know. Quite smooth, suave and sophisticated these days, aren't I?' His face became taut and he sighed. 'Sometimes, though, I thought I'd never make it.'

She hugged him. 'Well, that's all in the past now.'

He smiled at her. 'Yes, it is. We'd better get some sleep. We've got a big day tomorrow.'

Jenna switched the light off and snuggled into him.

'Quite a pair, you and I,' he said quietly. 'How do you fancy being the Olivier and Leigh of the Eighties?'

Jenna didn't know whether he was serious. So she didn't tell him that to share her future with Matthew would make her happiness complete.

18

'GOOD LUCK, MY JULIET, I'll see you on stage and tell you how much I love you again.' Matthew kissed her and went off to take his place in the wings.

Her heart was beating loudly as she sat in the crowded dressing room that all the female members of the cast shared. She could hear the subdued murmurings of the audience coming over the tannoy. Jenna was aware of the effect that the invited audience of directors, agents and critics could have on her career. She wondered if her mother had come, but she doubted it. She had sent the ticket to her, explaining she would be too busy rehearsing to come home for the next few Sundays, but she would love her to come to the play.

She hoped Charlie was out front, but recently he had been curiously distant. She understood that he was heavily involved in directing his own play, so she had left him alone, hoping he wasn't sulking about Matthew. She felt selfish about the fact that she wanted nobody to spoil her delicious sense of happiness.

The hum of the audience gently died as the poignant

sounds of the opening music were heard on the speakers. Her call came over the tannoy and she made her way to the wings. Matthew's voice drifted to her from the stage. Suddenly she didn't feel nervous any more.

When it was time for her first appearance, in her bedroom with her nurse, she calmly stepped out on to the stage and began to tell her tragic story.

Frankie, sitting in the audience, felt a sense of disquiet as she watched Matthew and Jenna together on the stage in front of her.

Two other people were sharing that thought with her.

Joyce sat watching her gifted daughter and knew immediately.

And Charlie knew too.

As Jenna sent the knife into her body, staggered towards Romeo and lay dying by his side, she knew without a doubt in her mind that she would do the same if Matthew were to leave her. The thought of life without him was as unbearable as Juliet's grief. There was an audible gasp from the audience as the curtain fell.

For a moment there was total silence. Jenna lay there, feeling disoriented and wondering if the audience had gone home. Then there was tumultuous applause and she was standing next to Matthew taking bow after bow.

Theo turned to Rudi to congratulate him. 'Marvellous, old chap! I told you that girl had enormous talent. I think we may have a new pair of young stars on our hands.'

At the party after the show, Jenna and Matthew were standing, arms entwined, in the centre of a large crowd of admiring well-wishers. They were both on a high. Three agents had offered Jenna their cards and asked her to contact them. Matthew was talking to a very well-known television director whom his new agent had brought along. It seemed he was interested in Matthew for a new weekly series beginning in September.

Matthew turned to her and squeezed her hand. 'We're on our way, darling.'

She smiled back happily as Theo approached them.

'Congratulations, you two. Super performances! So super, in fact, that a director friend of mine has just asked me whether you would be prepared to extend your time as the star-crossed lovers and appear for three weeks in his version at the Round House. It's a good venue and it would mean you'd get your Equity cards.'

'We'd – I mean, I would love to!' said Matthew, knowing he would need a card before he could think about appearing on television.

'What about you, Jenna?'

The thought of working with Matthew for an extra three weeks was an answer to her prayers. 'I'd love to as well.'

'Good decision,' Theo remarked. 'You can use it as an extra chance to get more people in to see your performance. I'll let Roger know tomorrow.'

Jenna saw a lonely figure standing nervously on the other side of the room. 'Excuse me,' she said, 'I've just seen my mother.' She walked towards her.

'Hello, Mother. I'm very glad you could come.'

'You were very good, Jenna.'

'Thank you. Would you like a glass of wine?'

'No, thank you.'

They stood in silence. Jenna saw Matthew coming over to join them. He held out his hand. 'Hello. I'm Matthew Valmont. It's very nice to meet you.'

Joyce took his hand as if it contained poison and shook it.

'Excuse me, would you mind awfully if you held this for me and I borrowed your daughter for two minutes? Please don't go away, I know Jenna wants to speak to you.' He gave his glass of wine to Joyce and dragged a surprised Jenna into a corner.

'I'm sorry, darling, but this really is urgent.'

'What is it?'

'Well, I know this may come as a huge shock to you and you can say no if you want. I love you, Jenna, and I want you to marry me.'

He pulled out a small box and gave it to her. She fingered the soft velvet of the box, wondering if she was dreaming.

'Look, I know that this is slightly rushed, but I couldn't think of a more romantic or fitting time to propose. And I know I'm sure. How about you?' He looked at her anxiously.

Of course she was sure. She loved him, even if they had known each other only a short time. She had given him her virtue and therefore it was only right that she married him.

'If you aren't going to say something, then open the box at least, darling.'

She did so. Inside was a delicate band of gold with a solitaire diamond sparkling brightly in the centre.

'Can I put it on your finger?'

'Yes.'

He slipped it on. It fitted her slim finger perfectly.

'My love, you've made me very happy.' He tugged at her hand. 'Come on, I want to tell everyone before they start going home.'

'Shouldn't we tell my mother first before we announce it to everyone?'

'We can speak to her afterwards.' Matthew had already pulled Jenna to the centre of the room. He clapped his hands for silence.

'Ladies and gentlemen! Romeo and his Juliet have an announcement to make. We have decided to rewrite Shakespeare's story and give it a happier ending. I'd like you to know that two minutes ago, Miss Jenna Shaw agreed to be my wife.'

A sound of glass breaking shattered the surprised silence and Jenna saw the white face of her mother with the shards of the wine glass she had dropped lying at her feet.

Frankie, who had just walked in, sucked in her breath.

People crowded round to congratulate them.

Charlie quietly left the room.

Frankie kept her thoughts on the subject to herself and marched across to hug her friend. 'Well, this is what you call an action-packed night, isn't it? I'll say one thing for your man, he hasn't hung around. I don't know what I'll look like in some frilly bridesmaid's get-up, but congrats anyway. At least someone will be watching out for you when I go Stateside.'

Jenna had not seen Frankie since her performance in

Blithe Spirit the previous night. Her father had taken Mimi, his agent, along to watch her.

'Frankie, has Mimi agreed to take you on to her books?'

'Yes. And I may have a part in a film, too,' she announced proudly. 'Anyway, I'll tell you all about it another time. You just enjoy tonight, kiddo. By the way, is your mom here? I think it's time we were introduced.'

'Yes, she is.' Jenna looked round but could not see her. 'Well, she *was*. Matthew, have you seen my mother?'

'I think I saw her leave, sweetheart,' said Matthew and turned his attention back to the director who was congratulating him.

'Never mind,' said Frankie, 'I didn't want to meet the old bat anyway. I'd have probably disgraced myself by saying "Christ" or "Jesus" and she'd have passed out from the shock. Are you staying with Matthew tonight?'

'Yes,' Jenna said distractedly. She was worried about her mother.

'Fine. Will I see you at school tomorrow?'

'Yes.'

'Have a fun evening. You two come round to the flat tomorrow night and we'll open a bottle of champagne.' She kissed Jenna and headed for the door.

People were starting to say good night. Jenna tapped Matthew on the shoulder. 'I can't see my mother anywhere. I'm worried.'

'She was probably just tired and nipped off home not wanting to disturb you. After all, she doesn't know anyone here.'

'Matthew, she's my mother and we just announced our engagement. Why didn't she come and at least say goodbye?'

'I don't know, Jenna.' She could hear the tinge of irritation in his voice. 'She'll be fine. Just relax and enjoy the night, will you?'

'I'm sorry, I'll have to go home and make sure she's all right. I'll see you back at the flat.'

Matthew sighed. 'Okay, Jenna, if that's what you want, I'll see you there later.'

He looked annoyed but pulled out a five-pound note from the pocket of his jeans. 'Get a taxi, I can't have my wife- and star-to-be getting mugged on the tube, can I?'

'I'll be as quick as I can.' She kissed him, rushed outside and hailed a cab.

Jenna stepped into the dark hallway. With relief she saw a crack of light coming from under the kitchen door. She opened it and stopped short when she saw her mother.

Joyce was still in her coat. There was a glass in her hand which she was filling to the brim with something that looked suspiciously like sherry. The bottle in her other hand was more than half empty.

'Mother, are you all right? Has something happened?' She put her arm protectively around her mother's shoulders.

'Don't you touch me!' screamed Joyce and pushed Jenna away.

She lifted the glass to her mouth with shaking hands and drained it in two gulps.

Jenna looked at the glazed eyes. Her mother was drunk.

'How could you, Jenna, how could you? Don't you see what you've done?'

'Mother, I . . .'

'You little whore! You've been sleeping with him, haven't you? Haven't you?' Her body was shaking violently as she stood up and walked towards Jenna who shrank back into the corner of the kitchen.

'You little tart, you've been sleeping with that no-good actor bastard. It's written all over you, you stupid little cow.'

Tears started to flow down Jenna's cheeks as her mother's voice went up a pitch.

'Are you pregnant, Jenna? I said, are you pregnant? Answer me, goddamn it!'

'No, mother, I'm not. You don't understand, Matthew and I . . .'

'Don't understand? Hah!' Joyce raised the bottle of sherry in her shaking hand and Jenna wondered whether her mother would strike her with it. Instead, she filled her glass again.

'Don't understand!' She was slurring her words. 'I'll tell you something, Miss Jenna Short or Shaw or whatever ridiculous name you're calling yourself, you know nothing about what I've been through for you. Nothing!' She spat the words out. 'And how do you repay me? You sleep with some scummy little actor who thinks he's God's gift to women. And you believe he loves you? You silly little fool, Jenna. He's a bastard, and he'll leave you, just the way I was left, with a whole lot of memories and nothing else.'

Joyce sank down on to a chair.

'You're twenty years of age, Jenna. You're a child! What do you know about love? I tell you now. If you marry him I never want to see you again.'

Jenna looked at her mother's flushed face.

'Please don't say that, Mother. You don't even know Matthew. I know he loves me.' The tears streamed down her face.

'Love, hah! Look what love's done for me. Go off and marry your Prince Charming, but I don't want you in my home a moment longer.'

'Mother, you're being completely unreasonable. I don't want to leave you like this. Can't we talk about it when you're feeling calmer?'

'I am calm and I know exactly what I'm saying. And I want you out of here now. Get out! Get out, you little whore! Do you think sex is going to keep your boyfriend faithful and happy? Your father was a bastard. They're all the same. They're bastards, all of them, selfish bastards!' She stood up, leaning on the kitchen table to support her shaking body.

'Now get out and don't ever show your face here again, you whore!'

Jenna fled out of the door and into the night, crying hysterically. Eventually she managed to hail a taxi and gave the driver Matthew's address. She sank back into the seat and tried to control her tears.

She had little idea of what she had done that was so

wrong. Matthew would never hurt her, she was sure of that. He was so gentle and caring and he told her how much he loved her a thousand times when they made love.

And she loved him. Surely that wasn't a crime?

19

CHARLIE THREW the remaining paper clips and broken pencils into the waste bin. He checked the room for the umpteenth time, then shut his battered case. He checked his watch. Ten minutes before he needed to leave for Heathrow.

He sat on the bed and sighed, thinking of the times she had sat here, looking exquisite in the dismal surroundings of his bedsit.

'Well, Charlie, old boy, you blew it!'

He spoke to the four walls that had listened silently to his frustrated rantings of the past two years. He knew he ought to be happy. After all, his play had received a lot of praise. He had immediately been offered a six-month season at the English Speaking Theatre in Frankfurt as director, with a clause in his contract that would allow him to write and direct two of his own works.

But his good news was overshadowed by the fact that Jenna was to marry Matthew. This had caused him the kind of grief he was able to write about in one of his plays, but found impossible to deal with in reality.

He was grateful for the opportunity to go abroad; maybe he could forget her there and get on with his career. He doubted it. Jenna had haunted his thoughts since he had first seen her on the balcony. He loved her, would always love her. Why he had never told her this, after the ample opportunities he had when she was alone with him in this very room, he could not fathom.

Maybe if he had . . . maybe.

Now she was lost to him for ever, to be married to that good-looking macho bas . . . He stopped himself, remembering he hardly knew Matthew. He couldn't work out whether he didn't like him because he had Jenna, or because his instincts were telling him that Matthew was not to be trusted. He would have no time to find out, for in three hours' time he would be out of the country.

During the last few painful days he had turned, as always, to the comfort of his pen and poured out the feelings that he had never been able to articulate to her on to the paper in front of him. It was beginning to shape up very nicely. Of course, the female lead character was Jenna . . . some time, perhaps in the future, he mused, still allowing himself to cling to some hope.

He had not been able to talk to her and he knew his congratulations would have sounded hollow. He had written to Jenna, praising her performance in *Romeo and Juliet* and hoping she would be happy with Matthew. He looked at the letter, thought for a moment, then tore it up and threw it in the wastepaper basket where it lay alongside the broken pencils. As a writer, he prided himself on trying to write truthfully and that letter was anything but.

He picked up his case and walked slowly down the stairs. 'Goodbye, my angel,' he murmured as he closed the front door for the last time and hailed a passing taxi.

'Jenna, honey, are you ready? The cab's waiting.'

Jenna looked around the lovely room that had been hers for nearly two years.

Tomorrow she was to be married to Matthew at Chelsea Registry Office and the two of them would then move into the airy flat they had found to rent in Little Venice.

The past month since leaving drama school had flown. They had gone straight into rehearsals for the production of *Romeo and Juliet* at the Round House, then performed every night for three weeks. She had loved every hectic minute of it. Various distinguished members of the profession had popped in to see the show, having heard on the grapevine that two new young talents from the British School of Drama were appearing in it and they had both received their Equity cards.

Matthew had been for an endless round of re-calls. Then three days ago the news had come through from his agent that he had got a large part in a new television series. There had been much excitement and champagne.

'I hope I'm not selling out for the sake of a regular wage packet,' he had told Jenna. She knew that his dream was to work at the Royal Shakespeare Company. However, his agent had assured him that he would be doing himself no harm at all by spending a year in the series, especially as it was to be shown on the BBC and would be viewed as a high-quality show. He would be established and directors would regard him as a 'bums on seats' box office draw in the theatre. And the money was excellent.

Jenna had visited the four agents who had given her their card and decided on Peter Cross. He had been in the business for over thirty years, knew everyone and kept his agency small and select. He knew each of his clients personally and had a reputation for nurturing young talent.

When Jenna had arrived at his untidy office in Soho, she had been confronted by a kind-faced man who reminded her of Mr Micawber, or the favourite uncle that she would like to have had. He immediately whisked her off to the nearest pub to interview her.

He had seen both her performance at drama school and at the Round House and thought that she was very talented. They discussed her future and the kind of work she envisaged herself doing. By the end of the conversation she felt convinced that this was the man to look after her fledgling career.

She was impressed that Peter refused to take any commission on work she did in repertory theatres, and only ten per cent of her earnings on television or film.

Since their meeting, Peter had successfully persuaded a number of prominent casting directors and producers to see her performance at the Round House, while he had filled her days with auditions for everything from a commercial advertising baby food, which she had got, to a fringe production of *Gotcha* by Barry Keefe, which she had not.

Only two things marred her happiness. The memories

of that terrible night with her mother and the fact that Frankie was leaving for Hollywood the day after the wedding. She had hardly seen Frankie over the past few hectic weeks, but her friend had made her promise to keep the night before she got married free. She was taking Jenna out on her hen night.

She checked her face in the mirror and went down the hallway, trying not to notice that Frankie's room was piled with boxes and bags. Daniel had decided to sell the flat when Frankie left and Jenna could hardly believe that it was the last night the two of them would spend together here.

Frankie looked her up and down. 'Good! You're wearing jeans. This is not going to be a night to dress up.'

Their cab drove through Soho and pulled up in front of a pub. It was a hot August night and the whole of London seemed alive and vibrant.

'Come on, hon, I'll get the first round. We're going on a quick pub crawl, then eating at Kettners at ten. The main aim of the evening is to get you as drunk as possible.' Frankie grinned as she pushed her way towards the crowded bar.

Jenna felt a hand on her shoulder. She turned to see Bettina. Jenna threw her arms round her friend.

'Frankie called me. I couldn't let one of the gang of three get married without me being around to send her off in style.'

Frankie came back with drinks and the three of them stood, giggling at the pleasure of being reunited.

'Okay, drink up and we'll be on to the next watering hole,' Frankie ordered.

At Kettners they drank champagne in the bar before going through to the restaurant to eat.

Frankie stood up. 'I'd like to propose a toast to Miss Jenna Short, who became Shaw and tomorrow will be Mrs Valmont. May you have many years of wedded bliss with the man of your dreams.'

'Thank you both.' Unsteadily Jenna stood up. 'And I would like to propose a toast to Frankie, who flies off in a couple of days to her first Hollywood film. I know she's going to be a huge success. And also' – she paused – 'I'd like to propose a toast to both of you for being the best friends I could ever have wished for.' Tears came into her eyes as she looked at Frankie, who had helped her mature as much as the school had done, and then at Bettina, who despite her own problems had always been there when she needed her.

'I hope that we never lose touch,' she added, raising her glass.

It was Bettina's turn to make a toast. 'To my two pals, who helped me pull through last year in one piece. Here's to your futures. I have a feeling you're both going to be big stars and I look forward to telling my children I knew you. Cheers!'

Eventually they made their way home to the flat, feeling happy yet knowing that a very special time in their lives had come to an end. They sat drinking coffee and chatting.

'I'll be at Langdale Hall for the next couple of months.'

'Are you going to stay up there?' asked Jenna.

'Yes, for the time being at least, until I've decided what to do. Actually,' Bettina's eyes twinkled, 'I've met rather a nice man.'

'You little snake! Tell us all about him,' said Frankie.

Bettina smiled coyly. 'When there's more to tell you, I promise I will. Now come on, chaps, I think it's time for the bride-to-be to get some sleep.'

Jenna's stomach churned as she realized that eleven o'clock tomorrow was fast approaching. The wedding was going to be a small affair, due to lack of funds and family members. Jenna had sent an invitation to her mother but was not surprised when she didn't receive a reply. Matthew had refused even to send an invitation to his father and neither of them had any other relatives they wanted to ask.

Jenna had just climbed into bed when she saw the door open.

'Are you awake?'

'Yes, come in.'

Frankie sat on the bed. She took Jenna's hand.

'Sorry to disturb you, but just in case I don't get a chance tomorrow, I just wanted to say thank you for a great two years. And to tell you that if you ever need anything, you know where I am and, as the song goes, all you have to do is call.'

Jenna saw tears appear in her friend's big eyes. She reached over and hugged her.

'I'll miss you, Jenna.'

'Oh, Frankie, and I'll miss you.'

'Just come and see me soon, okay?'

'As soon as I can.'

'See you tomorrow for the big day.' Frankie got up and walked to the door.

'Love you,' she said as she stepped out of the room and closed the door.

September 1980

Curtain Up

'Demons can charm you with a smile
For a while, but in time,
Nothing can harm you,
Not while I'm around.'

STEPHEN SONDHEIM,
Sweeney Todd

20

JENNA OPENED HER EYES and stretched. She checked the clock by the bed and remembered that she was meant to be at an audition at eleven thirty – in ninety minutes' time.

She leaped out of bed and drew back the curtains, taking a second to admire the pretty tubs of plants she had arranged on the balcony that overlooked the canal.

The day was bright and shafts of sunlight drifted into the room. She showered, pulled on Matthew's towelling robe and went into the bright white kitchen to make herself some coffee. She took her cup into the living room and sat down on one of the two cream sofas that had arrived a couple of days ago.

She was for ever asking Matthew if they could really afford the new things that seemed to arrive every week. He always took her in his arms and told her to stop worrying, because he was earning a good salary and had everything under control.

She went back into the bedroom, dried her hair and brushed it until it shone. She put on what she called her audition dress. It was plain, simple and neutral. It showed off her slim figure but made no statement about the girl wearing it. She hoped this would mean that the casting people could use their imagination to fit her into whichever role it was she was going up for.

'I will get this part. I will get this part, I will get this part,' she repeated as she ran downstairs to get a taxi to Wardour Street, where the audition was being held.

Her heart always beat faster when she was on her way to an audition. She knew that it was silly to be nervous of a ten-minute interview with a perfectly pleasant stranger. But it was the desperation of wanting to get the job and the ultimate feeling of failure when she didn't.

As an actress, there was nothing she could hide behind.

She took a deep breath, trying to put the next twenty minutes into perspective, walked through the doors and gave her name to the receptionist. She was handed a script and told to read pages three to eleven. She sat down and smiled at the usual collection of blondes whom she was starting to recognize. The same faces seemed to appear at every audition. She read through the script quickly and decided that everyone in the room was more suitable for the part than she was.

Her name was eventually called and she went into a small room where three people were sitting, drinking coffee.

'Hello, Jenna, I'm Irene Montague, the casting director. This is Ben Black, the director, and Chris Hughes, the producer.'

'Hello,' she said, shaking their hands and sitting down.

'Right.' Irene glanced at Jenna's short CV. 'What have you been doing lately?'

Jenna hated this question, for of course the answer was, nothing.

'Well, I've just finished making a commercial for washing powder.'

There was silence as they waited for her to continue. Eventually the director said, 'Done any film work, Jenna?'

'I did a corporate video for a car company three months ago.'

'Oh,' he said. 'Jenna, let me tell you a little about this film.'

Jenna listened. Then he asked her to read the script she had been given. She gave her reading all she could.

'Thank you, Jenna. We're seeing girls for the next couple of days and re-calls will be next week. We'll be screen testing at Elstree studios.'

Jenna stood up. 'It's been nice to meet you.'

'And you, Jenna. Thank you for coming in to see us. Goodbye.'

Jenna walked out into the watery sunlight of Wardour Street, sure that the audition had been a complete waste of time and energy.

She felt low and did not relish the thought of going back to the empty flat to spend the rest of the day alone. So she walked slowly down the road to Valerie's Patisserie in Old Compton Street to have a coffee and a sulk.

Jenna sipped the hot liquid. She would go mad if she didn't work soon. It was five months since she had finished *Romeo and Juliet*. At first Peter Cross had sent her to audition after audition. Then the telephone had stopped ringing. This morning was the first audition she'd had for a month.

She had started calling Peter every day. She hated doing it, especially when she knew she would get the usual: 'You're up for lots of things, dear, and we'll call you if anything comes in. Don't worry, it always takes time to pick up after Christmas.'

She had written letters to every casting director and regional rep director on the list provided by Peter, but only received the standard letter back thanking her for her photo and saying that they'd call her in as soon as something suitable came along.

Sometimes she hated Matthew. No, she didn't hate him exactly, but the fact that he was becoming a well-known face and something of a sex symbol to the teenage fans who watched the weekly BBC series made the fact that she was doing nothing even worse.

She remembered the day of the wedding when she had worn the beautiful cream two-piece Dior suit that had been Frankie's wedding present to her. The twelve of them had gone back to the then empty flat in Little Venice and drunk a lot of champagne. There had been no family, of course, and because of that, the friends they'd invited had made every effort to make the day special.

Matthew had borrowed a car which had been outrageously decorated by Frankie and Bettina. They'd driven off to a small hotel in Tunbridge Wells to spend three blissful days before Matthew had to return to start work.

Jenna ordered another coffee and remembered how

happy she had been then. Of course things were different now, she thought, morosely stirring her coffee. The fact that she wasn't working was making her feel bad-tempered and irritable. It had also started to make her feel very insecure about Matthew, who was receiving a lot of attention from the press and fan mail by the sackful.

Last night she had shouted at Matthew for no reason at all, then locked herself in the bathroom and refused to come out. Matthew had begged and cajoled her for two hours until he had given up and gone away. Eventually she had crept out to find him fast asleep in bed. Then she had felt horribly guilty and cried herself to sleep.

She couldn't fault Matthew. He was working very long hours at the studio, but would always listen to her while she complained about how miserable she was becoming. He would take her in his arms and tell her that something would turn up soon and then she'd feel much better.

She had suggested to him that she might get a temporary job, just to get out of the flat, but he had balked at the idea. He told her that she was a talented young actress and he didn't want his wife doing some menial job when he was starring on television.

She paid for her coffee and decided to walk along Regent Street to buy Matthew a present for being so horrid last night. Even that depressed her as she realized she would be spending his money, which was placed in the joint account they had opened just after they married.

Jenna walked into Dickins and Jones and bought a shirt for Matthew and then some beautiful silk underwear to cheer herself up.

On the tube home, she decided she would buy a bottle of Matthew's favourite wine, make something special for supper and put on her new underwear.

Jenna put on the radio and busied herself in the kitchen, singing along to the music and feeling a bit more cheerful. At six o'clock she put her new lingerie on, enjoying the soft feel of silk against her skin and knowing that Matthew would too. She shivered as she thought of the pleasures to come and liberally sprayed Chanel No 5 all over herself. Then she fixed herself a vodka and orange and sat on the sofa to wait for him to come home.

At half past nine she was worried that the meal would be spoiled. At half past eleven she tipped it into the bin. Her heart was beating steadily against her chest. He had never been home as late as this without telephoning her. She remembered how awful she'd been to him the night before and had just started to imagine all sorts of dreadful things when she heard the key in the lock.

Matthew walked into the lounge. 'Sorry I'm late, darling. We had to re-shoot the scene I was in first thing this morning and they left it until last.'

Jenna thought he was slurring his words slightly but she ignored it.

'Dinner is ruined.'

'Sorry, darling. I should have called you. Come over here and give your husband a kiss.'

She went to him and smelled the alcohol on his breath as she kissed him.

'Darndest thing happened today,' he said as he got into bed and switched the light off.

'What was that?' she asked coldly.

'You'll never guess who turned up to play my girlfriend in the show.'

'Who?'

'Paula, that's who.'

21

'HI POPS, HOW'S TRICKS?' Frankie kissed her father and sat down in the chair opposite.

'How are you, darling? It seems we haven't seen each other since London.'

'That's 'cos we haven't.'

'Well, I only got back to town last night and I went to stay with a friend of mine for the evening.'

Frankie wondered why her father had to lie to her. She had seen the picture of him stepping out of some night club accompanied by a new blonde bimbo in the *Los Angeles Times*. The caption said he'd returned from filming in the Rockies a week ago. She couldn't give a shit how many girls he screwed, but he always seemed to be embarrassed about it.

'Anyway,' he said, ordering a bottle of Chardonnay, 'I'll come back to the house with you after lunch. I'm going to be home for a couple of months.'

'Well, that's great, but I'm moving out tomorrow.'

Daniel looked hurt. 'Why, Frankie? That place is a mansion large enough to keep three families in comfort, let alone you and me.'

'I know. And that's exactly why I'm going, Pops. I'm twenty and I just want a small apartment that's mine and cosy. I don't like rattling around in that huge place by myself.'

'All right, if that's what you want. Remember, you can always come back any time you want.'

'Thanks, Pops.'

'So,' Daniel changed the subject, 'how are you finding life in the movie world?'

Frankie shrugged. 'It's okay. I enjoyed being chased around by three headless monsters and a couple of ghosts. I feel it's what all my classical training was for.'

'You have to start somewhere, Frankie, and for a first role, it wasn't half bad.'

'I know. And I enjoyed it. It's just that the script wasn't exactly Shakespeare, if you get my meaning.'

'Do I?' Daniel raised his eyes to heaven. 'God, the dross I've had to say over the years . . . sometimes I wish I'd stayed in London. At least I might have got a little more artistic satisfaction instead of this tacky commercial crap they roll out year after year.'

'It's funny,' Frankie mused, 'but the guy Jenna married was hailed at school as the new Olivier. He sold out like you, straight into some weekly soap.'

Daniel's heart jolted. 'Your friend Jenna has married?'

'Yes. Why? Does it bother you?'

'No, of course not. I mean, I'm just surprised, that's all. She seemed so young.'

'She is. Far too young,' Frankie agreed. 'Ridiculous, isn't it? Twenty-one years old and she's already looking forward to diapers. I just hope she doesn't forget about her career. She's a very talented actress. And I've never been sure about the man she's married.'

'What do you mean, Frankie?'

Frankie played with a lettuce leaf. 'Oh, I may be wrong but I pride myself on being able to know a rat when I see one. Jenna is so naïve. I've spent the past two years trying to wise her up but I'm not sure how much progress I made. The guy has got an ego to match the size of his dick, and that means it's big.' She giggled and didn't notice her father shudder. The thought of Jenna sleeping with anyone else was horrendous.

She had been constantly in his thoughts since he had met her. He'd thought of suggesting that Frankie invite her over to Hollywood to stay for a while. At least that way he would get an opportunity to see her again. But now she was married.

He ate as calmly as he could and listened to Frankie chattering on about the new film she was testing for.

'Listen, Pops, I've got to run. I'm meeting a friend this afternoon. I'll see you back at the house later, okay?' She kissed him and breezed out of the restaurant.

He ordered a large scotch and sat staring into space.

He had lost Blanche and now it looked like he'd lost Jenna too.

He slugged back the whisky.

Daniel Duvall was not a happy man.

22

'THEY WANT YOU for Chichester to do three plays in the season.'

The deep voice of Peter Cross came wafting down the telephone. Jenna's heart leaped and then sank.

'How long for?' she asked, biting her lip.

'It'll be four months in all. Don't you want to know the parts they've offered you before we discuss the length of your stay?'

'Yes, of course.'

'Well, they're all good parts: Masha in *The Three Sisters*, Ariel in *The Tempest* and Ginny in *Relatively Speaking*. What do you think?'

'I'm very pleased.'

'Good. Chichester has an excellent reputation. I presume you'll take it?'

'Yes, I will.'

'Right. I'll come back to you on the money. I should be able to get ten pounds more than the Equity minimum for you, and, of course, you'll get a subsistence allowance. It should work out at around eighty pounds a week. How does that sound?'

'Fine.'

'Right, my dear. I'll get back to them and sort out the contract. Rehearsals start in two weeks' time, on the tenth of March. Speak to you soon and congratulations.'

Jenna put the phone down and stared out at the canal. She felt completely confused. On the one hand, she knew she should be thrilled she would be working again, but on the other, it would mean leaving Matthew . . . Matthew, who was not arriving home sometimes until after she'd given up and gone to bed. Matthew, who swore that his returning in the early hours had nothing to do with Paula Franklyn joining the cast. He told her that he was an up and coming young actor and had to go out and socialize.

So, she was going away to Chichester and leaving her husband all alone in London with Paula.

She went to the drinks cabinet and poured herself a stiff vodka and tonic. She took a large slug and thought how ironic life was. The reason that she had been so depressed and insecure was because she had been out of work. Now she had a job, and a good one at that, she was panicking about leaving Matthew.

She was convinced he was having an affair with Paula. All the corny signs that were mentioned in women's magazines were there. She had found lipstick on his shirt and his interest in making love had diminished to such a point that she could not remember the last time he had taken her. He had changed in his attitude towards her. He was distant and on the few nights when he did arrive home before nine o'clock, he didn't ask what she had done during the day. He just ate his supper and stared at the television.

When she had tried to talk about it calmly and rationally, he had told her to stop taking her insecurity at being unemployed out on him, that she was being ridiculous. It would end with Jenna bursting into tears and locking herself in the bathroom. He didn't bother any more to try and tempt her out. The lines of communication between them seemed to have broken down.

Of course, if he was having an affair, then she could hardly blame him. She had not been fun to be with for the past few months. She poured herself another large drink and looked out at the barges bobbing along the canal beneath her.

Matthew, for a change, arrived home early that night.

She told him her news and he hugged her tight and looked genuinely thrilled.

'This calls for a celebration, darling. Get your glad rags on. I'm taking you out for dinner.'

She was tempted to ask him whether he was celebrating the fact that she would be out of his hair for four months, but she didn't want another argument.

They walked to a small fish restaurant where Matthew was immediately asked for his autograph by the young waitress.

'Here's to Chichester.' Matthew raised his glass.

'Matthew, I'm really not sure I want to go.'

He looked at her in amazement. 'Why ever not, Jenna?

You've been as miserable as sin for the past six months and now you've got a great job and you're not sure you want it?' He shook his head. 'Sometimes I really don't understand you.'

'I'll miss you,' she said quietly.

'I'll miss you too, sweetheart, but that's part of the profession. I mean, we knew we'd be spending time apart when we married, didn't we?'

She nodded.

'Look, you'll be so busy the time will fly. And I'll try and come down for the odd weekend and the opening nights.'

Her face brightened. 'Will you?'

'Of course, darling, as long as we're not filming.'

Matthew was loving and attentive for the rest of the evening. When they arrived home he picked her up and carried her into the bedroom, where they made love the way they used to when they were first married.

The tears poured down Jenna's cheeks as she waved goodbye to Matthew and the train chugged out of Victoria Station bound for Chichester. She cried most of the way there and thought of getting off at every stop and catching the next train back to Matthew and giving up acting for ever.

She found a taxi at Chichester station and gave the driver the address of the boarding house where she would stay for the next four months. The theatre had provided her with a digs list and she had managed to get a room in a house only five minutes' walk from the theatre. The cheerful face of Marge, the plump, middle-aged landlady, greeted her at the door of the house. Marge escorted her to her room, and explained the few rules.

'Breakfast is half past seven until nine, and if you want a meal before you go to the theatre at night, let me know. There's hot water available between six and eight every morning.'

Jenna thanked her and sat on the narrow bed. She stared round the dull room with its candlewick bedspread and peeling orange wallpaper. It reminded her of her room at her mother's. She had never felt so lonely and miserable in her life.

However, she cheered up in the next few days as she met her fellow actors and they went into rehearsals. But the nights were long and lonely. She had been unable to get a reply as she dialled and re-dialled Matthew's number on the pay phone in the narrow hallway. By the end of the week she had still not spoken to him. She got up at eight o'clock on Sunday morning and dialled the number.

A sleepy voice answered. 'Hello.'

'Matthew, it's me, Jenna. I've been trying to call you all week and had no reply.'

'Jenna, what the hell are you doing calling me at this hour of the morning? Christ! You know it's the only day I can lie in!'

She bit back the tears. 'I'm sorry. I just wanted to speak to you, that's all.'

He was distant and curt and her money soon ran out.

'I'll call you again soon. You've got this number, haven't you?'

'Yes, Jenna. Look, Jenna . . .'

The line went dead. She went back up to her room and spent the rest of the day miserably learning her lines.

The actress who was playing Irena and was living in the room across the landing knocked on her door in the evening and asked if she fancied going out for a drink. They walked down to the nearest pub where Jenna proceeded to drown her sorrows and woke up the next morning with a raging headache.

The three-week rehearsal period for the first play, *The Three Sisters*, passed quickly. Jenna became wrapped up in her part and did her best not to think about Matthew. She rang him twice a week, but he didn't call her.

She awoke on the morning of the opening, drew back the curtains and saw the sun shining for the first time since she had arrived in Chichester.

A mixture of happy anticipation and terror gripped her, due not only to first-night nerves, but also the prospect of seeing Matthew. She had spoken to him a couple of days ago and he had promised he'd be there. He planned to arrive by train just in time for the beginning of the show and Jenna would not see him until afterwards, at the first-night party in the stalls bar. He was going to stay the night with her, then get up early to dash back to the studios in London.

She went into the theatre at five o'clock and found a huge bunch of red roses waiting for her at the stage door. The card read 'All my love, Matthew'. As she made up in the dressing room, she began to feel better than she'd felt for ages. It was an opening night, and her husband was coming all the way from London to see her. Everyone in the cast was eager to meet the man that was becoming a well-known face on television.

The curtain went up and she forgot about Matthew sitting out front and lost herself in her role.

The applause at the end was rousing and Jenna came offstage on a high. Her heart was beating with anticipation as she slipped into the new dress she had bought.

At the stage door the doorman stopped her.

'There was a call for you earlier, miss. It was from your husband. He sends his love but he can't make it this evening due to his filming running over time. He says he's very sorry but he'll telephone you tomorrow at your digs.'

Something inside Jenna snapped. She swallowed the lump in her throat and marched upstairs to the first-night party, where she brushed aside the questions about the whereabouts of her husband, and sparkled for the rest of the night. She lapped up the compliments she got, flirted with the director, who was eager for her to accompany him back to the flat he was renting, and drank glass after glass of champagne.

Back at her digs, she fell into an alcohol-induced sleep, and staved off the depression that accompanied her hangover by going straight to the theatre and reading her excellent reviews.

She returned home after the evening performance to find a note under her door asking her to call her husband. She ignored it.

Jenna spent the next week going out every night with

other members of the cast and only when Marge stopped her in the hall and insisted she call her husband, who was apparently getting frantic about her, did she smile and pick up the telephone.

The tables were turned. Matthew was concerned, loving and deeply apologetic for not making the first night. Jenna was as calm and cool as she could manage.

He wanted to come down the following weekend to see her. She told him that she was so busy with rehearsals for *Relatively Speaking* and evening performances of *The Three Sisters* that she didn't have a moment to spare. Matthew sounded disappointed but said he understood. Jenna put down the telephone with a sense of triumph. She, too, could play games.

Matthew had been right. The four months passed very quickly. She'd settled down and had enjoyed being part of theatre life again. She'd also got some very good reviews. One national newspaper called her 'a face to remember for the future'.

A sense of dread filled her when she thought of returning to London. She had no idea what to expect.

23

AS JENNA OPENED THE DOOR to the flat, Matthew came running out of the sitting room. He hugged her tight and swung her round.

'God, I've missed you!' He kissed her, picked her up and carried her into the bedroom.

Her body pulsed with a need for him as he tore her clothes off and buried his head between her legs. His tongue played with her swollen clitoris until she thought she would explode with desire. She had to feel him inside her again. She reached down, grabbed his shoulders and pulled him up towards her. He entered her warm wetness with a sigh of pleasure.

'Oh God, Jen, I can't hold it any longer, come with me, now please . . .'

They didn't get out of bed for the rest of the day. They talked as they had not talked for months, with apologies and promises never to let the situation deteriorate again.

'Jenna, it's Bettina.'

'Bettina! How lovely to hear from you. Where are you?'

'Well, I'm in Yorkshire today, but tomorrow I'm coming down to London. Can you meet me for lunch? I have a favour to ask you.'

Jenna could hear the excitement in her friend's voice.

'Where do you want to meet?'

'Let's go to the little café across the road from the school. I'll meet you there at one tomorrow, okay? I can't wait to see you, Jen.'

'Me neither, see you tomorrow then. Bye, Bettina.'

She put the phone down and thought how nice it would be to get out of the flat. She had been back in London a month and was finding being out of work again more difficult than before.

'You're what!' Jenna spilled coffee down the front of her clean white shirt.

'I don't know why it's come as such a shock, Jenna. I mean, you did exactly the same this time last year.'

'I know. I'm just surprised because of Mark.'

'Jenna, I'll never forget him. But I've got to get on with my life.' Bettina's eyes had clouded and Jenna felt guilty for mentioning Mark's name.

'Who is he?'

'His name and full title is Frederick, Lord Roddington, but he's known as Freddie by everyone.'

'What does he do?'

'To be honest, I'm not exactly sure. I know he owns a lot of farmland down in Dorset and he's on the board of a bank that used to be owned by his family until it went public. He always seems terribly busy. He has a beautiful house in Chester Square that looks as though it hasn't been decorated since before the First World War, and a house in Cannes.'

'How old is he?'

Bettina blushed, 'Forty-eight, actually.'

'Bettina!'

'I know, I know. Ma was very worried when we first announced our engagement, but Pa adores him.'

'Do you love him?'

Bettina paused for a moment. 'Well, Jenna, if you mean do I love him the way I loved Mark, then no, I don't. But we're comfortable together and we make each other laugh a lot. Freddie's a bit of an old fuddy-duddy, really. He's never been married and was terribly shy when I first met him. I think he's always been a little frightened of women. He had a similar experience to me when he was younger, fell for a girl who, as Pa would say, was NQOCD – "not quite our class, dear". His parents refused to let them marry. So we have something in common.'

'You still haven't answered my question, Bettina,' Jenna persisted. 'Do you love him?'

Bettina sighed. 'Yes, I do, Jenna. Freddie and I suit each other very well. We each understand the way the other has been brought up. Unfortunately, we both learned very young that love is not enough.'

'So what was this favour you wanted to ask me?'

'Oh, of course. I wondered if you would be my matron of honour?'

'Bettina, I'd love to. When?'

'December the fifteenth, three months' time.' Bettina giggled. 'I think Ma and Pa want me up that aisle as quickly as possible before I change my mind! I've already telephoned Frankie and she's agreed to be a bridesmaid.'

'I can't wait to see her in a frilly dress!' Jenna laughed.

'Talking of dresses, I'll need you to see my dressmaker in London for a couple of fittings. I've asked Frankie to send her measurements over. We'll have to make any alterations the day before.'

'Are you looking forward to it?'

'Oh yes, of course. Ma has already decided to invite over three hundred people and chosen the flowers for the church. It's a dream for her. She just loves organizing.'

'What will you do after you're married?'

'Well, we'll move down to London and I will spend at least six happy months totally refurbishing the house in Chester Square. I can't wait to get my hands on it. Then, well, we intend to have sprogs as soon as possible, as Freddie is not exactly in the prime of life.'

'And what do you mean by that, my girl?'

'Oh no, don't worry, I checked his equipment was still fully functional before I agreed to marry him!' Bettina laughed. 'Anyway, enough of me. How's that gorgeous man of yours? I'm always seeing him on the television and in the papers.'

'He's fine. Well, we did have a few problems, but it's all sorted out now and we're really happy.'

'So you recommend married life, do you?'

'Yes, very much. The only thing is . . .' Jenna paused. 'I just get so frustrated and miserable when I'm not acting.'

'Jenna, you know that is part of being an actress, to be able to cope with the bad times as well as the good. Although I can understand how hard it must with Matthew doing so well. Anyway, don't worry, one day I know you're going to be very famous. Don't give up, Jenna.'

Jenna squeezed her friend's hand. 'Thanks, Bettina. I'm fine, really. Actually . . .' She checked her watch. 'I've got to run, as I have an audition at the BBC in Shepherd's Bush this afternoon and you just never know . . .'

'That's the spirit, old girl. Now, are you going to bring that husband of yours to the wedding? I quite fancy having a celebrity there.'

'I don't know, Bettina. They rehearse on Saturday so I doubt it.'

'Never mind. As long as you're there. Frankie said she'd be ringing you about meeting in London and catching the train up to Langdale Hall together.'

They stood up and Bettina kissed her friend.

'Keep that beautiful chin up and I'll be in touch about the fittings. Bye!'

Bettina went off to give her wedding list to Peter Jones, and Jenna to another fruitless audition.

24

'JENNA. OH, IT'S WONDERFUL to see you!' Frankie hugged her with such force that she could hardly breath.

'Here, let me look at you.' Frankie stood back and surveyed her. 'Not bad! It's good to see that you haven't gone to total rack and ruin while your old pal hasn't been around to keep an eye on you.' She hugged Jenna again and then grabbed her arm. 'Come on, I've got the tickets, I thought I'd treat us and we'd go first class as this is a special occasion. Let's go and get on the train.'

They made their way through Kings Cross, boarded the train and found themselves good seats.

'It's two hours to York, then we change and have a fifteen-minute wait before we get on the train to Harrogate, where Bettina is meeting us,' Frankie announced, 'so get started. You've got approximately two hours and forty-five minutes to tell me all about the past year.'

Jenna regaled her with most of the details of the past year. She said that Matthew and she had had a few problems a while back but that everything was just fine now . . . which was nearly the truth.

She didn't mention that they had started arguing again or that he often returned home late once more. She tried to put it down to her own insecurities, but her suspicions were roused.

Halfway through the journey, she had come up to date.

'So come on, Frankie! I'm absolutely dying to hear about life in Hollywood.'

'Well,' said Frankie, 'I've done three movies now and spent my entire time being eaten, raped and generally pursued by monsters of all shapes and sizes. But Mimi, my agent, has got me a screen test for a Woody Allen film. It's a great part and at least there's no way I'd be eaten and raped in that!' She laughed.

Jenna realized how much she'd missed her friend. She was looking fantastic; bronzed and fit from the California sun and very sophisticated in an Oscar De La Renta suit.

'I notice you didn't make straight for the smoking carriage.'

'I know, I gave up four months ago and I'm feeling so much better for it.'

'Well, you look wonderful, Frankie. Is life in Hollywood as glamorous as it's made out to be?'

'Yes and no. It's a lot of damn hard work, I can tell you. Anyway, Miss Shaw, you're just going to have to come over and see for yourself. They'd love you over there.'

'I'd love to come, Frankie, it's just that Matt . . .'

'That lover boy is here and you can't bear to be torn from his side for more than five minutes. I understand, Jenna.'

'How's your love life? Have you met anyone?'

Jenna was surprised to see a dreamy look come into Frankie's eyes, but it disappeared in an instant.

'No. You know me, Jen, I'm not the sort to fall head over heels for anyone. Look, we're arriving at York, grab your bags, will you?'

As they got off the Intercity and boarded the two-carriaged commuter train that would take them to Harrogate, Jenna wondered whether Frankie was telling the truth about her love life. Just for a moment, she had looked as though ... but if she didn't want to talk about it, that was fine.

'Look, there she is!' Frankie waved to catch Bettina's attention.

'Frankie!' yelled Bettina. The two girls had not seen each other for eighteen months and there was an emotional reunion on the platform. Eventually they climbed into Bettina's new Golf convertible, a wedding present from Freddie, and drove through Harrogate and out into the country.

Jenna was stunned at the beauty of the scenery on either side of her. She listened while Bettina regaled them with details about the wedding tomorrow.

'Ma is charging around in a complete panic about everything and Pa is just doing his best to keep out of the way. Look, there's the entrance to Langers.'

They drove through wrought-iron gates and along a narrow road. They stopped in front of Langdale Hall, an elegant mansion dating from the seventeenth century.

Frankie whistled. 'This is like a film set, Bettina. It's fantastic! Why on earth didn't we visit before?'

'I kept asking you both, but you were always too busy.'

'I can't believe that your family live here. What do they do with all the spare rooms?' asked Jenna.

'Fill them with wedding guests,' Bettina laughed. 'We have thirty-two bedrooms, but Pa closed the East Wing years ago as Ma couldn't cope with the hoovering!'

They took their cases out of the boot and made their way up the steps to the front door.

'Come on, I'll take you to your rooms.'

They walked through an imposing hallway and up a sweeping staircase.

'Who are all these people?' asked Frankie, nodding towards the portraits hanging on the walls.

'Oh, my ancestors,' said Bettina as they walked along a maze of corridors. Finally, she opened a door and led them into a room with a fire blazing merrily in an old Victorian fireplace. There was a comfortable single bed, an old-fashioned mahogany wardrobe and an ancient basin in one corner.

Bettina opened a door that led through to another room identical to the first.

'I think you'd better leave this door open, just in case our friendly neighbourhood ghost decides to put in an appearance!' She looked at two worried faces. 'Actually, he only comes out on a full moon and there isn't one tonight so you should be safe enough. Now, the bathroom is down the passage, pretty basic and absolutely freezing, I'm afraid, but it does the job. Pa has put central heating in the main rooms downstairs, but the funds didn't quite reach upstairs. Still, I got Tilly to light the fires so it's nice and warm in here. Just dump your things and I'll show you round.'

Frankie was gazing at the two peach-coloured gowns hanging on the wardrobe. 'I assume those are our get-ups for tomorrow,' she mused.

'Yes. Do you like them?' Bettina asked anxiously.

'Well, all I can say, my dear Bettina, is that I would only do this for you. A sugar and spice ladylike "dainty" is something I'm not.'

The girls laughed as they followed Bettina downstairs.

'This is the showpiece. Only used on special occasions.'

They were standing in an enormous sitting room. There was a Steinway grand piano at one end and a marble fireplace at the other. French windows along one side of the room looked out over beautiful rolling parkland.

They followed Bettina into a small cosy room. 'Ma and Pa use this as their sitting room most of the time.'

It had chintz curtains, a well-worn settee and numerous photographs of the family. Frankie picked up a photo of a very young Bettina with her mother, father and a boy in his early teens.

'Is this your brother?'

'Yes, that's Gerry, my protector in London. Some job he did! You never met him, did you? He'll be arriving later tonight from London. Come on, we've got masses more to see.'

Bettina led them down a long oak-panelled corridor and into the library, through the formal dining room with a table that could seat thirty, then back upstairs to show them the many grand bedrooms.

'Where do you sleep?' asked Jenna.

'Oh, my room's up in the eaves where the servants used to sleep. I much prefer it. Pa installed a bathroom and storage heaters so I'm virtually self-sufficient up there,' said Bettina as she led Frankie and Jenna downstairs.

'And now for the *pièce de résistance*, the ballroom. This is where the reception is going to be held.'

They walked through tall panelled doors into a room that was filled with countless tables covered in cream tablecloths. The high ceiling was painted in rich golds, blues and pinks, with cherubim sitting on white fluffy clouds sounding horns. The parquet floor was highly polished and the walls were painted a soft pink. The afternoon sun shone through the french windows, which were draped in extravagant peach moiré.

'This is magnificent, Bettina. How many people will be at lunch tomorrow?' Frankie asked.

'At the last count, two hundred and sixty-two. In the evening some of the tables will be cleared so we can dance.' She checked her watch. 'Now, the rehearsal is at five, which gives us half an hour to grab a sandwich before we have to leave. I would introduce you to Ma and Pa but God knows where they are at the moment.'

They drove the quarter of a mile to the picturesque church on the edge of the estate, where generations of Langdales had been christened, married and buried.

'Now, I'm counting on you two to keep the other six bridesmaids and two pageboys in order. Ma insisted we have so many. She thinks they look so romantic. Look, there's Freddie!' She jumped out of the car. 'Hello, darling. Come and meet Frankie and Jenna.'

She brought over a short, rather plump man. He had bright-blue eyes, a moustache and a ruddy complexion. He shook their hands. 'Glad to meet you both. I feel as though I already know you, I've heard such a lot about you from Bettina.' He spoke in a slightly gruff voice and seemed nervous. 'Come on, darling, let's get this over and done with.'

Bettina put her arm in his and marched off towards the church with her two friends following. The vicar was there to greet them, along with eight chattering youngsters.

The balding Freddie wiped his forehead with a large hanky, turned to Jenna and whispered, 'I'll be glad when all this is over and Bet and I are on the plane to Cannes. Never one for standing on ceremony myself.' He raised his eyes to heaven.

Frankie and Jenna took an instant liking to this rather shy older man who was to marry their friend.

'Pa, there you are! We've been waiting for you.'

A tall man with an aristocratic bearing came into the vestry.

'Sorry, Bettina, I got stopped by your mother on the way out, and you know that can be fatal.' The deep voice resonated around the church. 'She is on her way here with a Range-Rover full of flowers.'

The rehearsal got under way. A tiny bridesmaid who tripped over on her way down the aisle stopped crying only when Freddie produced a toffee from his pocket.

'We'd better get some of those for tomorrow,' Jenna commented.

'I favour a whip myself,' whispered Frankie as they marshalled the children into a pew.

Once the rehearsal was over, the two of them strolled out into the chill December evening. A middle-aged lady was walking towards them, carrying two enormous floral decorations.

'Bettina's mother,' Frankie whispered. 'Just look at that red hair and those eyes.'

'Hello. You must be Frankie and Jenna. I'm Henrietta Langdale. Please excuse me. I must have a word with the vicar about the flowers. I'll see you back at the house.' She disappeared inside the church. Jenna and Frankie got into the Golf and waited while Bettina said her goodbyes to Freddie.

'There's no formal dinner tonight but Ma has provided a buffet in the dining room,' Bettina told them as they drove back to the house. 'What say you we grab what we want, steal a bottle of champers and go to my room for a good gossip?'

'Great idea,' said Frankie.

While Jenna and Bettina organized the food and champagne, Frankie went upstairs to try on her dress. It fitted perfectly.

Jenna looked around Bettina's room. It had a sloping ceiling and a tiny picture window which she guessed would have a beautiful view of the surrounding countryside.

Bettina poured champagne into three glasses. 'Here's to us, reunited once more.'

'I'll drink to that,' said Frankie. 'And here's to your marriage! May you have years of happiness with Freddie, who, by the way, we both think is a sweetie.'

'Well, he's not exactly Robert Redford, but he's awfully kind and he's got a lovely sense of humour.'

'He's going to need it, being married to you!' Frankie laughed.

'Charmed, I'm sure. Anyway, what's happening to you, Frankie? I mean, with two out of the three of us married tomorrow, you'll be left behind.'

Frankie shrugged her shoulders. 'Come on, Bettina, I'm not exactly the marrying kind, now am I? So, what time do we need to be up tomorrow?'

'Early. Honestly, I'm so nervous! Every time I think of walking down the aisle with all those people watching me, my tummy turns over.'

'Some actress you'd have made,' Frankie smiled.

'I know. I have absolutely no regrets about having had to chuck it in. I mean, I enjoyed it while it lasted but I know it wasn't for me.'

'As long as you're happy, that's all that matters.'

They sat in the cosy room and chatted for hours until Bettina looked up at the small clock above the fireplace and gasped. 'Goodness, it's after twelve! Sorry, gang, but the bride is going to have to try and get some of the beauty sleep she so desperately needs.' She kissed them both. 'Thank you so much for coming, you don't know what it means to me to have you here.'

Having found their way back to their rooms, Frankie came and sat on Jenna's bed. 'You know,' she said thoughtfully, 'it's hard to believe that Bettina actually belongs to all this. She's so unpretentious, you'd never guess who she was if you met her in the street, would you? Not like that father of hers, I think he's a complete pig of a –'

'Thank you, Frankie, I get your drift,' Jenna laughed.

'I think I'll have terrible dreams tonight,' Frankie sighed.

'About the ghost?'

'No, about that peach monstrosity I've got to wear! 'Night, sweetie.'

Jenna was awake at eight. She drew back the curtains and gazed at the magnificent view. She had a sudden urge to go outside into the fairyland below her. The ground was covered with a coating of frost and the tips of the pine trees sparkled.

She pulled on her jeans and a large sweater and tiptoed downstairs to the front door. She pulled back a large bolt, opened the door and stepped out into the cold air. She wandered around to the back of the house. The gardens sloped away to give a clear view of the Yorkshire Dales beyond.

The scenery filled her with happiness. She strolled over to the stables, where she could see a groom already hard at work on one of the horses.

She patted the elegant black horse in the first loose box, and then walked down the whole line saying good morning to them all.

The groom, dressed in an old army sweater, riding boots and a cloth cap, did not seem to notice her.

'Gosh, I bet it's a tough life being a groom,' she said.

No answer came from the man. He carried on brushing the horse.

She tried again. 'I mean, up early every morning, come rain, come shine.'

He turned round and looked at her. He reminded her of someone but she couldn't place it. She noticed he wasn't wearing gloves and that his hands looked frozen.

'And who might you be?'

'Oh, I'm Jenna Shaw.' She took off her gloves, which were Matthew's, and offered them to him. 'Your hands look freezing. Here, take these.'

He stood staring at her in surprise.

'Come on, take them. I'm going back inside so I won't need them.' She shoved them into his hands. 'You should ask Lord Langdale to buy you a pair. I'm sure he could afford them. Goodbye.' She started to walk off.

'Goodbye, Miss Shaw,' he called. 'Thanks for your kindness, and I will tell His Lordship you said he should buy me a pair of gloves.'

Jenna hurried back to her room and huddled by the fire that had been lit in her absence.

By eleven, Frankie was still having her hair done and Jenna was struggling to cope with the baby bridesmaids.

When Frankie was ready, she looked absolutely stunning in the pale peach dress with her hair piled high up on her head and wreathed in Christmas roses.

The vintage Rolls Royce and the four Daimlers made an impressive sight lined up in front of Langdale Hall.

Bettina emerged, looking fresh and pretty. The hairdresser had been unable to completely control the flame-coloured locks and already wisps were escaping from the tight knot on her head. She had a small tiara nestling among the tulle of her veil, and her white satin gown, trimmed with ermine, was simple but stylish. She carried a large bouquet of red roses, which set off the white dress and made her look like a Christmas princess.

As Jenna watched Bettina take her father's arm and walk down the steps to her car, she thought her friend had a degree of poise and grace she'd never possessed before.

'I believe I'm travelling with you two. I think we're in the second car.' Jenna turned and saw Lady Langdale standing behind her. The three of them got into their car and set off slowly down the drive.

'I'm terribly sorry we've not had a chance to talk. It's been so hectic. Oh, I do hope it goes all right! I'm just glad I only have one daughter to marry off as I couldn't go through this again. Oh, goodness me, we've arrived already!'

Jenna and Frankie stepped out of the Daimler and started to unload the bridesmaids from the car behind.

Jenna kissed Bettina on the cheek. 'Good luck, darling!'

'Thanks, Jenna,' she said. 'I'm petrified!'

The church organ began to play William Walton's 'Crown Imperial'. Bettina took her father's arm, turned and winked at her friends, then set off down the aisle.

They ushered the bridesmaids into their allotted pew and sat down to let the marriage service begin. Jenna gazed at the twinkling lights of the Christmas tree and felt a lump in her throat as she heard Bettina repeat her marriage vows.

She had so much wanted this for her own wedding, but she'd had to make do with the bland unromantic service at the registry office. She prayed that Bettina would not encounter any of the problems she had experienced in her marriage as she walked into the vestry to witness the signing of the register.

They were soon outside and the church bells were ringing. As Jenna posed with the rest of the bridal party for the traditional photos in front of the church, she noticed a familiar-looking figure in full morning dress standing behind her.

Back at Langdale Hall, the guests moved into the ballroom, where there was vintage Dom Perignon champagne for everyone. Frankie and Jenna toasted the bride.

'Oh, thank God that's over!' Bettina squeezed their hands. 'Let me introduce you to my brother Gerard.'

'We've met, actually, haven't we?'

Jenna knew that she was turning red. She lowered her eyes and managed to nod.

Gerard smiled at her and moved away.

'Well?' asked Frankie.

'I met him in the stables this morning. I thought he was a groom. I gave him my gloves because his hands looked cold.'

'You did what?' cried Bettina.

'There's worse,' said Jenna, 'I told him he should ask Lord Langdale to buy him some gloves.'

Bettina wiped her eyes, 'Oh, Jenna, that really is the

funniest thing I've ever heard. Gerard a groom! When are you ever going to stop being so naïve? No, on second thoughts, don't stop. I haven't laughed like this in ages. Oh dear, my stomach hurts!'

The toastmaster announced that the wedding breakfast was served. They took their places at the long top table with the other members of the wedding party. Freddie's best man was placed between Jenna and Frankie.

'Well, I must say, it's not often that I sit down to eat between two such delightful young ladies. Name's William Bates, call me Bill.' They shook hands. Bill was in his late forties, tall, with a military bearing.

'Known Freddie since we were pushed in our prams round the park by our nannies. Solid chap. Never thought he'd take the plunge, though.'

As they dined on pâté de fois gras and fresh salmon, Jenna surveyed the guests. They were mostly middle-aged, the men in full morning dress and the women in beautifully tailored expensive outfits with hats to match. There was a lot of laughter from the tables as they drank copious glasses of Dom Perignon. Jenna recognized a number of famous faces.

Once the meal was finished, Lord Langdale, Freddie and Bill gave short, eloquent speeches. After the cake had been cut, Frankie and Jenna went with Bettina to help her change into her going-away outfit.

'Thank you so much for being here,' Bettina kissed them as they prepared to go back downstairs. 'Have you enjoyed it?' she asked anxiously.

'Yes. And the more champagne I drink, the more I

do,' Frankie said, laughing. 'The most important thing is, have you?'

Bettina's eyes shone. 'Oh, yes! I feel incredibly happy. Freddie is such a darling.'

The newlyweds were catching the evening flight to Nice. They had decided to spend their Christmas honeymoon at Freddie's house in Cannes.

Bettina was driven off down the drive in Freddie's Jaguar under a storm of confetti.

'Oh dear, Frankie!' Jenna giggled, 'I think I've had a little too much champagne.'

'Join the club. Let's sneak upstairs and get some shut-eye before the evening's festivities begin.'

They made their way to their rooms, collapsed on their respective beds and passed out.

'Jenna, come on, wake up.' Frankie was shaking her. 'They'll be sending the dogs to sniff us out if we don't make an appearance soon. We've been asleep for ages. It's half past eight.'

Jenna tidied her dishevelled appearance and they went down to the ballroom. The evening party was in full swing. A small band was playing and people were dancing.

The two girls grabbed glasses of champagne from a passing tray and saw Lady Langdale and Gerard heading towards them.

'I was wondering where you'd got to,' said Gerard. 'Jenna, as you were so kind to me this morning, I insist I have the next dance.'

'Oh yes, do! The more the merrier on the dance floor,

my dear,' said Lady Langdale. 'Off you go, you two, and I'll keep Frankie company. I'm desperate to hear all about Hollywood.'

'Go on, we'll be fine,' Frankie encouraged.

Gerard led Jenna to the dance floor.

'You know, Bettina was wrong about you.'

'What do you mean?'

'Well, she told me you were beautiful but she didn't say just how lovely you are.'

'You ought to have told me who you were this morning.'

'I know. It was very naughty of me. I apologize. I just couldn't resist it. Do you forgive me?' He looked down at her.

'I suppose so,' she said grudgingly. 'And I apologize for thinking you were a groom.'

'You can think anything you like as long as you'll have the next dance with me.' He whisked her off around the floor before she could refuse.

'So tell me. You're a married woman?'

'Yes.'

'And who is this swine that bagged you before any of us chaps could get a look in?' He smiled.

'My husband's name is Matthew Valmont.'

'Oh yes, now I remember Bettina telling me. Isn't he in some awful weekly soap opera?'

She could see his green eyes twinkling and decided she would not rise to the bait. 'As a matter of fact, he is. At least it's better than being a groom.'

'*Touché*, Jenna. Now let me get us both a glass of bubbly.'

LOVERS & PLAYERS

Jenna began to enjoy Gerard's company. He had a good sense of humour, was courteous and flattered her constantly. She noticed what an attractive man he was as they drank glass after glass of champagne.

As Gerard steered Jenna on to the floor for the last dance of the evening, she saw Frankie leaning drunkenly on Bill, the best man, her crown of flowers askew.

The band was playing 'Moon River' and a *frisson* of excitement ran up Jenna's spine as Gerard pulled her closer.

'Jenna, I hope you don't mind, but I'm going to have to do something,' he whispered, and kissed her long and hard.

She closed her eyes and enjoyed his kiss. Then guilt surged through her. She struggled out of Gerard's arms and hurried out of the french windows into the freezing night. The blast of cold air sobered her up. She realized she had done exactly what she was so scared her husband had been doing. She was no better than he was.

Something warm was put round her shoulders. 'Here, you'll freeze.'

She snuggled into the jacket Gerard offered her and tried to stop her teeth chattering.

'Look, I'm really sorry. I didn't want to upset you. It's my fault.'

'No, it's not, Gerard.' She had a sudden urgent desire to get out of this place, away from temptation. 'Listen.' She turned to him urgently. 'How late do the trains run? I need to get back to London tonight.'

'Well, as it's gone one o'clock in the morning, I don't

think there'd be much doing at Harrogate and, unless you want to walk the forty-odd miles there to check, I'm afraid you're pretty stranded. I tell you what, if you can bear to spend just a few more hours in this dreadful place, I'm going back to London first thing tomorrow. I'd be happy to give you a lift.'

'That would be very kind of you.'

'Right, I'll meet you downstairs at six thirty. And unless you want to turn us both into blocks of ice, can we step back inside, please?' He grinned at her and held out his arm.

She smiled sheepishly and let him lead her back into the ballroom.

She found Lady Langdale, who was busy saying goodbye to some of the guests, and thanked her for her hospitality. She explained she had to return to London early in the morning and that Gerard had offered her a lift.

'It's been our pleasure having both you and Frankie here. Thank you for being a super matron of honour and we hope to see you here again soon. By the way, Frankie went to bed a little while ago.'

Gerard escorted her upstairs to her room.

''Night, Jenna.' He kissed her chastely on the cheek. 'I'll see you bright and early tomorrow.'

The alarm clock went off at six o'clock and Jenna awoke feeling tired and hung over. She popped her head around the door to Frankie's room. Her friend was fast asleep. She wrote a note saying that she had had to rush back to London and would explain later.

Gerard looked incredibly fresh as he opened the passenger door of his sleek red Porsche.

Jenna liked him a lot, but she was going back to see the man she loved, to make sure that what had happened last night would not happen again. She sat back in the comfortable seat, enjoying the way Gerard controlled the car as they sped down the empty motorway.

Just before nine o'clock the Porsche pulled to a halt in front of the Little Venice flat. Gerard helped her out of the car and handed over her suitcase.

'Thanks, Gerard.'

'Any time.' He smiled at her. 'Maybe I'll see you again?'

'Maybe,' she replied. 'Bye, Gerard.'

'Goodbye, Jenna. Take good care of yourself.' He got back into the driver's seat. She waved as the car disappeared round the corner, then walked up the steps to the front door. The Sunday papers were still on the doorstep. She picked them up and walked up the stairs, quietly unlocked the door and tiptoed into the hallway. She took her shoes off and padded silently to the bedroom door.

The bedroom was in darkness. As she stepped inside, she tripped, lost her balance and grabbed at the dressing table, sending something solid crashing to the floor.

A hand reached out and turned on a bedside light. Two pairs of eyes stared at her in shocked amazement.

'Bloody hell!' said Matthew.

'Fuck!' said Paula and disappeared under the duvet.

Time ticked by as she stared at Matthew and he stared back. At last her legs managed to carry her from the bedroom. She grabbed her shoes and flew down the stairs.

25

THE TAXI DROPPED JENNA OFF outside the café across the road from the drama school. Despite it being a Sunday morning, the café was open and she went straight to the booth where the three of them had always sat and ordered a cappuccino.

Jenna held her thoughts at bay, not wanting to let them surface, trying to harbour the faint notion that she had dreamed it. She knew she hadn't. She had found her husband in their bed with another woman. Paula. And to think she had raced back because she had been feeling guilty about a kiss!

So now she knew. For definite. And she also knew she was going to leave him. She had to. Nobody could treat her like that. Nobody. Not even the man she loved.

Her thoughts gave way to tears as she wondered how she could possibly live without him. She started to recall all the beautiful times that they had had together. Then she stopped herself from being self-indulgent. She had to be strong.

First things first. She must go back to the flat and

pack some of her personal belongings. He wasn't having everything. She wondered whether she had any claim to the furniture, but brushed the thought aside. Furniture didn't matter, but a change of clothes and some money did. She checked her purse. She had just under five pounds but there was a hundred pounds hidden in her underwear drawer.

She ordered another coffee and considered her options. Under no circumstances could she go crawling back to her mother and admit she had been right about Matthew. Frankie was probably still at Langdale Hall, just about to leave for Heathrow to catch a flight back to Los Angeles. Bettina was on honeymoon. Charlie? Well, she hadn't heard a word from him in eighteen months. Gerard? After last night she knew he would misread her intentions.

Jenna decided she would have to check into a hotel and start job hunting first thing in the morning. After that . . . well she didn't know. What she had to do now was pluck up the courage to go back to her flat and be prepared to face Matthew and possibly Paula. She felt her stomach turn at the thought but she knew it had to be done. So she finished her coffee and got a taxi home for the last time.

She felt faint as she climbed the stairs. The front door was open. She went straight into the bedroom with her teeth gritted.

She was relieved to see that the bed was empty.

Matthew was standing by the window.

'I changed the duvet cover.'

Jenna did not reply. Instead she pulled her biggest

suitcase down from the top of the wardrobe and started to throw her clothes into it.

Matthew ran a hand through his hair. 'Jenna, what are you doing?'

'I would have thought that was pretty obvious. Why don't you leave me alone? Go and keep your girlfriend company.'

'She's gone.'

'Well, you shouldn't have thrown her out on my account.'

He walked towards her and took hold of her elbow. She wrenched it away.

'Please, Jenna, can't we sit down and talk? Please?'

'I really can't see much point in a post-mortem, or are you going to tell me how she dragged you into our bed and raped you?'

'Jenna, I don't want you to leave. I love you.'

'I must say you have a funny way of showing it.'

He sat on the bed, put his head in his hands and started to cry. 'Oh God, I know, I'm so sorry. Please don't leave me, Jenna, I need you.'

She tried not to hear the sobs and reminded herself that he was a very talented actor.

'Please, Jenna, I know how you must feel . . .'

'No, you don't, Matthew.'

'Okay, I don't, but won't you give me a chance to explain?'

'There's nothing to explain.' She shut the suitcase.

'Paula was after me from the minute she walked on to that set. She never left me alone, Jenna. I know I'm a weak man, but we've had a few problems, and, well, she was always there. She lives with another man, for Christ's sake! I don't love her. I don't even enjoy going to bed with her any more.'

Jenna flinched and walked into the sitting room.

Matthew followed her. 'I love you, Jenna. Please, give me a chance to make it up to you. I promise I'll never ever do anything like that again. I told Paula it was over this morning. I'll be home early every night and never give you another moment's worry ever, just please don't go!'

As he shouted the words at her, all her suppressed emotion came rushing to the surface and she couldn't keep the charade up any longer. She sat down on a sofa and burst into tears.

'Matthew, how could you?'

He shook his head and came to sit beside her. 'I don't know.'

'With her, of all people.'

He sat there as she cried. He tentatively put his arm round her. 'Please, sweetheart, give me one more chance. I swear I'll make it up to you. I can't take the pressure of this job without you.'

'Just do me one favour, Matthew. Tell me the truth. When did this all start again?'

Matthew sighed. 'All right. I suppose I owe you that at the very least. I started seeing her soon after she joined the cast. But I swear I wasn't sleeping with her.'

'So when did that start?'

'When you were in Chichester. I was lonely, Jenna, and under pressure. Paula understood because she's in the show as well. You don't know what it's like working to that timetable. We rehearse the scene for twenty minutes, then we film it. Mistakes are money and the cast can't afford to make them.'

Jenna shook her head. 'Look, I understand the pressure, but for God's sake, stop making excuses. You must have liked Paula to jump into bed with her the minute I was out of the way.'

'I told you when I first met you that Paula was good in the sack. And we'd been having so many problems, darling. I'm not trying to make excuses but that was a factor.'

'When I came back from Chichester, were you still seeing her?'

'No. The guilt was getting to me and Paula was making demands. I realized that I missed you and didn't want to lose you so I told her it was over.'

'So why did I find you in bed with her just now?'

'Jenna, you needn't believe me, and I won't blame you if you don't, but last night was the first time since I finished it months ago.'

'You're right, I don't believe you.'

'Well, I swear it's true. On Saturday evening the cast went out for a Christmas drink. One thing led to another. God, I'm sorry! I suppose I deserve it if you leave me. I was so frightened this morning that you wouldn't come back. It made me realize just how much I love you. Please give me another chance, Jenna. I swear I'll be a model husband. I really have learned my lesson.'

Jenna stood up.

'Are you going, Jenna? Oh, please don't go!' he cried.

She tried to collect her thoughts. At least she felt better for knowing. She also remembered that she had not behaved perfectly the night before.

Jenna turned to Matthew. 'All right, I'll stay. I expect you to sleep in here until I say you can come back to the bedroom.'

Matthew looked relieved. 'Fine, fine,' he muttered. 'Listen, how do you fancy getting out of here for Christmas? My friend John at the studio has a cottage in the country somewhere in Norfolk. He said I could have it for the Christmas week. I think we could both do with some time to ourselves, a sort of second honeymoon. Well?' he asked eagerly.

Jenna wearily turned to him. 'Let's take one day at a time. I don't know how I feel at the moment so we'll just have to see. If you'll excuse me, I'm going to have a bath.'

She walked from the room, hoping she had managed to salvage a little pride.

In the next few days, Matthew behaved perfectly. He brought flowers or chocolates home every night, helped her around the flat, talked enthusiastically about the audition she had the next day, and called the director all the names under the sun when she didn't get the part. He went to sleep on the sofa every night without a murmur.

Jenna was polite but distant.

On the fourth night by herself in the large bed, she

decided he had paid his penance. After all, there were only a few days left until Christmas.

The next morning Jenna told Matthew that she would go to the cottage in Norfolk with him. He was thrilled and telephoned his friend to arrange things.

Jenna began to look forward to getting away. She thought that it could be just what both of them needed to patch up the delicate threads of their relationship.

Matthew hired a car the day before Christmas Eve and they shopped for provisions late into the evening and came home with the car full of Christmas fare.

Matthew opened a bottle of wine back at the flat and handed Jenna a glass.

'Here's to the next few days.' Matthew stretched contentedly. 'It will be bliss to be away from the studio, out in the country with my beautiful wife.'

Jenna let him take her in his arms and kiss her good night, but she retired to the bedroom alone.

They set off early the next morning, hoping to avoid the heavy Christmas Eve traffic. Jenna turned the radio on and they listened to a carol service as they drove up the M11.

They stopped at a picturesque country pub on the outskirts of Cambridge, full of locals enjoying a lunchtime drink. They ate in the pleasant restaurant attached to the pub and drank glasses of mulled wine.

'Isn't this wonderful, Jenna?' Matthew's eyes were shining. 'It's the first time since we've been married that we've really had time to relax together. It's because of my job. I know many actors who are out of work would kill to be me, but look how our relationship has suffered because of it.'

After lunch they set off again towards Norfolk. Matthew stopped when he saw a garden centre advertising Christmas trees. They chose a small one and Jenna bought some decorations for it from the shop.

An hour later, after a few wrong turns, Matthew pulled up in front of a tiny thatched cottage. It stood completely alone, surrounded by a small wood on one side and rolling green fields on the other.

'It reminds me of the gingerbread house in "Hansel and Gretel".' Jenna surveyed the whitewashed exterior with small leaded windows. 'Isn't it gorgeous?'

Matthew emptied the car while Jenna explored the rooms. The flagstone floors were covered with bright rugs and there were nooks and crannies everywhere. There was an old, comfortable Chesterfield in the heavily beamed sitting room which was dominated by an inglenook fireplace.

Jenna helped Matthew unpack their provisions, made up the bed and struggled to light a fire.

'Ouch!' Matthew rubbed his head, having forgotten to duck below the doorway leading to the kitchen. 'I'll end up having a cerebral haemorrhage or become permanently hunchbacked by the end of this week.'

In the kitchen there seemed to be one important appliance missing. 'Matthew! There isn't an oven.'

'What?' Matthew came into the kitchen. 'Idiot, there it is. It's called an Aga.' He laughed and removed the two black-leaded covers concealing the hobs.

'Oh,' said Jenna. 'I thought that was some kind of boiler for the heating.'

He raised his eyes to heaven. 'Dear Lord! I've married a grockle.' He tickled her until there were tears streaming from her eyes, then showed her how to work 'the boiler', as the Aga was called from then on. Eventually, a kettle was boiled and they sat sipping tea in front of the sitting room fire.

'You really notice the silence here.'

Jenna nodded. 'Peace, perfect peace. I think it's because I'm a London girl born and bred that I have a yearning to live in the countryside.'

Later, she warmed some mince pies and Matthew opened a bottle of wine. Jenna could feel the tension of the past few weeks slipping away.

At five to twelve, Jenna went to one of the leaded sitting room windows and peered out. She looked up into the pitch-black night as the stars twinkled in the sky way above her.

She did not move when Matthew's arms encircled her from behind.

'Merry Christmas, darling!' He kissed the back of her neck gently. 'Do I have to sleep on the sofa tonight?' he asked quietly as he nuzzled her ear.

'No, Matthew.'

'Thank God for that, because if I don't make love to you tonight, I think I'll go mad.'

He led Jenna upstairs to the bedroom, with its low-beamed ceiling, and made love to her on the big wrought-iron bed.

Jenna was tentative at first, trying not to think of the other woman who had enjoyed the same pleasures, but as her physical instincts took over everything else was forgotten. They reached a heady climax and sank into each other's arms. Matthew held her tight as the tears trickled down her face.

'Please don't cry, Jenna. I love you so much and I'll never hurt you again, I promise.'

'I love you too, Matthew. I just feel frightened, that's all.'

'Why?'

She shook her head and settled down into his arms. But she knew exactly why. She couldn't live without him.

26

'AWAKE, OH SLEEPING BEAUTY.'

Jenna opened her eyes to see Matthew standing in his dressing gown holding a tray with a bottle of champagne, two glasses and a small gift-wrapped package on it.

'Ho ho ho, little girl, wake up and see what Santa has got for you this morning!' Matthew put the tray on the bed, opened his dressing gown and began thrusting his crotch towards her. She giggled. He opened the champagne and poured it.

'Cheers, my love. Now, are you going to open that parcel or not?'

She tore the paper off like an excited child and inside found a box with 'Van Cleef and Arpels' inscribed on the top. She knew they were a very expensive jeweller. She looked up at Matthew with a half frown.

'Matthew, you shouldn't . . .'

'Shut up and see what's inside, Jenna.'

She carefully opened the box and found a delicate gold filigree chain, strung with tiny pearls nestling next to twinkling sapphires and diamonds. There were earrings to match.

'Do you like it?' asked Matthew anxiously as he watched her fingering the necklace in silence. 'I know they're your favourite stones and I had it made up specially.'

'It's absolutely beautiful, Matthew, but it must have cost a fortune and –'

Matthew put a finger to her lips and proceeded to put the necklace on. 'Jenna, darling, you're my wife, and I'm a successful actor. If I want to buy you extravagant gifts, why the hell shouldn't I? Now, put it on and go and have a look at it.'

Jenna stared at her reflection in the mirror. The necklace was exquisite. 'It's wonderful, Matthew, but I don't think it exactly goes with my thermal pyjamas.' She laughed, and reached in her case for Matthew's present. She had very nearly taken it back to the shop and asked for a refund, but now she was glad she hadn't.

Matthew sat down on the bed and tore the paper from the box. His eyes lit up when he saw the watch inside and he immediately put it on. 'Thank you, darling, I'm thrilled.' He leaned over and kissed her.

'Now, I must get up and start cooking that turkey, otherwise we won't be eating it until Boxing Day.' Jenna laughed.

'Okay, okay, but have a glass of bubbly first.'

A lot of champagne later, Jenna managed to serve up a perfectly cooked bird.

'I'm impressed, Mrs Valmont. You know I'll expect this every night when we get back to London.' Matthew sipped his glass of Châteauneuf du Pape.

'I hope you have room for the superb plum pudding, made by me with a little help from Marks and Spencer.' Jenna put a large portion smothered in brandy butter in front of him.

Afterwards, having overindulged in both food and wine, they decided to go for a walk. They pulled on thick sweaters and coats and strode out, arm in arm.

'This must be the most perfect Christmas Day I have ever spent,' said Matthew with a sigh. 'Thank you, darling!' He pulled her close and they held each other in a long embrace.

'Can we go home?' Matthew asked coyly.

Jenna nodded.

She tentatively took him in her mouth. This was something she had found hard to do at first, but Matthew had gently encouraged her. She looked up at him, lying on the bed, eyes closed and moaning in pleasure. Now she enjoyed the feeling of control she knew she had over him. As her lips moved up and down over his penis, she felt it quiver. The power she felt turned her on.

'Faster, Jenna, faster, oh, God . . .'

She felt the hot, slightly salty liquid pump into her mouth and swallowed quickly.

'Jesus, do you know how good you're getting at that?' He pulled her up and kissed her. 'Now, madam, can I do you the same favour?' His tongue found her clitoris. Sensations of pure pleasure suffused her as her hips involuntarily rose up towards his mouth. Her orgasm took her by surprise in its intensity.

Eventually they arose from the bed and went downstairs wrapped in dressing gowns. They curled up in front of the fire and watched a James Bond film on television. When the film finished, Matthew turned the television off. He sat in silence staring into the fire.

'You know, I've been thinking about our future.'

'Oh yes?'

'Well, I really don't know how much longer I want to stay in the series. I mean, the money is great. But look what it's done to our relationship. Also, I've a yearning to get back to the boards.'

Jenna shrugged. 'If that's what you want, darling, then do it.'

'Well, my contract comes up for renewal at the end of February. I'll have to go and discuss it with my agent and see what she thinks, but I'm too young to get stuck in the series for ever.'

'I agree, but I know what it's like being unemployed. I'm not saying you would be, Matthew, but you haven't experienced it before. It could be very miserable with both of us out of work.'

'It may sound strange to you, Jenna, but I actually long to be miserable and out of work. At least I'll feel like a real actor for a change. I'd be able to lie in bed late occasionally.'

Jenna smiled wryly, thinking that the easy transition

from drama school to a secure job had made her husband naïve. Matthew had not yet experienced the self-doubt and loss of ego that was par for the course as more and more auditions fell by the wayside. However, she did not want to be a wet blanket. Matthew would discover for himself.

'If that's what you want, then it's fine with me.'

'And something else; I really do have a hankering to get out of London and move to somewhere like this.'

'What a wonderful idea! I adore it here. But what would happen if one of us got a regular job?'

'I don't see why we couldn't commute. Lots of actors do. And I know enough people at the studio who would give us a bed for the night if we were desperate. The low cost of renting outside London would easily cover the higher fares. I think we should sleep on it and discuss it again tomorrow.'

Jenna went to sleep under the feather-filled eiderdown dreaming of an idyllic future.

After seven blissful days and nights they had both made up their minds. The thought of going back to London did not appeal to either of them. They had already been into Thetford, the nearest town, visiting letting agencies to see what was available.

'This is probably a little too far away. I'm sure we can find something closer to London that isn't too expensive. You're going to have to do some detective work once we get back.'

Jenna nodded. She was getting into a tight black dress

that Matthew had bought for her in Thetford. It was New Year's Eve and they were about to leave to drive straight to a cast party being held in a hotel close to the studio.

'You look fabulous, darling, absolutely beautiful.' Matthew smiled. 'You'll knock 'em all dead in that.'

'I can't say I'm looking forward to seeing Miss You Know Who tonight.'

'Look, Paula will keep away and I promise I won't leave your side all evening.' He kissed her and took her in his arms. 'Just remember I love you, Jenna. Think of all the plans we've made for the future.'

She closed the cottage door slowly behind her and carefully locked it. She took one last look at the cottage, waved it goodbye sadly and got into the passenger seat next to Matthew. The car started first time and they drove off down the road.

The mist slowly turned to fog. Matthew drove along at a snail's pace.

'Do you think it's such a good idea to go back tonight? This fog is dreadful and it seems to be getting thicker.'

'It'll be all right once we hit the motorway. That's lit. I'm afraid we're going to be late, though.' Matthew sighed.

It took them an hour and a half to cover the eighteen miles to the motorway.

'It isn't lit, Matthew.'

'Well, we've come too far to turn back now. We'll just have to take it slowly.'

/ The driver of a lorry heading north was not following the same principle. He swerved to avoid hitting the car in front of him and lost control of his vehicle.

27

FRANKIE COULD HARDLY CONTAIN her excitement.

She checked her appearance in the mirror. The black leather trousers hugged her legs, accentuating their slimness and length. The grey muslin blouse did little to conceal the pink areolas that hardened as she thought of the pleasure to come.

She walked through the newly furnished apartment to the spacious kitchen. The champagne was chilling in the ice box and the canapés were waiting on the kitchen table.

Frankie went through the archway and into the sitting room and plumped up the cushions on the cream sofa. She stood and admired the effect that she had created in this room. The lighting was subtle, with spotlights placed to enhance the striking black and white framed prints and the many different varieties of pot plants.

She pulled out a Bruce Springsteen album from one of the built-in shelf units that lined a wall, and put it on the turntable. She knew it was June's favourite.

June . . . her lover of four months.

Frankie had been a lesbian since the age of sixteen when one of her father's girlfriends, a bisexual, had seduced her in the poolhouse. That day had both relieved and frightened her. Since then her sexual escapades had been limited, as she struggled to come to terms with what she was.

When Jenna had first come to live in the apartment with her, she had fantasized about her and felt ashamed of herself for doing so. Jenna was so innocent, so untouched. But quickly the attraction had turned into something deeper – an almost maternal feeling. She had felt bad about not telling Jenna what she was, but worried that she might be disgusted or threatened.

She had met June during her last movie. June was the chief make-up artist and Frankie had spent long hours in front of the mirror while June transformed her face from its natural state to looking ravaged, half-eaten and, finally, burned to a frazzle.

She had felt attracted to the diminutive blonde with the shapely figure and coarse sense of humour, but it had been June who had made the first move. On one occasion, as she was applying the latex to Frankie's face, she had brushed the back of her neck gently, then ran a hand over her breast so subtly that it could easily have been by accident. When Frankie had made no move to stop her, June had become less cautious and eventually asked her out for dinner.

Afterwards, they had gone back to June's apartment for a night of wonderful lovemaking. The older and more experienced woman had taken the lead. At last Frankie understood what the songs were all about. The insecurity that she had always dismissed as weakness in other women had caught her unawares. She was surprised by the new feelings that suffused her, emotions she had not experienced before.

Frankie was aware of the scandal that her relationship with June could cause. So they spent quiet evenings in Frankie's apartment, eating, listening to music and, of course, making love.

The thought sent tingles up her spine. She could feel herself moistening. She sat on the sofa and let her hand wander gently to her crotch, the sensation dulled by the layer of leather, but heightening her sense of anticipation. She stopped herself as her excitement rose, wanting to save the pleasure for the woman whose fingers knew her body so well.

The doorbell rang and she hurried to open it.

June looked well. Frankie wondered if she had had her hair lightened, for the short bob was glowing and made her bright-blue eyes stand out in her pretty, feminine face. Once more, Frankie realized the similarity between her lover and her best friend. Although June, with her full breasts and shapely figure, had none of the fragility of Jenna.

June hugged her and Frankie drank in her smell, revelling in the soft touch of her lover's hands as they caressed her hair.

'Come in and sit down. I got some champagne,' Frankie said, knowing that if she didn't remove herself from June's grasp, they would end up making love on the doorstep.

Frankie went quickly to the kitchen, opened the icebox

and removed the champagne. She uncorked the bottle and filled two Waterford flutes, then handed June a glass and sat down next to her.

'Thank you, darling. Did you have a good day?'

'Not bad. I went to a couple of meetings at Warner's. It looks as though the part's mine. Mimi called me an hour ago to confirm it.'

'Why, that's fantastic! Not bad? Honestly, Frankie, most actresses would be ecstatic. That's terrific, darling.' June put her glass down on the table and trailed her hand from Frankie's knee to her crotch. 'I love the trousers. Where did you buy them?'

Frankie tried not to watch the hand making slow circles around her most intimate area. She could feel the heat rising within her.

'Saks. In a sale. Half the original cost.' She knew that she was babbling but her mind was finding it impossible to ignore the erotic sensations that June's fingers were producing as they touched her.

She could resist no longer. She leaned forward to find those soft pink lips, with one hand automatically travelling to a tantalizing breast. Frankie sighed as she almost savagely squeezed it. She pulled up June's tight Lycra top and her mouth closed around a nipple. It hardened beneath her tongue.

June's hand was slowly unzipping her trousers and sliding down to Frankie's soaking wet mound. She gasped as the fingers found their target and began massaging her clitoris. Frankie's fingertips moved under June's skirt and caressed her thighs. She slipped her fingers inside June's panties and felt the contained heat. Frankie knelt down in front of June and pulled her panties off. Her head went between June's legs and she inhaled the familiar musky smell of her lover. She loved pleasing June, knowing that the favour would always be returned. June moaned as Frankie sucked hard, using her tongue to tantalize her. June's release was fast and, without waiting to recover, she tore the rest of Frankie's clothes from her body, eager to pleasure her in the same fashion.

Frankie closed her eyes as both tongue and finger were employed to bring her to an earth-shattering orgasm.

Later, they drank the rest of the champagne and ate the canapés.

Frankie felt happy and contented. For the first time, she felt that she belonged.

28

JENNA WOKE AND REACHED OUT for Matthew. Her arm fell into thin air. She opened her eyes. Blurry images appeared. She immediately closed them.

Some time later, she felt a hand on her arm. She opened her eyes again. A woman dressed in a nurse's uniform slowly came into focus.

'Hello, Jenna. You've been asleep nearly two days.'

Jenna tried to sit up.

'Don't try to move, dear,' the nurse advised. 'There's nothing to worry about. You just have a nasty case of concussion and some bruised ribs. You'll be up and about in a day or two.'

'Where's Matthew?'

'The doctor will be in to explain all that to you. Now, you just try to rest.' She walked out of the small room across from the nurses' station, glad she didn't have to be the one to tell the fragile, beautiful girl the terrible news.

'. . . and I'm afraid there was nothing we could do.'

Jenna lay staring at the doctor in disbelief. It couldn't

be true. Matthew couldn't be dead. If he was dead, why was she alive? Why hadn't He taken both of them?

'Jenna, I'm going to give you something to make you sleep,' the doctor said gently.

She hardly noticed as the needle entered her arm and her mind went blank.

'Bettina, how was your honeymoon?'

'Fantastic. We only arrived back from Heathrow half an hour ago.'

'Well then,' Gerard said, 'you won't have read yesterday's or today's paper, will you?'

There was a pause. 'No, why?'

Gerard cleared his throat. 'Look, I'm sorry to tell you this the minute you get back, but Jenna and her husband were in a car crash three days ago. A lorry jackknifed in bad fog and hit them head on.'

'Oh, God!' Bettina gulped. 'Are they badly hurt?'

'I'm afraid Matthew is dead. It's been splashed all over the papers because he was in that series on TV.'

'And Jenna?'

'She escaped relatively unscathed, according to the press reports. She's in some hospital in Cambridge.'

'I'll drive down and see her immediately. Do you know which hospital she's in?'

'One of the papers mentioned she was at the General in Cambridge, but you'd better check to make sure.'

'Oh, Gerard, she'll be in a terrible state. I'd better call Frankie, too. Thanks for letting me know. The poor thing has no one. Her mother won't even speak to her any more.'

'Send her my love, won't you, Bet? Bye.'

Bettina felt a lump rise to her throat as she looked at the thin, white-faced girl sitting by her bed staring into space. She walked towards Jenna and put a hand on her shoulder.

'Hello, Jenna.' Tears came to her eyes as Jenna reached out her arms and Bettina hugged her.

'I'm so, so sorry, darling.'

'Thank you, Bettina. It's lovely to see you.'

Bettina didn't know what to say.

'I'm going home tomorrow,' said Jenna, trying to smile.

'That's good news, isn't it? I can drive you to London. You can come and stay in Chester Square with Freddie and me.'

'No thanks, Bettina. I mean, I'd be grateful for the lift, but I want to go home to our . . . my flat.'

'Jen,' she took a small cold hand in hers. 'Just remember, you've always got Frankie and me.'

Jenna wouldn't let her hand go. 'Bettina, what will I do without him? I love . . . loved him so much. Why him?' She moaned.

Bettina felt helpless. 'Jenna, you mustn't think like that. There's no rhyme or reason for these things. I know you must be wondering why you're alive and Matthew . . . Well, you just mustn't punish yourself, darling. It won't help anyone, least of all yourself.'

'But we had so many arguments and wasted so much time. I was awful to him.' Tears streamed down her face. 'And then we had such a wonderful Christmas and everything was sorted out. We had so many plans . . . Oh, Bettina, he was only twenty-four!'

The nurse popped her head round the door and noted the distress on her patient's face. 'I think Jenna needs to rest now,' she said.

'Of course. Now, you take care. I'll be here tomorrow to pick you up and take you to London.'

Jenna released Bettina's hand and smiled her thanks.

When Bettina had gone, Jenna asked the nurse for some of those nice tablets that made her sleep and took the cruel world away.

Joyce had read about the crash in the papers. She had spent two days pondering what to do. Jenna was her daughter and her first instinct was to go immediately to the hospital.

But then she remembered the last time she had seen Jenna and the way she had shouted at her that night.

In the end, she decided not to go to the hospital. She doubted if her presence would help Jenna. She bought a card that said 'With Deepest Sympathy' and sent it to Jenna's flat. She would leave it at that. The next step had to come from Jenna.

Besides, she also had problems of her own.

Matthew's funeral was held at the Actors' Church in Covent Garden and he was buried in a graveyard not far from the flat in Little Venice. Most of the cast of his television series were there, including Paula, crying copiously. The press had turned out in force as well.

LOVERS & PLAYERS

Jenna was supported by Freddie and Bettina. Her eyes were dry as she watched the coffin being lowered into the ground. She threw a red rose on to the casket and walked away. She had already said her goodbyes to Matthew. Today was just a surreal circus to be endured. She knew Matthew wasn't in that hole in the ground. He was somewhere else, high above her, looking down and smiling at her.

'Mrs Valmont, Jenna, if there's anything we can do at all, let us know,' the series director said insincerely. He wandered off with one of his actors, deep in conversation about tomorrow's shoot.

As she had arrived at the funeral, a middle-aged man in a dirty jacket, scuffed shoes and with the stench of alcohol on his breath had introduced himself to her as Matthew's father.

As Jenna gratefully stepped into Freddie's car for the drive back to her flat, she saw him standing by the grave, surrounded by reporters. She hated his hypocrisy; beating his son when he was alive and basking in his reflected glory when he was dead. She had refused to speak to any reporters, although they had hounded her constantly since she left the hospital.

They arrived back at the flat, where Bettina had organized sherry and sandwiches for close friends of Matthew. Jenna watched her friend deftly distributing drinks and felt enormous gratitude. Bettina had been a tower of strength, taking over all the arrangements for the funeral and making sure that Jenna was seldom left alone.

Bettina was worried about Jenna. When she had

collected her from the hospital, the doctor had asked her to come into his office. He had suggested someone keep a careful eye on Jenna, since she was still suffering from shock. So Bettina had slept on one of the sofas for four days.

'Tell her to come and stay with us, Bet darling. There are more than enough bedrooms at Chester Square.'

'She won't, Freddie. I keep asking her but she always says she wants to stay at the flat.'

Freddie shrugged his shoulders and took a sherry from the tray Bettina was holding.

When all the guests had left and Bettina was busying herself with the washing-up, Jenna came into the kitchen.

'Listen, Bettina, I can't tell you how grateful I am for your staying with me and making all the funeral arrangements, but there's no need to stay any more. I'm feeling better and I'll be fine by myself, honestly.'

Bettina breathed a selfish sigh of relief but then checked herself. She studied Jenna's pale face and thought that she did look slightly better.

'Are you positive?'

'Yes.'

'All right, but I'll be round to check on you first thing tomorrow. And you have our telephone number, don't you?'

Jenna nodded. 'I'm so tired after all this, I'll just take one of those tablets and pass out.'

Once Bettina and Freddie left, Jenna poured herself a

large vodka and collapsed in relief on a sofa. She downed that and poured herself another.

She wandered through the flat to the bedroom and found one of Matthew's big jumpers to put on because she was cold. The familiar smell of him almost brought the tears that she had not yet shed, but she stopped herself. She made another vodka and looked at the huge pile of post that at some point she would have to open. Not tonight, maybe tomorrow.

She could not explain the way she felt, the guilt that was inside her. Why had she lived while he had been taken? Why couldn't it have been her? Matthew was so young, so full of life, with so much to live for. He hadn't deserved to die and she didn't deserve to have to carry on without him.

As she remembered, the pain became too much, so she reached for the vodka bottle again and washed down two sleeping tablets. She went into the bedroom and lay down, hoping that sleep would come quickly.

29

'FRANKIE, IT'S BETTINA. How are you?'

'Oh, fine, I'm just fine. How's Jenna? I feel so bad about not being able to make it over for the funeral, but we were right in the middle of filming.'

'Actually, Jenna is what I'm calling about. I'm at my wits' end. It's been six weeks since the funeral and she just can't seem to pull herself out of it. She isn't eating and I know she's drinking too much because I keep finding empty vodka bottles in the bin.'

'Shit, it sounds as if she's in a pretty bad way. Every time I call her, she just answers in one syllable.'

'Tell me about it. Look, the problem is that I'm pregnant and –'

'You're pregnant? Congrats! And why is that a problem?'

'Well, Freddie has talked to the doctor and they're worried because my blood pressure is high. So Freddie is insisting I go and stay in our house at Cannes until the birth. In fact, he won't take no for an answer.'

'Sounds like a swell idea to me. So what's the problem?'

'Jenna is. If I go to Cannes, there's going to be nobody around to keep an eye on her and I was wondering . . .'

'You were wondering if I could pop over to Jenna-sit?'

'In a nutshell, yes.'

''Course I will. Sounds as though she needs a bit of sense knocked into her. But I'll only be able to stay a week or so 'cos I start a film in three weeks' time.'

Frankie put down the telephone and sighed. She wanted to go and see her buddy and help her if she could, but it would mean leaving June and when she got back she would be straight off to Nevada on location for two months.

Well, it couldn't be helped. She called reservations and booked a flight.

The doorbell rang and Jenna wondered who on earth it could be. She had kissed Bettina goodbye yesterday and had settled down to another night of blissful inebriation. She knew that Bettina would not be coming round this morning, since she had flown off to Cannes with Freddie. So Jenna had not bothered to get dressed or take a shower. She had been relieved when Bettina had told her she was going to Cannes because it meant she wouldn't have to go through the pretence of making herself presentable and waiting for Bettina to go before she could make for the vodka bottle.

The doorbell rang again. She pulled on her dressing gown and went downstairs to peer through the glass pane in the front door.

She could not believe who was standing there. She opened the door.

Frankie did her best not to show how shocked she was at the appearance of her friend. Jenna, always slight, was now pitifully thin. Her usually glowing skin had turned a sallow colour and there were huge dark shadows under her eyes.

'Hiya, kiddo! How are you?'

'I'm fine, Frankie. What are you doing here?'

'What do you think I'm doing here, standing on your doorstep with a suitcase? Are you going to let me in or have I dashed all the way from LA to spend the week outside?'

Jenna's heart sank. She was glad to see Frankie but she preferred to be alone in her private world of vodka and memories.

She led Frankie upstairs and into the flat. Jenna quickly shoved an open vodka bottle in a cabinet. Frankie pretended not to notice.

'I'd kill for a coffee and some toast.'

'Well, I can make you coffee, but I'm afraid I'm running a little low on food.'

'Fine, I'll run across to the supermarket and pick up some supplies. Anything you want?'

Jenna shook her head.

Frankie nodded grimly and set off across the road. She bought freshly baked bread, soup, cartons of orange juice and anything else she thought might tempt her friend to eat.

And she's damn well going to, even if I have to personally shove it down her throat, she thought as she marched back to the flat.

Jenna had changed into a pair of jeans that hung off her and a dirty white T-shirt. She had made coffee for both of them and was slumped on the sofa staring into space.

Frankie busied herself in the kitchen making toast spread thickly with butter and honey.

'Right, I want to see all that eaten up,' she said in her best matronly voice.

Jenna nibbled at a small corner.

Ten minutes later the conversation was still being maintained by Frankie and all but a tiny crust of the toast lay uneaten on the plate.

'Jenna, you must eat. You're wasting away.'

'I'm fine, Frankie, just not very hungry.'

Frankie lost her temper. 'Bullshit, Jenna! Have you taken a good look in the mirror lately? You look awful!'

She grabbed Jenna by the arm, pulled her to the full-length mirror in the bedroom and stood her in front of it.

'Take a look, Jenna, and I mean a real look. What's happened to you? Do you think Matthew would like it if he saw you falling apart like this? You're damn well killing yourself!'

Jenna wrenched her arm away and ran to the cabinet in the lounge. She pulled out the vodka bottle but Frankie was too quick for her. 'Oh no you don't! You've had too much of that already.'

'I need it, Frankie. Please, give it to me!' She tried to grab the bottle back but she was so weak that Frankie brushed her arm away.

'Tell me, Jenna, do you want to die? Is that what it is?'

'Yes, yes! I should have died with him.'

Frankie watched Jenna as she sank to the floor and the tears started to come; proper, healing tears that were long overdue, tears that had to flow before she could recover. Frankie put her arms around Jenna and held her.

Hours later, when Jenna was all cried out, Frankie picked her up and half carried her to the bedroom and laid her on the bed.

'Listen, Jenna. I'm going to make you some soup and you're going to eat it, okay?'

Jenna nodded forlornly. When Frankie had left the room, she rose slowly from the bed, went over to the mirror and took the first proper look at herself since Matthew died. Frankie was right. The haggard face in the mirror hardly resembled the beautiful girl of six weeks ago. She felt faint and only just managed to stagger back to the bed without passing out.

Frankie brought in the hot soup and spoonfed her like a baby. It took a long time, but only when the bowl was empty did Frankie say, 'Right, I want you to get some sleep, and without those tablets you're shoving down your throat with vodka every thirty seconds.' She smoothed Jenna's lank hair away from her face. 'Frankie's here to look after you now, so you just get some rest and then we'll talk, okay?'

Jenna nodded and smiled properly for the first time since Matthew's death. When Frankie shut the door, she fell into a deep sleep, unprompted by anything except sheer exhaustion.

After three days in Frankie's care, Jenna was looking a

little more like her old self. Frankie looked after her with the tenderness that her mother had never shown her. She cooked dishes designed to tempt Jenna's feeble appetite back to life and was there by Jenna's side if she awoke from another dreadful nightmare.

Little by little, Jenna managed to talk. Slowly she unburdened herself of the pain, grief and guilt.

'Sweetie, asking why he was taken and not you is like asking why a two-year-old child dies of some terrible disease and a monster who rapes and murders women lives until he's a hundred. There's no answer to that question and you mustn't punish yourself trying to find one.'

She knew Frankie was right and, slowly, she could feel herself regaining her strength and a little of her zest for life.

Frankie dragged her out on the fifth day, saying she needed advice choosing some clothes. Jenna was glad to get home to the safety of her flat, but she had enjoyed the afternoon out.

'You know I've got to go back the day after tomorrow, don't you?'

Jenna nodded.

'Why don't you come with me? I know I'll be away filming for a while, but you could stay in my apartment and see LA.'

'No, Frankie. I've got to face reality here. I can't run away.'

'I understand, but any time you need to, just hop on a plane. Come on, let's both have an orange juice to celebrate your recovery and the start of my film.'

Frankie poured the orange and handed a glass to Jenna.

'Cheers, hon. Now, you promise me you won't start back on the vodka?'

'I promise I won't.'

'Good, because it doesn't cure anything. So what are you going to do when I'm gone?' Frankie asked.

'Well, for a start, I'm going to open all those,' Jenna pointed to the huge pile of post that had sat unopened for seven weeks. She guessed most were sympathy cards and she hadn't been able to face reading them.

'Well, that's a beginning. And what next?'

'Ring my agent to let him know I'm still alive.'

'Fine. And then?'

'Get some kind of a job to earn some money.'

'Congratulations! I think you've decided to live again.'

The next day there was an emotional goodbye on the doorstep. Jenna watched Frankie's taxi disappear round the corner before she went back inside.

She definitely felt better. Strength was returning to her as each day passed. If Frankie hadn't turned up, God knows what would have become of her. She made herself a coffee and settled down to open the mail.

She sorted the post into piles, separating the personal letters from what were obviously bills, and began with those.

Half an hour later, Jenna went to the drinks cabinet, poured herself a stiff vodka and sat on the sofa staring at the pile of letters on the table in front of her. There were four letters from the bank, wanting immediate proposals for payment of the five thousand pounds overdrawn on Jenna and Matthew's account, and a final demand on their joint American Express card. Jenna picked up the statement and saw the hundreds of pounds spent at expensive London restaurants and nightclubs and a thousand pounds at Van Cleef and Arpels. There were also letters from all the utilities such as gas and electricity, and a note from the landlord demanding immediate payment of the last two months' rent on the flat.

Jenna drained her glass and poured herself another large vodka. Night was falling and the cold chill of fear was coursing through her veins.

In a state of shock she totted up the total amount she owed. She managed a wry smile. If she and Matthew had had separate bank accounts . . . but they hadn't. She would also have to find a way to pay the credit card bills that Matthew had run up at all these places she didn't even know he'd been to. He had certainly never taken her to any of them.

The pedestal on which he'd been in her mind since his death came down a good few feet as she knew he couldn't have been there by himself. Paula. She pushed it from her mind. He was dead and gone and she couldn't ask him. She'd just have to give him the benefit of the doubt and believe his claim that the affair had been over months ago.

Six thousand, eight hundred and forty-three pounds.

She stared at the figure and reached for her drink, then firmly pushed it away. She had a lot of telephone calls to make. Tomorrow she was going to need a clear head.

Before going to bed for what she guessed would be a sleepless night, she opened the sympathy cards that she had earlier put to one side. She gazed at the card from Joyce. Inside she had just signed it 'Mother'. There was something cold and unemotional about the one word, as if Joyce hardly knew her. Jenna threw it into the wastepaper basket. She had no energy to waste on a mother who so obviously didn't give a damn about her.

At three o'clock in the morning she took two sleeping tablets. They refused to do their job and, rather than staring at the bedroom ceiling, she rose at seven and started making a long list of people she had to contact.

Jenna made appointments to visit her bank manager, her agent and some temporary recruitment agencies who were advertising in the local paper for office staff.

Then she called a house-clearance firm to come and give her a quote for the furniture.

In the afternoon she took a tube to Piccadilly and went into Van Cleef and Arpels. The manager was sympathetic when she explained her predicament, but told her that he could only buy the jewellery back at a third of what Matthew had paid for it, and that was a generous offer. That evening, the house-clearance firm offered her two thousand pounds cash for the entire contents of her flat. It was a ridiculous price, but she was desperate. When they had gone, she worked out that after selling everything she owned, she would still owe around four and a half thousand pounds. Grimly, she decided that her wedding ring would have to go, too.

Jenna forced some soup down her throat and wondered

for the umpteenth time what had possessed Matthew to go so deeply into debt and why on earth he hadn't told her about it. She knew it was a question that she could never get an answer to.

The bank manager was sympathetic but firm. The money had to be paid back or things would start getting nasty. There was little advice he could give her except to find a job quickly.

Her agent was about as much help as her bank manager, although he did take her to a nearby pub and buy her a drink.

'I'm sorry, darling, but until something comes up, there's nothing I can do.' He patted her hand. 'Don't worry, I'm sure something will.'

She told him she was going to have to go out and get regular employment and was thinking of going back to her job as an usherette at the Globe. He looked horrified.

'Darling, that's fine when one's a drama student, but when you're an up-and-coming young actress you don't want to be seen selling ice creams to the director you may have auditioned for the previous afternoon. You have an image to preserve. Why don't you go and tuck yourself away in some anonymous office and do some filing until something turns up on the theatrical front?'

So she trudged round the employment bureaux.

'Sorry, love, we're a bit slow at the moment and you have no typing skills. But give us a ring in a few days and we'll let you know if anything has come in.'

Jenna didn't have a few days. She went and sat in a

dreary café in Soho and had a lukewarm coffee as she pondered what she should do next.

She had to think of where she was going to live because she couldn't afford to stay in the flat any more.

As she walked out of the café, she saw a grubby notice in the window. It said, 'Waitress wanted. Apply within.'

She sighed. If she hadn't come up with any better ideas by tomorrow, she would come back.

The next morning, once the furniture had been removed, she went back to Van Cleef and Arpels and exchanged her jewellery for three hundred and fifty pounds. The manager offered her a further two hundred for her wedding and engagement rings. With a lump rising in her throat, she accepted it. Then she went straight to her bank and paid a thousand pounds into their joint account. After that, she purchased some postal orders with what remained of the money and spent the rest of the day putting them in envelopes. She addressed and posted letters to her landlord, American Express and the gas and electricity boards. Feeling better that she had managed to clear the majority of the smaller debts, she ran to catch the last post and walked back home to work out how she was going to pay the remaining four thousand pounds back to the bank.

She looked round the eerily empty flat and did not relish the thought of spending the night there on the mattress. But at least she had a roof over her head, which was more than she might have the next week. She had put a note in the envelope addressed to her landlord, telling him she would be moving out in a week's time and asking that the deposit they had given him be used to cover this month's rent. She had ninety pounds in cash left, which would keep her going for little more than a couple of weeks. She had to find a job quickly.

The telephone jangled, echoing noisily in the empty room.

'Hi, Jen, it's me. How are ya, kiddo?'

What Jenna wanted to say was 'Matthew has left me in huge debt, I'm stony broke and about to be thrown in jail 'cos I can't pay it back. Also, I've just sold my furniture, have no job and nowhere to live next week.'

But she knew it wasn't fair. Frankie had done enough already and this was her mess. Besides, she did have some pride.

'Oh, fine, how about you?'

'You sure?'

'Yes, honestly, Frankie.'

'Not back on the booze?'

'No, Frankie.'

'Getting enough sleep and eating properly?'

'Yes, Frankie!'

'That's great. Listen, I called to let you know that I'm off on location to Nevada tomorrow, so if you need to call me, ring my answer service. I'll get back to you as soon as I can but I don't know what the telephone lines are like in the middle of the desert.'

'Don't worry, I'll be fine.'

'Any work on the horizon?'

'Oh, a couple of things look quite hopeful,' Jenna lied.

'Well, keep your spirits up, sweetie. It sounds as if

you're doing great. I'll call you as soon as I get back. If nothing else, I should come back with a great tan! Bye, Jenna.'

'Goodbye, Frankie.'

She put the receiver down and sat in the middle of the deserted flat. She felt frightened and completely alone. There was no one to turn to now, only herself.

She put her coat back on and walked down the road to catch a bus to Piccadilly Circus.

'I saw your advert in the window. Who do I need to speak to?'

The gum-chewing waitress pointed to a short, dark man standing behind the counter. 'He's the boss. Name's Leo.'

Jenna walked over to him. 'Excuse me, but I'm here about the job in the window.'

The fat Italian looked her up and down and said, 'Got experience waiting tables?'

In desperation she lied and said yes.

'So you know how much hard work the job isa?'

'I don't mind hard work.'

'Good. But the hours are long.'

'Could you tell me what I'll be paid, please?'

'Two pounds an hour. But if you good, you earn extra money in tips.'

'When can I start?'

'I give you trial tomorrow. Be here at eight.'

'In the morning?'

'Yes. Is a that a problem?'

'Oh, no,' she said quickly. 'I'll see you tomorrow.'

Leo watched the beautiful girl walk gracefully down the street. He wondered what on earth she was doing coming to work for him.

30

JENNA WAS AT THE CAFÉ by ten to eight. The manager introduced himself as Mr Leon. 'But calla me Leo. And this is Marilyn, our other waitress. She teach you the way things work around here.' Leo went back to the kitchen leaving Jenna with a tall, thin, black girl.

'Hi, what's your name?' asked Marilyn.

'Jenna Shaw.'

'Done much of this before?'

'To be honest, no. Could you show me what to do?'

'Sure, Jenna, I'll show you the ropes. Just follow me around and I'm sure you'll pick it up. First, though, you need to get yourself into one of these scummy uniforms. There's a spare hanging in the ladies' bog.'

'Thank you.'

Jenna found the dirty toilet at the back of the kitchen and put on the bottle-green nylon dress and stained white apron. It was far too big for her and smelled of fried food.

'Okay, you take the orders from the punters and write down the menu number on this pad. For example, if they ask for egg and chips, that's number four on the menu. Then you put them on that spike for the chef. When he's cooked your order he puts it on the warmer over there and you take it to the punter. Don't worry about the till today, I'll teach you how to use it tomorrow. All right?'

Jenna nodded nervously. For the rest of the morning she ran from the kitchen to the tables, trying to look as though she knew what she was doing.

'So what's your story, eh? Actress, dancer, model, or boyfriend left you pregnant?' asked Marilyn as Jenna carried a mixed grill from the kitchen.

'What do you mean?'

'Well, there has to be a reason why a girl like you winds up in a dump like this.'

'Some of the above, but not the pregnant part, thank God,' she said, smiling.

'We all gotta suffer for the sake of our art. Jonnie, my man, is a film director waiting for a break. 'Course, he can't work, got too many people to see. He's just finished film school, so I help him out by working here to earn some dough. Are you here 'cos you're desperate for money?'

Jenna nodded.

'Well, you ain't gonna become a millionaire in this joint. The wages are pathetic but at least it's steady money every week.' Marilyn glanced at her. 'It just so happens that I might know of somewhere that you can really make decent money.'

'Really, where?'

'The place I work in the evening. 'Course, it may not be quite your style.'

'Anything's my style at the moment, Marilyn. I'm really desperate for money. What's the job?'

'I suppose you could call it a sort of public-relations role really. See you later, alligator.' And she disappeared off for her lunch break.

By the end of the week, Jenna was completely exhausted. She left the flat in Little Venice at seven in the morning, spent the entire day running around the café taking orders, and arrived home after eight in the evening. Her feet were blistered and her back ached. But she had little time to think of her plight, having only one aim; to earn as much money as quickly as she could.

However, sitting on the mattress on the floor of the flat on Friday night, counting out her meagre wages plus the tips she had made, Jenna felt terribly depressed. Sixty pounds for an unrewarding, miserable slog. Panic rose in her as she did her sums. The money she had earned was hardly enough to provide her with food and a roof over her head, let alone make any inroads into her debt, and in four days' time she had to be out of the flat.

She was tempted to blow some of her hard-earned money on a bottle of vodka. But sense said no, so she had a bath and spent another sleepless night.

On Saturday morning she bought the local paper and checked the rooms-to-let section. She spent the rest of the weekend trudging around a selection of squalid rooms whose seedy landlords all wanted a month's deposit and a month's rent in advance. She did not have that kind of money.

On Sunday night, she went to the nearest pub and

treated herself to a glass of vodka. Desperation was setting in. Her hand shook as she lifted the glass to her lips. She didn't know what she was going to do. Everything seemed so hopeless.

There was only one thing for it. She would have to go back to her mother's and ask her to take her in.

'Oh, God,' Jenna moaned under her breath. The thought of having to crawl back on bended knee filled her with horror. She remembered the sympathy card, devoid of emotion, and seriously wondered whether her mother would be prepared to have her.

She walked slowly back to the flat and let herself in, thinking that, unless a miracle occurred, she'd have no choice. She'd have to go back home.

Marilyn noticed her drawn face the next morning. 'What the hell is wrong with you? Your pet dog died or something?'

'Sorry. I've just got a few problems, that's all.'

Marilyn raised her eyes to heaven. 'Haven't we all, sugar?' She started to move away but turned back. 'Look, if you need to talk, we could go to the pub after work and you can tell Auntie Marilyn all about it.'

Jenna smiled gratefully. She really needed to talk to someone. 'Thanks, Marilyn. That would be great.'

'Okay. Now buck up before you add another problem to your collection and get fired for not doing any work.' And she hurried off to serve a waiting customer.

'So you see, I really am in a mess,' Jenna finished. She hadn't meant to tell Marilyn everything, but it was such a relief to talk to someone; and alcohol had loosened her tongue and the whole story had come out.

'Now let me see. You're homeless, penniless, husbandless and motherless – in more ways than one!' said Marilyn, looking at the four empty glasses in front of Jenna. 'Are you sure you can't go back to your mum?'

Jenna grimaced. 'It's a long story, Marilyn, but I think it would just about finish me off if I had to do that. But it looks like that's what I'll be forced to do, if she'll have me.'

'Well, I might be able to help. I've got a flat. It's only small, mind you, but it does have a boxroom that's crammed with my junk. I suppose I could clear that out and you could come and stay with me.'

'Marilyn ... really? Are you sure? That sounds wonderful.'

'Hang on a minute, Jenna, you've not seen it yet. It's hardly big enough to swing a cat in. You can have it if you want it, though. There's an old mattress in there that you can sleep on.'

'If you're sure you don't mind, I'd be very grateful. It would only be for a while, until I sort myself out,' said Jenna, relief written across her face.

'Yep, I could do with some extra pennies myself, and the rent's very cheap if it's halved. I spend a lot of nights at Jonnie's anyway, when I'm not working at the club, so it'll work out fine for both of us. It's just off Tottenham Court Road. You'd better come and have a look.'

'No, it's okay, I'm sure it'll be fine. Would you mind if

I moved in tomorrow night? Only, I have to be out of my flat by then.'

'That's what I call cutting it fine. But yes, that'll be all right, though you'll have to clear out the room yourself 'cos I'm working at the club tonight. Talking of the club, I'd better take you down to meet Lily. If you have as much debt as you say, you can pay it off in no time working down there.'

'If you earn so much at this club, why do you work at the café as well?' asked Jenna curiously.

'I told you, I work at the café to give Jonnie some money. The dosh I earn at the club is for me. I'm not gonna do both for much longer, though, I'm bloody knackered.'

'What exactly do you do there?'

'I'm a hostess, except it don't have much to do with flying,' Marilyn giggled, finishing her gin and tonic.

Jenna had no idea what being a hostess entailed. 'Well, I'll see how things go, but thanks for the offer.'

'Okay, dearie. I gotta run. I'll see you tomorrow at the café and give you a set of keys. Bye.'

Jenna just managed to close the two suitcases. Everything she had in the world was crammed into them. She was leaving the mattress, since she had no money to move it to her new home. She wandered around the deserted flat, remembering some of the beautiful moments she had spent here. She thought of the happy girl who had moved in. A new husband whom she adored, a glittering career and a whole lifetime to look forward to. Twenty months later she was leaving with virtually nothing.

She picked up her suitcases.

'Goodbye, my darling. God bless,' she whispered as she shut the door behind her for the last time and headed for the bus stop.

31

JENNA LUGGED HER SUITCASES up the narrow staircase to the small landing in front of Marilyn's front door. She looked in her handbag for the keys that Marilyn had given her at work earlier in the day.

She unlocked the door and stepped into a narrow hallway. She put her suitcases down and took a look round the flat. She was pleasantly surprised at what she found. There was a kitchen, which was basic but functional, a sitting room with bright posters and floor cushions, a bathroom that was spotless, Marilyn's bedroom and her own broom cupboard. Jenna sighed as she looked at the amount of clutter that she would have to remove before there was room for her to sleep. Marilyn had left a note and some cardboard boxes, telling her it was fine to fill them and leave them in the hallway for her to sort out later.

Jenna set to work and three hours later had managed to clear enough space to lay the old mattress on the floor. She had also salvaged a chair and a broken mirror from the junk. When she had piled the remaining clutter into the boxes and put them outside, she scrubbed the walls and swept the floor. She put the sheets and a pillow she had brought with her on the mattress, then stepped back to admire her handiwork.

'Well, it's not much, but it's home.' Jenna smiled wryly as she put the photo of Matthew on the floor next to her pillow.

Feeling filthy, she ran herself a bath and soaked in the tub. As she put some of her toiletries in the bathroom cabinet, she was amazed to see the number of bottles of pills on the shelves. She went to the kitchen and made herself a cup of tea, which she took into her room. She settled down on the mattress, sipped her tea and gazed up at the cracks on the ceiling.

At least it was a roof over her head. She looked at the photo of Matthew and a lump came to her throat. She swallowed hard, switched off the light and fell into an exhausted sleep.

'Sleep well, then?' Marilyn came into the kitchen, yawning.

'Yes, thank you. What time did you get in last night? I didn't finish clearing out my room until two in the morning.' Jenna handed Marilyn a cup of coffee.

'Yeah, well, I didn't leave the club until late.'

'Oh. I was wondering, Marilyn, if the money is as good as you say it is, I might ask you to get me an interview.'

''Course I will, sugar. Why don't you come with me tonight? I'll introduce you to Lily and she can explain exactly what the job entails.'

'It's nothing, well, illegal, is it?'

'No, the club is licensed and I don't think it's run by the Mafia,' Marilyn laughed. 'Just bring some pretty underwear with you and I'm sure Lily will let you start tonight.'

'Pretty underwear?'

'It's not as bad as it sounds. Just come with me and see what you think. You don't have to work there if you don't want to, but you're the one who says you need the money. Come on, we're gonna be late.'

Jenna ran to her room and rifled through her case to find the silk camisole and french knickers that she had bought to please Matthew. Surely there could be no harm in looking?

The café was always packed first thing in the morning and Jenna was glad to get to ten o'clock, when it calmed down until lunchtime.

She didn't know whether she was just tired or stupid that day; she had managed to drop a plate of scrambled eggs, then mixed up a bill and had an irate customer swearing that he'd only ordered a coffee. When she had sorted it out and the customer left, she breathed a sigh of relief.

As she took a sip of cold tea, she heard a familiar voice.

'I want a cup of coffee and the – Jenna!'

She jumped and turned to see Gerard Langdale looking at her in astonishment.

'What the hell are you doing here?'

'Earning my living,' she said, feeling her cheeks burn in embarrassment.

'Well then, in that case, you can take my order. I'd

like the cooked breakfast and some toast with my coffee, please.'

She muttered 'Okay' and hurried off to ask Marilyn to take the order over to him. It was bad enough having to work in the café without having Gerard Langdale gloating at her plight. She ignored him as best she could and thankfully watched him leave.

'What's he to you?' asked Marilyn. 'He refused to pay the bill until I asked you what your telephone number was. As it's the same as mine, I gave it to him.'

Jenna groaned.

She followed Marilyn down a narrow flight of stairs with garish red velvet wallpaper on either side. It looked and felt seedy. Jenna wished she hadn't agreed to come. She tried to calm herself with the thought that she could always turn back up the stairs if she didn't like it. And she did need the money so badly.

At the bottom of the stairs a scantily clad woman sat behind a desk smoking a cigarette.

'Hi, Marcia,' the woman said to Marilyn.

'How ya doing, Jane? I brought a new recruit with me. Her name's, er, Jennifer.'

'Mm, pretty, ain't she? Should do well.'

Jenna felt Jane's eyes on her. She blushed and felt like a piece of meat ready for auction.

'Come on. Let's take you to meet Lily. See ya later, Jane.'

Marilyn led her through some double doors and into a small deserted bar furnished with comfortable easy chairs.

'Why did Jane call you Marcia and you introduce me as Jennifer?' Jenna whispered.

'It's just better if no one knows your real name, that's all.'

'Why can't they know my name?' Jenna persisted.

'Look, don't worry about it. There's Lily.'

Marilyn led her down some stairs from the bar and into a dimly lit room. Jenna could see booths in which shadowy figures were sitting. There was a small dance floor in the centre of the room. They walked across it to a booth in an alcove at the back. Sitting there was an extremely thin woman of indeterminate age doing some paperwork. She had short bleached blonde hair and was heavily made up. She wore a Lurex catsuit and was adorned with heavy gold jewellery that hung from her ears, neck and arms.

Marilyn pushed Jenna down on to the red velvet-covered bench opposite the woman.

'Hi, Lily. This is my friend Jennifer. She wants a job here.'

'Is that right? Done this before, Jennifer?'

Jenna shook her head.

'Good. We don't like girls who have. They get bad habits. We need more blondes. When do you want to start?'

'Tonight,' said Marilyn quickly. 'She's brought her gear with her.'

'Fine. Is she clean?' Lily asked, looking at Marilyn.

'As a whistle. She's living with me.'

'Maybe you'll pick up some of her good habits,' Lily drawled sarcastically. 'Okay, Jennifer, I'm sure you'll do very well. Marcia, bring her back when she's dressed.'

Jenna followed Marilyn to a tiny changing room in which a dozen girls of different nationalities were in various stages of undress.

'Right. Get your gear on, sugar.'

'Well, I don't think that . . .'

'Come on, Jennifer, you're here now. Try it for a night. If you don't like it, you don't have to come back, do you?'

'I suppose not.' Jenna reluctantly pulled her camisole, french knickers and suspenders out of her bag. She slowly put them on.

As she was doing this, she noticed the sly glances of the other girls.

'You'll do well, the Arabs love blondes,' said a Spanish girl with an enormous cleavage hanging out of a tiny bra.

'Come on, I'll take you back to Lily. You'll need two pounds for the entrance fee.'

Marilyn led Jenna back to Lily, who took her two pounds and wrote her name down at the bottom of a long list. She looked up at Jenna, taking in her silk lingerie. She smiled. 'Very nice, dear. Now go and sit over there with Marcia and she'll tell you the rules.'

Jenna gratefully sank into the relative privacy of the booth. Having to walk around dressed like a tart when only Matthew had seen her like this made her feel completely degraded.

'Don't look so worried. It's not that bad, and we're last in the queue, so you'll probably just be able to sit and watch tonight.'

'What queue?' asked Jenna.

Marilyn explained that the girls were on a rota, and

those who arrived at the club first and signed in earliest got to entertain the first punters as they came into the club.

'What time do the girls get here, then?'

'They start coming in about four.'

'And what do they do until the punters arrive?'

'Sit and wait, dearie. You'll have to get used to that. The club doesn't start filling up until after eleven. We have to make the punters buy as much champagne as possible. We drink with them, dance with them and make them feel good. For that the club pays you a hostess fee, but what you get from the punter depends on what you offer him. We're not supposed to sleep with them, but the money can be really good.'

'For God's sake, Marilyn, surely you don't do that, do you?'

Marilyn looked away. 'Course not. I've got Jonnie, haven't I? Anyway, that's the score here. It's not so bad, is it?'

'It sounds awful,' Jenna said honestly. 'I think I need a drink.'

Marilyn shook her head. 'No go, sugar. We're not allowed to touch alcohol until we're bought a drink by a customer. As we're last in the queue, that drink is a few hours away.'

Jenna looked at the goose pimples appearing on her skin. It was chilly and in her skimpy outfit the cold was biting into her. She checked her watch. It was only eight o'clock. Another three hours at least of sitting in the dark, dreading what she would have to do.

Marilyn chattered away to her, then disappeared off

to the ladies' with another girl, leaving Jenna alone. She watched with morbid fascination as a party of Oriental gentlemen entered the room and the girls who were first in the queue moved towards them. Within seconds the men were being led to a booth and a magnum of champagne was brought to their table by a waitress. Loud music started beating out of the sound system. Then into the centre of the dance floor came a young woman in a long black velvet cloak brandishing a leather whip. The pace of the music changed to a slow erotic beat. The girl began to move to the music, cracking her whip. The cloak came off, revealing a skimpy bikini. The girl was making suggestive movements, running her hands over her body. Suddenly, and to Jenna's surprise, her bra came off. The girl continued dancing. Jenna watched transfixed as she ground her crotch towards the table at which the Japanese sat with their hostesses.

The stripper's routine came to an end and she disappeared behind a screen.

A hostess in a G-string brushed past her and leaned down to whisper in her ear.

'Don't sit there looking so stuck up, love. We're all the same in here, you know.'

Jenna's cheeks burned. The girl was right. They were all there for the same reason, because they had no choice. She was an actress, wasn't she? And she had a job to do.

The club was starting to fill up. Two or three of the Japanese were dancing with their hostesses, hands roaming all over the girls' bodies. Jenna felt sick.

She saw Lily walking towards her.

'A guy has asked for you. Come with me and say hello.'

Reluctantly Jenna followed Lily to the bar, noting the bitchy glances from some of the girls who had arrived hours before her.

'This is Jennifer, the girl you asked for.'

Jenna looked at the short, fat Arab with moles growing on his jowly face. His arm went around her and she fought an urge to shudder.

'What would you like to drink, Jennifer?' the Arab asked.

'Champagne,' Lily said under her breath from behind her.

'Champagne, please.'

'Would you like to take your lady and sit down?' Lily encouraged him.

Jenna discovered later that a punter must sit down in a booth before the club would pay her a hostess fee.

The Arab nodded and Lily led them to a booth. He sat far too close for Jenna's liking. His arm slid around her bare shoulder and a hand started to glide up her thigh. She put her hand over his to stop it.

'Oh no, you mustn't stop me. I've paid for you, and like all things I own, I can do what I like with you,' he said in a thickly accented voice.

Somehow, she made it through the rest of the evening. The champagne flowed and the waitress kept asking Jenna if she wanted more. She shook her head. After an hour of trying to keep the Arab's hands away from the private parts of her body, she excused herself. As she made her way to the ladies', the waitress grabbed her.

'Listen, love, you never say no to more champagne. There's a pot plant by every booth. When the punter isn't looking, you pour what you have in your glass in there. Or pour it on the floor, take it to the loo and empty it. It doesn't matter how you do it, but keep your glass empty so he'll have to buy another bottle.'

Jenna nodded. When she reached the ladies', Marilyn appeared out of the toilet, looking glazed.

'How you doing?'

'It's awful, Marilyn!'

'You'll get used to it. It'll all seem worth it when he tips you at the end of the evening. Be nice to him, Arabs tip well. Want some of this? It'll help you relax.' She opened her hand to show a small bag of white powder.

Jenna guessed it was some kind of drug. 'No thanks. I'll cope.' She gritted her teeth and went back to her groping, drunken Arab.

Marilyn was right. At the end of the the evening, the Arab gave her a hundred-pound tip. Then he offered her a thousand pounds if she'd accompany him to his hotel.

She declined and scurried off to the changing room in search of Marilyn.

'Not bad for a first night. There aren't many girls who make that when they're new,' said Marilyn as they walked back to the flat. Jenna didn't reply.

As she wearily lay down on her mattress, revulsion surged through her. What she had done tonight was only one step away from prostitution. But what choice did she have? She worked out how many nights it would take to clear her debts if she always did as well as she had done tonight. She reckoned two months. The thought comforted her. She closed her eyes and fell into an exhausted sleep.

32

'JENNA, IT'S GERARD. Where have you been? I've telephoned every night and you're never there.'

It was Sunday evening. Jenna had slept most of the day, trying to recover from the punishing routine of café and club. The last person she wanted to speak to was Gerard.

'I'm sorry I haven't been sitting by the telephone waiting for your call,' she said irritably, 'but I do have to work to earn a crust, you know.'

'What? Twenty-four hours a day? It's okay, Jenna, you can tell me if once again I'm too late and some other guy has managed to beat me to it.'

'No, Gerard, I promise you. I really have been busy. I'm at the café all day and then I . . .' She thought quickly. 'I'm doing a play in the evening.'

'Great. When can I come and watch it, then take you to dinner afterwards?'

Jenna smiled wryly. 'Oh, you really wouldn't want to see me in this. It's only a tiny part and the venue is hardly West End. In fact it's in the back room of a pub and I haven't told a soul I'm doing it.' She lowered her voice conspiratorially. 'I really would prefer it if you gave it a miss. I'm a bit embarrassed about it, to be honest.' She hoped that would shut him up and swiftly changed the subject.

'How's Bettina?'

'Glowing, but getting bored with being in Cannes. She misses you and sends her love. Honestly, Jenna, you'd think that it was the first baby ever to be born, the way Freddie's clucking over her. Her blood pressure is down so don't be surprised if she slips from Freddie's clutches and arrives in London to see you. So, Miss Elusive Busy Person, when can this poor desperate man beg a couple of hours of your company?'

'Really, Gerard, I'm up to my eyes at the moment – I'm not being difficult but I . . .'

'. . . I can't fit you into my diary for at least the next three weeks!' He laughed good-naturedly. 'All right, what if I call you in a couple of weeks' time to see if your social secretary can squeeze me in somewhere?'

Jenna breathed a sigh of relief. 'That will be fine. And thanks for ringing, it's nice to hear from you.'

'Take care and . . . Jenna?'

'Yes?'

'I really was sorry to hear about your husband.'

She bit back the tears. 'Yes, well, thanks. Bye, Gerard.'

Jenna put the phone down and buried her head in a cushion to stem the tears. She blew her nose and went to the kitchen to make some tea. Thankfully, she had little time to think of the past. During her two weeks at the club, she had slowly come to terms with what she was doing. At first, she had treated every punter as a potential rapist. Then, after a couple of nights partnering well-mannered gentlemen who only wanted to sit and talk, she began to relax a little.

Jenna discovered that she was a good listener, and often heard them pour out their problems. Her understanding and gentleness paid off. Her tips were good and a couple of men had returned again and asked specifically for her. She had learned to deal with the ones that drank too much champagne. She discovered that if she treated them like naughty little boys and put on her best motherly voice, they would apologize and ask her forgiveness. She always adamantly refused offers to go back to their hotel or flat. She had to admit that the money they offered her was tempting, but she could only lower herself so far.

She took her tea into the bedroom and picked up the photo of Matthew. She wondered whether she would ever be able to rid herself of the dreadful emptiness.

Jenna heard the front door open and listened as the familiar footsteps trod their usual route straight to the bathroom. The door was locked and she knew that Marilyn would not emerge for ten minutes or so. And when she did, her eyes would be glazed over.

All in all, Marilyn was a mystery to her, with her regular trips to the bathroom and her boyfriend who had never yet appeared at the flat.

The other night, while Marilyn was changing at the club, Jenna had noticed huge bruises on her ebony skin. She said nothing. Although they shared a flat, their relationship was far removed from the closeness she had shared with Frankie. Marilyn often disappeared when she had finished at the club, telling Jenna she was going to Jonnie's place.

There was a tap on her door.

'Come in,' called Jenna. Marilyn appeared, eyes glassier than ever, but looking pleased with herself.

'I want you to do me a favour, Jenna. A friend of mine is coming into town tomorrow and I'm meeting him after I've finished at the club. If Jonnie calls to find out where I am, just tell him I'm asleep with a bad headache and you don't want to wake me. Okay?'

Jenna shrugged and said, 'Okay.'

Marilyn looked relieved. 'Thanks. He, er, has a bad temper and doesn't like this friend of mine and I don't want to get him angry. I'm going to sleep. See you tomorrow.'

Jenna did the same. Before drifting off, she wondered whether the 'friend' was a punter from the club who helped finance a rather expensive habit.

Jenna was growing up fast.

33

'JESUS, WHO'D BE A MOVIE STAR?,' Frankie growled, mopping her forehead with an already damp tissue. The heat from the desert was making the cast and crew short-tempered.

Frankie was sick of having sand in her hair and the tap water that reduced to a trickle as soon as she got into the shower. She had not spoken to June for five days and the pain of being without her served to heighten the frustration she felt.

Frankie lay on the bed in her camper van and thanked God that at least she had brought a decent supply of grass to while away the monotonous evening hours. They had been filming in the desert for five weeks and the only evening entertainment was to screw whoever was in the next-door camper. However, since Frankie was in love with June, this was not tempting.

She lay there smoking dope, willing the time to pass as quickly as possible.

'Damn Mimi for making me do this ridiculous piece of shit!' she shouted as she ground the joint out in the ashtray.

Frankie knew that her agent had been right to push her to do the film. The director was a young hotshot by the name of Curt Waltham. He had recently won the Palme d'Or award at Cannes with a low-budget but brilliantly contrived film that had received huge critical acclaim. *The Heat Is On* was his first Hollywood film and the publicity surrounding it was enormous. Frankie's role was a welcome departure from the lowbrow horror films she had done so far and Mimi was hoping that it would launch her into the league of legitimate actresses.

Mimi had been her father's agent for years and knew everyone. She was adamant that Frankie should keep her relationship with June a secret.

'Jesus, honey! How can you expect men to accept you as a major Hollywood sex symbol if they know you're a dyke? All the male film stars of the Fifties who were gay found a nice little wife to protect their image. Why don't you do the same and get a husband?'

Frankie had shaken her head vehemently. She didn't want to weave a complicated web of deception. That was a dangerous game to play. However, to keep Mimi happy, she did reluctantly agree to be seen at parties and premieres with a stream of well-known male faces. June didn't seem to mind.

In the desert, Frankie had tried to ignore the constant attempts by Curt to seduce her. A couple of days ago the situation had reached crisis point when the young director had appeared in her camper at three in the morning. Frankie had stifled a scream and ejected the drunken Curt with a cutting tirade meant to make him never come near her again. Instead it had seemed to fire his ardour. Frankie wondered whether he really did find her irresistible or, more likely, he had screwed every other female on the set.

It's amazing that the whole of Hollywood isn't hospitalized with this AIDS thing, she thought. Yet she knew that the number of people infected with the newly discovered killer disease in Tinsel Town was far higher than the public realized. Well, that was one problem she didn't have, thank God. She wondered how Jenna was doing, alone in London without Matthew. She must call her as soon as she returned to LA.

Oh, well, she thought, closing her eyes to encourage the sleep that she knew would evade her. Three more days and I'll be back in June's arms.

34

IT WAS SUNDAY and Jenna was spending the day trying to recover from the rigours of the previous week. Although totally exhausted, she felt triumphant. She only had to earn another thousand pounds and she would be out of debt.

She was surviving on three hours' sleep a night and the work at the café became harder each day. She had contemplated giving up her job at the café and only working at the club. But once her debts were cleared, she was determined to leave the club and she would need the job at the café to provide a regular, if small, income. So Jenna soldiered on, comforting herself with the thought that as each day passed, she was nearer to achieving her goal.

The hours spent at the club waiting for the punters to arrive had become invaluable. She used the time to rest and think. The desolation of her life had given her a hunger for success that had been missing when she was with Matthew. She was determined to put her career back on track.

She called her agent's office every Friday to keep in

touch but there never seemed to be any auditions for her to attend. She had decided that once she had cleared the debt, she would use one night's tips to have a really good set of photos done. She also planned to find a new agent. She could hardly blame Peter Cross for not finding her work after the way her dedication as an actress had waned since Matthew died. She decided it would be better to make a fresh start. Once her evenings were free she could spend time writing letters to casting directors and even take a few acting classes at the Actors Centre. She felt rusty and insecure about her skills as an actress.

Jenna went over to the old record player in the sitting room and put on Prokofiev's *Romeo and Juliet*. She had found the record in a second-hand shop and splashed out.

The music soothed her and she closed her eyes.

The front door opened and Marilyn came into the sitting room.

'Hello, dearie. How's things?'

'Oh, you know, Marilyn. I'm just exhausted, that's all. I can't wait to leave the club.'

Marilyn looked at her thoughtfully. 'Well, what would you say if I told you I knew a way that would enable you to leave the club tomorrow?'

Jenna looked sceptical. 'Oh yes, and what's that?'

'Well, don't sound so enthusiastic, will you? If you don't want to be in a film and get paid lots of money, then that's fine by me.'

Jenna was interested enough to ask Marilyn to tell her more.

'A friend of Jonnie's has asked him to direct a film. They

need a couple of girls, so naturally Jonnie suggested me and I suggested you. It's not exactly Hollywood, but they've got backing, so the money's good.'

'How much?' asked Jenna, before she could stop herself.

'A grand each, and Jonnie's getting three, so maybe I'll be able to leave the club as well.'

The magic figure. 'Tell me more,' said Jenna.

After interrogating Marilyn as best she could, Jenna began to believe the project was genuine.

'Look, I've done one before. They're a good crowd and we really have fun. It won't be quite what you're used to, you being a professional actress and all that, but it's only one evening's work and the money is fab. I described you to Jonnie and he's really keen to use you. He thinks we'll contrast well.' Marilyn shrugged. 'Anyway, it's up to you, dearie. Just let me know tomorrow.'

Jenna went to bed and thought about it. One more week at the club and a thousand pounds would not only pay off her overdraft but would allow her to have her photos done and still leave money over for things like rent. And she felt sure that Marilyn's boyfriend would not have her involved in anything untoward.

The next morning, in the kitchen, she told Marilyn that she would do it.

The following Sunday, Jenna's nagging doubt surfaced and grew in intensity as she arrived in a taxi with Marilyn at the old warehouse that Jonnie was using as a makeshift studio. It was on the south side of the Thames among a sad clutter of empty buildings. Jenna glanced at Marilyn. She was stoned out of her mind.

'I hope you're going to relax, Jenna. Jonnie won't like it if you're uptight on film,' Marilyn commented as they climbed the crumbling stone stairs.

'Are you sure this is all right, Marilyn? I mean . . .'

'Stop worrying, dearie. Jonnie wouldn't let me do anything that he didn't approve of, now would he?' Marilyn giggled but the joke was lost on Jenna.

At the top of the stairs they entered a barnlike room. It was dark, the windows had been covered with black felt, but Jenna could see bright lights shining from behind a screen at the far end of the room. Out of the gloom she saw a figure coming towards them. As he came nearer, Jenna could make out a tall, thin young man with long greasy hair tied back in a ponytail.

'Hi, babe,' he said to Marilyn and offered her a drag of the reefer he was holding. She took it and passed it to Jenna, who refused. She noticed Jonnie raise his eyebrows to Marilyn, who shrugged and introduced Jenna.

'Good to meet ya, Jen babe.' He smiled, showing a set of uneven teeth. 'Marilyn was right. You're perfect. What a contrast!' He winked at Marilyn.

'Er, Jonnie, I'm sure Jenna could do with a drink of something to warm her up a bit.'

The two of them exchanged a glance. 'All right, darlin', I'll get something organized. Follow me and I'll show you where you can change.'

He took them into a small room full of old furniture and plastic cups overflowing with cigarette butts.

'Park your arses and I'll get you that drink. Bloody freezing in this place,' and he disappeared out of the room.

'When do we get our scripts?' asked Jenna.

'Oh, well, probably in a minute,' said Marilyn, looking a little uncomfortable. 'It's one of those arty films where no one says much.'

'Marilyn, I'm really not sure about this, I . . .'

'Stop worrying. You'll be fine.' Marilyn started rolling a joint.

'What are we wearing?'

'Dunno. Jonnie'll tell us in a minute.'

Jenna bit her lip as Jonnie reappeared.

'There we go, girls, a nice big vodka and tonic, with an extra large measure for Jenna, who looks as if she needs it.'

Jenna knew that she shouldn't be drinking before she went on set, but she was cold and nervous, so she gulped it down. The liquid had a strange, bitter aftertaste, but as it slipped into her system, she began to feel a little better.

'They'll be ready for you in fifteen minutes,' Jonnie was saying. 'Don't worry. Once we get on the set, I'll explain exactly what I want you to do.' He turned to Jenna. 'Have you done this sort of thing before?'

'Well, I played Juliet at drama school and everyone seemed to think that I . . .' Jenna's mouth did not seem to be working properly and she forgot what she was trying to say. She felt incredibly sleepy. She heard a familiar but distant voice saying, 'I told you she'd be great, didn't I, Jonnie?', and an unfamiliar one replying, 'Yeah, fantastic body, the company'll be well pleased. Bloody uptight, though. I thought you said she'd done this before.'

'Oh, she'll be fine now. Look at her, she's completely out of it.'

'Yeah, well, let's get on wiv it. You get 'er gear off and I'll 'elp you carry 'er to the set.'

Jenna opened her eyes but closed them quickly as a harsh light bore into her pupils. Someone close to her moaned.

The pain between her legs was unbearable. She opened her mouth and screamed.

'Fuck! Stop the camera. For God's sake shut the bitch up!'

The naked man lying on top of Jenna rose slightly, balled his fist and swung at her face. She passed out.

Jenna focused slowly on Matthew's photograph. Her head throbbed and her body ached.

She eased herself upright, looked down and saw that she was dressed. Her wrists were badly bruised.

'Marilyn, Marilyn . . .' The words were no more than a hoarse whisper.

Jenna stood up and leaned against the bedroom door. She moved unsteadily across the hall to Marilyn's bedroom and knocked. There was no reply so she opened the door. She took a step into the room and looked around.

A strange, bruised face stared back at her from the mirror hanging on the wall. She groaned, sank back on the bed and buried her head in her hands.

'Oh, Marilyn, what happened? Where are you?'

After a few moments she looked up and saw that Marilyn's belongings were gone. The wardrobe doors hung open and it was empty.

She didn't understand. Anything.

Except that she was totally alone.

35

CHARLIE STRETCHED HIS ARMS above his head and yawned contentedly. He looked down at the last sentence of the play he had just completed and smiled to himself. He stared out of the small window, saw that the sun was rising and heard the birds starting to sing. It was five in the morning and he had been at work all night.

He got up from his desk and lit a cigarette. He took a long drag and exhaled slowly. He knew that this was the best thing he had written so far. He wasn't surprised since he had written it for her and she always inspired him.

Charlie had enjoyed the past eighteen months in Frankfurt. He had been able to hone his skills as a director and make mistakes away from the glaring eyes of the media. He had directed two of his own plays and they had been well received by the German press. But he knew that he was ready to move on.

Three weeks ago he had been offered a six-month contract by the Lancaster Playhouse. The resident artistic director had left and they needed a stand-in while they found a new, permanent director.

Charlie had been hesitant when they had come over to Germany, seen his work and offered him the job. But eventually he had decided he should take it. It would get him back to England and give him a base to sniff out other possibilities.

After so many months the image of Jenna was still firmly in his mind. Time had not dulled the love he felt for her, and although he had tried to forget her, knowing she was a married woman and out of his reach, it had been to no avail.

He wondered if she was happy. He hoped so.

Jenna held Matthew's photo and stared at it through her tears.

She had been out of the flat only twice in the past week, and that was to buy more vodka to help keep the nightmare at bay. She was living in the kind of never-never land induced by shock, lack of food and the alcohol she had once more returned to. Being drunk meant that she didn't have to feel the pain.

She had no idea what time it was. It must be night, she thought as she peered through the curtains and looked at the black sky outside. She scrabbled around the floor to find her purse. She looked inside and saw it was empty. She let out a strangled cry of dismay and threw the purse across the floor.

She staggered to her feet and maniacally went through the pockets of her entire wardrobe looking for change. There was none. She saw the jeans she had been wearing on that dreadful night, flung in a corner. She picked them up. To her surprise she felt the crackle of notes in one of the back pockets. A scruffy piece of paper fell out with them. 'For services rendered,' it said.

'Oh God!' She groaned and slumped back on the mattress to count the notes.

There was a thousand pounds. She lay back and closed her eyes. She had enough to buy at least six months' supply of vodka. 'No!' she said out loud. That cash was no better than blood money. If she kept it, it meant that she was accepting payment for doing something so despicable that she wanted to murder the bastards that had made her do it. On the other hand . . . She sat up. They had made her do it. They had drugged her and used her, then left her to die for all they knew.

She fingered the money and for the first time in a week a glimmer of hope appeared. Maybe she could pay off her debts and make a new start after all.

Jenna sank back on the mattress with a groan. Then again, maybe it was easier to buy another bottle of vodka and stay where she was, in her nice secure state of inebriation. At least then she would not have to face those dreadful memories . . .

She slept, she didn't know for how long, but she woke feeling a little better. Her head felt heavy and woolly but for the first time in a week she wasn't drunk.

Unsteadily, she stepped under the shower and let the water awaken her senses further.

She shivered as she emerged and thought that she was going to faint. She lay down again. What she needed was to put some food inside her.

Slowly, she dressed her complaining body in a tracksuit. She found some paracetamol in her handbag and swallowed three with a glass of water.

There was a tin of soup in the kitchen, which she opened and warmed in a saucepan. Nausea hit her as she forced the soup down and drank two cups of sweet tea. Exhausted, she lay down again, dozed, and woke later feeling strong enough to make it across the road to buy some proper food. She scrambled eggs and made toast.

Jenna's head was slowly clearing and the meal she had forced down was restoring a little of her strength. Where was Marilyn? After all, this was her flat. Why hadn't she returned?

Then she remembered that Marilyn had told her she had done one of those films before. So she must have known exactly what Jenna would have to do.

'How could you, Marilyn?' she groaned. But Marilyn had an obsession that blinded her to everything else.

It was midnight and she knew that to recover she must sleep. When she awoke, the sun was shining through her uncurtained window. Jenna ate breakfast and took a cup of coffee into the sitting room. She had to decide what she was going to do. Jonnie deserved to be punished for his crime and she considered going to the police. But this was not a feasible option unless she could find Marilyn. On her own she had no proof at all.

She fought an urge to pack her suitcases and leave the flat immediately. That was silly; she needed a roof over her head until she sorted things out. The money that had nearly cost her her life to earn needed to go straight into the bank. It would clear the remainder of her debt and set her free to start again.

When Jenna had put the money into the bank and closed the account, she walked away feeling brighter. She vowed never to owe another penny for as long as she lived. The anger that was starting to stir inside her was fuelling her determination to put her life back together. She walked past a pub and with huge restraint did not go in. That must also be in the past.

Once back at the flat, Jenna did some calculations. She had seventy pounds to her name, but no debts. It was a lovely feeling. She would not go back to the club but maybe she could beg Leo to take her back. If he wouldn't, she was sure she could get a job as a waitress somewhere else.

A week later, when Jenna was feeling stronger and the bruising on her face was almost gone, she ventured out to see Leo at the café. It was full of lunchtime trade. She glanced around and saw Leo shouting orders, but she could not see Marilyn.

Leo caught sight of her, gave her a glare, and carried on telling off a waitress whom Jenna had not seen before. She walked towards him and waited patiently until Leo had finished berating the waitress.

He turned to walk away. Jenna called his name. He turned, looked at her and muttered something in Italian before marching into the kitchen. Jenna followed him.

'Leo, please, I know you're angry, but I can explain.'

'I don't want to hear your silly excuses. You and Marilyn disappearing off the face of the earth and leaving me with no staff, and now you come waltzing back saying you can explain, *pah*! I don't want to hear.' He turned his back on her.

'Listen, it's not how you think. But please, Leo, have you seen Marilyn?'

Leo heard the urgency in Jenna's voice. He turned around. 'I thought you lived with her?'

Jenna shook her head.

'Well, I haven't seen her since the last time I saw you, sorry. Hey, you're not in any trouble, are you?'

'Not exactly, I just need to find Marilyn. You don't know where her boyfriend lives, do you?'

'Hey, *bambina*, I was her employer, not her probation officer,' said Leo, smirking at his own joke. 'Sorry, kid, can't help you.'

'That's okay, Leo, it was worth a try. And I really am sorry for leaving you in the lurch. I, er, had problems at home.'

Leo's face softened further. He could never resist a helpless female and this one was *bellissima*, so fragile.

Jenna said goodbye and started to walk out of the café.

'Hey, kid?'

Leo's voice stopped her.

'If you want your job back, it's yours. There's always a space for a hard worker ina my café.'

'Thanks, Leo, that would be great,' she said.

'See you tomorrow then, usual time.' Leo smiled. There was something about that girl, something special. He wondered what kind of trouble she was in.

Jenna went back to work at the café the following

morning. That evening she gritted her teeth and went to see Lily at the club. Lily had not seen Marilyn either.

The landlord came round to collect the rent and asked who Jenna was. She asked him if Marilyn had been in touch, but he said no and told her that if she wanted to stay there, she'd better have her name put on the rent book. Jenna did so. She also moved her things into Marilyn's empty bedroom, which at least had a proper bed. She knew she could only afford the rent by herself for a short time and she would soon have to look for something cheaper.

The weeks passed. Jenna found she was still feeling queasy in the mornings and faint at work. She put it down to shock.

May brought the start of the tourist season and Jenna found her tips at the café increasing. She decided that she was looking well enough to have some new photographs taken to send to other agents and to put in *Spotlight*, the actors' casting directory.

Jenna went to have her hair cut and arrived in Paddington for the session with Mike, a photographer who had taken pictures of Matthew. The three hours stimulated her and boosted her ego, as Mike showered her with compliments.

The following day she went to see Peter Cross, her agent. He took her to lunch and said that he was concerned he didn't seem to be doing very well for her.

'It might be better, dear, if you had a change. I don't want to lose you, but going with someone else might alter your luck.'

Jenna agreed and thanked Peter for what he had done,

then ran to the ladies' to throw up for the second time that day.

The contact sheets arrived through the post the following morning and she pored over each picture, trying to decide which photos were the best. After work she dropped the sheets back to Mike, having marked the ones she wanted. When they came back in a couple of days, she would take them to Denbry Repros in Charing Cross, where they would print the original photo fifty times.

On the bus back to her flat she leafed through a copy of *The Stage* and checked in the auditions section. There was little there that was suitable for her, mostly cruises and the odd fringe production. She worried that she would have problems finding a good agent unless she could invite them to see her in something.

That evening, Jenna made a list of ten agents she thought might be suitable for her. When she got her fifty photos she would start sending them off, not only to prospective agents, but to casting directors who might be able to use her.

A couple of days later, Jenna passed out cold at the café in the middle of the kitchen. She awoke to find herself in an ambulance on the way to casualty.

'Well, Mrs Valmont, you'll be pleased to know that there is nothing wrong with you at all.' The kindly, fresh-faced young doctor smiled reassuringly.

Jenna breathed a sigh of relief.

'You're six weeks pregnant.'

Jenna stared at him as though he had made some terrible mistake. 'I can't be pregnant, my husband is dead.'

The doctor looked perplexed. 'Well, Mrs Valmont, you don't have to have a marriage certificate to get pregnant, do you now.'

'No, you don't understand! There's no way that I can be pregnant. I haven't, well, I haven't since my husband died.'

'And when was that?' The voice was suitably sympathetic.

'Oh, just after Christmas. So you see, it can't possibly have happened, you must be wrong.'

'Oh, come now, Mrs Valmont, six-week-old foetuses do not get there by themselves.'

'Look, it really isn't how you think,' she said lamely.

The doctor was looking at her as though he thought exactly that.

'We're all human, Mrs Valmont, and it's not unusual to take comfort when bereaved. Anyway, I can assure you that there is no doubt, you're definitely going to be a mother. Now, take this letter to your GP. There are antenatal classes you should attend, and you must . . .'

Jenna didn't go back to work, but straight into the nearest off licence.

Her resolve in pieces and too numb to think, she went home and found the photos from Mike on her doormat. She sat, throwing back the vodka and tearing the pictures into tiny pieces.

36

'I MUST SAY I am most impressed with this play of yours. I really think it has possibilities, Mr Devereaux.'

The overweight impresario drained his dry martini as Charlie listened with baited breath.

He had sent a copy of his 'Jenna play' to four or five West End producers and Harold Kidd had been on the telephone two weeks later to ask Charlie if he'd come down to London to discuss it over a drink.

'Obviously it's very unusual to put on an unknown playwright's work in the Avenue, but I may just be prepared to take a chance if we can get some big names interested in doing it. And of course, a well-known director.'

Charlie's heart sank. 'I'm sorry to be churlish, Mr Kidd, but I make it a rule to direct all my own work. I believe it stops conflict between what I write and what is presented on the stage.'

Harold Kidd frowned. 'Do you think that established actors would be prepared to listen to a young, inexperienced director? You'll be eaten alive, my boy.'

Charlie shrugged his shoulders. 'That's a chance I'll

have to take. If you need reassurance, why don't you come up to Lancaster and see the play I've just directed? It got pretty good reviews.'

'I've read them, but, yes, I might well do that. Anyway, to get back to the play. We would look to October to put it on. I happen to know there's an available slot on the Avenue at that time. That gives us six months. It means we're going to have to move pretty quickly. What do you think?'

'I'm delighted, obviously, but I'm standing my ground on the direction front.'

'I'll think about it, Mr Devereaux, and I'll be up to Lancaster some time next week. Excuse me, but I have another appointment. It's good to meet you, and I hope that we can work together to both our satisfaction. Good day.'

Charlie ordered another gin and tonic from a passing waiter. 'You cracked it, old boy, you cracked it!'

There was one problem that was dulling his excitement. The play was a *tour de force* that had been written specifically for one lady in the starring role. Jenna. He had named it *Angel in Hell*, the title inspired by the memory of her looking so beautiful against the tawdry background of his bedsit. It was her play and since he had been back in England, he had scanned *The Stage* to try and find her name but he had never seen it. He supposed she could have given up acting but doubted it. At the very least he should try to find her and sneak her in for the audition. After all, you never knew . . .

Charlie tried not to let it spoil his day. He was a

very lucky young man about to be given a shot at his dream.

And why not? It's a damn good play! He smiled to himself.

Unable to sleep, Jenna lay on the bed knowing that she was cursed. She asked Him what she had done to be so badly punished but He didn't reply. He never did.

All her rekindled hope had been brushed away in an instant by what the doctor had told her. She had been able to fight back before but this ... this was something she couldn't fight.

And she was tired of fighting. Like a soldier who thinks the battle is over but then sees another army emerge in the distance, she knew she was beaten.

She thought of her mother who had borne an obviously unwanted child and resented it all her life. She knew that she could never do that to a baby of her own. That would be the ultimate cruelty, to replay the childhood devoid of the love that she had so craved when she was young.

She had gone over and over the possibilities in her mind and had come up with no solution. Throughout her childhood, the nuns had warned about the murder of unborn babies. Abortion was not an option she could consider. How could she murder complete innocence? The guilt would live with her for ever.

She felt a strange bond with the thing growing inside her. It had not asked to be born into a world that didn't want it, just as she hadn't.

Although her mind was whirling, there seemed to be only one solution. She could not give this child life, and yet she could not destroy it, punish it for something it had not done.

So full of grief and pain, she came to a decision.

Jenna moved slowly towards the bathroom, a half-empty bottle of vodka in one hand, a glass in the other. She placed them on the floor and opened the cabinet. She took out five small bottles and closed the door. A pale face with misery etched on to it stared back at her from the mirror.

Jenna quickly looked away, sat down on the floor and tipped the contents of the bottles out until they formed a large pile. They looked like sweets. She licked one and tasted the sugary coating.

She filled up the glass with vodka and swallowed the green and yellow pill. Then she chose another. A red one this time.

Jenna was surprised how easy it was. There was no pain as the pile in front of her diminished, only relief at having found an answer to her problems.

Once she had swallowed all the pills, and the vodka bottle was empty, she wondered what she should do while she waited to die.

She thought of saying a prayer, but could not remember one.

Suddenly, the pain hit her. It was coming from her stomach. It was excruciating.

'Please, let me die now,' she moaned. 'Oh, God, help me!'

She writhed around the floor, clutching her stomach.
She could feel the baby dying.
'I'm sorry, I'm so sorry . . . Oh, God . . .'
The pain stopped as everything went black.

37

MARILYN STIRRED and looked at the clock beside her. It was five o'clock in the morning and Jonnie was snoring loudly next to her. She lay there sweating, then started shivering violently.

He was a bastard. She hadn't been allowed anything since yesterday afternoon because he had said she'd been a bad girl. He had hit her hard, then locked her in the bedroom.

Somewhere in her confused mind she knew she should go, but she loved him. And she was dependent on him to give her what she craved.

Marilyn could see the key in the lock. Jonnie must have been drunk when he came in last night because usually he hid it somewhere so that she couldn't get out while he was asleep.

She crept towards the door. At every creak of the floorboards she flinched, petrified that he might wake. She knew what would happen then. When Jonnie got angry, he got aggressive, just like the night they had made the film.

She had told Jonnie that Jenna had made films like that before. She thought he'd be pleased that she'd found him such a beautiful girl to star in his film.

Marilyn had thought that Jenna would be fine once they had fed her a little something to warm her up, but then Jenna had blown it all by screaming at the vital moment. Jonnie had been furious.

'I thought you told me she'd done this kind of stuff before, you stupid bitch!' A harsh slap scorched her cheek. 'You know this stuff is illegal. What if she goes to the police? What then, you fuckin' stupid cow?' The next punch made her fall to the floor, clutching her stomach in agony.

'I'm sorry, Jonnie, I'm sorry. I thought she'd be okay once we'd given her something.'

'Jesus, Miss Prim couldn't have taken anything before in her life, the way she reacted to those pills I put in her drink.'

Jonnie paced the deserted warehouse and looked at Jenna, still passed out and tied to the bed on the set.

'We gotta get her home before she wakes up. And you'll 'ave to move out and come and stay with me. She don't know where I live, does she?'

'No, Jonnie, honest.'

'I suppose that's something. She fuckin' ruined the film, fuckin' screamin' 'er head off at the crucial moment, I can't use that. I'm gonna have to reshoot the whole bloody scene. I know what we'll do. We'll take 'er home, you can move yer stuff out while she's still passed out and we'll give 'er the thousand pounds with a receipt. Then if she decides to go to the police, she won't 'ave no proof 'cos she won't be able to find you, and if she screams rape and they do believe 'er, we can say that we paid 'er and she took the money.' Jonnie nodded. 'Yeah, that's the best thing to do. If the company gets wind of this they'll friggin' kill me. They've already had an investigator from the Vice Squad sniffin' around. If your mate goes to the police they might put two and two together. Christ, Marilyn! You could get me in the slammer for this, you silly bitch!' He turned and slapped her hard across the face.

'No, Jonnie, please . . . *stop*!' Marilyn cowered.

'Get 'er dressed and make it quick.'

Once Marilyn had put Jenna's clothes on, Jonnie had put her over his shoulder and carried her to his car. They drove back to the flat and Jonnie had dumped Jenna on her bed and watched her while Marilyn packed her things. Jenna started to stir.

'Marilyn, let's get the fuck out of 'ere, she's waking up.'

'But Jonnie, I need to get some things from the bathroom –'

'I'll buy you a fuckin' toothbrush tomorrow, for Christ's sake. Just get those cases downstairs.'

And they had left.

Marilyn reached the door. Holding her breath, she turned the key and heard the click as it opened. She pulled the door towards her. It creaked open. She thought all was lost as Jonnie stirred. But he sighed, rolled over and was still.

She quietly closed the door behind her. Her coat was hanging on the peg in the hall and she put it on over the filthy T-shirt and jeans that she had not taken off for days.

Once outside, she didn't stop running until she was safely down the road. She turned a corner and leaned against a wall to catch her breath.

She'd done it. With any luck she could get to the flat, take what she needed and be back before Jonnie woke up.

She walked hurriedly down the deserted street, praying that Jenna had not emptied the bathroom cabinet.

38

'SO, ANY IDEAS ON CASTING?' asked Harold.

Charlie was sitting in a comfortable chair at the Garrick Club, sipping a gin and tonic. He was feeling extremely pleased with himself. Harold had come up to see the play he had directed at Lancaster. He had met Charlie in the bar afterwards and told him that he was impressed but needed time to think and could they meet in London next week?

Charlie had arrived at the Garrick twenty minutes ago and Harold had just told him that he was willing to let him direct *Angel in Hell*. The Lyric Theatre on Shaftesbury Avenue had been booked for the end of October, which gave them just over four months to assemble a cast, a production team and have the play rehearsed and ready for the opening night.

They drew up a list of well-known actresses who they agreed would be good to play the part of Mrs Simpson, the mother.

'Of course, my first choice would be Glenda Jackson, but I called her agent and he said she's booked solid for the next year.'

Charlie was disappointed. Harold ordered more drinks and they continued discussing each character in the play.

'And now we come to Christina herself. I think we're going to have a few problems casting her. We must get her right because the whole play revolves around her.' Harold sighed. 'How many young actresses do you know with the innocence of the Virgin Mary, the sex appeal of Monroe and the talent of Ashcroft? We'll get every young blonde from here to the States wanting to audition.'

Charlie nodded. He knew exactly who possessed those qualities. 'I have someone in mind, but I have to check to see if she's available,' Charlie said lamely.

'Well, there are a couple of girls who are worth seeing.' Harold mentioned a couple of names.

Charlie looked doubtful. 'What about trying to find someone new? Launch a young star and all that?'

'*Gone With the Wind* style, you mean? A nationwide hunt for the next blonde Vivien Leigh? Well, from a publicity point of view it's not a bad idea, but watching hundreds of talentless nobodies performing their party pieces is not my idea of fun. Look, I'll get the script off to a couple of agents who look after the girls I mentioned and we'll do a week of open auditions to see what we can find. But we've got to have this cast by the end of next month if we're to stand any chance of opening in September.'

Charlie nodded in agreement. Jenna was proving elusive. He'd tried her agent, who told him that he no longer represented her but had given him a telephone number. He had rung it, only to discover that she had moved out over four months ago and the people renting the flat in Little Venice had no idea where she had gone. He had tried calling her mother, who also only had Jenna's old address. Joyce had coldly informed him that she had not heard from Jenna in two years and didn't care to think where she might have ended up. He still had Bettina and Frankie to try, but they were proving difficult to get hold of.

Charlie refused to believe that Jenna had disappeared. Anyway, he'd keep trying and prayed that he'd find her before it was too late. Someone had to know where she was.

Jenna could hear voices drifting towards her. She felt very peaceful. She wondered if this was heaven. She smiled, glad that she had decided to remove herself and her baby from the pain of living.

She opened her eyes slowly and looked around her.

Jenna let out a low moan as she took in the stark hospital room. There was a tube hanging above her that entered her wrist.

'Oh, God, I couldn't even kill myself,' she groaned.

Then she remembered and moved her hand down to her stomach. All she could feel was a gnawing pain that was increasing the more she came to.

A nurse loomed above her. Jenna wanted to ask her what had happened to her baby, but before her mouth could form the words, she drifted off to sleep again.

'You're a very lucky young woman,' said the consultant. 'If someone had called an ambulance any later than they did, you wouldn't have been here to tell the tale.'

Jenna was sitting up in bed the following morning, having woken and demanded that the nurse tell her what had happened to her baby. The nurse had immediately gone to fetch the doctor.

'What about my baby?'

'I'm afraid it had already started to miscarry before you arrived here, due to that concoction you fed yourself. We were only just in time to save you. You were haemorrhaging very badly so we had to make a decision and put your life first. We needed to stop the bleeding and get your stomach pumped as quickly as possible.' He looked for a reaction on Jenna's face. She was staring blankly at him. 'There's no need to worry. We gave you a D and C – that's a general clean-up of your womb to prevent further infection. Your stomach will feel very sore for a while from the pump and you'll be on a drip for a couple of days until things settle down in there, but you should be up and around within a week. Have you any idea who found you? You need to say a very big thank you to them.'

Jenna shook her head.

'Where on earth did you get that cocktail of pills? You certainly weren't taking any chances, were you?'

A large tear appeared and made its way lamely down Jenna's cheek. Remorse, thought the doctor. Good, at least that was a healthy sign.

'Anyway, it's not my job to find out why or how. Our psychiatrist will be popping in to see you. Standard practice when people try to commit suicide. The good news is that there is no reason why you shouldn't have another child as soon as you're stronger. By the way, can we contact anyone for you? We also need to know your name: the person who called the ambulance just gave the address. When they found you they had no time to play detective. Well?'

There was no reaction from Jenna.

'What is your name and do you want your next of kin contacted?' he said, used to prompting patients in shock.

'Jenna Valmont, and I have no close relatives.'

'All right. Now you just try to rest as much as possible, and I'll be back to see you tomorrow.'

Jenna sank back on to the pillow and closed her eyes. She felt completely numb.

A couple of hours later, she heard someone softly calling her name. She opened her eyes and saw a woman in a colourful gypsy skirt and an ethnic headscarf sitting beside her bed.

'Hello, Jenna. I'm Darinka Sovek, your psychiatrist.'

Jenna didn't answer.

'It's all right, I'm not going to ask you any questions now. I just wanted to introduce myself. The doctor tells me that you have no one you want us to contact. Is that true?'

Jenna nodded.

'Okay. Well, I'll be back tomorrow to see whether you're feeling like talking, but if you need me before, just ask the nurse and I'll be with you in a jiffy.' Darinka squeezed Jenna's hand. 'Just remember, you're not alone any more. I'll see you tomorrow.'

A slight smile appeared on Jenna's lips as she looked up into the kind brown eyes.

'Thank you,' she said.

39

CHARLIE WAS FRANTIC. Four weeks on and auditions for the part of Christina were on second re-call and still not even a sniff of Jenna.

He was sitting having his tenth cup of coffee in the back row of the stalls at the Lyric Theatre, listening to the umpteenth bad reading of Christina's biggest scene. The rest of the show was cast, with a superb collection of actors drawn from the elite of British theatre. If they couldn't find their Christina in the next seven days, Harold was going to cast one of the young actresses that he had been keen on from the start. Charlie had seen both of them read Christina and he knew that they were wrong. They were brash and too worldly-wise to play the naïve, beautiful young daughter. He had called Frankie's agent in LA and left his telephone number. Apparently, Frankie was filming in the desert and was virtually uncontactable.

There was just one hope left. He had managed to get hold of Bettina's telephone number by asking Theodore Holmes for Lord Langdale's number. Bettina's mother had answered the phone and told Charlie that Bettina was in Cannes awaiting the birth of her baby. She had given Charlie the Cannes number.

Charlie threw his plastic cup under the seat in front of him, and whispered to the stage manager that he was popping up to the office in Wardour Street for half an hour. He walked along Shaftesbury Avenue, knowing that Bettina was the last hope he had of tracing Jenna.

He sat down at a desk in Harold's office, picked up the phone and dialled. It rang and rang. Charlie was just about to put down the receiver when a breathless voice answered.

'*Allo, ici* Bettina Roddington.'

'Bettina! Thank goodness you answered. It's Charlie Devereaux.'

'Charlie! How wonderful to hear from you. How on earth did you get this number?'

'Your mother kindly gave it to me. Listen, Bettina.' He drew in a breath. 'You don't by any chance know where Jenna is living, do you? I desperately need to contact her and no one seems to know where she is.'

'I've absolutely no idea. Since I've been in Cannes I've tried ringing but she seems to have moved out. She was pretty cut up after Matthew died, you know.'

'What? Matthew is dead! When?'

'Oh, Charlie, I'm sorry. I assumed you knew.'

'I've been out of the country for nearly two years. What happened?'

'They were in a car crash on New Year's Eve. Matthew was killed but Jenna wasn't hurt. As to where she is now, I really can't help you. Have you tried Frankie in LA?'

'Bettina, believe me, I've tried everyone. I don't understand it. She can't have just disappeared, I –'

'Wait a minute,' Bettina cut in. 'I'm sure Gerard said something about seeing her in a café ages ago. Maybe he has her telephone number.'

'Can you give me Gerard's number? It really is urgent.'

'Of course. Have you got a pen? I'll give you his work and home numbers.'

Charlie scribbled the numbers down.

'He's usually home by eight. Try him then. It's nothing serious, is it?'

'Well, it's not life or death, and nothing to worry about, but it could make a hell of a difference to both of our careers.'

'Well, good luck! If you find her, give her a good spank from me for not keeping in touch.'

'Rest assured, Bettina, I most certainly will.'

'Well, Jenna, I think I can say with a fair degree of confidence that we can let you go home tomorrow.' Darinka smiled encouragingly. 'How do you feel about that?'

Jenna shrugged her shoulders. In the three and a half weeks she had been in the hospital, she had been able to cocoon herself from reality. 'I don't honestly know, Darinka. I mean, it's all very well coming to terms with what's happened while I'm in here, but I don't know how I'll cope by myself. The thought of having to go back to that flat scares me.'

'Jenna, you have to face the outside world some time and I think you're as ready as you'll ever be. We don't want you to become institutionalized. You've been here long enough.'

Jenna nodded. She tried to imagine how she'd cope without Darinka's shoulder to cry on. In their first sessions together it had taken hours of coaxing from Darinka to get her to even utter a couple of words. Jenna had been numb, unable to release any emotion for fear of what it might do to her. The nightmare of the past six months was locked tight inside.

Darinka, a woman of seemingly endless patience, had refused to give in when Jenna would not talk. She had no idea what kind of trauma she had been through, but whatever it was, the pain needed to be released before she could begin to recover.

After a week of staring across her desk at a silent, tight-lipped girl, she was beginning to lose hope of reaching her. Then she had a stroke of luck.

She had gone home to her flat in Barons Court feeling depressed at the lack of progress she had been making. She made herself a cup of camomile tea and decided to unpack a couple of chests that were still standing in her hall, even though she had moved into the flat six months earlier. As she took an old teapot from its newspaper wrapping, she saw a familiar face staring up at her. It was Jenna clutching a posy of flowers with a tall, handsome man standing by her side. The picture had obviously been taken on her wedding day. The difference between the smiling girl in the photo and the shrunken, unresponsive figure that sat opposite her every day at the hospital was stark. She read the paragraph under the photo.

'Oh, dear,' she sighed when she had finished it. 'Poor Jenna.'

The next day, Jenna sat, silent as usual, opposite her.

Darinka tapped her pen on the pad in front of her. 'Jenna, why don't you tell me about Matthew?'

Darinka wondered whether she had done the right thing when Jenna's agonized eyes met her own.

'How do you know about Matthew?'

'I read about him in an old newspaper. I'm very sorry he died, Jenna.'

She knew she had found the key. The cry came from deep inside her patient. It was pitiful to hear, the cry of a wounded animal.

'Why did he die? Why take him and not me? Oh, God, I murdered my baby as well . . .'

Darinka let the tirade of jumbled thoughts pour out. Jenna didn't know it, but she had just taken her first step on the road to recovery.

From that day, Darinka was able to help Jenna deal with the guilt she felt about killing her child.

'The whole reason I tried to kill myself was so I wouldn't have to have an abortion. It seems that I ended up doing exactly that.'

'What about the father?' asked Darinka. She watched Jenna shudder.

'I really can't talk about that. Ever.'

'Jenna, were you raped?'

'I'm sorry, I don't want to talk about it.'

After repeatedly coming up against a brick wall as far as this was concerned, Darinka was convinced that Jenna had indeed been raped. She wanted Jenna to admit it so that they could at least try and find the man and prosecute him. Darinka knew that this would ease Jenna's guilt, help her realize that it was not her fault, but Jenna refused point blank to talk about it. Darinka had seen this before and without the victim admitting the crime, there was no way forward.

Apart from that, Jenna was responding well. She had admitted the fact that she turned to alcohol when faced with problems. Darinka had sent her on a short alcohol-rehabilitation course. However, once she got back to the problems of the outside world, well . . . Darinka thought of all the progress she had made with patients under her care, and the satisfaction it had given her when they had walked from the hospital capable of leading a normal life. Then the depression when they were readmitted six months later . . . She prayed that this would not happen to Jenna.

'Now remember, whatever you do, don't under any circumstances reach for that bottle. You know that it won't solve anything.'

Jenna shook her head. 'I'm determined not to.'

'That's what we like to hear. I've contacted Leo at the café and he's prepared to let you go back part-time until you're stronger. I think he has rather a soft spot for you.' She smiled.

'Do you think so?'

'I do. And it's very important to think about getting that career of yours back on the road. You're very young, Jenna, and I'm sure you can start again. Don't let me down, will you?'

'I'll try not to.'

'Good. Now, I'm going to do something I'm not supposed to do and give you my home telephone number. If things get really rough, give me a ring. And I suggest you get in touch with those friends of yours. I'm sure Frankie and Bettina will be worried about you.'

Jenna turned the key in the lock and let herself into the dark, freezing-cold flat. She picked up the post from the mat and checked to make sure that Marilyn had not returned while she had been away.

She knew what she must do first. She got some disinfectant and a rubbish bag and began to clear up the mess in the bathroom. She threw away the empty bottle of vodka and the pill bottles. Then she scrubbed the dried blood from the linoleum.

She made herself a cup of coffee and went into the sitting room, trying to remember what Darinka had said about returning home and coping with the memories.

'The first night will be the worst. If you get through that without reaching for the bottle, you're doing fine. It will get easier, Jenna, I promise.'

But as Jenna sat staring into space, the memories closed in on her. She wanted a drink dreadfully, dreadfully badly.

'No, Jenna, you mustn't,' she told herself and got up, knowing that she must not sit there and think.

So she scrubbed the kitchen until it was gleaming. Then she started to clear up the mess in her bedroom, but the need for a drink would not depart.

She went into the sitting room and checked to see if there was any vodka left in the cupboard. There was half a bottle. It was no good. She couldn't get through tonight without it.

'Just one small drink and from tomorrow I swear I won't touch it,' she promised herself. Jenna poured the vodka into a glass and lifted it to her lips. Before she could take a sip, the telephone rang.

She put the glass down and nervously picked up the receiver.

'Hello.'

'Jenna?'

'Yes?'

'It's Charlie.'

It was the telephone call that changed her life.

40

SHE SAT IN FRONT OF her mirror and carefully applied Leichner number five pancake on to her face. She added a layer of blusher on each cheek. Then she surrounded her eyes with kohl liner.

Jenna giggled at her reflection when she had finished. She looked like an over-made-up tart but she knew that on the big stage under the glare of the lights she would look completely natural.

Her dresser came in carrying another large bouquet and a pile of telemessages. Her dressing room was overflowing with cards, gifts and flowers. No one seemed to have forgotten her. Jenna thought how ironic it was that two months ago she had been so alone, without anyone to turn to.

She looked at the exquisite spray of red roses. They were from Charlie. She smelled them and asked her dresser to put them in a vase.

She opened the telemessages. There was one from Theodore Holmes and Rudi Gregorov and another from Frankie telling her to 'Knock 'em dead, kiddo!' Frankie had jetted over to be at her friend's first night and Daniel, who had just finished filming on location in Cornwall, was staying on specially to see the play before he flew back to Hollywood tomorrow. Bettina, who had given birth to twin boys, three weeks ago, had sent flowers and a note apologizing for not being able to attend.

Jenna wondered if her mother would come. She had sent her a ticket plus an invitation to the first-night party at the Waldorf and a note asking if they could 'forgive and forget', but there had been no reply.

'Ladies and gentlemen,' a voice came over the tannoy, 'this is your half-hour call.'

'Is this really happening?' Jenna asked her reflection in the mirror. She was still waking up in the morning and pinching herself. It was hard to believe that the nightmare of the past few months could have dissolved so quickly.

After he had spoken to her on the telephone, Charlie had driven straight over to her flat.

'Jenna, I can't tell you what a relief it was to hear your voice. Where on earth have you been?'

'Oh, I'll explain another time.' She made them both a coffee, having poured the rest of the vodka down the sink straight after Charlie's call.

'Now, tell me what this is all about.'

Jenna listened as Charlie explained.

'So you see, Jenna, it really is the eleventh hour.'

'Well, I'm awfully flattered, Charlie, but I haven't done any acting for ages. And nobody has ever heard of me. Are you sure you want me to audition?'

'Do I? My sweet angel, I wrote the damn thing for you. Now, let me tell you the plot . . .'

Jenna sat and listened. The story was about a young girl who is hunted down by her real mother who had her adopted at birth. Christina has no idea that the parents she has loved and trusted for her entire life are not her real mother and father. The play centred on the havoc that is wreaked on the whole family when the real mother makes an appearance.

'Well? What do you think?' said Charlie.

'I think we'd better sit and read it.'

'Yes. Now listen, it's final re-calls tomorrow for Christina. We've got a lot of work to do tonight. We must have Christina's big speech perfect by eleven o'clock tomorrow.'

'Tomorrow? Oh, but Charlie . . .'

'No buts, you're going to be brilliant.'

So they read the play through, Jenna reading Christina and Charlie reading all the other characters. She was stunned by the play. It was superb. As for the role of Christina, no wonder every young actress in town wanted it. It was the role of a lifetime. And the end . . . the end was both shocking and stunning.

Jenna put down her script. There were tears in her eyes.

'Charlie, it's magnificent.'

'Thank you, my dear. Now let's get to work on the scene with Christina's mother.'

They had spent the rest of the night going through the scene. At five o'clock, as Jenna's eyes were closing, Charlie put her to bed. He kissed her chastely on the cheek. 'Sleep well, my angel. You have nothing to worry about tomorrow, or rather today!' and he had fallen into a deep sleep in a chair in the sitting room.

He was up at nine, waking her with tea and toast.

'Get that inside you, my girl. You're looking far too thin and pale for my liking.'

Charlie chose what she should wear and they walked to the Lyric Theatre on Shaftesbury Avenue.

He introduced her to Harold, and Jenna chatted to him nervously about her past work.

'All right. Can you go up on the stage and read the scene for me, Jenna?'

'Go on, my angel, show them what you can do,' whispered Charlie.

Jenna climbed up on the big stage and gave the performance of her life. Charlie felt a lump in his throat as he watched her. Harold leaned over to him.

'I think we just found our Christina. She's marvellous. Where on earth did you find her?'

Harold insisted on running through another couple of scenes before he called Jenna down and asked her if she would like to play Christina.

Her eyes shone with happiness. 'I'd love to, Mr Kidd.'

'Good. Who's your agent? We'll call them this afternoon and negotiate money.'

'Well, I don't actually have one at the moment.'

'I know a very good one,' said Charlie, smiling 'Her name's Lindsay Bates and she represents me. She has an excellent reputation. I'm sure she'd be happy to take you on.'

'Fine. Ring her and take Jenna across to her office as

soon as possible. I want to get this thing sown up. We go into rehearsal in two weeks' time.'

Charlie had called Lindsay and arranged to take Jenna over that afternoon. Then he had insisted on taking her for a celebratory lunch at L'Escargot. Jenna raised her glass of mineral water. There was no need for alcohol now. 'Thank you, Charlie.'

'Don't thank me, my dear. If I hadn't found you the play would have been a shambles. I'm counting on you to win me the Play of the Year award.'

Jenna liked Lindsay immediately and was amazed when she called her to tell her how much money they were offering a week.

'We'll push for a little more. I know you're a newcomer but you are playing the lead.'

Jenna worried for the rest of the day that Harold might change his mind if Lindsay asked for more money. She would gladly do the play for free. But Lindsay rang the next day to say she'd negotiated another fifty pounds a week. Jenna was to come into the office where the contract would be waiting for her to sign.

Later that evening, back at the flat, she telephoned Darinka.

'My goodness, that's marvellous, Jenna! Aren't you glad I kicked you out of the hospital when I did? I hope I get a first-night ticket.'

'Of course you do. And Darinka, thanks for everything. I'll see you soon.'

'As long as it's on a stage and not in a hospital. Goodbye Jenna, and congratulations.'

Darinka put down the receiver and smiled. Maybe her job was worthwhile, after all.

Rehearsals got under way. Jenna was overawed to be at the helm of such a respected cast. There were times when her confidence sagged, when Charlie insisted on running a scene over and over and she would go home tired and demoralized. But the times when she got it right and Charlie dropped a few words of praise in her direction made it all worthwhile. Not only had Charlie written a masterpiece, but his skills as a director soon won the respect of everyone in the cast. He was completely professional in rehearsals, but would often pop round to see Jenna in the evening to chat about the play.

'Charlie, now that I'm earning some money, I want to find somewhere else to live.'

'I'll come and help you look if you like.'

'That would be lovely. Could we go this weekend?'

'Sure.'

They concentrated on looking for flats near the theatre so that Jenna could walk home in the evenings. After seeing more than a dozen possibilities, they were shown one that she loved the minute she walked through the door. The one-bedroomed flat was on the top floor of a recently built block just off Neal's Yard in Covent Garden.

Jenna moved in the following weekend.

Charlie watched the colour return to Jenna's cheeks as her confidence grew. Her performance as Christina was becoming more powerful as each day passed.

He did not mention how he felt. She needed space. He could sense that. He would bide his time.

'Ladies and gentlemen, this is your fifteen-minute call, fifteen minutes, thank you.'

Jenna's dresser was holding out the simple dress that she wore for the first scene. She stepped into it, unable to believe that in under twenty minutes she would be out on stage in front of a thousand people. And a posse of critics waiting to tear her to shreds. She was not nervous for herself, but worried about letting down the distinguished cast that had given her so much help and support.

There was a knock at the door.

'Come in,' she said.

Charlie entered and gave her a hug.

'Oh, Charlie! I can't believe this is it.'

'My angel, you will be superb. I know it, the cast know it, and by tomorrow, the rest of the world will know it as well.' He tipped her chin and looked into her eyes. 'My sweet Jenna, I wrote this for you. All you have to do is be your own perfect self. Best wishes, my dear.'

'Act One beginners on stage, please, Act One beginners, thank you.'

Her heart skipped a beat. Charlie left the room and Jenna took a couple of minutes to compose herself. Then she made her way along the passage and into the wings. She stepped on to the stage and took up her opening position. As she stood there, she heard the audience fall silent.

The curtain glided silently up into the flies.

She remembered Charlie's words. 'I wrote this for you, Jenna, just be your own perfect self . . .'

Her dressing room was bursting with well-wishers. Jenna hugged Frankie tightly to her, then kissed Daniel, Theo and Rudi.

'We'll let you get changed and see you at the Waldorf. You were terrific, Jenna, I'm so proud of you.'

When everyone had left her dressing room, Jenna sat down with a sigh of relief. She felt completely exhausted. Her dresser bustled in with her freshly ironed gown. Harold had managed to get it on loan from Yves Saint Laurent for Jenna to wear to the first-night party. She felt like a princess as she slipped it on.

Charlie knocked softly and stepped into the room. The vision in front of him took his breath away. Jenna looked exquisite in the midnight-blue tulle dress. Maybe tonight he should tell her how he felt . . .

'May I have the privilege of escorting you to your first, first-night party as Queen of the West End?'

'Of course.' Jenna piled her blonde hair on top of her head and secured it with pins.

She put her coat round her shoulders and followed Charlie out to the taxi.

It pulled up in front of the Waldorf.

'Just before you go in to be crowned, I –'

The door was opened and a flashbulb went off in their faces.

'Sorry, Charlie, you were saying?' They stepped out of the cab.

'I . . . just wanted to tell you that you were perfect tonight.'

'Thank you.' Jenna kissed his cheek and they went inside, Charlie once more berating himself for his loss of courage.

The party was being held in the grand marble banqueting suite. As Jenna and Charlie entered, there was a spontaneous round of applause. People clustered round Jenna. She had an aura that night which drew people to her, wanting to be close to the girl who had risen from nowhere to take the West End by storm.

Charlie watched with pride. And love. Then he too was surrounded by admirers.

'We're witnessing the birth of a new star tonight. Look at the way people want to be near her. She has that special something that marks out greatness.' Theo's eyes were misty. He could only count on one hand the times he had watched this happen before.

Jenna was smiling for the cameras and chatting to the people around her, but inside she wished she could leave with Frankie and go home to her new flat. She felt completely drained. However, this was a very special night, so she allowed herself a glass of champagne and enjoyed the attention she was getting. She turned and saw a small familiar figure standing nervously by the entrance, in the same dowdy coat she had worn ever since Jenna could remember.

'Excuse me, my mother has just arrived,' she said to Harold. She walked tentatively towards her.

'Hello, Mother.' Jenna was at a loss for what to say.

'Hello, Jenna. I've not come to stay. I just wanted to tell you that I thought you were very good.'

'Thank you, Mother. I . . . I'm very glad that you could come. Before you go, can I introduce you to Charlie, the writer and director? And I'm sure Frankie would love to meet you. She's over there, the girl with the raven hair. Please come and have a quick drink and say hello to them,' Jenna urged.

Why not, thought Joyce. As she moved forwards, a face, hidden before, came into view. Older now, but still as magnetic as ever. Then he was masked again as someone stood in front of him. Joyce thought she might faint. It was over twenty years since she had last seen him. She had to get out of here before he saw her.

'No!' The word tumbled out before she could stop it.

Jenna looked at her in amazement.

Joyce tried to compose herself. 'Sorry, it's just that I feel very out of place here and I have to be at work early so I must go home.' She was already moving towards the door.

Jenna looked hurt.

'All right, Mother, don't worry. Thank you for coming. Mother?'

'Yes, Jenna?'

'I really am glad that you came. Would it be all right if I came and visited some time?'

Joyce looked at her daughter. The similarity, now that she was older, was remarkable. He must have seen it too.

'Mother?' Jenna was waiting for a reply.

'I should think so, if you have time.' She forced a smile.

Jenna planted a kiss on her cheek. 'Take care, Mother, I'll see you soon.'

Joyce hurried out of the Waldorf and along the road to the bus stop, her mind in a whirl. What had he been doing there? She needed to get home to think.

She closed the front door of her flat and went straight into her bedroom. She found the key and unlocked the bottom drawer of her dressing table.

There, right at the back of the drawer, sat the black safety box. She took it out and sat on the bed.

She unlocked it and laid the contents on the bedspread.

Joyce had never stopped loving him. Never. But she hadn't been able to forgive him. Or the girl standing next to her in the faded black and white photo.

She wept. She wept for herself, for the years of hell he had given her. The two people she had loved most in the world who had conspired to hurt her more deeply than she thought humanly possible.

She wept for Jenna, an innocent victim who had never known that she had been born as a living reminder of the man who had broken her heart and, subsequently, her life.

She wept for the girl whom her daughter so strongly resembled, for the first time feeling sorrow for the life that had been cut so tragically short, feeling the love that she had once felt for the girl replacing the bitterness and hate that had festered for so long inside her.

She cried for a long time, and then, feeling a little better, went to the bathroom to wash her tear-stained face.

Time was short. She knew that. The cancer that had been growing inside her for two years was starting to win the battle. She had known that she was in trouble when the doctors had told her that the tumour they removed was malignant, but they had been hopeful then that they had caught it in time.

After nearly a year of treatment the cancer had spread. The doctors had told her that there was little more they could do.

She might have years or she might have months.

Whichever, Jenna had to be told.

It was time.

41

'HEY, THIS IS CUTE!' Frankie was admiring Jenna's flat, filled with flowers from Jenna's many first-night bouquets.

'Now how about we do some serious shopping this morning? And I'll treat you to lunch at Joe Allen to celebrate those stunning reviews.'

Frankie had arrived the morning after the party, laden down with every paper she could get her hands on. She had checked them quickly in the newsagent's and then bought a bottle of champagne.

Frankie polished off most of the bottle while reading out particularly flattering excerpts.

'"Jenna Shaw is like a breath of fresh morning air after watching the same faces on the West End stage for years,"' read Frankie. '"Miss Shaw's talent is only equal to her beauty. She heralds the arrival of a new breed of young actors rising to fill the footsteps of the stars of the Fifties that up to now have been left so empty." "Shaw is a real find; congratulations to the producers for being brave enough to give Christina to a hitherto unknown actress."'

'I think they liked you.' Frankie grinned. 'So, get into something that befits a new star and let's hit the town!'

'I haven't got any decent clothes, Frankie.'

'Fine. Rest assured you will have by tonight.'

Frankie's eyes gleamed as she escorted Jenna down New Bond Street and South Molton Street.

'I can't afford this,' hissed Jenna, standing in the middle of Browns in a beautiful pink silk suit.

'Honey, I'm lending you the money for now. You've got to have decent clothes if you're going to be a star.'

They sat in Joe Allen, surrounded by boxes and bags. Frankie had made Jenna stay in the last outfit she had tried on, an Ungaro two-piece that had cost the earth, but that Frankie had insisted she buy.

'I'm going to end up on the slippery slope back to bankruptcy if I'm not careful,' said Jenna as she tucked into her Waldorf salad.

'With those reviews, I don't think you'll have to worry about money ever again!'

The whole restaurant, full of theatrical people, had turned to stare as she walked in. Suddenly, overnight, she had become a star. She could not believe that a profession, so cruel at the bottom, could be so kind and generous at the top, with no rhyme or reason as to who was at which end.

After all, if it hadn't been for Charlie . . . She shuddered to think what might have happened.

People whom she didn't know were approaching their table and showering praise and good wishes upon her. Frankie had also been seen by an admirer and Jenna watched her friend as she dealt professionally with the eager fan, who wanted to know what her next film would be.

There was something different about Frankie. She still displayed the same enormous zest for life; but there been had change. Jenna wanted to ask her if there was a problem. It was only an instinct, but she was sure something was wrong.

'Okay, kiddo, it's three o'clock. I'm taking you home and putting you to bed for a rest. You've got a performance tonight and you look exhausted from all this excitement.'

Jenna lay down, positive she would not be able to sleep as adrenalin was still pumping through her system. But before she knew it, Frankie was waking her at six o'clock with a cup of tea.

After the show that night, Frankie met Jenna at the stage door and they walked to Jenna's flat, picking up a pizza on the way.

'This is just like old times!' Frankie laughed. 'Except for one thing. I see you're off the booze.'

'Yes. I had a problem after Matthew died, as you know, and it didn't get any better once you'd gone back to the States. I'm fine now, but, apart from the odd glass, I'm trying to steer clear.'

Frankie nodded approvingly. 'Good girl! So, Jenna, tell me, where did you disappear to for all those months?'

Jenna sighed. 'It really is a long story and I don't want to bore you with the gruesome details. It was to do with money, mainly. I ended up having to do things that, well, were very unpleasant.'

'Jeez, Jenna, you weren't out on the streets looking for business, were you?'

Jenna laughed. She didn't want Frankie to know how close to the truth she'd just come. 'No, waitressing, that sort of thing, but it's all over now. I feel very lucky to have been given a second chance.'

'Honestly, Jenna, you really should have come to me if money was that tight. You know I'd have helped.'

'I know, but it was something I had to sort out for myself. Let's leave it at that, shall we? So, how's your life, Frankie?'

'Good, good,' she said, lying. 'I got this big film called *The Heat Is On* premiering soon. It's a really great role and my agent swears it's going to take me into the big time.'

'That's fantastic, Frankie! So you'll be a star, will you?'

'Well, I don't know about that,' said Frankie. 'I've been offered the lead in Curt's next film, though. We start shooting in two weeks so I'm keeping busy.'

'You don't sound very enamoured. Isn't life in Hollywood all it's cracked up to be?'

'No. It's just a lot of hard work with very little time to enjoy any of the money you make. And worst of all,' Frankie sighed, '. . . you seem to be the public's property with absolutely no privacy.'

Jenna knew then that Frankie's problem had something to do with her personal life. It was obvious that she did not want to discuss it. Jenna understood completely.

'How's your father?'

'Okay. At least, he seemed fine last night and when he said goodbye to fly back this morning.' She shrugged. 'Since I moved to my apartment I hardly ever see him. We're not exactly the perfect father and daughter, you know. Mind you, he's always asking about you. He got terribly upset when I told him that Matthew had died. Said he knew how it felt, 'cos he'd been through it with my mother.'

'Do you ever wonder what your mother was like?'

'Nope, not really. I was so young when she died that she isn't someone that I've ever missed. And Pops has never spoken about her to me. I think it upsets him too much. I've no idea what she looked like and have never really wanted to find out.'

'I know what you mean,' Jenna cut in. 'I used to dream about my father coming to find me when I was small, but then I grew up. It's strange that if you're born without things that other people take for granted, you don't really miss them. Not that it wouldn't have been nice to have a father. Anyway, I've managed without one for all these years. Now tell me, have you met John Travolta? I think he's gorgeous.'

Frankie kept Jenna enthralled with Hollywood gossip until she saw her friend yawning.

'Bed for you, madam. You have two performances tomorrow and it's three in the morning. Do you mind if I stay on your sofa for the night?'

''Course not.'

'Why don't you come out to Hollywood in a couple of months' time and see it for yourself?'

'I'm two nights into the play and you're persuading me to take a holiday,' Jenna laughed.

'All right, but come over as soon as you can. I miss you, kiddo.'

'And I miss you, Frankie. Sleep tight.'

42

THE FOLLOWING TWO WEEKS were hectic, with Lindsay constantly on the phone asking Jenna if she could go to a photo session or an interview. The journalists wanted to know what she ate for breakfast, whether she exercised regularly and who her boyfriend was. She began to understand what Frankie had meant when she had said that you had no privacy. Jenna was guarded about her past, worried that someone might make the connection between the girl who had worked at the club and the new young star of the hottest show in town.

After a month, things quietened down. Jenna got into a routine of waking late and having a leisurely breakfast while deciding what she would do with her day. She went to art galleries, museums and for walks in Regents Park. She was always back at her flat by four thirty to have an hour and a half's rest before the night's performance.

Jenna was careful with her money, placing several hundred pounds a week in a high-interest building society account. Her experiences of the past year had given her a healthy respect for the damage debt could do. She allowed herself a more than adequate allowance to live on each week, and watched with pleasure as the money in her account grew. After all, who knew what might happen when her contract came up for renewal in six months' time? It was a fear that was a little unfounded since, thanks to the excellent reviews, the show was booking two months in advance. However, she knew that meteoric as her rise had been, her fall could be just as fast.

Charlie would often ring her in the morning and ask her out to lunch. She enjoyed his company and loved having him back in her life.

'I've shown a rough draft of my new play to Harold and he's very interested. It will be a challenge for you, Jenna. The part is the antithesis of Christina.'

'When you've finished it I want to read it. I love the idea.'

'Mmn, well, you do seem to have this ability to inspire me to genius, although there have been no offers from Hollywood yet. Never mind, I suppose I can't have the large villa *avec* heart-shaped Jacuzzi and be recognized as a decent playwright too!'

'Oh, I'm sure one day you'll have that, Charlie,' said Jenna, laughing.

And how I'd love to have you share it with me, he thought.

Charlie was still at a loss to know how to change the wonderfully close relationship they had as friends into that of lovers. He was scared that if he chose the wrong time and messed it up, he might lose her for ever. He knew that the signals he received from her were those of a girl who needed a friend and nothing more. His only comfort was that there was no other man in her life, so he filled the gap that was there and hoped no one stepped in to take her away from him. He didn't think he could bear that.

'Have you heard from your mother, Jenna?'

'No, I've tried to ring her, but she never seems to answer the telephone.'

'Well, you never know, she could be having a rampant affair with her boss and can never be bothered to get out of bed.'

The thought of her mother having a torrid affair with anyone was enough to make Jenna laugh out loud.

'I don't think so somehow. If I haven't managed to contact her by the end of the week, I'll go to the flat and see her. After all, she did come to the opening night. I think that was some kind of a peace offering.'

'Good idea. Want me to come with you?'

'No, it's all right. I think I can just manage to hold my own now.'

After another week of unanswered telephone calls, Jenna tried again very early in the morning. The telephone rang and rang. Finally she called directory enquiries and asked for the telephone number of the company where her mother worked. Joyce had always been adamant about not being called at work, but Jenna was getting very concerned. A woman in personnel told Jenna that her mother had left six months ago.

It was most odd, but Jenna tried to remind herself that it was over two and a half years since she had spoken to her mother properly. Things in Joyce's life might well have changed. Maybe Charlie was right. Maybe she did have a lover and had disappeared off to some sunny clime. Jenna thought it unlikely, but she was not her mother's keeper and could hardly blame Joyce for not letting her know if she was going away.

She would just have to keep trying.

Jenna was removing her make-up and looking forward to a hot bath and an early night after the two Saturday performances when there was a knock on her dressing room door.

'Come in!' she shouted.

A familiar figure stood in the doorway.

'Bettina!'

'Jenna, you were marvellous, darling! Freddie and Gerard are with me and they thought so too. Listen, can we take you to dinner? We've booked a table at a Thai restaurant round the corner and we'd love you to come.'

'That would be great,' said Jenna, seeing the hot bath and early night disappearing out of the window.

The food was excellent and the three of them raved about Jenna's performance.

'Of course, if it hadn't been for me helping Charlie find your number, none of this would have happened, so I take a huge part of the credit for your success,' Bettina said, laughing.

Gerard was subdued all evening.

'Are you all right, Gerry?' Bettina asked.

'Oh yes, I'm absolutely fine.' He smiled.

The truth was that he felt tongue-tied in front of Jenna. She had grown even more beautiful and had matured beyond belief since he had last seen her.

He wanted her. He wanted her more than he had wanted anything in his life.

'So, we'll be in London for the next six months at least. You must come and see the twins, they're just adorable, and they both look like Freddie!'

'Poor things,' muttered Freddie.

They kissed goodbye and Gerard asked tentatively if he could offer Jenna a lift home.

There was not a taxi in sight and Jenna didn't feel like walking. 'Thank you, that would be very kind.'

'It's lovely to see Bettina so happy. I think motherhood and Freddie suit her,' Jenna said as they drove the short distance to Covent Garden.

'Yes, I think they suit each other very well.'

They pulled up in front of Jenna's block of flats.

'Thank you so much for the lift, Gerard,' she said, stepping out of his Porsche.

'Well, you can return the favour. I'm going to a recital at the Albert Hall tomorrow night. Will you come with me?'

'Oh, Gerard, Sunday is the day when I recover from the week and don't even bother to get dressed. Thanks for the offer, though. Goodbye.'

She closed the car door and disappeared inside.

Gerard sat in his car for a while, thinking about Jenna.

She wasn't going to escape that easily again.

On Monday night Jenna walked out of the stage door and

stood signing autographs when she saw Gerard casually standing on the other side of the road.

He walked towards her and she knew she was trapped.

'I've booked a table at Kettners and we're going to be late.'

He put his arm around her waist and started marching her along the road.

'But I —' Jenna tried to protest.

'No buts, a chap can take only so many refusals. Anyway, you owe me one. If it hadn't been for me giving Charlie your number you'd probably still be working in that awful café.'

In spite of herself, Jenna had a lovely evening. Gerard was very good company and a complete gentleman. After dinner they went to Annabel's. He drove her home, giving her a quick peck on the cheek before driving off.

When he arrived at the stage door again the following evening, asking if she fancied a steaming bowl of noodles at an excellent nearby Chinese restaurant, she said yes. And again the night after that. By the end of the week she had seen him every night. He hadn't laid a finger on her. Not once. And each time she saw him she relaxed more.

Two weeks later the telephone rang at midday. It was Lindsay, her agent.

'I've got some very good news. You've been nominated for a SWET award in the Most Promising Newcomer category for your performance as Christina.'

'Lindsay, that's fantastic!'

'Plus Sheila Hall has been nominated for Best Actress

for her performance as your mother, and *Angel in Hell* is up for Best Play.'

'Charlie will be thrilled. Thanks for calling, Lindsay.'

Jenna immediately tried ringing Gerard at his office but he was out at a business lunch and not expected back until three.

It struck her as she put down the receiver that she had automatically called Gerard before anyone else. She sat down and thought about this. Was she growing fond of him without realizing it? Why had she started feeling disappointed on the odd night that he was not standing at the stage door to greet her? She stood up and paced the floor.

She thought of Charlie, with whom she had developed such a close bond during the play, and wondered about her feelings for him. She loved Charlie, there was no doubt about that. He was like the big brother she had never had. They shared an artistic and emotional bond forged from the years when they were both struggling to free themselves from the restrictive chains of their past.

The relationship had never progressed beyond that and Jenna felt that Charlie saw her as nothing but his best friend. At least, he had never hinted that he might feel differently, so she assumed he didn't.

She sighed. So what was stopping her letting the relationship with Gerard develop?

Gerard picked her up as usual after the show and they went to try a new Italian restaurant tucked away in the back streets of Soho.

When Jenna told him of her nomination he ordered champagne. 'So, what does SWET stand for?'

'The Society of West End Theatre. The awards are the most prestigious in the British theatrical world.'

'Well, here's to the new Vivien Leigh!' he said, raising his glass to her.

Jenna watched him across the dimly lit table. He was looking extremely handsome in a beautifully cut dark-blue blazer. He had taken after his father with his strong profile, but he had his mother's twinkling eyes, just as Bettina did.

After dinner they walked to Ronnie Scott's and sat listening to jazz. Later, he drove her home. As she got out of the Porsche, she said, 'Gerry, I was wondering if, as a sort of celebration for me being nominated, you might like to come round here on Sunday for a late lunch.' She felt herself blushing.

Gerard's face brightened. 'Jenna, I'd love to. What time?'

'Oh, about threeish.'

'Great, I'll see you on Sunday then. Sleep tight.'

'And you.'

Jenna waved and disappeared into the building.

Gerard watched her as she went inside. 'Yes!' he said, and started the engine. He put a tape into the machine, turned up the volume and sang to the music as he drove off.

His patience had paid off. He had had his doubts as he sat night after night with a table separating them, giving her a chaste kiss on the cheek before he went back to his flat to sleep alone and dream of her. He had wondered if his dreams would be the only time he took her passionately and felt her perfect body against his.

He had known it must come from her.

And at last it had.

43

FRANKIE'S CAREER WAS SOARING. Her spirit was not. June had refused to go to the premiere of her latest film, *Shock*, using the excuse that it was too dangerous for them to be seen together.

'Bullshit!' Frankie had raged at her. 'You just don't want lover boy to know about us.'

June would not argue. She quietly told Frankie she was being paranoid and that she was going back to her apartment until Frankie decided to be sensible.

Frankie burst into tears as she heard the door close.

June always managed to make her feel like a spoilt child. She wiped her tears away, put on a trouser suit, and drove downtown. The attendant took her car keys and put her Mercedes into the car park as she went into Ma Maison. She could see Daniel was already seated at a table waiting for her.

'Hello, darling.' Daniel stood up and kissed her. 'Can I get you a drink?'

'Sure. A large vodka on the rocks with a twist, please.' Frankie sat down and removed her sunglasses. Daniel noticed her red eyes.

'Is anything wrong, Frankie?'

'No, I'm fine, Pops, just a bit tired from the last weeks of filming, I suppose.'

'Why don't you take a holiday? It would do you good to get away.'

'Maybe.' The thought of leaving June alone was unbearable.

'When do you move into your new house? It's pretty soon, isn't it?'

'Yep. It'll be final next week and I'll move in when the decorators move out.'

Frankie, encouraged by her agent, had decided to invest some of her money and buy a house. She and June had visited a selection of properties and found a house called Orchid Villa – the last owners had had a hothouse full of them. The four-bedroomed, two-bathroomed villa was not particularly large by Hollywood standards, but it had a big pool and was in a secluded spot with beautiful views.

Most important of all, June had loved it. They had spent hours discussing the decor and the work was very near completion.

Then, a week ago, June had announced she wouldn't be moving into Orchid Villa.

'Why the hell not, June?'

'It means I have to drive an extra ten miles to the studio. You know how terrible the traffic is these days. I'm going to stay at my apartment on Mulholland Drive for now.'

Frankie had been heartbroken. There could only be one

reason why June had changed her mind. She tormented herself with thoughts that the stories she had heard on the Hollywood grapevine were true. They had begun three months ago when June started work on a new film. Someone at a party had mentioned that the director, Nigel Forster, was having an affair with one of his make-up ladies. Frankie's informant did not know her name, but when he described what she looked like, Frankie knew it was June.

Frankie had always been very insecure about the fact that June had been married when she was younger. She had slept with men as well as women. Frankie, never having done that herself, found this difficult to handle.

'I just don't understand, June. You knew from the start that the drive to the studios would be longer. It's because of Nigel Forster, isn't it?'

Frankie watched closely for a reaction on June's face. There was only anger.

'I don't believe you'd listen to the gossips! You of all people, Frankie, with a father who apparently spends his life in bed with someone different every night.'

'Then why have you suddenly changed your mind?'

'I've told you. While I'm working on this film, I want to be nearer the studio.'

'I'll get a car to collect you every morning.'

June shook her head and placed two bowls of chilli on the table. 'No, Frankie. I'll come up when I can, but for now I'm staying put.'

'You just don't want lover boy to know you're a dyke.'

'Oh, for God's sake, Frankie! Stop being silly and come and eat.' June sat down at the table while Frankie continued to pace the room.

'So you're denying it?'

'Damn right I am. Nigel has become a great friend and, yes, we do spend a lot of time together but, honey, if you stopped being so ridiculously insecure, you might just notice that I'm a one-woman woman. And that woman happens to be you.'

'So why won't you move in with me to the house that *we* chose?'

June sighed and put down her fork. 'Darling, I'm sorry, but until you've calmed down a little we shouldn't discuss this, okay?'

And that was that. June would not be swayed. Frankie was moving into Orchid Villa by herself.

Daniel watched his daughter. 'Are you sure you're all right? You're looking awfully pale and I'd guess you've lost weight.'

Frankie nodded. It worried her that her problems were showing. 'Yes, Pops. I told you, I'm just tired.'

Daniel didn't believe her. Although they had never been close, he cared for his daughter. And he knew what Hollywood could be like. The people in it were like piranha fish, ready to eat anybody who could not keep them at bay.

Daniel wondered if it had something to do with Frankie's personal life. Mimi had hinted to him that his daughter was gay and that she was worried that news of her unusual love life might leak out. Mimi would keep quiet, not wanting a whiff of scandal to touch her client's successful career or her commission on that success.

Whether he was right or wrong, Daniel would not pry. Frankie probably assumed he would be shocked, but he had seen so much since his arrival in Tinsel Town that as long as Frankie was happy, he didn't give a damn what her sexual preferences were.

'Okay, darling. Just take it easy when you move. Don't overdo it, will you? I expect to be invited up for dinner once you're settled in.'

'Of course, Pops.'

'I'm afraid I've got to go. I'm doing an interview for Channel Two at four. You stay here and finish that salad you've hardly touched. Call me with your new telephone number.' Daniel got up from the table and kissed her on the cheek.

'Will do, bye.'

Frankie picked at the tuna on her plate.

She was beautiful, rich, successful and very unhappy.

44

GERARD DROVE TO Jenna's flat and parked his car. He pressed her intercom button. The front door unlocked with a click.

He took the stairs two at a time, hardly able to contain his excitement.

Jenna, looking radiant in a simple Laura Ashley dress, met him at her door.

'Hello. I bought a bottle of champagne.'

'Oh, how lovely! Come in.'

He followed her into the flat. A table was laid for two and there was a delicious smell emanating from the small kitchen.

'Something smells good.'

'Wait until you've tasted it.' She giggled. 'Want a drink? I've got lager or wine.'

'I think we should open the champagne. After all, this is meant to be a celebration.'

'Fine. I'll have mine drowned with orange juice if you don't mind.'

Gerard opened the bottle and poured their drinks while Jenna busied herself in the kitchen.

'Nice place you've got here.'

'Yes. It's only big enough for me but I like it. Can you sit at the table, Gerard? I'm going to serve up. I do hope you like garlic. I'm afraid I rather overdid it.' She smiled as she put down a plate in front of him.

'Mm, this tastes wonderful. A great cook as well as a brilliant actress. Here's to you winning that award. I don't think the competition stand a chance.'

They ate chicken in a cream sauce, followed by fruit salad and cheese.

'It's wonderful living so close to Soho. The delicatessens have such a fabulous range of food. I'm sure I've put on pounds since I moved here.'

Gerard's eyes took in her slim figure. 'I don't think so, Jenna.'

She blushed. 'Would you like some coffee?'

'That's a good idea.'

As they drank their coffee, Gerard suggested they go for a stroll round the piazza.

They wandered through the still-busy streets. The November day had been bright, but now evening had fallen there was a chill in the air and Jenna shivered. Gerard put his arm around her and she snuggled closer to him. They bought hot chestnuts from a wizened vendor and watched the last street performer. Jenna shyly slipped her small hand into his as they strolled home.

Jenna took their coats and hung them up. Gerard was looking out of the large picture window and she went and stood next to him. He put his arm around her and carried on gazing out of the window.

'Jenna, you can say no, and I won't be offended, but I have a desperate desire to kiss you. Would you mind?'

She shook her head. 'No, I wouldn't.'

Then she was in his arms.

'Oh, God! Jenna!' He groaned as they broke away. He saw a look of fear come into her eyes.

'Look, it doesn't matter if you don't want to ... I mean, I ...'

She covered his mouth with a kiss, knowing that if he didn't take her now ...

He undressed her slowly, trying desperately to contain the passion he had held inside for so long. He made love to every part of her body, kissing her porcelain skin tenderly. When he knew she was ready, he entered her gently and she cried out in pleasure. Afterwards they lay there, Jenna cocooned in his arms, still shivering from the strength of her orgasm.

She felt a wave of gratefulness and affection for the man who had replaced her fear with happiness. He had restored her feelings as a woman. The past was exorcized as she went back into the world of natural physical pleasure.

After that first night, the two of them became inseparable. They divided their time between her place in Covent Garden and Gerard's Knightsbridge flat.

He asked her to spend Christmas at Langdale Hall. Jenna wanted to say yes immediately, but felt she must speak to her mother before she agreed. Her efforts to contact Joyce had been curtailed by her developing relationship with Gerard. But she was determined to talk to her soon. She tried telephoning repeatedly but with no success. Then, one night at the theatre, just as Act One beginners were called, her mother answered the phone.

'Where have you been, Mother? I've been worried.'

'Hello, Jenna. I, er, had a small operation and the doctor said it was a good idea to get out of London, so I went to stay with a friend in the country.'

Jenna did not know of any friends in the country, but was relieved to hear her mother's voice.

'Are you okay now?'

'Yes, I'm fine.'

Jenna's money was running out and she had to get on stage.

'Mother, I've got to go, but I'll be round to see you tomorrow morning. Bye.' She put the receiver down before Joyce could say anything and hurried to the stage.

Joyce washed her hair and applied some make-up. She chose a large, baggy sweater. There was no need for Jenna to know. She had put the child through enough. This was perhaps her last chance to make amends.

She had been in and out of hospital for two months, undergoing chemotherapy. It had left her pitifully thin and weak. She had to go back in over Christmas for more tests. She wasn't quite sure how to hide this from Jenna.

The doorbell rang, and Joyce walked towards it, her hands shaking as she opened the door. It was not just her illness that made her shake, but the fact that she had decided she must tell Jenna all those things that had been kept from her for far too long.

'Hello, Mother.' Jenna took in the thin face and the sunken eyes that no make-up could disguise.

'Hello, Jenna. Come in and I'll make us a cup of tea.'

'How are you feeling? Are you sure this operation was nothing serious?'

'No, dear, just a woman's thing. It's knocked the stuffing out of me a bit, that's all. Sit yourself down.'

Jenna sat at the kitchen table. She saw that nothing in the flat had changed.

'There you are, and I bought some of those biscuits you used to like so much.'

The sight of the biscuits that had been such a treat when she was a child brought a lump to Jenna's throat.

'So how is the play going?' Joyce asked.

'Very well. I've been nominated for an award. It's for Most Promising Newcomer.'

'That is good news. Congratulations!'

'Mother,' Jenna said, uninterested in talking about herself, 'why have you left work?'

Joyce was prepared for this. 'Oh, I decided that after twenty years of doing the same thing, I should leave and have some fun.'

Jenna was taken aback at the word 'fun' coming from her mother.

'I can always go back if I want, but I have a little money saved and I thought that it was about time I spent it.'

Although this sounded perfectly plausible, Jenna had lived with her mother for too long to be totally taken in.

This must have shown, for her mother continued, 'Look, Jenna, I know I must sound very different from the last time I saw you, but when you went away, I learned some very hard lessons. I . . . I want to say that I'm sorry for the way I behaved over Matthew. It was selfish and silly and I apologize.'

'Oh, Mother, that's okay. Let's just forgive and forget, shall we? Try and start afresh?'

Joyce smiled and nodded. 'Jenna, a friend from church and I are hoping to go away for Christmas, but I said I'd wait and see what you're doing.'

Jenna breathed a sigh of relief. However much her mother had changed, the thought of spending Christmas alone with her in the flat was not attractive.

'Well, actually, Mother, I've been invited by Bettina's brother, remember Bettina?'

Joyce nodded.

'To spend Christmas at Langdale Hall.'

'Are you seeing him?'

Jenna smiled at the old-fashioned phrase. 'Yes, quite regularly, actually.'

'Is it serious?'

'Yes, I think so.' Jenna sighed. 'The trouble is, I feel so guilty because of Matthew.'

'Jenna, never dwell on the past. People spend their lives wishing things could have been different and wasting the time they do have. I mean . . .'

Now was the moment. She knew she should seize it, but her courage failed her.

'Yes?' Jenna looked at her expectantly.

'I mean . . . you have to make the most of life, don't you?'

'That's true,' said Jenna, taken aback by her mother's new philosophy.

The moment had passed. Joyce had let it slip through her fingers. She did not have the strength or the courage to try again.

'I'm afraid I'm going to have to leave in a minute. We have a matinée on Wednesdays. Why don't I pop round next week with your Christmas present?'

'No, Jenna. We'll be away by then.'

'All right. Then maybe we can arrange something in the new year. You could come round to my flat for Sunday lunch.'

'Yes, that would be nice, but we might be away for a while.' Joyce walked with Jenna to the door.

'Have you decided where you're going?'

'Er, yes, Scotland.' It was the first place that came into her head.

'Well, have a wonderful time, and Merry Christmas!' Jenna kissed her mother.

'Thank you. And you, dear.'

She watched Jenna until she turned the corner and disappeared from sight.

She knew she would never see her daughter again.

Joyce shivered as the cold December air whipped through her frail body. She closed the door, returned to the kitchen and sat down. After a while, she felt strong enough to walk to the bedroom. She unlocked the bottom drawer of her dressing table and took out the black box.

She spread the photos on the bed. She was dying and maybe it was best if the past died with her. Today had been the last chance to tell Jenna, to explain, but she had not been able to do so.

She smiled as she thought of the pretty, successful girl that had just left and prayed that God would protect her once she had gone. Her only regret was that she had never told her daughter that she loved her.

Joyce went into the kitchen and found a box of matches. She collected the contents of the black box from the bedroom, went into the living room and knelt down in front of the fire. She placed the photos in the grate and lit a match. She watched as the flames devoured the only clues to her daughter's birthright.

45

THE DAY DAWNED CRISP and bright. Jenna was grateful that Christmas Eve had fallen on a Sunday so she did not have a performance.

Gerard arrived outside Jenna's flat in his Porsche at nine o'clock and they sped up the motorway to Langdale Hall, arriving just in time for lunch.

Gerard carried her suitcase into the hall. Jenna followed, stopping to admire the tall Christmas tree decorated with twinkling white lights.

'Bettina told me how fussy your mother is about finding the perfect tree,' Jenna said, smiling, as she followed Gerard upstairs to a guest room rather grander than the one she had stayed in the year before.

'Yes, she is, but doesn't it look super? Now, powder your nose or whatever it is you women do and I'll see you downstairs. By the way, this leads to my room.' Gerard winked as he opened an internal door and disappeared through it.

Jenna hung up her ball gown and a new suit she had bought to wear on Christmas Day. She brushed her hair and applied some lipstick. As she walked down the stairs, looking at the holly and the hundreds of Christmas cards strung up everywhere, a sense of well-being enveloped her. She was going to have the sort of Christmas that she had always dreamed about.

'Jenna! I'm so glad you were able to come,' said Bettina as Jenna entered the formal sitting room full of people drinking sherry. 'Ma and Pa have invited a few guests around for lunchtime drinks. You'll probably recognize some of them from my wedding. Here, have a glass of sherry and come and meet Sebastian and Toby, the terrible twins.'

The two babies were gurgling happily in their carrycots, watched over by their grandmother.

'It's lovely to see you again, Jenna, and congratulations on your success in the play. William keeps promising I'll be allowed down to London to see it, but something always seems to crop up.'

Jenna smiled. 'Well, Lady Langdale, I can get you some complimentary tickets if you would like me to.'

'Oh, that would be smashing, then William would have no excuse. And by the way, dear, please call me Henri – that's short for Henrietta – everybody else does.'

'Freddie, look, it's Jenna!'

'Hello, my dear, and a Merry Christmas to you.' Freddie kissed her.

'I think your two sons are beautiful, Freddie.'

'Dear girl, thank you for those kind remarks, but personally I have to admit that . . . I totally agree with you. They are adorable, aren't they?'

'Nearly as adorable as my baby.' Jenna heard Gerard's voice and felt an arm slip around her waist.

Freddie coughed and raised his bushy eyebrows. 'I see you two know each other.'

'Jenna,' said Bettina, interrupting. 'I hope Gerry told you there's a Christmas Eve dance tonight. It's a tradition going back ages. The whole of Yorkshire seems to attend! Did you bring your best frock?'

'Yes, he did tell me. The wardrobe lady at the theatre lent me a gown.'

'Oh, good.'

Gerard cut in. 'Come on, darling, let's go and get something to eat from the buffet. I'm famished and I'm sure you must be too.' He led her into the dining room.

'Gerry, good to see you, old man.' Lord Langdale slapped his son on the back before turning to Jenna. 'Miss Shaw, how delightful to see you again.'

Jenna looked at Lord Langdale. She still found it difficult to warm to the man who had treated his daughter so harshly. She thought how lucky he was still to have Bettina's respect.

'Thank you for having me to stay for Christmas.'

'Our pleasure, my dear. I'm of the opinion that there can never be enough pretty women in the house.'

Jenna blushed and moved away.

The pink satin and tulle gown that the wardrobe mistress had suggested fitted Jenna perfectly.

There was a knock on the door and Bettina came in.

'Jenna, you look like a fairy-tale princess.'

'I love your dress, Bettina.' Jenna admired the heavy emerald velvet gown.

'It's Yves St Laurent. I bought it in Paris last year when I was six months pregnant and this is the first time I've been able to get into it.' Bettina laughed. 'I'm sure Gerry won't get a look-in tonight, the locals haven't seen anything like you in years.' She came over to the dressing table. 'You will be kind to my brother, won't you? It's just that I know he's rather smitten and I'd hate to see him get hurt.'

'Oh, Bettina, I wouldn't hurt him for the world.'

'Do you love him, Jenna?' She could see Bettina's serious face reflected in the mirror.

'I . . . well, yes, I think I do.'

Bettina's face brightened. 'Well, thank goodness for that, because I know he loves you. Come on, the future Lady Langdale had better get her backside downstairs and greet the guests!'

'The future Lady Langdale' . . . the words rang in Jenna's head as she walked down the stairs. Marriage had never been mentioned by Gerard. Surely Bettina's romantic mind was working overtime . . .

Gerard stood by the front door next to his father, greeting the guests. He turned to see what it was on the stairs that everyone was staring at. He caught his breath as he saw Jenna in a stunning pink ball gown, seemingly floating down the stairs towards him. She smiled at him. Jenna, his Jenna! He reached for the small box in his dinner-jacket pocket. The feel of it reassured him. By the end of tonight, Jenna would be his for ever.

Jenna was immediately surrounded, everyone eager to

talk to the enchanting young actress whose face they had seen in the papers.

'I've seen the play, Miss Shaw, and I thought you were quite charming. May I have the next dance?'

As Jenna was whirled round the floor time after time, she thought how ironic it was that this gathering of wealthy, titled people should be so interested in her, a fatherless child from a council flat in Hornsey.

The ballroom looked magnificent with its grand chandeliers throwing light on the formally dressed guests. Jenna truly felt like Cinderella. After accepting dance after dance, she searched the room for her prince. She spotted him, excused herself from a puffing colonel and set off towards him.

'Darling! At last! I thought you were never going to get off the dance floor.' Gerard was standing with a group of friends.

'There you go, some orange juice with the smallest amount of champagne to cool you down.' Gerard handed her a glass.

A striking girl in a very short black cocktail dress was hanging on to Gerard's arm.

'So you're the famous Jenna?' she drawled. 'We've all been *dying* to meet you.'

'This is Camilla Hamilton, daughter of one of my father's oldest friends.' Gerard glanced fondly at Camilla. 'She has just managed to secure herself a modelling contract to launch a new range of cosmetics.'

Jenna glanced at the flawless skin and perfect figure. She felt a twinge of jealousy.

'If you've had time to draw breath from dancing with every other man in the room, can I have the pleasure of my first dance this evening?' Gerard grinned at her and led her towards the dance floor.

'I haven't had a chance to tell you how radiant you look tonight,' said Gerard, holding her close.

'Thank you, darling. I think your friend Camilla is very beautiful.'

'Oh, Cam's not bad. She's the same age as Bettina and we all used to go riding together in the school holidays. She was my first girlfriend. Fifteen minutes to go until Christmas. I fancy some fresh air. Will you join me?'

Jenna nodded and followed Gerard out of the same doors through which she had run away from him over a year before.

It was a frosty night, but the sky was clear and the stars were twinkling brightly. Gerard's arms went around her.

'Oh, Jenna, I remember the last time we stood here together. You were crying and asking me to take you back to London immediately.' Gerard smiled at her. 'I think I fell in love with you then but there was nothing I could do about it. Now there is. Darling, will you marry me?'

Gerard fumbled in his pocket and produced the small box. He opened it to reveal a ring, in the centre of which was a gleaming sapphire, nestling in a cluster of tiny diamonds. He took her left hand and slipped the ring on to her fourth finger.

'Jenna, please say something.'

Jenna was staring up at the sky, remembering Matthew, and wondering if he was looking down on her. Then she thought how wonderful it would be to have a man who would love her always. A man who could give her the security and comfort that she had had only briefly in her life.

'Sweetheart, if you're worried about your career, don't be. There's no reason why you should give up while I'm working in London and Pa's up here playing lord of the manor.'

'Yes, Gerard. I will marry you.'

He took her in his arms and held her.

'Merry Christmas, my love.'

'Merry Christmas, Gerard.'

'Come on, I want to break the good news to everyone before they leave.'

46

FOR HOWEVER LONG she lived, Jenna would always remember that Christmas at Langdale Hall. It was magical.

Just after midnight, Gerard had silenced the band and announced their engagement. There had been an audible gasp, then a surge of clapping. People surrounded them.

'Jenna, I was right.' Bettina hugged her tight. 'Congratulations and welcome to the family!'

Jenna watched out of the corner of her eye as Gerard talked to his father. Her heart started to pound as she remembered what had happened to Bettina when she had tried to marry someone unsuitable. Lord Langdale turned towards her. She looked at his solemn face in trepidation.

'Well, Jenna, as I seem to be the only man that hasn't had the pleasure of kissing my son's fiancée . . .' He took her hand and kissed it. 'Gerard told me this afternoon that he was going to ask you and I gave him my full blessing. I think you'll make a very beautiful Lady Langdale.

I told Gerard it rather reminded me of Rainier and Grace Kelly.'

He laughed and Jenna relaxed a little.

'I'm afraid this isn't quite the palace in Monaco and certainly doesn't have the warmth of that part of the world, but we like it. Glad to welcome you into the family, Jenna.'

'Thank you, Lord Langdale, I –'

'Call me William,' he smiled.

'Thank you, William,' Jenna blushed. 'I promise to do my best to make Gerard happy.'

'That's the ticket. I think my son is getting jealous so I shall wish you a happy Christmas and see you in church tomorrow morning.'

'Oh, you two, it's so romantic,' Henri arrived with Gerard and kissed Jenna. 'I hope you'll both be extremely happy together.'

'Thanks, Ma, I'm sure we will be. Won't we, Jenna?'

'Yes, Gerard,' she said, smiling.

Later, Gerard crept through the adjoining door and they made love.

'I'm so happy, darling! I've been planning tonight for ages.'

He kissed her and crept back to his own room.

Jenna lay sleepless, pondering why she was able to marry Gerard with the full approval of his family when Bettina had been forbidden to marry Mark. She found it hypocritical and felt rather guilty about it. After all, Mark would not have inherited a title as she would. But then, the Cinderella syndrome rarely happened to men. In a world striving for equality, she wondered why not.

Gerard woke Jenna in the morning and they made love again. Then they drove to the church and sat together in a pew at the front. When the service was over and they had walked from the church hand in hand, Jenna asked him if he knew she was Catholic.

'Of course,' said Gerard, opening the door of his Porsche for her. 'I asked Bettina, just to make sure you weren't a member of some strange sect that allowed you to marry five husbands at the same time! If you want a Catholic priest in attendance at the service, I'm sure that can be arranged.'

'You seem to have thought of everything, darling.'

'Bankers are taught to prepare the ground carefully.' Gerard smiled.

When everyone had returned to Langdale Hall, there was mulled wine and a stack of presents waiting to be opened in the sitting room. Jenna was embarrassed that everyone in the family seemed to have bought her something. She opened the package from Gerard and found a slim gold Piaget watch engraved on the back with 'J,ILY,G'.

At one o'clock, Camilla and her family arrived to join them for lunch.

'I didn't get a chance to say congratulations last night. I hope the two of you will be very happy,' Camilla said without enthusiasm.

The festive fare in the grand dining room was devoured hungrily. The main topic of conversation was what date Gerard and Jenna would set.

'Do you want to go for a walk, darling? I feel so stuffed, I could use a little exercise.'

Jenna nodded and they wandered outside.

'We've got some plans to make.'

'I know.'

'When would you like to do the dirty deed, so to speak?' asked Gerard. 'As far as I'm concerned, the sooner the better.'

'Well, I'll have to speak to my agent about getting some time off from the play, otherwise you'll be a grass widow within hours,' Jenna laughed.

'What about the beginning of April? That gives us three months. I'm sure Ma will be happy to handle most of the arrangements; in fact, she will thrive on it.'

'April will be fine. Around then I might be coming out of *Angel in Hell* to do Charlie's new play, so we could perhaps fit the wedding in between.'

'Look, Jenna, there is one thing I wanted to mention.'

'Yes?'

'I know this sounds odd, but could you just play down the fact that you'll be carrying on as an actress in front of my father? It's just that he's a bit of a traditionalist. He'll be fine once he gets used to the idea, but I think it's best that we don't mention it at the moment.' Gerard looked embarrassed.

'You haven't told him I'll be giving up, have you?'

'No, but I think he assumes it.'

'I can't do that, Gerard. Not when things have just started to go so well.'

'I know that, Jenna. Once we're married there's nothing

he can do. And the main thing is I'm perfectly happy to live in your shadow and become known as Mr Shaw.'

They started walking back towards the house.

'All right, but I don't like lying.'

'You're not lying, just not shouting the truth from the rooftops. Anyway, let's forget that now. Pa has said he'll give us something towards a new house in London. If I sell my flat we really should be able to find something very nice. I want us to start looking as soon as we get back . . .'

That night, once Gerard had left her bed for his own, Jenna pondered some of the things she had not told him. She had worked as a hostess in a seedy London club. She had been raped and become pregnant. She shivered and wished she could tell Gerard, but she didn't have the courage.

When Jenna arrived back in London, she called Frankie.

'Well, well, well,' drawled her friend. 'It doesn't surprise me. Gerard had the hots for you at Bettina's wedding. He didn't waste any time, did he?'

'Frankie, you don't think I'm rushing into this too quickly, do you?'

'No, I don't. Life is short. If you're happy, go for it, but don't expect me to bow and scrape just because you'll get a title one day.'

'You don't think Matthew would mind?'

'Matthew is dead, but I can tell you someone who's living who won't be too pleased. Have you told him yet?'

'Told who?'

'Don't play the dumb blonde with me. Charlie, of course.'

'Oh, I'm sure Charlie won't mind as long as I'm doing his next play.'

'If you say so, kiddo. I've not got to put on another flowery get-up, have I?'

'No, but I want you to be there.'

'Of course. And good luck for those awards.'

'Thanks. I'm sure I won't win.'

'Wait and see. I'll speak to you soon, okay?'

Jenna put the telephone down. She tried her mother's number but, as she expected, there was no reply. She pulled out some writing paper from a drawer and wrote Joyce a letter, telling her about her engagement to Gerard. She posted it on her way to the theatre.

After the performance, Jenna was coming out of her dressing room when she bumped into Charlie.

'How was your Christmas?' she asked him.

'Good, and yours?'

'Wonderful. I got engaged to Gerard Langdale, Bettina's brother.'

She looked for a reaction on his face. There was none.

'Congratulations. I've got to go, I'm meeting Harold to discuss the new play. Presumably you'll be carrying on with your career, will you?'

'Oh yes, it won't change anything.'

''Night then, Jenna.'

'Bye. See you at the awards ceremony.'

'Yes.'

Charlie walked out of the stage door and dived straight

into a pub across the road. He ordered a double gin, swallowed it in two gulps and ordered another. He had blown it again. God, he wanted to shout and scream and rip the place apart with his frustration and anger.

He wanted to take Jenna in his arms and tell her that he was the one who loved her the way no one else ever could. The words flowed from his pen unchecked, and yet he could not bring himself to tell the girl he had known for four years that he loved her.

Charlie hung his head in dismay. He knew he had never given a hint of how he felt and because of this, he had lost her for a second time.

Then he thought about the letter he had received that very morning. Perhaps it was not such a silly idea after all.

The following Sunday, the Café Royal was jam-packed with every luminary in the British theatrical world.

It was the night when the business bestowed awards on the business. The cast of *Angel in Hell* were seated at one of the central tables. It was obvious who the nominees were. They ignored the food in front of them in favour of large quantities of wine. As well as the eight-strong cast, Harold Kidd, the company manager, and the set and lighting designers were there, too.

'Not long to go now, Jenna,' said Sheila Hall, nervously looking at her watch. Sheila played Jenna's mother and had been nominated for Best Actress.

'Thank goodness! I'll just be glad when it's all over. Won't you, Charlie?'

Charlie nodded silently. He was nominated three times, for Best Play, Best Director and Most Promising Newcomer, the section in which he was competing against Jenna.

It had been a company joke that by the law of averages he should win one. Jenna knew that he was only concerned about winning Best Play.

She glanced at him sadly. The special relationship they had worked so hard to build again was crumbling. They had looked forward to this night so much and yet he hardly spoke to her.

Silence fell as a well-known television presenter welcomed them. The curtain went up on a number from one of the nominated musicals.

Hearts started to race as the winners were announced and a cheer went up from the *Angel* table as Sheila Hall won the award for Best Actress.

'And the award for Most Promising Newcomer goes to . . .'

There was an agonizing pause as the envelope was opened. Jenna reached for Charlie's hand but couldn't find it.

'Jenna Shaw!'

The applause was thunderous as she stepped on to the stage to receive the award.

'Thank you, ladies and gentlemen. This award should also go to the company of *Angel in Hell*, who helped and encouraged me throughout. And especially to Charlie Devereaux, who wrote such a wonderful play and gave me the chance to play Christina. Thank you, Charlie.'

Gerard watched the ceremony on television. He saw the look in her eyes as she thanked Charlie. He wondered . . . no, surely he was just being insecure. All actresses were emotional about their peers on nights like this. He put the thought out of his mind.

Joyce watched the ceremony in the day room at the hospital. Tears of happiness ran down her face. She was puzzled, though. Mrs Tab, her neighbour, had visited her today and brought the post. She had read the letter from Jenna, feeling happy that her daughter had become engaged to a man she cared for. But, as she watched the television, she wondered why Jenna was marrying Gerard when she was so obviously in love with the playwright.

Jenna returned to her table just as Charlie's name was announced for Best Play.

'I'd like to thank everyone concerned with *Angel in Hell*. Without such a fine cast I wouldn't be standing here tonight. Thank you.'

Jenna hugged him as he arrived back at the table. He distanced himself from her for the rest of the evening, knowing he couldn't trust himself to speak.

Unusually, Charlie didn't come into the theatre to watch his play during the following week.

47

WITH ONLY EIGHT WEEKS to go to the wedding, which was scheduled for the twelfth of April, Jenna's life became a mad whirl of activity.

She was quite happy to let Henri make most of the many decisions.

'I was thinking of salmon for the entrée, the same as at Bettina's reception. What do you think, Jenna dear?'

'That'll be fine.'

'How is your dress coming along?'

'It's looking lovely,' replied Jenna.

'Good. Now, what colour flowers would you like in the church? I was thinking of light pink and yellow, they're such fresh spring colours.'

These conversations took place at least every other morning. As well as fittings for her dress and house hunting with Gerard, Jenna was doing her usual six nights a week in the play.

'I know you're tired, darling,' they were having supper at Gerard's flat after the show, 'but do you think you could manage half past nine tomorrow to have another look at the house in Glebe Place? I realize it's early, but if we don't make a decision this week we'll lose it.'

Jenna nodded wearily. 'Okay.' She had seen so many houses, each one of which most young brides would give their eyeteeth to live in, that she was totally mesmerized.

'You do like it, don't you?'

'Very much, Gerry.'

'Good, because I think it's the one to go for. The price is competitive and the location is superb.'

The next morning they drove to the house and agreed with the agent the offer Gerard would put forward. Afterwards, he drove her to Chester Square to see Bettina.

'See you later, darling. I must go and do some work.'

Jenna and Bettina had coffee at the kitchen table while Mrs Eaton, the nanny, took the twins for a walk to the park.

'I just can't understand why Charlie is behaving the way he is. He hardly speaks to me any more.'

'Oh, come on, Jenna, stop being so naïve. The guy is jealous. He's in love with you. Always has been, if you ask me.'

Jenna shook her head. 'I think you're wrong, Bettina. He's never said anything to make me feel that.'

'Then you're blind as well as stupid,' Bettina laughed. 'Don't take it so seriously. He'll get over it.'

'I hope so, Bettina. I'm terribly fond of Charlie. I'd hate to lose him as a friend.'

'Not too fond, I hope?'

'Of course not!'

'Good. Actually, there is something I want to talk to you about. I hope you won't feel as though I'm interfering or anything.'

'Of course not, Bettina. What is it?'

'Well, I just wonder if you know exactly what you're taking on. I mean, one day you'll be Lady Langdale and then you really won't be able to act any more. You know that, don't you?'

Jenna nodded. 'Yes, Gerry and I have discussed it, but I'm sure it'll be years before I become Lady Langdale.'

'Let's hope so. But when it does happen, even Gerry will have to give up his job. Running the estate is a full-time occupation, you know. And your role as his wife will be, too. I'm just worried that if your career continues to soar and then suddenly you have to give it all up, you'll be miserable for the rest of your life. I'm sorry, Jenna, I just wanted to say it, that's all.'

'That was some speech.'

'I know, but, Jen, you have no conception yet of the restrictions that will be put on your life once you join our family. You have to be very – well, how shall I put it – discreet about everything you say and do. It's been bad enough for me. I mean, I'm only the daughter, but you're going to be Lady Langdale. Believe me, Jenna, when I say it can be tough.'

There was silence. Bettina studied her hands. Eventually she stood up.

'I'm sorry, Jen. I'm sure everything will be fine if you love him. And you do, don't you?'

'Of course I do. And I appreciate what you've said. I'm

beginning to understand what I'll be taking on, so please don't worry.'

'You don't think I'm interfering, do you?'

'Don't be silly. I'm just grateful that I'm going to have you for a sister-in-law. You can give me advice when the going gets tough.'

'Anyway, Pa keeps comparing you to Grace Kelly, and she seemed to cope very well. Now, on to more practical matters. Ma wants you to wear the family tiara . . .'

Jenna waved goodbye to Bettina from her taxi.

Her friend was right. She did have some thinking to do.

48

CHARLIE CRUSHED his tenth cigarette of the day into the ashtray. He had to make a decision.

He had been avoiding Jenna, but now that Harold had given the go-ahead to put his new play, *Tired of Living*, into production, it was going to be impossible to avoid her any longer. Harold wanted Jenna to finish *Angel in Hell* in a month's time, then two weeks later start on rehearsals for the new play.

Since he was directing the play, Charlie would be put through the torment of seeing her every day. He didn't know whether he could stand that.

But Jenna was not his only problem. He was growing increasingly unhappy with the rewrites that Harold was asking him to work on.

'This is just going to end up as another piece of West End commercial claptrap!' he had said to Harold the day before.

'Bums on seats, my boy, that's what we're talking about. That first scene is still not right. Go home and try again.'

Charlie, having been perfectly happy with the original version, had spent most of the night staring at a blank page.

He opened the drawer and retrieved the embossed letter from the Canadian embassy. He read it for the hundredth time. The way he felt right now, the proposition was very tempting.

Working with a group of actors, hand-picked by him. Spending time devising a play from scratch, à la Mike Leigh and Peter Brook. In total artistic control. On top of that, it would all be paid for by the Canadian government. They were offering it to him on a plate as long as he was ready to sign a five-year contract.

What the hell, he thought, and dialled the number at the top of the letter. After all, it could do no harm to meet the cultural attaché and find out more.

At the very least it was an option.

If he couldn't have Jenna, then he didn't want to hang around and watch while someone else did.

He spoke with a secretary at the embassy and made an appointment to meet the attaché in two days' time.

He lit another cigarette and took a deep draw.

He hoped that fate would help him make a decision.

'Jenna, my love, sorry to wake you at this time of night.' Gerard's voice sounded tense. 'It's Pa. He's had a bad heart attack and I've got to drive up north straight away.'

'Gerry, I'm so sorry. How bad is bad?'

'Well, from what my mother says, he . . .' Gerard's voice cracked. 'His chances aren't good. Listen, I'll call you from the hospital in Harrogate when I know more. I love you.'

Jenna put the receiver down and reached for the alarm clock. It was four thirty in the morning. She got out of bed and filled the kettle for a cup of coffee. There was little point in trying to sleep.

She sat there, sipping the hot liquid, and watched the sun rise over Covent Garden. Later that day, she was having lunch with Lindsay to discuss her contract for *Tired of Living*. The wedding was less than four weeks away. Selfishly, she wondered, if Lord Langdale did die . . . no, she mustn't think like that.

Feeling rotten for thinking about herself when Gerard was suffering so much, she prayed that his father would live. After all, he had looked very healthy last time she had seen him and modern medicine could work wonders . . .

At half past eight, she showered and put on her best underwear. She was going to a final fitting for her wedding dress and the seamstresses in the plush salon intimidated her.

The telephone did not ring again and she was tempted to call the hospital in Harrogate before she went out, but thought better of it. He'll ring when he has news, she said to herself, and closed the door to her flat.

'You really do look beautiful. The off-white suits your pale skin. It doesn't look so stark.'

Jenna was standing in front of a large mirror while Elizabeth, the designer, made last-minute alterations to the gown. It was unusual, made of heavy cream satin, with a tight-fitting bodice encrusted with hundreds of tiny seed pearls. The V of the waist tapered into a skirt that was not full but shaped down into a four-foot train that cleverly showed off her slim figure.

As she stood there, things that she must do ran through her mind. Of course, it would all be cancelled if . . .

She had sent an invitation to her mother, but had received no reply. She had tried telephoning continually, but so far Joyce had not answered. Jenna made a mental note to phone her again this afternoon.

'All right, Jenna, you can take the dress off now. I'll call you when it's ready to be picked up, probably some time next week. We could deliver it but I'd prefer you to try it on once more.'

'Thank you, Elizabeth. It really is beautiful.'

'I just wish all my customers did justice to my designs the way you do.'

Jenna changed and caught a taxi to Joe Allen, where she was meeting Lindsay.

'So you're pleased; I thought you would be.'

'Very.' Jenna picked at the Waldorf salad in front of her.

'The money is almost double what you got for *Angel*, and you've got that two-week break before you go into rehearsals. So you can get married and swan off to some foreign clime for your honeymoon. They've also agreed, after hours of haggling, to put your name above the title.'

'I'm impressed, Lindsay.'

'That's why you pay me fifteen per cent of everything you

earn. Just occasionally, agents do justify their commission.' She smiled.

'So I only have three weeks of *Angel* left to go.'

'Yes. Will you be sad to finish?'

'Definitely. I think Christina will always have a special place in my heart.'

'Although you must agree that the role of Sarah is more of a challenge?'

'Without doubt. *Tired of Living* is really going to stretch me.'

'Well, you're really what they call "hot" at the moment. They're prepared to put rehearsals back by a week so you can have a two-week honeymoon. But they do want this contract signed, sealed and on their desk in a week's time. That's no problem, is it?' Lindsay looked at the frown that crossed Jenna's face.

'I hope not.'

'Is something wrong, Jenna?'

'Gerard's father, Lord Langdale. He had a heart attack last night.'

'Oh, Jenna, I am sorry.'

'I just feel so helpless, being here in London.'

'Has Gerard driven up to be with him?'

'Yes.'

'Jenna, might this affect your career?'

'To be honest, Lindsay, I don't know. I've told you before that when Lord Langdale dies, Gerard will inherit the title and we'll live at Langdale Hall.'

'Well, let's not pre-empt things. I'm sure he'll be all right.'

'Obviously I want to discuss the contract with Gerard before I sign it.'

'Fine. Here's a draft to show to him. If you come in to sign next Wednesday, it gives you a week to review it. Let me know in the meantime how things are going with Gerard's father.'

'Okay.'

'Try not to worry, Jenna. I'm sure he'll pull through.'

'I hope so, Lindsay, I really do.'

The telephone rang at twenty past three the following morning. Jenna picked it up, her hand shaking.

'Jenna, it's me. He died twenty minutes ago.'

'Oh, God! Darling, I'm so sorry. Is there *anything* I can do?'

'No, but we need to talk as soon as possible. I've got to spend tomorrow up here helping Ma with the usual nasty formalities. I'll drive back to London in time to pick you up after the curtain.'

'Darling, I wish I was there with you.'

'So do I, Jenna, so do I. I'll see you tomorrow night.'

'All right. Please take care of yourself and drive carefully.'

'I will. Good night, darling.'

'Good night, Gerard.'

Jenna slowly replaced the receiver.

'Oh, Jenna, I just can't believe this has happened.' Gerard sank into the sofa and Jenna handed him a large whisky. 'Everything was working out so perfectly and now . . .'

'How are Bettina and your mother coping?'

'They're both very cut up. It was the speed that was so dreadful. One moment Pa was tying his shoelace, the next he was on the floor having the attack. Freddie is with them at Langdale Hall, holding the fort until my return. Ma wants the funeral as soon as possible. It'll be next week, either Tuesday or Wednesday. Jenna, come and sit down beside me.' He patted the seat. She sat and Gerard turned to her and took her hands in his. 'Sweetheart, you know what my father's death means, don't you?'

Jenna nodded, not trusting herself to speak.

'Ma has insisted that the wedding take place as planned. She was adamant about it, actually. However, beyond that – oh, dear, I don't know how to say this, Jenna . . .'

'You don't have to, Gerard. I understand completely.'

'You see, it would just be so impossible for you to continue as an actress. I have to go and live at Langdale Hall to supervise the farm and the family's other business interests in the area. I'm afraid the role of my wife is going to be a full-time one, too. Especially in the coming months. I tried to think of ways round it on the journey down here. I toyed with the idea of suggesting you just do this next play, but I suspect that then there would be another and another.' Gerard sighed. 'There is an option open to you, Jenna. I will understand if you don't want to marry me. It breaks my heart to say those words, but it's the most important decision you'll ever make. It must be the right one.' Gerard ran a hand through his hair. 'God, what a nightmare this is! Anyway, I'm not going to ask you to make a decision tonight. I want you to think it over. Oh,

Jenna, I'm trying to be calm about this but . . .' He put his head in his hands and started to sob.

She reached for him and cradled him in her arms as the sobs became louder. He buried his head in her lap and she rocked him gently, whispering words of comfort.

'I need you, Jenna, now more than ever. Please don't leave me.'

Lack of sleep, shock and emotion had got the better of him. Tormented though she was, Gerard needed to be comforted, fed and put to bed. She removed the whisky, knowing that it would only act as a depressant, and replaced it with a mug of hot tea.

'Come on, darling, please eat this. It'll make you feel better.' She fed soldiers of buttered toast to him like a baby, than insisted he went to bed and tried to sleep.

She tucked him in and sat on the bed next to him.

'Jenna, I'm sorry. I was determined that I wouldn't put you under any emotional pressure. I want your decision to be as unbiased as possible.'

She stroked his forehead. How could she leave him now?

'Darling, I love you. And when I said I would marry you I took into account the fact that one day I'd have to give up my career. It's just come sooner than expected, that's all.'

The anguished expression lifted slightly from Gerard's face.

'I want to be with you wherever you are.'

'Please, Jenna, take your time. If you're not sure . . .'

'I am.' She silenced him with a kiss.

'So you still want to marry me?'

'Yes.'

'Thank God! I think if I had lost you on top of my father, I'd have gone insane.'

'Now, will you close your eyes and try and get some sleep?'

He grasped Jenna's hand. 'I love you, darling. I'll make it up to you, I promise.'

He slept.

Jenna switched off the light and tiptoed out of the room. She went to sit in her favourite chair by the window.

She had just sacrificed the greatest love of her life.

49

THE FOLLOWING TUESDAY, Gerard picked Jenna up after the show and they drove up to Langdale Hall. The funeral was at eleven the next morning.

They arrived just after midnight. Bettina was waiting up for them.

'Jenna, it's so good to see you. Thank you for coming. It means a lot to all of us.'

The three of them went into the small sitting room where coffee and sandwiches were waiting.

'How's Ma?'

'Asleep, with a little help from some tablets. She's been better today. I keep asking her questions about the wedding. It seems to be what's keeping her going.'

'I think that goes for all of us.' Gerard squeezed Jenna's hand.

After checking the arrangements for the following morning, Bettina told Gerard that he was looking tired and that he should go to bed.

'All right, I take the hint,' Gerard smiled. 'Good night, Bettina, 'night, darling.' He closed the door behind him.

'Jenna, I wanted to have a chat, as tomorrow I'll have my hands full and you have to rush straight back to London. I really wanted to check that you're, well, happy, I suppose.'

'Yes, why shouldn't I be?'

'Oh, come on, Jenna. It's a hell of a big decision you've just had to make. And remember, I've known you since the day you arrived at drama school. I know better than Gerry how much your acting career means to you.'

'Well, it wasn't an easy decision to make, Bettina, but I just happen to be in love with your brother.'

'He didn't emotionally blackmail you, did he? I mean, he wouldn't do it on purpose.'

'No, he didn't. As a matter of fact, Gerry was incredibly fair. He said he quite understood if I wanted to cancel the wedding.'

'Okay, Jenna. It's not my place to interfere, but I love both of you so much. As long as you've done it for the right reasons. Because I can tell you now, the whole thing will be a disaster if you haven't.'

'Please, Bettina, I'm very tired. You can rest assured that I don't intend to be a sacrificial lamb, however much Catholic guilt I may have.'

Bettina blushed. 'Forgive me. I promise not another word will be said on the subject. I may be totally biased, but I'm sure you've made the right choice.'

Jenna lay in bed and thanked God that she'd trained as an actress.

The funeral was a sad, sombre occasion and Jenna was

relieved that she had to hurry to Harrogate from the church to catch a train back to London.

The next morning she called Lindsay to say that she needed to come into the office to see her.

'Well, Jenna, I can't say that I'm happy about it. But it's your decision and you're obviously clear about what you're going to do. What a choice to have to make!' Lindsay sighed.

'Yes. It wasn't easy, but I've made it, so that's that. Will you call Harold and tell him? Please send him my apologies. I feel dreadful about letting him down, especially as he gave me such a big break with *Angel*.'

'I'll call him as soon as you leave. He'll be terribly disappointed. What about Charlie?'

Jenna couldn't face speaking to him just yet.

'I'll call him myself, but I think I'll leave it until tomorrow. I'm dreading speaking to him.'

'I can understand that. You two have been so close and Charlie seems to use you as his inspiration. He'll be devastated that you won't be doing the play. I'll phone you later to let you know what Harold's said. And just remember, any time you want back in, give me a call. Casting directors always have time to see a "Lady".'

'Thanks, Lindsay. I'll see you at the wedding,' Jenna kissed her. 'And thank you for everything.'

'ACTRESS BECOMES LADY OVERNIGHT,' the *Daily Mail* reported the next morning. The article told the story of

Jenna giving up her promising career to marry the new Lord Langdale.

'Miss Jenna Shaw, who came from nowhere to win the Society of West End Theatre's Most Promising Newcomer award, for her startling performance in *Angel in Hell*, will give her last performance this Saturday before giving up her career to marry Lord Langdale at a glittering wedding on the twelfth of this month. It is rumoured that the Prince and Princess of Wales will be among the guests attending.'

Jenna read the article in horror. Charlie! She had been working up the courage to call him since she had woken up. If he had seen the article . . . She picked up the phone and dialled his number. It rang and rang.

When Charlie had received the telephone call from Harold to let him know that Jenna would not be doing the play, he had gone out and got very drunk. He had returned from the pub and fallen asleep on the sofa. He woke up to a stinking hangover and the telephone ringing. It stopped before he got to it. He drank a lot of black coffee, showered and dressed. He knew what he must do.

He put a call through to the Canadian embassy to confirm that he had decided to take up their offer. Then he went to see Harold at his Wardour Street office.

'I think you're a fool, Charlie my boy. Burying yourself in the middle of nowhere for five years. Has this got something to do with our leading lady's decision to quit the business?'

'No, Harold.'

'Okay. But I'm not blind, Charlie. Take it from me, women aren't worth it. Won't you reconsider?'

'I'm sorry, Harold. I've made up my mind.'

'Well, that's it then. I suppose there's nothing more to be said. You're a talented fool. Let me know when you're out of purdah. I might even consider staging one of your plays again.'

Charlie spent the rest of the day making arrangements for his departure. He booked a plane ticket for Saturday, which gave him a few days to tie up loose ends. There was no point in hanging around in London any longer than necessary. Now the decision was made, he wanted to get the hell out as soon as possible.

As for Jenna, well, he had been out a lot and she might have telephoned. He supposed he could go to the theatre to say goodbye . . . but no, he couldn't face seeing her. What would he say to her? That he was flying thousands of miles away because she was marrying another man?

Hardly.

He had lost her. Words were pointless now.

50

THE CURTAIN FELL on Jenna's last performance in *Angel*. Her last performance ever, Jenna thought, as she accepted the engraved Waterford rose bowl from the cast.

She had hoped that Charlie might turn up at the party backstage to say goodbye to her and toast her forthcoming marriage. But she wasn't surprised when he didn't.

The champagne did not taste as refreshing as usual.

'I'd exchange all this for what you're getting,' said Sally, her understudy, who was taking over the role of Christina.

Jenna said her goodbyes and went back to her dressing room. She packed away her make-up and the cards that she'd hung round her mirror. She sadly closed the door behind her and walked down the corridor.

'Bye, Bill, and thanks for everything,' she said to the stage doorkeeper.

'Goodbye, miss, and congratulations. Oh, miss?'

'Yes?'

'I nearly forgot. Someone brought a letter in for you

earlier and said I was to be sure to remember to give it to you. And there was me nearly forgetting. Here you are.'

She took the brown envelope and stuffed it into her pocket.

'Bye,' she said to the theatre as she stepped outside and walked up Shaftesbury Avenue, the bright lights a blur through her tears.

Jenna arrived home, relieved that Gerard was up north still sorting things out; she wasn't at all sure he'd like to see her so miserable five days before their wedding. He was coming down to London in two days' time to drive her up to Langdale Hall and her life would change completely.

Jenna took out a bottle of vodka and poured herself a large drink. She remembered the fan letter Bill had given her as she was leaving the theatre. She went to the bedroom and fumbled in her coat pocket, found the envelope, then settled in her favourite chair by the window. She sipped the tasteless alcohol and felt the liquid warming her as she opened the letter.

At first the contents didn't register and she could not make head or tail of the words in front of her. She read it again. Slowly she started to understand. Her hand trembled as she drained the remaining vodka in one.

'Five grand Miss La Di Da, otherwise every paper in Fleet Street gets a copy of that "revealing" little video you did a while back. Eleven tomorrow morning,

Victoria Station, platform seven. Bring the money and you get all the copies. Don't try no funny stuff. Wouldn't want Lord Lover Boy to know he's marrying a whore now would we?'

Jenna let out a low moan. She opened the drawer and found the book that would tell her how much she had in the building society. She also checked the amount in her current account. Altogether she had six thousand, four hundred and sixty-five pounds. Enough to pay Jonnie and buy a one-way ticket out of England. There was no question of what she had to do. If she called the police, Jonnie would make sure the video caused maximum embarrassment to the Langdale family. She couldn't put Gerard through that. She couldn't stay and marry him now, living in fear every day that her dreadful past would leak out. She would be living a lie.

She was a whore. And whores didn't marry into one of the most respected families in England. She'd known all along it was too good to last.

The truth was that one could never escape from the past.

Not ever.

The taxi pulled into Victoria Station at ten to eleven. Jenna asked the driver to wait as she had three large suitcases with her. She walked over to the post box and posted the letters addressed to Gerard and her mother. She walked towards platform seven, checked her watch and felt for the envelope tucked safely in a pocket of her handbag.

She saw him, a large carrier bag in his left hand. He saw her and smiled.

'You got my note, then?'

'Just give me the tapes. Here's the money.'

'Open the envelope and show me what's in it.'

Jenna opened it and showed him the wad of notes inside.

Jonnie seemed satisfied. He grabbed the envelope and put it in a pocket of his jacket. Then he handed the carrier bag to her.

'Sensible girl. Couldn't have that kind of filth coming out, now could we?' He grinned.

Jenna stared at him. 'I warn you, if you've tricked me and I discover that there's another copy of these tapes and you try to use them, I'll make it my business to find you. I'll use every penny I have to make sure you're put behind bars for the rest of your life. I believe rape, porn films, drugs and blackmail can add up to a lot of years. You got that money because I don't want to hurt someone I love. But from now on, there's only me. So keep looking behind you, Jonnie.'

Jenna turned and hurried out of the station to her taxi. As she did so, she saw a refuse lorry, its iron jaws eating the waste that the men were throwing on to its rear. She stopped, thought for a second, then went over to it. She threw the carrier bag on to the back of the van and watched as it was crunched. When she was satisfied that the bag had been destroyed, she got into the taxi.

'Heathrow airport, please.'

The cab moved off along the busy street. Maybe she ought to have checked that the tapes really were the ones she had paid five thousand pounds to own, but she couldn't face that. It might destroy her.

'Frankie, thank God you're home! Listen, I'm afraid that plans have changed slightly. The wedding's been cancelled. Sorry? Oh yes, it's to do with Gerard's father, but I'll explain more when I get there. What? Yes, I'm at the airport now, catching the two o'clock BA flight to Los Angeles. Can you pick me up? Great. I'll see you then, bye.'

The aeroplane took off on time and Jenna watched as the familiar countryside disappeared under a veil of clouds. She hoped she wouldn't see it again for a long, long time.

Someone else had taken off at the same time, hoping the same thing. Marilyn sat beside him, drugged and only partially aware of what was happening.

''Ere's to your mate.' Jonnie raised the can of lager. 'Bloody glad I saw that picture of 'er in the paper. Paris is the only home for creative minds like mine.' He grinned. 'This is where our life begins, Marilyn. This is what I've been waiting for.'

The two giant birds soared high above the clouds, taking the betrayed and the betrayer far away from their field of combat.

April 1983

Interval

'Off into the world we go,
Planning futures, shaping years.
Love bursts in and suddenly,
All our wisdom disappears.'

DON BLACK AND CHARLES HART,
Aspects of Love

51

'IT'S *SO* GOOD TO SEE YOU!' Frankie clasped Jenna to her. A tall man with Frankie took the three suitcases and made off towards the exit.

'The limo's outside. I thought I'd meet you in good old Tinsel Town style.' Frankie grinned.

'Good God!' said Jenna, as they climbed into the back of the white Mercedes stretch limousine. 'Is this yours?'

'Nope, it's Pops's, but I borrowed it to collect the brightest star of the West End as she makes her first visit to Hollywood.' There was a pause as Frankie studied her friend. The limousine pulled smoothly away from Arrivals and headed for Hollywood.

'You okay, honey?'

Jenna stared out of the window. 'Yes. I'm fine.'

'When you called I was just packing my case for the trip to England to watch you get married, yet here you are in LA. What's happened?'

'It's a long story, Frankie.'

'Is the wedding just delayed because of Gerard's father?'

'No. It's off altogether.'

'Oh, dear.' Frankie looked at Jenna's impassive face and decided she'd better drop the subject.

'Anyway, it's great to see you. I missed ya, kiddo.' She squeezed Jenna's hand.

They arrived at Orchid Villa just as the sun was setting.

'Oh, Frankie, isn't this beautiful?' Jenna exclaimed as she hung over the balustrade and gazed at the view over the valley.

'It's not a bad little shack. Come inside and I'll give you the guided tour.'

Orchid Villa was spacious and elegant. The tiled floors and big windows gave it a Mediterranean feel.

'You must be becoming quite a celebrity to have this place,' Jenna remarked as they sipped freshly made daiquiris by the pool.

'Well, not quite Meryl Streep, but getting there.' Frankie laughed.

In truth, Frankie's career was rising rapidly. Mimi was now sending her a couple of scripts a week and she was able to pick future projects carefully. Her next film, in which she was going to star with her father, was due to start shooting in six weeks' time.

As for the rest of her life ... June was again away on location in Rome, working with Nigel Forster. Frankie didn't want to think about that.

The two girls ate chilli and salad, prepared by Juanita, Frankie's housekeeper, and spent a relaxed evening sipping wine by the fire. Frankie wanted to ask Jenna exactly what had brought her to LA, but she could see her friend did not want to talk yet, so she left it.

Hours later, the telephone by Frankie's bed rang. She looked at her watch. It was seven thirty in the morning. She picked up the receiver.

'Hello, Frankie Duvall speaking.'

'Is Jenna there with you?'

'Hello, Bettina.'

'Is she?'

'Yes.'

'Oh.'

There was a short pause.

'Have you any idea what happened?' Bettina sounded tense and exhausted.

'I'm afraid not. She only arrived last night.'

'Has she said anything?'

'No, Bettina, not yet. But I'm sure she will, given time.'

'Gerard's distraught.'

'Oh, dear,' Frankie bit her lip.

'I just don't understand it. When I saw her last week she was fine. Why on earth has she run out on him?'

'Look, Bettina, I know no more than you do.'

'Does she seem upset?'

'Yes, she does.'

'Gerard received a letter this morning saying that she wanted to continue with her career, but it sounded so unlike Jenna.'

'Absolutely. I have to believe that what she's done, she's done for a very good reason. We're both going to have to trust her.'

'I'm trying, Frankie, believe me. But you can imagine the uproar it's caused here. I feel completely torn. I love Jenna but, Frankie, you should see my brother . . .' Bettina's voice faded away.

'There's nothing I can say. All I can do is suggest that I call you if Jenna starts to talk. But I think at the moment Jenna needs a friend, not an interrogator.'

'Okay, Frankie. I'd prefer it if you don't tell Jenna I called. I just had a feeling that she'd run to you.'

'I won't tell her. You take care of yourself and that brother of yours. You don't think he's going to come across here, do you?'

'Well, I must ring him and tell him where Jenna is. I have to, Frankie.'

'Yes, of course. Just ring me if he's likely to put in an appearance.'

'I will. Thanks, Frankie.'

Bettina put down the phone and dialled Gerard's number. There was no reply.

She tried it again and again and then later, throughout the evening. At one o'clock she gave up and went to bed.

In the week that followed, Frankie insisted that she show Jenna all that Hollywood had to offer. They went shopping on Rodeo Drive, to lunch at the Ivy and Ma Maison, then down to the Beverly Hills Hotel for cocktails. Jenna was fascinated by the glamour of the place.

Frankie seemed to know everyone. Jenna was astonished and proud of the celebrity status Frankie had acquired. The maître d's gave her the best tables and the assistants in Saks and Yves St Laurent fell over themselves to serve her.

'Honestly, Frankie, I can't believe that you know so many famous people. I feel completely star-struck.'

The two of them were in the Polo Lounge having an early evening drink and Michael Caine had just come over, kissed Frankie and asked after her father.

'Oh, Michael used to rock me in my cradle. He and Pops are great buddies, both being English and all. Anyway, tomorrow we have to find you something stunning to wear. I'm taking you to your first Hollywood party on Saturday night and I want you to look gorgeous.'

The following day Frankie took Jenna into I. Magnin, where they found a white Galanos sarong that Frankie pronounced perfect and insisted she buy for Jenna.

'I can't let you do that, Frankie. It's over two thousand dollars and –'

'Shut up Jenna. I thought we went through all this at school. I'm buying it for you and that's that.'

The party was at a palatial house in Bel Air. At the entrance to the grounds they were stopped by a uniformed guard who asked for their names and checked them against a list.

'Okay, Miss Duvall, take the car up the drive and Bernie will park it for you. Have a good evening.'

'My God, Frankie, this isn't a house, it's a mansion!'

'Yeah, it's a nice place. Clark Gable lived here once. Come on.'

Frankie ushered Jenna up the steps and into an opulent hallway lit by one enormous crystal chandelier.

'Frankie, darling, wonderful you could come! And this is the friend we've heard so much about? Introduce me, Frankie, do,' gushed a woman in bright mauve chiffon and smothered in diamonds.

'Melissa, this is Jenna Shaw. We were at drama school in London together.'

'Welcome, Jenna, you look beautiful. Now, Frankie, you take this young lady through to the pool where we're serving champagne. Have a good time, Jenna!'

'Thank you. It's very kind of you to have me.'

'A friend of Frankie's is a friend of ours. See you later,' Melissa turned to greet the next arrivals.

Frankie propelled Jenna through a string of magnificent rooms and out on to a floodlit terrace.

'Melissa is the wife of Henry Blumberg, the biggest TV producer in town. Film mixes with TV these days, although ten years ago, the film people would not have been seen dead near them, but TV has a lot of power here now. Have some champagne. Cheers!' Frankie raised her glass and downed it in one.

'Now, who can we introduce you to that's really important?' Frankie giggled. 'Of course, they all believe they're mega important but . . . ah, I see Jackie coming towards us. She's casting director for that hospital soap we caught on TV the other night. It's slipping in the ratings and they're thinking of axing it.' Frankie had reduced her voice to a whisper.

'Hi, Jackie, how's things? May I introduce you to Jenna Shaw? Jenna, this is . . .'

By twelve o'clock, Jenna had been introduced to so many

people that her head was spinning. Everyone in Hollywood seemed to be there.

A small jazz band was playing and Frankie had been pulled on to the floor to dance. Jenna sipped her champagne and half listened to a group of young actors bitching about the lack of good roles for men under forty. She walked slowly across the veranda and stopped at the edge of the terrace. She leaned against the ornate railing and stared into the darkness beyond.

A sense of aloneness engulfed her, heightened by the glamour of the people that surrounded her. She had run from the pain, believing she could leave it behind. Now she realized that the pain was deep inside herself and no amount of running could free her from that.

Two men watched her across the terrace, the three of them unaware of each other.

Daniel, who had just arrived with a nineteen-year-old starlet, gazed at the solitary figure silhouetted in the moonlight. Blanche was back.

Don Steiner studied her with an intensity that came from years of looking through a lens. He felt exhilarated. She was perfect, just perfect.

'Jenna, you *must* test!' Frankie paced round the pool. 'No one, but no one, turns down the offer of testing for the second lead in a Don Steiner movie! Especially when you'd be working with me.' She stopped and glared at Jenna.

'Look, Frankie, I understand what you're saying, but I'm really not sure what I want to do at the moment.'

Frankie threw up her hands in despair. 'Jesus fucking

Christ! There are a million girls who would willingly screw the Hunchback of Notre Dame to get a Steiner test, but oh no, not Jenna Shaw. Don sees you at a party, doesn't even speak to you and calls Melissa at eight thirty the next morning to find out who you are. He wants to test you immediately and you want to fucking think about it!' Frankie sat down, put her head in her hands and sighed deeply. 'Look, Jenna, I can't say anything more, but it's just stupid to turn the test down. Jesus, you don't have to take the goddamn part if they offer it to you. Opportunities in this town come once if they come at all.' She stood up. 'I'm meeting Pops for lunch and I've got to run. Are you sure you won't come with me? Maybe he could talk some sense into you.'

Jenna shook her head. 'Thanks for the offer, but I think I'll stay here. Give him my love, though.'

'Suit yourself. When I come back I want you to have made the right decision, okay?'

Jenna smiled and nodded. 'Okay, I'll think about it.'

'Good. Now have a swim. Maybe that'll bring you to your senses. See you later.'

Jenna watched as the white Mercedes Sports disappeared around the corner. She knew Frankie was right, but during the night, unable to sleep, she had made up her mind to go back to England. She had no idea what she would do when she got there, but it certainly didn't involve acting. She had pondered the possibility of going back to college, somewhere far away from London and starting again. She wanted anonymity, no pressure, and peace.

She dived into the pool. Last night the idea had given her comfort. It sounded safe and painless.

Jenna swam length after length. The cool water started to clear her head. The physical action of using her body against the gentle water emptied her mind and eventually she climbed out feeling refreshed.

She sat in one of the padded pool chairs, closed her eyes and enjoyed the sensation of the cool droplets of water drying on her skin. The idea of returning to England, having been presented with such an opportunity here in Hollywood, began to seem ridiculous.

Jenna stood up and walked inside. She paused in front of the full-length mirror and looked at her reflection.

Blonde hair, already gently lightened by the sun; a lithe body, perfectly shaped; blue eyes, shining bright and clear in her delicately sculptured face.

'Jenna Shaw, you really do look beautiful,' she said to the mirror.

She went to the bar in the corner of the sitting room and found a half bottle of chilled champagne. She poured herself a glass and went back to the mirror. She toasted her reflection.

'Jenna Shaw, this one's for us!' She downed the champagne in one.

52

'ARE YOU REPRESENTING HER? Because if not, I wanna call the person who is.'

'I'm representing her. Frankie Duvall brought her in yesterday to meet me,' Mimi drawled into the phone. 'Presumably you have good news?'

Donald Steiner impatiently paced his stark living room, portable phone tucked into the crook of his neck, beer in one hand, cigarette in the other. Why didn't the goddamn woman get on with it? He hated all this game-playing with agents. Most of them were girls from small towns who had gone to secretarial school and slowly moved in on the business. They made themselves indispensable in the office and in the bedroom, eventually having their name added to the list of directors and then to the name of the agency. He hated all the power they possessed. Money and art were never pleasant bedfellows, but he knew that one needed the other, especially in this town, and Mimi represented the three people he needed to indulge himself in his passion.

'Good news for you, my dear, considering the commission

you charge these poor talented artistes. I want Jenna Shaw for *Rosie*.'

Mimi smiled. To represent the three leading characters in the new Don Steiner movie was quite a coup, quite a coup. She kept her voice casual. 'If she agrees to do it, what are the terms?'

'I'll talk exact terms later, but you know the company won't cheese-pare, even if I spent most of last night and countless bottles of champagne getting them to agree to take an unknown. I just want her agreement in principle, okay?'

'Hardly an unknown, Don. She does have the lead in the most successful West End show in three years on her credits.' Mimi trod carefully. She knew how unusual it was to have a director of the calibre of Don Steiner speaking to her personally about an actor. Usually, the call was made by one of the hordes of senior secretaries in the contracts department. Still, she wanted as much as she could get. That was her business.

'Okay, Mimi, call me by five and let me know if she wants it.'

The telephone went dead in her hand.

'Jenna, smile for the nice little photo man,' said Frankie through clenched teeth. Daniel shepherded Jenna and his daughter past the paparazzi and inside the restaurant. The maître d' led them immediately to their table.

'A bottle of Dom Perignon would be suitable for the occasion, I think, Jacques,' Daniel smiled.

'Of course, Mr Duvall.' The maître d' hurried away and returned with a bottle of chilled champagne.

'Right, the first toast is to Jenna, for being in this town for three weeks and landing a plum role in a movie. Here's to success, Jenna!' Daniel raised his glass. 'And here's to the three of us and the success of *Rosie*. It'll be the first time the press won't be able to accuse me of having an affair with my leading lady!' They all laughed.

'Two more weeks and the fun stops. We start hating the wardrobe lady, get pissed off with the cameraman and scream for the director to be replaced immediately,' said Daniel. Of course he didn't mean it, not really, but twelve-hour days, working with a bunch of overinflated egos in a confined space, could be rough.

'Mimi always says that the best day of an actor's life is the day you're offered the part. And it's all downhill from there. I think she's got a point. Of course, it's still new for you, Jenna. Are you enjoying it?'

'Yes. But I'm worried that I won't come up to scratch and they'll slate me when the film comes out.'

'I doubt it. Don Steiner is not a man to take a gamble. Anyway, I saw the test, and I don't think you'll have too many problems, my dear. But you must learn to ignore the press. They only build you up to pull you down again. According to the newspapers I have fifteen illegitimate children, of all colours and creeds. I've been near death four times due to bouts of heavy drinking, I've screwed countless models but at the same time have a secret gay lover that I keep hidden in a fabulous apartment in the hills and visit three times a week! Seriously, Jenna, just be careful. These people can be very cruel, and if you're not used to it, it can really hurt. That's why we all have press agents. Has Mimi sorted that out yet?'

'Yes,' Frankie cut in. 'She's got Loni, the same as me.'

'Good. Loni may be an irritating little shit when he calls you at four in the morning to check out a story, but he's one of the best. He'll look after you.'

'Well, at least you have the advantage of having us around to wet-nurse you,' said Frankie. 'My advice is, keep your mouth shut, keep your head down and don't smoke anyone else's cigarettes.'

Jenna's eyes widened. 'I don't smoke, Frankie.'

'Fine, then don't start, 'cos it may not be just tobacco you find in it. *Comprende?*'

Jenna nodded, trying to take in all they were telling her. Since her screen test two weeks ago she had felt as though she was living in a dream. When Mimi had called to tell her the part was hers and had mentioned figures, Jenna could hardly believe it. They were going to pay her almost a hundred thousand pounds. It was a drop in the ocean to most people there, but to Jenna it meant security and control over her life.

Frankie had been fabulous, helping her through the surge of interest from the press when they heard she was in the film. There had been articles in the British newspapers about her too. Jenna knew that this would back up the letter she had written to Gerard. Of course, she hadn't planned for this to happen, but there was little she could do.

'So, what do you make of Hollywood so far, Je–' Frankie's voice broke off as she stared at a group of people who were entering the restaurant. The colour drained from her face. Jenna watched as Frankie tried to regain control and picked up her drink. Her hand shook and she had to put the glass down.

One of the women who had entered in the group was making her way towards their table. She was small, with a full figure, blonde hair and bright-blue eyes. She kissed Daniel and then Frankie.

'Hi, how are you both?' She spoke in a deep, husky voice.

Daniel replied before Frankie had a chance to speak. 'Fine, we're just fine. Yourself?'

'Tired. We only just arrived back from Rome a couple of hours ago and you know what plane food is like, so we came straight here from the airport.' She glanced at Jenna. 'You must be Jenna Shaw. Frankie has told me so much about you, I feel I know you already. Congrats on the film.' The woman put her hand on Frankie's shoulder. 'I'll call you tomorrow,' she said softly. 'Ciao.' And she went off to her table on the other side of the room.

Frankie signalled to the waiter to fill her wine glass.

Jenna was so intent on watching Frankie that she had not realized Daniel was talking to her.

'Sorry, what did you say?'

'I said, young lady, that all stars in the making need their beauty sleep. As do old stars who don't want "the sad passage of time" mentioned in the reviews of their latest film.' He glanced at Frankie. 'I think it's time we all made a move.'

Jenna lay awake that night wondering why Frankie had reacted so strangely in the restaurant. Frankie had been silent on the journey back to Orchid Villa and had gone straight to bed when they got home.

Jenna turned over and closed her eyes. She was just drifting off when she heard a faint noise coming from somewhere in the house. It sounded like a kitten crying for its mother. She sat up, got out of bed and put on a robe. She opened her bedroom door, fumbled for the hall light, and stood trying to identify where the sound was coming from.

It wasn't a kitten. It was Frankie.

Jenna opened the door to Frankie's room and peered in. Frankie was sitting, still fully dressed, in the middle of her large bed, surrounded by sodden tissues, overflowing ashtrays, and a half-finished bottle of whisky.

Her mascara was spread around her eyes and she looked so childish and woebegone that Jenna almost wanted to laugh. She walked towards the bed and Frankie looked up, startled. She stared at Jenna for a moment, and Jenna thought she was going to speak, but instead she burst into another flood of huge, hiccuping tears.

Jenna went to her and put her arms round her. She held her tight until the sobbing had abated and then said, in her most matron-like voice, 'Well, we can't have this, can we? If you don't tell me what's wrong I'll have to shout "Abandon bed!" before we drown in the tears.'

This brought a kind of snivelly laugh from Frankie.

'Now, come on, tell Auntie Jenna all about it.'

She held Frankie's hands and cleared some of the hair from her face. Frankie looked at her.

'But I'm always the auntie,' she said in a tiny, offended voice.

'Not tonight, honey. Anyway, Rudi always made us reverse roles in improvisation, so just think of this as an exercise to improve your acting. Okay?'

Frankie sniffed. 'Okay. But I can't tell you. I can't tell anyone.'

'Listen, madam, you always made me tell you everything, and I will take great offence and give you no juicy info on my life if you feel you can't talk to your best buddy. Look, I'm a big girl now and I can take it, whatever it is. I've been through a lot myself in the past year. Things that hurt so much I wanted to die. In fact, I nearly did.'

That made Frankie look up.

'I'll do a deal with you. If you tell me what the problem is, I'll tell you why I'm here. I think that's a fair swap, isn't it?'

'I suppose so.' Frankie shrugged.

'All right, I'll go first.'

Jenna told Frankie as concisely as she could what had led to her arrival in LA. She tried to keep her emotion at bay, but a couple of times a lump rose in her throat and she had to pause to collect herself.

'So that's the story. And I trust you to never tell another living soul. No one else must ever know.'

Frankie had stopped crying and looked shocked and penitent. 'God, Jenna, and here was me thinking I had problems! Why the hell didn't you contact me when all this was happening? I tell you, if I ever get my hands on that Jonnie bastard, I swear I'll kill him. Personally, I think you should have gone to the police.'

'I've explained why I couldn't, Frankie. The whole of the Langdale family would have been affected. They guard their privacy so closely. And after the death of Gerard's father, I couldn't risk putting them through the media uproar that would have occurred if that bastard did go public.'

'What did you say in the letter to Gerard?'

'Just that I'd changed my mind and decided I wanted to continue with my career. I thought it was something he would believe and might stop him coming after me.'

'Poor Jenna! It seems so cruel.'

'Well, I can guess what they all think of me back in England now I'm doing this film. It looks as though I'm a callous, hard-hearted bitch. I'm sure Bettina will never speak to me again. Anyway,' Jenna sighed, 'I've been lucky enough to be given another chance here. Now, do you feel ready to tell me your problem?'

'Oh dear, Jenna, I really don't . . .'

'Is it a man?'

Frankie immediately burst into tears again. Jenna presumed she had hit goal.

'Frankie, you've always told me what shits men are, and I must say I'm inclined to agree with you, so it's not the end of the world if he –'

'Jenna! It's not a man. I only wish it was.' She sank back and buried her head in the pillow. 'Look, I'm sorry. I know we made a deal, but you really wouldn't understand. Why don't you go back to bed? I'll be fine tomorrow.'

'I think it's unfair considering I've just poured out my heart to you, but if that's what you want, I'll go.' Jenna decided to have one last try. 'It's to do with that woman in the restaurant, isn't it?'

Frankie looked up. She sighed deeply and spoke in a weary voice. 'Yes, all right, it's to do with that woman in the restaurant. I happen to be hopelessly, fatally in love with that woman. I am a dyke, a lesbo, a queer, whose love object is having an affair with a *man*. So, now you can go pack your bags and call a cab and leave your woman-eating ex-friend alone with her hideous perversion.'

Frankie sat there quietly, calmly, with no more sign of tears in her eyes. Jenna stared at her thoughtfully.

'So, if I leave you alone, you won't start that horrible racket again or try anything stupid like jumping out of the window?'

'No, I'll be fine. I suggest you go to the Beverly Hilton. The rooms are nice there,' she said in a flat voice.

'Okay, I'm going.'

'Okay.'

'But only if you swear not to cry for as long as it takes the kettle to boil.' She went into the kitchen and came back with two cups of Earl Grey tea.

There was relief in Frankie's eyes.

'Now, drink this. The English always have a cup of tea in moments of crisis.' Jenna sipped her tea. 'You know,

I'll bet the *Titanic* went down with every English person on board holding a teacup.'

'So you really don't mind if your friend is slightly on the weird side and prefers women?'

'Frankie, in the past year I've begun to think they may be the safer bet!' Jenna smiled. 'Now, I suggest you move over and make room among the tissues, so I can get comfortable and you can tell me the whole story.'

'You don't feel funny getting into bed with a dyke?' Frankie asked sheepishly.

'Nope, because you really aren't my type, and even if you were, I make it a rule never to sleep with my friends.'

Frankie smiled. 'Jenna Shaw, you're turning into some lady!'

53

AT FIRST, THE FILMING OF *Rosie* had been a nightmare as Jenna struggled to learn a set of techniques completely alien to her skills as a stage actress.

During the first week, she was positive that Steiner was going to re-cast, as he called 'cut' for the tenth time. He walked over to her, put his arm round her shoulder and led her away from the set.

'Listen, my love, you have to remember that the camera is right up your bloody nose and picks up every hair follicle on your face. Please try to keep things smaller. Think, don't act, and you'll be fine. Okay, let's try again.'

They did. And again and again, until by the end of the week Jenna was at her wits' end.

It was Daniel who saved the day.

Jenna was sitting in the studio canteen dejectedly sipping her umpteenth cup of tea when a voice said, 'Hey, aren't you Jenna Shaw, the new star of that Steiner film *Pansy*?'

Each day the production was named a different flower by Daniel.

'I like that one. It seems kind of suitable considering all the namesakes working on the thing. Mind if I join you?'

Jenna shook her head. Daniel sat down opposite her and put his head in his hands, gnome style.

'You know, you're not the only actor in the world who's had to make the transition from footlights to camera. Let me tell you, I found it just as hard as you. Until I got a good piece of advice. Want to hear it?'

Jenna nodded.

'Well, it was when I was making my first film, and the director was despairing of me. One day a famous actor came down to the set. His name was Charles Laughton. After he had watched the take, he whispered something to the producer and pointed at me. Of course my heart sank and I was convinced he was asking which trash can they'd dug me out of. But then Laughton came over to me and put his hand on my shoulder. "Feel it in your gut and let it dribble out through your eyes, my boy. That's the secret of a great film actor," he said and patted my back. I never saw him again. He died soon after, but for me those words were the difference between success and failure. Think about them.'

Daniel got up, smiled and disappeared out of the canteen.

The advice worked. She didn't know why, but it made the difference and suddenly she was able to get through the day with sometimes only a couple of takes on each scene. Her confidence grew and Steiner began to smile a lot more. She forgot about giving up and started to enjoy the challenge of being perfect on the first take. Occasionally, she even managed that.

LOVERS & PLAYERS

Jenna began to relax about what she was doing. Daniel shared many of his scenes with her and a bond started to develop between them. They had a scene in which she had to kiss him. She was extremely embarrassed about this, but Daniel made silly jokes and winked at her before each take and she soon relaxed. They took to lunching together in the canteen. Frankie would join them occasionally, although she usually met June, who was working in another studio on the lot. Jenna didn't pry, but presumed that things had worked out between them since Frankie spent most nights at June's apartment. Jenna missed her at Orchid Villa, but was glad to see Frankie looking happier.

Jenna was taken home by a studio limousine at about half past eight. She would have a shower, then fix herself something to eat, usually a TV dinner that she could heat in the microwave. She'd watch some television while she ate. Then she would go to bed with the next day's lines for company. At half past ten, Jenna switched out the light and fell asleep. Her alarm went off at half past four, and the limousine would be waiting outside at five o'clock to take her on the half-hour journey to the studio.

She was due in make-up at five forty-five, where they would begin the long process of washing and styling her hair and expertly applying her make-up. At approximately seven o'clock she'd make her way to the canteen to find some breakfast. Then she would go to her trailer on the lot where her costume for the day's shoot was waiting for her to put on.

Once she was dressed, she would settle down until she was called on set by one of the floor managers who rushed around the lot with their walkie-talkies. Sometimes she was needed straight away, but on other days it could be four o'clock in the afternoon before she was called.

At first, the boredom of hanging around with nothing to do except go over and over her lines drove her mad. It gave her too much time to think. But then she discovered the daytime soaps on the TV in her trailer and quickly became an addict.

Frankie would sometimes pop in to say hello, but she was on set most of the time and Jenna could only stand back and admire the consummate performance that she was turning in.

The film was the story of a young girl, played by Jenna, who falls in love with her best friend's father, played by Daniel. Frankie was playing Rosie, the title role. It was her film, and explored how her life falls apart as she watches the affection of her father and best friend being gradually removed from her and poured into each other.

Frankie found the story line unnerving. In real life Jenna *was* her best friend and she watched with mixed feelings as the relationship between her father and Jenna developed. However, with things sorted out with June and feeling guilty for leaving Jenna on her own so much, she felt she couldn't complain that Daniel seemed to have taken her under his wing.

The night after meeting June in the restaurant, Frankie went straight round to June's apartment. She demanded to know the truth about her relationship with Nigel Forster.

'For Christ's sake, June! Don't treat me like an idiot! I've heard all about the end-of-shoot party at the hotel.

Apparently you were making out with him in the pool in front of the entire crew.'

June said nothing.

'You've become such an item I'm amazed you haven't returned wearing a fucking engagement ring!'

Still June didn't reply. Frankie sank down into a chair and put her head in her hands. 'I presume, as you're not denying it, that it's true. Why, June? Why?'

'I'm so sorry, Frankie. I didn't mean it to happen. You know what it's like on location. You're thrown together.'

'Literally, from the sound of things,' Frankie moaned. 'Can you imagine what it's been like for me here, having to listen to all the gossip? I'm devastated. I feel like a complete fool, especially as I can never compete with a man. Are you gay or not?'

'Yes, I am. And I love you, Frankie.' Tears appeared in June's eyes. 'I can't explain why I had an affair with him. I didn't enjoy the sex at all.'

Frankie shuddered. 'I'm going home. I can't take any more.' '*Please* don't go, Frankie. I need you. I promise I'll make it up to you. It'll never happen again.'

'How can you say that?'

'I know it won't, that's all. I never want to do it again, and it's shown me how much I love you.'

'Oh, God!' Frankie burst into tears. She knew she should get the hell out now and save herself more pain. But she couldn't. June was her life.

June came over and held her tight. 'Please don't cry, Frankie. I'm sorry for hurting you, I truly am.'

June's mouth covered Frankie's. At first she tried to

resist, but as June's tongue probed her lips open and slipped into her mouth, she could not help but respond. June's hands slipped underneath her sweatshirt. Her fingertips caressed Frankie's nipples.

'Come to bed with me, Frankie. Let me show you how I can love you.'

Frankie let June lead her into the bedroom. June gently removed Frankie's clothes and then her own.

'Turn over, darling, you need relaxing.'

Frankie rolled on to her stomach and June sat astride her. A tingle ran down her spine as fluid was poured on to her skin. June's hands began massaging her shoulders, using sweet-smelling oil to create a heat that soothed, but also fired Frankie's ardour. June worked down her back, kissing her buttocks and sweeping her hands tantalizingly along Frankie's inner thighs. She turned Frankie over, sprinkled more oil and began to massage her breasts.

June worked down until she was massaging Frankie's lower belly. Then her hands slipped between Frankie's thighs and pushed her legs apart. June's head went down to Frankie's soaking mound. Frankie moaned. June's tongue probed. Frankie orgasmed noisily, then lay panting as June stroked her.

Frankie arrived at the studio the next morning looking pale and tired. She felt drained. After they had made love again, she had agreed to give the relationship another try, knowing that her obsession with June would lead her down the road to more pain, but that she was helpless to resist.

Daniel was in seventh heaven. Sometimes he had to pinch himself to stop calling her Blanche. It wasn't just the way she looked. It was the way she used her hands to express herself; the way her eyes shone when Daniel praised her performance; and the gentle way she had started to tease him as her confidence with him grew. Of course, he knew that she was not Blanche. Blanche had been dead and buried almost twenty-four years.

He was surprised that nobody had commented on the similarity between them. But then, it was a long time ago and Blanche had always insisted on keeping out of the limelight. And of course, when she died, any photos he had of the two of them together had been removed and packed away.

He grew to respect Jenna's wit, her intelligence and, of course, her talent. He knew where she was headed and he prayed that it would not destroy her.

Don Steiner walked to the centre of the set. He eyed the cast sternly.

'Okay, it's a wrap. Congrats, everyone!'

There was a lot of hugging and kissing as the actors felt relief at having come to the end of what had been a tough three months. Especially for Jenna. Steiner came over and kissed her. 'Congrats, Jenna, we made it!' He gave her a hug. 'Just remember me when you're big box office and I'm still trying to make a crust.' Steiner smiled and went off in search of Frankie.

'Well done, sweetheart,' Daniel shook Jenna's hand

and then pulled her into his arms. 'We made it, didn't we?'

Jenna smiled, nodded and wandered off to her trailer to pack. She had never felt so confused about a man in her life.

54

FOR THE FIRST MONTH after finishing the film, Jenna had been content to relax at Orchid Villa. Occasionally Mimi would call her and ask her to go meet a producer or director, but they never followed through with an offer. By the third month, her days started to drag. She met Mimi for lunch and told her she was getting worried about being out of work.

Mimi was unconcerned. 'Honey, let's wait until the film comes out and we get you some exposure.'

'I seem to be going for very few auditions at the moment.'

'That's partly my fault. I could send you on more but I don't want you to do rubbish. I think you've got a very big career ahead of you and it's silly to ruin it by taking anything that comes along. Just be patient, Jenna, and wait until the film opens. Even after that, you'll have to be careful. As far as people in this town are concerned the first film can be a fluke, just a piece of good luck. It's the second film that really establishes you.'

'I'm sure you're right but I'm not very good at doing nothing.'

'Honey, enjoy the freedom while you can. In four months the film is premiered. It's being rushed through in time for the Oscar nominations and you'll be launched into a round of promotional stuff that'll make you long to have a moment to yourself.'

Mimi was right. After the premiere of *Rosie* in December, Jenna was inundated with requests for interviews and photo sessions. The film received a mixed reception from critics and public alike. But it was the kind of film that people discussed and urged their friends to go and judge for themselves. One thing everyone who saw the film agreed on: Frankie Duvall was superb and many were convinced that she was going to win an Oscar nomination. Jenna's performance was praised, with the critics predicting great things for the future.

Jenna was offered a lead in a mini-series and a TV film. Mimi refused to let her consider either.

'I'm sorry, darling, but they're not right for you. We have to wait until the right thing comes along. Just try and be patient.'

Jenna tried. But much of the time she was by herself at Orchid Villa and she was lonely. Frankie spent most of her time at June's apartment.

So she turned to Daniel. They had started to lunch together once a week.

'How's your week been?' he asked, as the maître d'settled them at a table in the Ivy.

Jenna shrugged. 'All right, I suppose.'

'Oh dear, the glitz of this town is wearing thin already, I see.'

'Do I sound that depressed?'

'Yes.'

The waiter brought a bottle of iced white wine and some soda. Daniel poured two spritzers.

'What's wrong?'

Jenna took a sip of her drink. 'I'm bored, that's all. Mimi is determined that I don't do anything until she finds me the "perfect vehicle", as she calls it.'

'That's a compliment, Jenna, believe me. She obviously thinks you're headed for the big time, otherwise she'd have had you in some mini-series faster that you could blink. Mimi knows what she's doing, Jenna. Trust her.'

'I do, Daniel, but she keeps sending me to meet people and whetting my appetite. I was offered a role in *The Oil Barons* two days ago. It would have been at least three months' work.'

'It's television, my darling, even if it is the number-one soap in the ratings. Mimi wants to establish you in films.'

'I know, but when I do go to an audition, there seem to be three times the number of pretty blondes that used to be up for parts in London. Won't I get left behind or just forgotten if Mimi keeps saying no?'

'You've just answered your own question. There are millions of wannabes in this town. Mimi thinks you have real talent and is trying to keep you separate, give you an identity.'

'I'm sorry, Daniel. I don't mean to complain and Mimi

has been very good to me. To be honest, I'm not sure I'm cut out for Hollywood. I seem to know a lot of people but, apart from you and Frankie, no one who I could ring up and chat to. I know this town has been good to me, but I'm not sure whether I like it very much.'

'You're talking to the converted. I hate this town with a vengeance, but unfortunately, I'm too old to change my life and there's really nothing else I can do as well as I can make films.'

'What about going back to the theatre?'

'It was my first love, but to be honest, my darling, I've grown used to the security of being able to do another take if the first is no good. I'd be absolutely petrified to get up on a stage now. And everyone would be waiting to tear me to shreds, so I'm playing it safe.'

Jenna sighed. 'I understand. But although I enjoyed the experience of making *Rosie*, I prefer the buzz of a live audience. I'm not sure whether I want to concentrate on films for the rest of my life.'

'Jenna, just look at the number of Hollywood actors who have been on Broadway. These days you're able to mix your career. And the good thing about becoming famous through films is that you get all the plum roles on stage offered to you. Just take one day at a time. You're very young. A lot of people here, including myself, think that you'll rise right to the top one day.'

Jenna blushed. 'Thank you, Daniel. You're right, of course. I've just had a lot of problems in the last few years and since I was a child I dreamed of being an actress and playing all the great roles. My mother was livid when I told her I was going to drama school.'

'Why?'

'I'm honestly not sure, Daniel. I've spent years trying to work it out. I think she's resented me from the day I was born. I presume it had something to do with my father.'

'You don't know who he was?'

'No. My mother would never talk about him. But he must have hurt her pretty badly. I always swore that I would never end up bitter and twisted like Joyce, my mother, has done.'

'Your mother never married?'

'No.'

'That was very unusual in the late Fifties, wasn't it?'

'Yes. But I don't know why she didn't. She never talked about the past.'

'Didn't you want to find out who your father was?'

'When I was younger, yes. I used to dream that when I was older I'd find him and he'd be like Daddy Warbucks in *Little Orphan Annie*. Then I grew up and realized that if he had wanted to see me, he would have found me, and I decided to forget about him the way that he'd obviously forgotten about me. Anyway, I had nothing to go on. I don't even know his surname.'

'Is Shaw your mother's name, too?'

'No, I use a stage name. My mother's name is Short. In fact it was Frankie who changed the Short to Shaw in our first term of drama school. She said it sounded far more actressy!'

'You said your mother's name was Joyce, didn't you, Jenna?'

'Yes. Why?'

'Oh, nothing. I . . . I used to know someone years back called Short. Look, Jenna, I have to make a move now. I have . . . I have an interview with the *LA Times*. I'd forgotten all about it. Sorry to rush off. I'll see you soon.' Daniel hurried out of the restaurant, leaving a bemused Jenna at the table.

He downed his fifth whisky in as many minutes. Unbearable memories were engulfing him. He knew that there was no one else to blame. He must suffer the pain as a man who kills another must suffer for his wrongs. He had escaped his punishment for twenty-five years. The memories were winning and Daniel couldn't stop them as they dragged him back into the past.

55

DANIEL DUVALL WAS BORED. The mind-numbing task of pouring endless coffee into the tiny espresso cups made his head ache as much as the deafening music.

It was September 1955, and the Heaven and Hell espresso bar in London's Soho was always packed. Daniel worked there as a waiter and he was rushed off his feet from the moment he arrived. Most of the other staff were like him, out-of-work actors and actresses.

He usually worked upstairs in Heaven. Soft music played and white clouds were painted on the ceiling. Downstairs in Hell, the lighting was low, the music loud and the black walls were painted with red flames. Today, one of the waiters had called in sick. The bastard was probably off to an audition, Daniel mused. So he was replacing him in Hell for the day. How apt, he thought, as Tennessee Ernie Ford's 'Sixteen Tons' blasted out of the jukebox yet again.

He was also pissed off because it meant that he would not be able to serve the girl with the blue eyes who had started coming into Heaven about two weeks ago.

He thought that she was the most beautiful girl he had ever seen. She had long blonde hair, which Daniel was convinced did not come out of a peroxide bottle, and huge blue eyes. She looked so innocent, with her ponytail and neat, white ankle socks.

Daniel had never had a problem getting women before. He knew all the waitresses fancied him and he had not been slow to take advantage of the fact. With his black hair, piercing chestnut eyes and smile that turned women's knees to jelly, he was a good-looking man.

But this girl was different. Daniel had really pushed out the boat, using his best chat-up lines and the smile – tried out in front of the mirror every day for two years until he didn't think it could be bettered – but the girl was having none of it. She smiled at him when he cracked a joke but then returned immediately to her conversation with her companion.

Of course, if she had batted her eyelashes at him and started falling for his charm, his interest would have disappeared. He would have probably screwed her and forgotten about her. But as his charm elicited no reaction from her, he decided he was in love with her.

This may have been partly because he was reading *The Importance of Being Earnest*, and he thought she would make the most perfect Cecily, with him of course playing Jack. He was an artist and artists did things like fall hopelessly in love with beautiful girls who hardly noticed their existence.

By eavesdropping on her conversation, he had eventually discovered that she was at the secretarial college round the corner. He decided the only thing to do was to hang round outside like Freddie in *Pygmalion*.

So, at half past four that afternoon, when his shift at the coffee bar had finished, he walked up to Tottenham Court Road and stood outside the entrance of the college.

Within minutes she came out and walked right past him, chatting to a friend. He set off behind them. They walked down to Cambridge Circus, then set off along Shaftesbury Avenue, Daniel keeping a discreet distance behind them. When the two girls arrived at Piccadilly Circus, they stopped to gaze in the windows of Swan and Edgar, and Daniel had to slow up. The blonde girl was pointing to something on display in the window. She giggled and the two of them disappeared inside the department store.

Daniel sighed, went down to the Underground to catch the tube back to his bedsit in Clapham, and played 'True Love' on his old gramophone until his neighbour banged on the door.

The next day, back up in Heaven, the girl did not appear. Daniel managed to change his shift for the following day. He went back to the college and waited for her to appear. At a quarter to five the girl emerged. She walked towards him.

'Hello,' she said shyly.

For the first time in his life, Daniel Duvall was at a loss for words. 'Hello' was all he could mumble.

She stood there, waiting for him to say something else. When he remained silent, she smiled at him and walked off down the road.

In bed that night, Daniel made up his mind that

tomorrow he would ask her out. Tomorrow he would tell her that he was no ordinary waiter, but the boy who had been the best Hamlet that the British School of Drama had ever seen. Everyone had said so. So what if he'd been out of work? Even Laurence Olivier, who at this very moment was playing Macbeth at the Shakespeare Memorial Theatre in Stratford, had struggled when he first left drama school. Daniel had read that Olivier had resorted to inserting advertisements in *The Stage* and the *Daily Telegraph*, reading 'Laurence Olivier. At liberty'.

This type of story consoled Daniel. He knew he was headed for the big time. He just needed one break, that was all.

He had auditioned the week before for Birmingham Rep. It had gone well. Birmingham had a reputation as a breeding ground for young talent – Olivier himself got his first professional job there. Daniel felt this was a good omen.

He walked between the cracks in the paving, knowing that if he stepped on one, they would cast someone else. He ran to reach a lamppost before the big red bus passed it, because if the bus got there first, he would not be getting on that train to Birmingham. He felt the same about the girl. If he could have her, he was sure he would get the job.

The following day she emerged from the college as usual. Daniel thought that she looked even prettier than he remembered. He was sure she was wearing lipstick. She glanced in his direction, then set off at a quick pace down the road. Daniel knew that luck was in his favour because she was alone. He caught up with her and kept pace beside her. She glanced at him and said hello. He said hello back and again felt completely tongue-tied.

They reached the tube station. The girl said goodbye, and started down the steps.

Daniel was spurred into action. He caught her arm.

'Listen, please don't go yet. Come and have a coffee with me. My life may be in danger.'

She smiled, shook his arm away, and started down the steps.

Daniel filled his lungs. It was now or never.

'If thou leavest me now,' he proclaimed, letting all Rudi's voice-production lessons take wing, 'I must go from this place, and take my own life!'

Everyone on the steps turned round and stared. Except for the girl, who carried on.

'In other words, I love you and if you don't have a coffee with me, I'll top myself.'

She had reached the bottom of the steps. She turned and stared up at him. After a moment's hesitation she started to climb the stairs back to him. When she reached him, she stopped.

'What's your name?'

'Joyce Short.'

'I love you, Joyce Short. Now how about that coffee?'

Daniel saw her every night for two weeks. He was convinced that he was in love with her. It was three days before Joyce would allow him to hold her hand, and another four days before she would let him kiss her at the cinema while watching *High Society*.

They had gone to see Tommy Steele and his Steelmen

at the 2I's espresso bar, and Joyce had stopped being so shy. She had smiled and laughed and pulled Daniel up on the tiny floor to dance with her. He held her close on the last dance and she had put her arms round his neck and snuggled into his shoulder. Back at his bedsit, Joyce had allowed him to touch her small, pink breasts. Then she had insisted on going home. It had been another week before he made the journey under her skirt and touched the tops of her stockings. It was at the cinema during *Night of the Hunter* when, locked in a passionate embrace, Daniel's fingers had finally made it into her panties. It was also the day he had been told that he had got the job with Birmingham Rep. He insisted on taking Joyce to a pub after the film and buying them both a drink to celebrate. Joyce got tipsy. Back at his bedsit, he undressed her slowly, but by the time he entered her he was so filled with pent-up passion that he disgraced himself.

Daniel felt like a complete bastard. She had been a virgin and he had treated her like a whore. To make it up to her he said, 'You know I love you, Joyce. Come with me to Birmingham.'

Joyce went into college the following day and handed in her notice. She wrote to her parents, telling them that she was in love with Daniel and would marry him as soon as they had enough money. She knew it was pointless going home to see them in their small Warwickshire village and trying to explain. What she was doing broke every rule. But Daniel was worth it. Joyce was sure of that.

Daniel was shocked when Joyce told him what she had

done. He hadn't expected her to take him literally, but he'd asked her and there was little he could do.

They rented a small, seedy flat five minutes from the theatre. It reminded Daniel of the stage set from *Look Back in Anger*. Daniel went off every day to rehearse his small part as the Duke of Aumerle in *Richard II*. Joyce supplemented his meagre wage by taking temporary work as a typist. The two of them had little money, but Joyce always had a smile for him when he came home from the performance and had become eager to learn how to please him in bed.

After the six months in Birmingham, Daniel was offered a season at Sheffield. After Sheffield, Manchester. Joyce came with him, comforting him when he worried that he would never make it out of the repertory circuit, and telling him how handsome and talented he was when the local reviewers ignored his performance.

But in Bristol, Daniel began to change. Instead of going straight home to Joyce, he started going out with the other actors in the company to one of the small underground clubs that stayed open until four in the morning. He would not return home until the early hours. Joyce had found herself another secretarial position in an office and had to be at work by eight thirty. She would wait up until after midnight, then retire sadly to bed.

Sometimes Daniel would wake her up to make love to her. If she suggested that he might be a little drunk, he would become aggressive. He would throw things across the room and on more than one occasion she thought he would hit her. Usually he exhausted his anger and frustration by entering her. She would lie there, a dead body beneath him, until he was finished. He would roll over and fall into a drunken sleep while Joyce bit back the tears until the dawn broke. She knew she was losing him. The smile disappeared from her eyes and her pretty face became pinched and thin.

While at the Bristol Old Vic, Daniel won his first major role, as Malvolio in *Twelfth Night*. His leading lady, Mathilda Delahaye, had flaming red hair and green eyes. Daniel had never met a woman like her. She had been in a hit play in the West End and had shot to fame instantly at the age of twenty-four.

Mathilda's career had not progressed since that early success. She had married a well-known older impresario, but had been divorced by him acrimoniously two years later. He had spread the rumour that she was trouble and no one wanted to employ trouble in their theatres. So Mathilda was employed only by those directors who knew they were about to retire and who appreciated the way in which Mathilda showed how grateful she was.

One evening the cast of *Twelfth Night* were assembled in a Chinese restaurant after the show, when Daniel felt a hand on his thigh. The hand began to move higher. He looked to his left. Mathilda was talking avidly to the actor on her other side.

Her hand gently undid his fly and slipped inside his underpants. The touch of her fingers upon his cock was such a shock that he nearly spilt his wine. He was glad the restaurant was poorly lit and that most of the cast had been drinking for some time. The hand extracted his cock and then moved slowly up and down, touching it in exactly the right places. Mathilda was still talking to the actor next to her. Her hand was moving faster now. He knew he could not contain himself for much longer. Mathilda turned to him, waving a hanky and said, 'You asked for a hanky, Daniel dear?'

Daniel didn't go home that night.

Joyce knew but kept quiet. She had no choice. She loved him and if she lost him she would have nothing. She maintained her silence in the ensuing months as she accompanied him round the country. After Bristol his roles continued to get larger and the critics began to notice him.

In the spring of 1957 Daniel auditioned for the Shakespeare Memorial Theatre. He was offered a season with a string of good parts. He moved with Joyce to Stratford upon Avon, where they rented a cottage a brisk ten-minute walk from the theatre.

Joyce decided to surprise Daniel one night and went to meet him at the theatre. She walked the short distance and waited at the stage door.

She watched through the double doors as he came out of his dressing room. His back was turned to her as he put his arms around a girl and kissed her full on the mouth.

Joyce sat on the platform shivering with cold. The train to London was forty-five minutes late. She was the only person on the platform. She wanted to cry, but she wouldn't. She would go back to London and get a job and forget about him. Yes, she loved him and the thought of life without him was unbearable.

But she had some pride. And she couldn't take any more.

The train pulled into the station. Joyce watched as the passengers alighted. Her resolve failed her. She waited for the train to pull out of the station. Then she stood up and walked through the deserted streets in the direction of the cottage.

Daniel was all she had.

The new season brought him *Hamlet* and instant fame. Joyce watched as the papers catalogued Daniel's ambitions, what he liked to eat for breakfast and where he bought his clothes. But they never mentioned her. His new agent, Al Alperstein, had told Daniel it was not good for his image to have a live-in girlfriend. Al wanted every woman who came to see the show to believe that he was available.

Joyce didn't like Al. He was one of the top agents in London and was always arriving with another casting director to see Daniel's performance, but she didn't trust him. She didn't like the way Daniel hung on his every word. Joyce knew that Al would love to see the two of them part. Al was building a star. And stars were built on sex appeal as well as talent.

Daniel again began to stay out until all hours. He always had a valid excuse, 'this director wants to take me for dinner' or 'my agent tells me that the guy he's bringing tonight has me in mind for a Hollywood film'. Joyce reluctantly acquiesced and never asked why she had to sit at home alone. At least he came home, which was something. But she knew he was slowly slipping away and there wasn't a thing she could do to stop it.

One day in early October, there was a knock at the front door of the cottage. Joyce opened it and there, standing on the doorstep, was her sister Blanche.

Joyce experienced a rush of contrasting emotions, just as she had at home. Part of her was pleased to see her younger sister. And the other part . . . well, she was ashamed as a pang of jealousy shot through her as she saw just how beautiful Blanche had become.

Joyce watched her walk gracefully across the room and take off her coat, to reveal a body that had matured perfectly. There was only a year between them but it had always been Blanche who attracted attention. When they were children, people would stop her mother in the street, completely ignore Joyce and ooh and aah over Blanche. With her naturally blonde hair, flawless skin and big blue eyes, she really did look like the little angel people told her she was.

Joyce had wanted to hate her, but Blanche was so kind and gentle that she couldn't.

During her time with Daniel, Joyce's inferiority complex had faded. She had started to see herself in the mirror and realized that she too was a pretty girl. But as she looked at Blanche, she felt once more like a second-rate version of her beautiful sister.

'Joyce, I can't tell you how good it is to see you,' she said in her soft voice. 'I've missed you so much.'

'How on earth did you find us?'

'Well, Mum and Dad eventually told me that you'd run

off to marry an actor called Daniel Duvall. And I saw his name in all the papers when he was chosen to play Hamlet. My college organized a trip to see the play today and I explained to my teacher I wanted to visit my sister and I'd make my own way home. After the performance I went round to the stage door. The doorman gave me your address and here I am.' She smiled.

'Oh,' said Joyce. 'How are Mum and Dad?'

'Fine. I still don't think Dad's got over the shock of you running off with Daniel. When he got the letter you wrote he went mad. He said he didn't ever want you in his house again. Mum was okay, but she has to stand by Dad. I think it's terribly romantic. And for Daniel Duvall, I'd have done the same. I think he's gorgeous. When did you get married?'

'We didn't. We, er, decided to wait until Daniel's career took off and he was earning more money. We'll probably do it at the end of his season here.'

Blanche's eyes widened. 'Living in sin? Gosh, Joyce, how decadent! I don't think I'll tell Dad that. You know what he's like, being Catholic and all.' She lowered her voice. 'Is he here?'

'No. Daniel doesn't usually come home between performances.'

'Oh, well,' Blanche did not hide her disappointment. 'It's you I came to see. How are you?'

'Fine,' lied Joyce.

'Gosh, I bet it's exciting living with a famous actor! I'm sure you get to meet some really interesting people.'

Joyce nodded. 'Oh, yes. Sometimes.'

Blanche's nineteen-year-old blue eyes sparkled. 'I'm studying drama now. It's only at the local college in Warwick but I'm really enjoying it. When I told my friends that my sister was marri– living with Daniel Duvall, they all fell over! All the girls are in love with him.'

Joyce smiled. What else could she do?

There was a strained silence. Blanche wandered around the room. She picked up one of the framed photographs from the mantelpiece.

'Gosh, the girls would be amazed if they could see this photo of my sister with Daniel Duvall. Where was it taken?'

'Clifton.'

'Could I take it to show them?'

'Yes, so long as you send it back.'

'Course I will. Can we go and meet him at the stage door?'

'If you want. But he won't be finished for a couple of hours.'

'That's okay. We can have a cup of tea and a long chat before we go. I want to hear all your news.'

Joyce knew all was lost the minute he set eyes on her.

As soon as Blanche shook hands with him by the stage door, she stopped being the young, innocent schoolgirl and became a woman that Joyce knew was impossible for men, least of all Daniel, to resist.

Daniel suggested the three of them go across to the Dirty Duck for a drink. Joyce sat in silence as Blanche and Daniel discussed the theatre. Blanche told him about the play she was in at college.

'We ought to try and see it, Joyce,' Daniel remarked.

'Oh, would you come?' said Blanche excitedly.

Joyce escaped to the ladies'. When she got back, they were putting on their coats.

'I have to catch the train back to Warwick,' Blanche explained.

'I said I'd walk her to the station. There's no need for you to come, Joyce,' said Daniel quickly.

'Take care, darling. It's been lovely seeing you. We must keep in closer touch from now on. Goodbye.' Blanche kissed her.

'See you at home, darling.'

Joyce walked back to the cottage alone.

Daniel arrived home half an hour later, commented on what a sweet kid Blanche was, then took Joyce to bed and made love to her. Daniel did not mention Blanche's name again and, as time passed, Joyce wondered whether she had overreacted.

The run of *Hamlet* came to an end and Daniel suggested they stay at the cottage while he decided whether to sign for another season in Stratford or take one of the other roles that Al had lined up for him. He told Joyce that he needed to visit London to discuss his options with Al.

'Listen, sweetheart, I'll only be gone a few days. I would take you but you'd be so bored with me disappearing to business meetings all the time. I really think it's better if you stay here.'

Joyce, as always, acquiesced.

'Take care, sweetheart. I'll call you when I can. Love you.' Daniel kissed her goodbye and went off to catch the train to London. He did not return after a 'few days'. He did not telephone either. After two weeks, Joyce was frantic. She called a few of Daniel's London friends but they had not seen him. She tried Al constantly, but he was was always 'in a meeting'. Joyce implored his secretary to make sure he phoned her back, but he didn't.

A month after Daniel had gone to London, an airmail letter arrived.

Joyce recognized the writing. Her hands shook so much, she could hardly open it.

Dear Joyce,

This is the hardest letter I think I will ever have to write.

First, you should know that I still love you. You have to understand that in no way did I ever want to hurt you but something happened two months ago that was so powerful. At the very least, you deserve to know the truth.

I fell hopelessly, irretrievably in love with Blanche the moment I saw her. And she with me. We both, at the beginning, tried to ignore it. But it was just too strong for us to resist. We met in London and, well, decisions had to be made.

I was offered a good part in a film in Hollywood, along with a five-year contract. Blanche and I decided that I should take it and she should come with me. We thought that, under the circumstances, it was better to get away to give us all a chance to get on with our lives. We will be married next week, in Las Vegas.

We both feel terribly guilty for what we've done. But Joyce, you are young and beautiful with your whole life ahead of you. I'm sure that you'll quickly meet someone else.

I enclose some money. If you need more, please contact Al at his office. He knows that you may call and has agreed to let me know if you do.

Please forgive us.

Love,

Daniel

Three days later Joyce went to the doctor to get something to help her sleep. He insisted on giving her a full examination. Five days later, the doctor told her she was pregnant.

She called Al to ask for Daniel's address. He told her to send any letters to him and he would forward them.

When her letter arrived, Al opened it and read the contents. Al thought for a while before tearing it up. He dropped the pieces in the wastepaper basket.

Al was getting fifteen per cent of Daniel's earnings in the States and Daniel had just signed a five-year contract with United Artists to make four films. Al didn't want that going down the tube for the sake of some ex-girlfriend who was probably not pregnant anyway.

When Joyce did not receive a reply from Daniel, she moved out of the cottage, took a train to London, and managed to get a council flat in Hornsey. On the twenty-fifth of September 1958, in the maternity wing of the North Middlesex Hospital, Joyce gave birth to a baby girl.

The baby was named Jenna Mary.

The father's name was not on her birth certificate.

56

THROUGH THE WHISKY, and the memories, things began to fit painfully into place. Daniel knew that it was too much of a coincidence that Jenna had a mother named Joyce Short. The startling resemblance between his dead wife and Jenna was evidence enough. He had a call to make.

Al had retired years ago. He'd been old when he'd first taken Daniel on to his books. But he was still alive and drinking as much scotch as usual. Daniel usually took him to dinner when he was in London.

He called the number. The seconds ticked by as the phone rang. Eventually Al answered. Daniel asked the question that Al had been dreading for over twenty years. Al felt relief as he related information he should have imparted far too long ago. He listened to the strained, furious voice that berated him with words he would remember for the rest of his life.

He deserved them all. Daniel knew it and he knew it.

But that was the profession, and they both knew that, too.

Daniel woke, still fully clothed, early the next morning. He was about to reach for the bottle lying on the floor next to his bed when he decided that a sauna would be of more use.

As the heat struggled to cleanse his system, so his thoughts began to come with greater clarity. Not only did he have another daughter, and Jenna a father, but Frankie had a sister she deserved to know about.

He had no idea what name, if any, was on Jenna's birth certificate but it was obvious that Jenna was completely unaware that he was her father.

Daniel wondered if he should try and contact Joyce. Had she not realized that Jenna's best friend was also his daughter? Surely it was inconceivable that Joyce didn't know?

He decided against contacting Joyce for the present. She would not welcome any communication from him, he was sure of that, having hurt her the way he had. She would be a last resort if he failed to find anything to prove to Jenna that he was her father.

He came out of the sauna, showered and put on an old tracksuit. He climbed the stairs two at a time, opened the trapdoor to the attic and pulled down the steps.

He switched on a light and searched for the old suitcase. When he had last moved he had put it up here.

He found the suitcase and opened it. The faint smell of Blanche's Chanel No 5 came floating up at him. He gasped, the perfume bringing back a wave of memories. Daniel started removing clothes, books and photographs, praying that he would find the one thing that would give his newfound daughter proof.

There were photos of Blanche with Daniel. A dreadful shot taken on their wedding day. There was also a photo of the two sisters which he put to one side, knowing that that would go some way towards convincing Jenna his story was true.

Then he found the framed photograph of Joyce and himself that Blanche had taken from the mantelpiece of the cottage in Stratford and never returned.

He put everything back into the case and went downstairs clutching the photographs.

He took a framed photo of Frankie and Jenna in a still from *Rosie* from a shelf in the sitting room and put it alongside the others.

Joyce, Blanche, Jenna, Frankie.

Four women whose lives had been affected by his selfishness.

Joyce, who had borne him a daughter that by some twist of fate had been an identical version of the sister who had treated her so callously.

Blanche, who had never forgiven herself for hurting the sister she loved.

Frankie, whom he'd shunned for her entire childhood, for his own selfish reasons.

And Jenna, who'd been an innocent victim of the sins of her father.

Was there a way to repair the damage? He did not know. But he knew he must try. First he would attempt to repair the harm he had done to his relationship with Frankie.

Jenna? Well, he must think more carefully. He didn't want to cause her any more pain. But maybe they could establish a relationship and build a bridge to Joyce.

Daniel knew only that he had been given a chance to make amends and he intended to take it.

57

'JENNA, IT'S DANIEL. Is Frankie home?'

'Hello, Daniel. I'm afraid Frankie's out at the moment but I'm expecting her back shortly.'

'Well, can you have her call me when she gets home? I just want her to know how thrilled I am about the Oscar nomination.'

'I know. It's wonderful, isn't it?'

'Well, she deserves it. And can you ask her if she could cancel everything tonight and meet me here at eight. I want to take her out to celebrate and I won't take no for an answer.'

'Fine. I'll tell her.'

'Thanks, Jenna. Bye.'

Frankie's reaction was predictable when she arrived home and Jenna told her about Daniel's request.

'Oh, Jenna, I was going over to June's tonight to celebrate. She goes away on location tomorrow and I won't see her for ages.'

'Honestly, Frankie, you've seen June every night for goodness knows how long. Your father wants to take you out to celebrate. You're always complaining that he never calls and now that he has, you're moaning about it.'

'Okay, you've made your point. I get your drift, you're coming across loud and clear.' Frankie smiled. 'I'll call June and tell her that I'll be round afterwards.'

Jenna sighed and went back to the script that Mimi had sent her to read.

Frankie walked through her father's house and found Daniel in the sitting room in front of a roaring log fire.

'Hi, Pops, how are you?'

Daniel stood up and hugged his daughter.

Frankie was nonplussed at this unusual show of affection.

'Congratulations, darling! I can't tell you how thrilled I am. You deserve it. We all knew it was your film.'

Frankie sat down. 'Oh, it was nothing. I haven't won it yet, you know.'

'Have some Dom Perignon. Just getting nominated is a major achievement for a twenty-three-year-old.' Daniel smiled. 'Here's to you, sweetheart. You've made your father a very proud man.' Daniel handed her a glass of champagne. 'To success!'

Frankie took a sip. 'Thanks, Pops.'

He took a deep breath. 'Frankie, look, I'm not quite sure how to say this, but I feel that I owe you an apology.'

'What for?'

'I don't feel that I've been the father I should have been. I do love you, but I've never been quite sure how to show it. I just want us, somehow, to be closer.

But I'll understand if after all this time you feel that's impossible.'

Frankie stared at her father.

'You don't know anything about your mother. That's completely my fault, as the pain of talking about her after she . . . well, I just couldn't.'

Frankie managed to murmur 'I understand'.

'She was so beautiful and we were so happy. Oh, God! Frankie, I just went crazy. I wanted to run from everything that was a reminder of her, and as you were our daughter, I ran from you and never seemed to quite manage to come back. I'm so sorry for that. Please forgive me. I've been incredibly selfish and I know how cross your mother would be with me for treating you so badly. But I really do love you, Frankie. Can we start again?'

Frankie sat silent and still, as if in shock. Then, suddenly, she was in his arms and they were hugging and holding each other.

'Frankie, if you want to ask anything about your mother, I'll be glad to tell you.'

'What was she like?'

Daniel talked to her about Blanche, finally releasing the pain he had held inside for so long.

'I will never love another woman as I loved your mother for as long as I live,' he finished.

Frankie began to understand. Sympathy replaced animosity as she realized that her father had suffered too.

'Oh Pops, if only you'd talked to me!'

'I know, Frankie. We've wasted so much time.'

Frankie nodded. 'The times I've wanted to ask for your help and advice.'

'I've known that there's been something wrong for a while. Can you talk to me about it?' Daniel asked cautiously.

Frankie shrugged. 'I don't think you'd understand.'

'I think that's where you're wrong, darling. I have a feeling that I'd understand very well what it's like to be in love. Especially as it's a woman you're in love with.' Daniel waited tensely to see how Frankie would react.

'Did Jenna tell you? She was sworn to secrecy and –'

'No, Jenna didn't tell me. I guessed when we met her in the restaurant that night. I'm afraid it was written all over you. Don't worry, no one else knows.'

'Oh Pops, it's so hard . . .'

Daniel listened as Frankie told him about the problems she was having with June.

'Tomorrow she's going away on location with Nigel for two months and I'm going to be worried sick every night until she gets back.'

Daniel looked at his daughter. 'Frankie, you have two choices. You either sit around for the next few weeks feeling miserable and worrying night and day about whether June is behaving herself, or you say, right! I can't do anything about it even if I wanted to. And you just get on and enjoy yourself as best you can.'

Frankie nodded. 'I know. I'll do my damndest to get on with things but, honestly, I'm smitten.'

Finally, at half past one in the morning, they said good night.

'Thank you, Frankie, for making it so easy for me.'

'And thanks for listening to me, Pops. It felt good to talk to you about it.'

'Just you remember, if you have a problem, you come and see me and we'll try and sort it out together. And look after that other young lady who lives with you. I know you've been neglecting her lately.'

Frankie looked guilty. 'Yes, I have. Don't worry, she'll get my full attention in the next few weeks.'

'And after that, my girl, even when said make-up artist arrives back?' Daniel raised his eyebrows.

'I'll try, I promise.'

Daniel waved as the white Mercedes disappeared round the corner.

The first step was accomplished.

Now he must find a way to tell his other daughter the truth.

58

'I JUST CAN'T BELIEVE what you're saying, Frankie. You're telling me that you're not coming to the party in honour of the Oscar nominees because June is flying in tonight?'

'Yep. That's about the size of it,' Frankie said stubbornly.

'Why can't you see her tomorrow? Surely one night won't kill you?'

'Jenna, I'm sorry, but I haven't seen her for two whole months and some crummy party doesn't stand a chance against a night of passion with June.'

'Well then, why can't you invite her as well?'

'Oh, come on! You know exactly why.'

'Okay, but couldn't you go and see her afterwards?'

Frankie shook her head.

'I give up, Frankie, I really do.'

Frankie shrugged, then turned pale as the telephone rang. She rushed to pick it up and Jenna made a hasty exit from the room. She didn't want to hang around and listen to her lovelorn friend whispering sweet nothings down the receiver. She ran a bath and poured plenty of sweet-smelling oil into the water.

She climbed in, closed her eyes and pondered the party ahead. Once out of the bath, she dried her hair and painted her nails. Then she wandered into the sitting room in her wrap to find Frankie slumped on the sofa hugging a cushion.

'Well?' she enquired. 'What's wrong?'

Frankie went to the bar and poured herself a large vodka.

'Want one?' she asked Jenna disconsolately.

'No, thanks. Come on, Frankie. What did June say?'

'Nothing much. Just that she's exhausted and thinks she may have gone down with some kind of stomach virus. I'm seeing her tomorrow. She's having an early night and so am I.' She slugged back the vodka and poured herself another.

Jenna sat down. 'Okay. Now you have no excuse to miss the party so go and find a dress. You're coming tonight if I have to drag you there.'

'Nope. No can do. I promised June I'd have an early night.'

'Screw June!'

'I only wish I could!'

'Honestly, Frankie! You're incorrigible! So you're going to let your best friend traipse along to this shindig all alone? Huh! Some friend!'

Frankie looked guilty.

'Look, I know I'm way behind June in the popularity stakes, but what about all those times we dreamed of a night like tonight when we were at drama school? And you have an Oscar nomination, for God's sake! Just remember, my girl, this time next week, that statuette may be sitting on someone else's mantelpiece. You'd better enjoy being one of the "maybes" because once you've lost, who's going to remember you were nominated? Nobody, I'd imagine.'

'That was quite a speech, Miss Shaw, and I would certainly have given it at least a nomination, if not the award.' Frankie sighed. 'You're right. I have been behaving like a first-class pain in the arse and I apologize. You win. I'll go and get dressed.'

Jenna breathed a sigh of relief as Frankie disappeared off to her bedroom. She emerged thirty minutes later in a black dress made only of beads, which tinkled as she moved. She wore a matching skull cap.

'God, Frankie!' Jenna drew in her breath. 'You'll be the sensation of the evening in that.'

Frankie smiled modestly. 'Well, kiddo, you don't look so bad yourself.'

Jenna wore a simple midnight-blue sheath that hugged the contours of her body. She had a string of pearls around her neck and her hair was piled elegantly on top of her head.

They got into Frankie's Mercedes. Before she started the engine, Frankie turned and put her hand on Jenna's. 'Thanks, kid. I needed that talking-to. I love you very much, you know.'

'And I love you.'

The Mercedes roared out of the drive.

At least three hundred people were crowded into the ballroom at William Rossi's home. He was one of Hollywood's most successful producers and his recent film had received three Oscar nominations.

Jenna saw Daniel and fought her way through to him. She reached up and gave him a peck on the cheek.

'Hello, darling. How are you?' He returned her friendly kiss. Butterflies danced in her stomach. It was a feeling that had started to occur regularly when Daniel kissed her.

'Ah, two of my favourite stars together,' Mimi purred. She pulled Jenna close and whispered in her ear. 'There's someone I want you to meet tonight. He's directing a great script in which there's a wonderful part for you. He is *très, très* interested. So when I come and get you, put your sexiest smile on your face, okay?'

Jenna nodded and tried to stop herself giggling. Occasionally she could not believe that she was actually in Hollywood. Everyone spent more time performing in real life than they did on the screen.

She noticed Frankie was surrounded by a crowd of male admirers. She was performing consummately and the men were entranced. Jenna pondered how ironic life was.

Frankie was thinking the same. She liked men a lot, but she could never stop that feeling of revulsion when they touched her. She would rather be sharing a pizza with June at home than be the centre of attention of this group of men. But she had resolved to try and have a good time and was almost succeeding when she saw June float through the door on *his* arm. June had lied to her because she had wanted to come here with *him*. Frankie excused herself from her admirers and made her way to the bar. She ordered a double Bloody Mary, because that was how she felt: bloody. She downed the drink and ordered another.

There was only one thing to do. Fight fire with fire. It was time to come out of hiding and show June that Frankie Duvall could also play dirty.

She flirted outrageously and by twelve o'clock, any man that she chose would be hers for the night. She decided on Ron Berini, a thin, intelligent young actor whom she had worked with a while ago. She found him as attractive as she found any man and offered him a ride home.

She sailed past June with Ron's arm firmly around her and waved a cheery good night. June's face turned pale and it was obvious that she had not noticed Frankie until then.

She started the Mercedes and sped off down the drive. She felt guilty about not saying good night to Jenna but knew that Daniel would give her a lift home.

They arrived at the villa and Frankie poured brandies for both of them. She sat next to Ron and knew that she must move quickly, otherwise her resolve would weaken.

She kissed him full on the mouth and let his hands roam her body. She moved swiftly into the bedroom and took her clothes off. He was excited, she could see that from the way his small dick stood to attention. She took it in her mouth, knowing vaguely what to do but having no real experience. Ron did not seem to notice and groaned in pleasure.

'God, you're gorgeous! Do you know how I've fantasized about this?'

Frankie did not know or care to know and quickly

silenced him with a kiss. What June could do, so could she.

His hands were kneading her breasts. Frankie closed her eyes and tried to imagine June's soft feminine fingertips gently caressing her nipples, but it did not work.

He had a hard time entering her because she was so dry. He finally managed and launched himself into a series of what reminded her of press-ups. Frankie only felt pain. She stifled a cry, which came out like a groan and Ron took for pleasure.

'I'm gonna come,' he cried, 'I'm gonna join you, baby, here I go!'

Ron collapsed next to her.

'Was that as good for you as it was for me?' He stroked her thigh.

Frankie murmured a 'yes'. The only thing she could think about was climbing into the shower and scrubbing her body hard.

As she stood up she saw the blood on the white sheets. Ron saw it too.

'Hey, you're a kinky beast. Most girls don't like screwing when they have their period. I love it. It adds sensation, if you know what I mean.'

Frankie smiled falsely and hurried to the bathroom. Let him think what he wished. There was little point in telling him that he had just relieved her of her virginity.

She scrubbed her body viciously in the shower, but still came back into the bedroom feeling unclean.

Ron was asleep. She padded into the sitting room and grabbed a bottle of brandy. She downed one glass of brandy after another and started to cry softly. When the bottle was half empty she had a desperate urge to have another shower. She got unsteadily to her feet and wobbled to the sitting room door. Then she stopped.

No. A shower wasn't enough. She needed to submerge herself in gallons and gallons of clean, cold water.

She pulled on a coat and grabbed her car keys.

The engine purred to life. Frankie steered unsteadily out of the drive.

The nearby beach was in darkness. As Frankie stumbled over the dunes she was guided by the sound of the waves. She hardly noticed the biting February wind as she reached the edge of the ocean. She took off her clothes and shoes and walked naked into the sea.

The current pulled her farther and farther away from the shore. She stopped swimming, rolled over and gazed up at the black sky.

She closed her eyes and let the waves engulf her.

She heard a voice. A gentle, perfect voice. And it was calling her name.

She knew whose voice it was. She lay in the water remembering the safety and security of the place where she had started life.

The tension disappeared from her body.

'Daniel, have you seen Frankie?' Jenna asked, having just noticed June.

'I think I saw her disappearing out of the door a while back. It looked as though she was with someone.'

'Oh, well, maybe she went home. I can understand why. Have you seen who's here and who she's with?'

'Yes. And I'm worried, Jenna.'

'Me too. God knows how Frankie will take this. I'm going home to see if she's all right. Can you give me a lift if Frankie's taken the car?'

'Sure.'

The chauffeur stopped the limousine in front of Orchid Villa and Jenna got out.

'If there's a problem, call me.'

'I promise. Good night, Daniel.'

Jenna let herself in and nervously tiptoed to the closed door of Frankie's bedroom. She was relieved to hear the sound of snores. 'Thank goodness,' she whispered and retreated to her own room.

Jenna was woken by a loud banging. She opened her eyes. The banging continued, louder than before. She pulled on her robe and went to investigate. She walked to the front door and opened it to find a uniformed policeman on the doorstep and another in the patrol car in the drive.

'Is this Francesca Duvall's residence?'

'Yes. Is anything wrong?'

'Unfortunately there is,' the policeman replied.

'I'll go and get Miss Duvall. I think she's still asleep.'

'Sorry, ma'am, but I think you'll find that she isn't.'

'I'll go and see.' Jenna hurried to Frankie's bedroom. She knocked on the door and then opened it. A naked man was standing in the middle of the room rubbing his eyes.

Jenna checked the kitchen, bathrooms and pool. There

LOVERS & PLAYERS

was no sign of Frankie. She went into the sitting room. The officers were both there, looking at a photo of Frankie.

'She wasn't there, was she?' said one of them to Jenna.

'No, she wasn't. Please, can you tell me what's going on?'

'Are you a relative of Miss Duvall?'

'No, but I'm a close friend and I live here with her.'

'I'm sorry to inform you that we had a call early this morning from a man who had found the naked body of a woman on the beach about three miles from here. What we presume to be the victim's Mercedes was found abandoned farther up the beach. The investigating officer recognized the face from her films. We checked the computer and found that the car was Miss Duvall's. Of course, we'll need a positive identification but . . .'

The words became a blur as Jenna tried to make sense of them. Frankie dead on a beach? No, they must be wrong. She was a strong swimmer.

'I don't believe you. It must be someone else.'

The officer nodded sympathetically. 'Maybe, but we're pretty sure it is her. As we said, we need a relative to identify her.'

'Oh, my God!' Jenna put her head in her hands. 'Have you contacted her father?'

'No. We came straight to the address that the car was registered at. I think you better call him. Is there anyone else home at present?'

Jenna thought of the stranger in the bedroom. 'Yes, there's a man I don't know in her room.'

The officer nodded. 'I think I'd better have a word. Now, Miss – sorry, I don't know your name?'

'Shaw. Jenna Shaw.'

'Can you contact her father? I'm afraid he's going to have to come with us to the mortuary to identify the body.'

Jenna nodded. She picked up the receiver with shaking hands and dialled Daniel's number.

An hour later they arrived at the morgue. Jenna insisted she accompany a white-faced Daniel to identify the body.

Daniel signed the death certificate and drove them to his house. They didn't speak. They couldn't.

They sat for hours, Daniel holding tightly to his surviving daughter; Jenna mourning her best friend and the half-sister that she had never known she had.

59

'AND THE AWARD FOR Best Actress goes to...' The ageing film star fumbled with the envelope. '... Frankie Duvall!'

The entire auditorium rose as one. Daniel, tears streaming down his cheeks, stepped up on the stage to accept the award for his dead daughter. It took five minutes before the audience could be persuaded to sit. Then Daniel spoke.

'Ladies and gentlemen, I accept this award on behalf of my daughter, Fran –' His voice broke. He collected himself and started again.

'I accept this award on behalf of my daughter, Frankie Duvall. As I'm sure you know, she tragically drowned a week ago. All of you who knew my daughter will know I speak the truth when I say that she was a wonderfully warm-hearted, generous, beautiful person and ...' He paused to wipe his eyes. 'And now she is gone.'

Daniel's voice strengthened. 'I know that, if she had lived, she would have gone on to become one of the great actresses of our time. And I cannot think of a more perfect way to mark the end of a brilliant but tragically short career than for her to receive an award that is coveted by so many but awarded to so few. So on behalf of my daughter, Frankie Duvall, I say: thank you, goodbye and God bless.'

There was silence as Daniel descended the stairs. Then tumultuous applause as they cheered and clapped for the girl they would never see again.

Jenna sat silently in her chair. When Daniel returned she hugged him to her, so proud of the friend that she only wished was sitting in the empty seat next to her.

The past week had been a nightmare. Daniel had hardly been able to speak. So it had been Jenna who had arranged the funeral, Jenna who had arranged for a secretary to deal with the stream of flowers and letters of sympathy that arrived daily, Jenna who had received the grief-stricken June, whom Daniel refused to see. And it had been Jenna who insisted that Daniel accompany her to the Oscar ceremony and, if Frankie won, collect the award on her behalf.

She had dealt with the police who had at first suspected foul play and had ordered an autopsy. But when the pathologist had found the huge amounts of alcohol in Frankie's system and not a mark on the body, he had concluded that Frankie had swum out too far and been caught by the strong current. The coroner had recorded death by misadventure and dropped the case.

For Jenna and Daniel, the great mystery was the young

actor who had been in Frankie's room. He swore he had made love to Frankie, then fallen asleep immediately afterwards. The story had leaked out and, of course, it had looked wonderful in the newspapers. It had meant that Frankie's sex-symbol image was preserved and assured she took her secret to the grave.

Once the Oscar ceremony was over, it took Daniel and Jenna an hour to get out of the theatre. When they eventually arrived at Orchid Villa, Jenna asked Daniel if he would like to come in for a coffee.

'Make it a large cognac, sweetheart,' said Daniel, slumping on a sofa.

He took the glass from Jenna, who went to sit quietly beside him. Daniel sat in silence.

'Daniel, please listen to me. We both loved her very much, but you're torturing yourself. What would Frankie think of you behaving like this? She wouldn't want you to suffer the way you are.' Jenna put her arm round his shoulders and kissed his cheek. 'I'm going to get ready for bed. You're welcome to stay here for the night. I need to sleep and I think you do too.'

Daniel turned and watched her disappear from the room. He picked up the heavy statuette sitting on the table in front of him and traced his fingers along its contours. He put it back on the table and sighed. Jenna was right. He was torturing himself. One of his daughters had died, never knowing she had a sister. Now that he had lost one daughter, he was petrified that, if he told Jenna the truth, he would lose another.

But he knew he had to face the inevitable. Jenna *must* know. Not because she could find out any other way – if Joyce had not told her by now, he doubted she ever would – but because he owed it to her to put his feelings aside just for once. If he lost her, then that was the price he should pay for his sins.

He waited for her to come back into the room like a man condemned. His heart raced as she returned, looking fragile and pale in a silk dressing gown. This week had been hard on her, too.

It was now or never. He crossed to her.

'Jenna, I . . .'

She looked surprised at the anxiety written across his face. 'What is it?'

'Look. Sit down. There is something I must tell you. The thing is, I . . .'

The telephone rang. Jenna picked up the receiver.

'Hello.'

'Er, yes, is a Miss Shaw there?'

'This is Jenna Shaw. Can I help you?'

'Oh, er, yes. Sorry to bother you, dearie, but your agent give me the number of Miss Duvall's 'ouse. She said you lived 'ere.'

'Who is this, please?'

'This is Mrs Tab, as lives next door to yer mum.'

Jenna's face remained impassive as she listened to what Mrs Tab had to say. She jotted down her telephone number on a piece of paper. 'Thank you for ringing me. I'll be in touch as soon as I've made the necessary arrangements.'

She put down the receiver and slumped into a chair.
'What's happened, Jenna?'
'I have to go to London. My mother is dead.'

60

JENNA'S LOSS SHOOK Daniel out of his own sorrow. He booked two first-class tickets to London on the next available flight. He needed to be with her. It was the least he could do.

He had been unable to tell Jenna of her birthright. She looked so fragile and pale, he thought the news might break her. But at least he could perform his fatherly duties without her knowing, and help her bury the woman who had given birth to his child.

The funeral was held in the small Catholic church that Jenna had visited as a child every Sunday. There were few mourners.

Jenna had been numb at the funeral, unable to feel anything. But as she sorted through her mother's meagre belongings, she sobbed for the woman she had spent so much of her life trying to please. She cried for the years the two of them had wasted and for the miserable existence that Joyce had led. She had died as she had lived – alone. Jenna felt terrible for not being there to comfort her at the end. She wondered, if life had been different for Joyce, whether they could have been friends. But something had happened to Joyce that had ruined her ability to love.

Having given Joyce's belongings to a local charity shop, Jenna wandered round the deserted rooms of the small flat for the last time. It was the end of an era. Time to put the past behind her and take what she wanted before it was too late.

She closed the door sadly behind her and caught a taxi to the Hilton, where she and Daniel were staying. Her mind was made up.

Daniel sat in the bar waiting for Jenna. Since they had arrived in London, Daniel had held his breath, expecting Jenna to confront him with evidence she had found in a drawer as she emptied her mother's flat.

He saw her walking towards him. Every man in the bar turned to look at her as she sat down opposite him.

'Okay, buy me a vodka and tonic. I've finished sorting everything out, so we can fly back tomorrow.'

Daniel ordered drinks. 'That's good news. I know how unpleasant it must have been.'

'Yes, it was. I just feel so dreadfully sorry for my mother. She was an intelligent woman. She could have done so much more with her life. Whatever it was that happened to her prevented her from enjoying life and I can't help but feel bitter at the way it made her feel towards me.'

Luckily for Daniel, the drinks arrived. He raised his glass. 'To the future!'

Jenna smiled at him. 'Yes. Here's to us.' She drained her glass. She was going to need a little Dutch courage tonight, for it was she who must make the first move. Out of the tragedies of the past few weeks, the bond between Daniel and herself had grown. And Jenna wanted more.

They went downstairs and ate in Trader Vic's. At the end of the meal Jenna plucked up her courage.

'Would you like to come to my suite for a drink? I don't feel like being alone just now.'

Daniel nodded. 'Of course.'

They stepped out of the lift and Jenna unlocked the door to her suite.

She poured two generous whiskies and sat next to Daniel on the sofa.

'I just want to say how grateful I am that you came with me. I really couldn't have got through without you, Daniel.' She looked straight into his eyes and leaned forward.

Daniel, being a professional in the game of love, should have noticed the look in her eyes, but all he could see was his beautiful daughter smiling at him. So when she kissed him full on the mouth, with such force and passion that he literally had to tear himself away from her, he let out a shocked 'Noooh!' He quickly moved away from her and sat in a nearby armchair with his head in his hands. When he looked up, Jenna was staring at him in horror and shame.

'I ... I'm sorry. I just, well, I thought ... Look, please go now. It's my fault. Please go.' She started to cry.

He wanted to comfort her as a father, but he could not, so he sat there, uncertain of what to do.

'Please go. I should never have thought that you felt the same way I did. I'll get over it. I usually do.'

'Jenna, I do love you. I love you more than anything. But I . . . I . . .' Daniel searched for the words.

'It's just that you don't want me in that way. I understand.'

'No, Jenna, you really don't understand.' Daniel braced himself. The time had come. She had to know.

'Jenna, I'm going to tell you a story that you ought to have known a long time ago. I will tell you as honestly as I can, leaving nothing out, and then you can make your own decisions. Please believe everything I say. I'm telling you this because I love you so very much and have not told you before because I'm a selfish old man and did not want to lose you.'

So he told her, watching her face change from astonishment to shock and then finally to anger. When he finished, the two of them sat there in silence. Then Jenna stood up.

'I believe you. I don't need or want to see the photos because even a bastard like you couldn't make up a story like that.' Her eyes blazed. 'You destroyed my mother and you nearly destroyed me. Well, *Daddy dear*, I promise you one thing.' She spat out the words. 'If you ever try to contact me again I'll make sure every home in the world knows what a bastard Daniel Duvall really is. "I didn't know I had a child" must be the oldest line in the book. Surely, if you're half the actor you pretend to be, you could have thought up something more original than that!'

Jenna walked towards him and slapped him across the face. 'Get out of my room and out of my life *now*!'

Daniel stood up and left the room.

Jenna crumpled on to the floor and sobbed. It was the best performance she had ever given. All she had wanted to do was run into his arms and make up for all the years they had wasted. But she couldn't. She owed her mother. And, like her mother, she'd loved him too.

When Daniel woke the next morning, he was informed that Miss Shaw had checked out. So he did the only thing he could. He went to Heathrow and got a flight back to the one place he fitted in.

61

WHEN JENNA HAD WALKED OUT of the Hilton Hotel at eight thirty the following morning, she had hailed a taxi and given the address of her London bank. Since the bank did not open until nine thirty, she had installed herself in a nearby café and read a newspaper. She was the first customer through the door when the bank opened.

After asking to see the manager, she had sat in his office and explained that she wished to close her account immediately. The manager had confirmed that 'Miss Shaw' had over ninety thousand pounds in her deposit account.

'I can close the account now but it will take us twenty-four hours to get that amount of money for you. If you really want it today, the best I can do would be five thousand in cash and a cheque covering the remainder. You will of course be penalized for such a quick withdrawal. Are you sure you can't wait for the money?'

'Yes, I'm quite sure I want the money now. Five thousand in cash and a cheque will be fine. I'd like the cheque made out to Mary Short.' She wrote it down for him. 'It's my maiden name, not my stage name. Here, it's on my passport,' Jenna showed him.

At one o'clock she was sitting in a first-class compartment on a train headed for Leeds. The cash and cheque were tucked securely into the pocket of her handbag. She just had to get away from London, and Leeds sounded safe and anonymous.

She never got there. The train broke down at Leicester and everyone was asked to get off and wait for the next train to Leeds, due in two hours. Jenna went into the buffet and sipped a lukewarm cup of tea. A scruffy young man came and sat opposite her. Every time she looked up he was staring at her. She thought of the large amount of money she was carrying. She was also beginning to feel dreadfully tired. She went to the station forecourt, found the information desk and asked for the name of a nearby hotel. The clerk told her that the Grand Hotel was a two-minute walk away.

Jenna found the hotel and booked a room for the night. She asked the receptionist to put her cheque, cash and passport in the hotel safe. A porter showed her to her room. Once he had gone she sank exhausted on to the bed and closed her eyes.

When she awoke, it was nine o'clock the next morning. She felt rested and hungry. Room service brought her a large cooked breakfast of the sort only found in English hotels.

She took a bath, then felt like some fresh air. She stepped out of the hotel and strolled up Granby Street.

After walking for ten minutes she came to a large expanse of beautifully kept grassland.

Jenna sat on a bench and tried to collect her thoughts.

Yesterday her only concern was to get as far away from Daniel as possible. Now, here she was, in a town that she had no connection with wondering what she was going to do with the rest of her life.

There was only one thing she was sure of. The 'business' corrupted. It took artistic people and sacrificed them on the altar of money and fame. It drained them and used them until they didn't know who they were.

Jenna thought of what it had done to her. What it had done to Frankie, her mother and her father. She wanted no more of it.

She sat on the bench for a long time.

There was no going back. She had to try and start again. But where? How? What should she do?

She had enough money to help her make a new life. What other skills did she possess? She remembered how her mother and the nuns had suggested she should go to business college. Her exam results had certainly proved that she possessed an aptitude for figures.

Where should she live? Jenna looked around at the pleasant park and shrugged. She supposed here was as good as anywhere.

She wandered back to the hotel and booked in for the rest of the week. That would give her the time to look round Leicester.

She needed to change her appearance. The last thing she wanted was someone recognizing her.

She found a hairdressers and asked the stylist to cut her long mane into a short bob. Then she went to a chemist's and bought a hair colorant. She went back to the hotel and dyed her hair a mousy brown. She darkened her eyebrows to match.

When Jenna looked in the mirror, she was astonished.

'How do you do, Mary Short,' she said.

The following day, she opened an account in the name of Mary Short and deposited the cheque and most of the cash, just keeping enough to pay her hotel bill.

Then she set about thinking what she was going to do with her life.

A visit to the main library in the centre of the town gave Jenna a list of possible courses at local colleges that looked interesting. However, as it was late March, these full-time courses were almost into the summer term and she was told by the lady at the library that it would be September before she could enrol for the start of a new course.

'Why don't you try one of the night-school courses? There are plenty that only run from term to term.' The lady handed her a sheaf of leaflets and Jenna went back to the hotel and studied them. She decided to try a basic typing course for a term. The skill would always come in useful and it would be a gentle entry back into the world of learning.

The next step was to find somewhere to live. She found a pleasant flat to rent in an area called Stoneygate, a ten-minute bus-ride from the city, enrolled on her typing course and moved in.

Jenna spent her days looking round houses for sale. She

felt she needed to make her decision to stay in the town as permanent as she could and the security of owning her home appealed to her.

After a month of house hunting, she found a pretty Edwardian terraced house that over-looked the park she had sat in. It needed extensive renovation and repair, but she bought it for thirty-five thousand pounds and paid cash.

For the following three months, she spent her time supervising the renovation work necessary to transform the house back to its original splendour. Once the builders had installed central heating and a new kitchen and bathroom, Jenna left her rented flat and moved in. She scoured the many antique and second-hand furniture shops for bargains and by the middle of August, she had completed the transformation.

Having thoroughly enjoyed her typing course, she felt confident enough to enrol on a full-time business course at a local college of further education.

In September she began the course and found that she loved it. And she enjoyed coming home and spending the evenings poring over an essay by the fire in her cosy sitting room.

One Saturday afternoon in November, she was sitting in a tea shop feeling pleased with the print she had found in the shop next door, when the girl opposite her said 'Shit!' in a very loud voice.

Jenna looked up. An unusual but striking face stared back at her. The girl had very pale skin, made paler by the extravagant use of bright-red lipstick. Her green eyes were a little too close together and her long brown hair fell almost to her waist.

'Bollocks!'

'Is something wrong?' asked Jenna.

'Yep. I've left my purse in the laundrette.' The girl emptied the entire contents of her large bag on to the table. She shook her head. 'I wonder if they'll let me do the washing-up.'

Jenna laughed. 'You've only had a cup of tea. I'll lend you the money.'

'Would you? I'll take your address and send it to you.'

'Don't worry. I think I can run to thirty pence.'

'No, I always pay my debts. Here, write down your address.' She handed Jenna a piece of paper and a chewed pencil.

'Thirty one Clarendon Park Road. That's just round the corner. If you're in tonight I'll bring it round.'

'Yes, I will be, but you really don't need to worry.' Jenna said as she paid the waitress for the two cups of tea.

'My name is Hilly O'Neal. I'll see you at seven with the dosh. Thanks again.'

Hilly walked out of the door and Jenna went home, never expecting to see the girl again.

At half past seven the doorbell rang. Hilly was standing on the doorstep, looking bedraggled.

'Here's your money.'

'Thank you. But you shouldn't have bothered, especially in this terrible weather. Why don't you come in until the rain eases up?'

'If you wouldn't mind.'

Hilly came in and dried off in the sitting room while Jenna made some tea. Hilly chattered away about her course at the local polytechnic, where she was studying knitwear design. Then about her family.

'I'm the baby girl. All the rest are boys. Four big brothers. It's amazing I'm not horrendously spoilt. They treat me like a little doll.'

Jenna poured more tea as she heard about the airline pilot, the journalist based in South Africa, the actor in Canada and the youngest, who was a policeman. She discovered that Hilly was a Gemini, which was the reason she constantly changed her mind about everything from boyfriends to the colour scheme in her bedroom.

At ten o'clock, Hilly glanced at her watch. 'Oh dear, doesn't time fly when you're having fun? I'd better go. Thanks for the tea. Listen, why don't you come round to my place tomorrow? I've hardly let you get a word in edgeways this evening, have I?'

Jenna laughed. 'I enjoyed it, Hilly. And I'd love to come round.'

'Great. Would eight be all right? Good. Bye, Mary.'

Jenna went to sleep looking forward to seeing Hilly again.

The two girls started to see each other regularly over the next couple of months. Hilly was very easy to talk to and Jenna found herself relaxing more and more in her company. At the end of January, Jenna asked if Hilly would like to move into her spare bedroom as a lodger. Hilly said yes immediately and arrived a week later in a borrowed Beetle full of her things.

The house that had been so quiet came alive with Hilly's presence. She fell in and out of love every week. And each short-lived love affair had a song to go with it. Hilly had a cassette which she called 'These I have loved' and when she was feeling depressed she would play the tape, which ranged from Led Zeppelin to Richard Clayderman.

Flamboyant and eccentric by nature, she said exactly what she thought no matter where she was. She was also a very talented twenty-one-year-old. Jenna had seen some of her knitwear designs. They had an originality and freshness that could not be taught.

'What are you going to do once you've finished your course?' asked Hilly one evening. 'I don't wish to offend, but I don't exactly see you as the office-bod type. Come to think of it, I don't see you as a Mary either. Mind you, I'm a Hilda, really, so there we go.'

The thought of Hilly being christened Hilda made Jenna giggle. 'I don't know yet,' Jenna mused. 'Anyway, I've still got four months to think about it. It's only March. I love the course, though. What about you?'

Hilly shrugged. 'Well, I suppose it's off to some huge conglomerate to start at the bottom and wait until they fire me three weeks later because I won't work in acrylic. I mean, what I'd really like to do is to go into business by myself. You know, have a little shop where I sell my knitwear. Trouble is, I haven't got a bean to put into it and wouldn't know where to start as far as the business side is concerned.'

That night Jenna lay in bed and thought about their conversation. Hilly was right. She would soon have to decide what she wanted to do. She had been thinking of applying to Leicester University and doing a law degree. But Hilly had just given her an idea.

After making various preliminary enquiries she decided the time had come to ask Hilly for her opinion.

Jenna booked a table at a local restaurant and over dinner outlined her idea.

'Well, what do you think?'

'Mary, you've just described my dream. What do you think I think?'

'You like the idea, then?'

'It's outrageous, but yes, I love it.'

'Don't get too excited yet. I've still got to examine it more thoroughly.'

'I know, I know. But, oh, wouldn't it be wonderful?'

'Yes, Hilly, it would.'

Jenna's idea was to open a small boutique from which they would sell an exclusive range of knitwear, designed by Hilly. In the following weeks Jenna went to see her bank manager, an accountant and several estate agents. With the help of the accountant, she drew up a rudimentary business plan and painstakingly checked and re-checked the figures. If the project went ahead, every penny she had left in the bank would be needed, so it was crucial that the figures be realistic.

Jenna believed Hilly had a real talent that, if marketed correctly, could yield both of them a good living. This was confirmed when Hilly won the Best Original Knitwear Design award at her polytechnic and two thousand pounds. Soon afterwards she was offered a job by a high-profile chain store in the knitwear-design department. Jenna knew the time had come to make a final decision.

'Okay, Hilly, make yourself comfortable and listen to what I've got to say. What you have to know is that I'm not a financial expert. I'm going to be learning as I go along. I want us to start small. Apparently the first year is the toughest and the time when most small businesses go under. If we can get through that, we'll stand a chance. What the accountant has suggested is that we set up a limited company, each owning half the issued shares. That will protect our personal assets if we do go under. What I can't offer you is security like the other job you've been offered, but you will be your own boss.'

'Mary, as far as I'm concerned there really isn't a choice. If things do go wrong, I'm sure I'll be able to find a job with a large store in the future. But not before I've given this a damn good try. And by the way, here's something to go in the kitty.' Hilly waved her cheque for two thousand pounds at Jenna. 'How are we going to finance this?'

'Well, if you put in that two thousand and I put in the same, that gives us a share capital of four thousand pounds. I was also planning on making the company an interest-free loan of twenty thousand pounds from my savings.'

'So you're willing to take a chance on me?'

'If you're willing to do the same.'

Jenna went to open the waiting bottle of chilled champagne.

'You weren't pre-empting this by any chance, were you?' Hilly laughed.

'No, I thought we could console ourselves with it if we'd decided against it. But as we haven't, here's to – Oh, Hilly, we've not chosen a name yet.'

'Shit, that's a rather important point we've forgotten. Any ideas?'

'What about Milly? It uses both our names and it sounds young and fresh.'

Hilly repeated it a few times. 'I like it, Mary. Right, then, here's to Milly Limited!'

They raised their glasses.

62

FOR THE NEXT FOUR MONTHS the two girls lived, breathed and worried over Milly.

Jenna had found them premises in a newly built plaza in the city centre. Although the rent was more than she had wanted to pay, Jenna felt location was critical and the plaza was filled with other small boutiques, so their shop would catch a lot of passing trade.

While Jenna worked on the interior of the boutique with a designer, Hilly installed herself in the small studio-cum-office above the shop and set to work. It had been decided that to begin with, Hilly was going to design each sweater individually, with a range of ten following a particular theme. She favoured bright primary colours with intricate patterns knitted into each one. They had invested in one knitting machine, which they installed in the studio. If the business expanded, they planned to farm the extra work out to knitters who worked from home.

'How much do you think we ought to be charging per sweater?' asked Jenna one evening.

Hilly shrugged. 'Well, some sweaters take me two

days to make, some two weeks. I suppose we price accordingly.'

'We can't become outrageously expensive or we'll scare the customers off. On the other hand, because we're giving each customer a one-off, and we have to make them appreciate that, we must charge more than chain-store prices. We're aiming at the upper end of the student market and young working women. How about we set a middle price of forty pounds and work up or down from that?'

Hilly nodded. 'That feels about right. The quality of the wool we're using is second to none. Let's hope that once they've bought one and seen how well it wears, they'll come back for more.'

By the end of August, the boutique was almost finished.

The workmen had left a week before and Jenna had been busy making finishing touches. She had asked Hilly to come downstairs and take a look.

'So what do you think, Hilly?'

Hilly wandered around, taking in the curtains that Jenna had hung in a pretty pastel flower print in the window in front of the shop and across the changing rooms. The walls were cream, the floor stripped pine and there were baskets of dried flowers strewn around the boutique.

'I feel as though I'm in a country cottage.'

Jenna was pleased. That was the exact effect she had been trying to create.

'You don't think it's too twee, do you?'

Hilly shook her head. 'No, Mary, I don't.'

'When I was on that business course, one of the lecturers said that finding a strong image was essential. As you're making sweaters out of a natural product and everyone seems to be becoming so conscious about the environment, I thought this would give the shop the right image.'

'Seriously, Mary, I think its fab, I really do.'

'It'll look even more fab when we start filling the shelves with something we can sell.'

The grand opening was set for September the twentieth and they sent out invitations to anyone they could think of.

'Are you ready for this?' Hilly asked Jenna nervously.

It was ten to six in the evening of the twentieth and the two of them were standing in the boutique dressed in sweaters emblazoned with 'Milly'.

'As ready as I'll ever be.'

Jenna took a deep breath and unlocked the door. She peered out. The plaza was deserted. 'Don't all rush in at once,' she remarked.

At half past six they were still sitting by themselves.

'Fancy a glass of sparkling wine?' Jenna surveyed the thirty bottles lined up on the bar.

'Why not?' Hilly answered morosely.

They finished their glasses in a second and Hilly poured them another. 'Where is everyone?'

Jenna shrugged. 'I don't know. Have faith, Hilly. I know they'll be here.'

She was right. At seven o'clock a friend of Hilly's from the Poly arrived with a group of eight others.

Jenna breathed a sigh of relief. By half past seven the shop was crammed with people.

At nine the last person left. They had sold almost every sweater in the shop.

The two girls hugged each other and danced round the shop.

'We did it!'

'They raved about my designs.'

'Who said it was going to be difficult? Just look at these empty shelves!' said Jenna.

They both went to bed that night dreaming about Milly boutiques opening around the world.

The following day they came down to earth with a bump. Jenna sat in the boutique all day and served four customers, three of whom did not buy anything. The next two weeks followed in a similar vein.

'Don't worry, I'm sure that once the cold weather arrives people will be crying out for our sweaters.'

Jenna shook her head. 'I don't know, Hilly. The point is that once they're in the shop, one out of ten customers buys. They all seem to love the product.' She went back to her figures. 'What we need is fifty people every day to walk through that door. Then we'd sell five sweaters a day, which would adequately cover our costs and eventually start to show a profit. The trouble is, for every day that we sell little or nothing, it's going to take us longer to get into profit.'

Two weeks turned into three months and still the trickle of customers was slow. Jenna put a halt on ordering any more wool and suggested Hilly use up what she had and stop at that. They had stock piled everywhere and money was dwindling as Jenna paid out for advertising, rent, rates, electricity, telephone and other seemingly endless bills.

Jenna knew that if things didn't pick up soon they could last only another six months. She had tried everything she could think of, but short of accosting people in the street and dragging them by force into the shop, there was little more they could do.

'We just need exposure. I know the product we're selling is second to none.'

It was Saturday night and the two of them were making their way through a large bottle of cheap supermarket wine.

'Well, I come to the end of the wool next week. Then what do I do?' asked Hilly.

'You can come and play "I spy" with me in the shop to while away the long hours of boredom.'

Their January sale improved turnover a little but by February Jenna was thinking of closing the boutique down.

'I'm so sorry, Hilly. Maybe it's me. I had no real experience. I thought the money we had would last much longer than it has done. And I didn't expect sales would be quite as bad as they have been. We'll give it until the beginning of March and then, well, we're going to have to close.'

Hilly nodded sadly. 'Mary, you've done everything you can. It's not you. If it's anything it must be that my designs haven't appealed to people. At least we gave it a shot.'

The following Wednesday a young girl walked into the shop.

'Hello,' she said to Jenna. 'I'm from the Leicester Haymarket Theatre. Someone at the polytechnic told me about your boutique and I was wondering whether you could help us out.'

'We can try,' said Jenna.

'Well, we're doing a musical in which the director has decided that each member of the cast needs to have an individual design on the front of his sweater and his or her name on the back. It's a statement thing. I can explain in more detail if you think you might be able to help us. They'll have to be made in very light-weight cotton as it gets very hot under the lights.'

Jenna nodded as if she had no idea that this was the case.

'I'm sure we can help you. Why don't you pop upstairs and see Hilly? She's our designer and if you explain what exactly it is that you want, she should be able to come up with something.'

'Fine. Our wardrobe department just doesn't have time. We need twenty individual sweaters and they have to be finished in about three weeks. Is that possible?'

The girl went upstairs to see Hilly and Jenna sat with baited breath until she reappeared.

'Hilly is coming over to the theatre this afternoon to see the director. She thinks she can do them in time. Do I talk price with you?'

'Yes, but let's wait until Hilly has seen the director and we know exactly what he wants.'

Four weeks later the musical opened to rave reviews. Hilly's sweaters looked magnificent. Jenna took out a full-page advertisement in the programme and held off closing the boutique for another month.

A week after the show opened, the trickle of people coming into the shop turned into a steady flow. In April Jenna took more money than she had in the six months since Milly opened. Everyone wanted a sweater with their name on like those they had seen in the play.

Until now Hilly had been able to produce enough sweaters by using their one knitting machine. But as demand grew, they put an advert in the local paper asking for experienced knitters who could work from home. Leicester was a knitwear town and they quickly found five ladies who had machines and produced good-quality work.

Jenna employed a pleasant young girl named Sophie to help her in the shop so that she had a little more time to devote to the mounting paperwork.

Things became more hectic when Hilly was asked to design a new batch of sweaters for the musical's transfer to the West End.

'If things go on like this, we might even see a profit this time next year,' said Jenna jubilantly one night. The musical had started off a chain reaction, and people were beginning to travel substantial distances to buy a sweater from Milly.

'Are you going to come to the opening night, Mary? I think you should.'

Jenna shook her head. She was not ready to step back into a theatre just yet.

'No thanks, Hilly. I'm up to my eyes in re-orders and I have the accountant coming in next week. You go and have a good time.'

'Spoilsport,' murmured Hilly.

'I think you ought to start looking for an assistant. We've got a backlog of over fifty orders all wanting individual designs and more coming in every day.'

'Okay. I'll go to the fashion show at the Poly next month. I'm sure I can find someone there.'

Hilly chose a young man whose ideas followed the same themes as her own. Jenna liked the quiet, shy Ari who seemed prepared to work the same long hours as Hilly. Only a month later did she glance up from her cashbook for long enough to realize that that Hilly and Ari were having an affair.

Occasionally Jenna missed the time she used to spend with Hilly, but she found her increasingly heavy workload stimulating and time-consuming.

And she had big plans.

63

A YEAR AFTER MILLY had opened its doors, Jenna ordered champagne in the restaurant of the Grand Hotel.

'This is a touch extravagant, isn't it, Mary?' Hilly said.

'I think we deserve it. Last month we finally went into profit.'

Hilly and Ari both cheered.

'And I have something else to show you.' Jenna handed a large brown envelope across the table to Hilly, who tore it open and surveyed its contents. Her eyes lit up. 'Look, Ari, it's the plans for a boutique in Covent Garden. Oh, Mary, you sneak! Why didn't you tell me?'

'I wanted to make sure it was possible first. I knew how disappointed you'd be if it fell through. We've had a stroke of luck with the premises. They're trying to encourage small businesses to move into the development, so we can get the lease at a very reasonable price. It's a good moment to expand, with the economy looking set to grow. The bank is falling over itself to help us. Of course, I need the okay from you as the other shareholder in the company before I sign the –'

'Yes, yes yes!' cried Hilly, as Jenna knew she would.

'This will take an awful lot of organization. If possible, I want the new boutique open by in March. Also, how would you two feel about moving to London? There's a large room above the shop that would make a good studio for you both to work in.'

'Well, I think we could handle that.' Ari laughed.

'I'll move into the space above the shop here, since I'm beginning to need more of a proper office than my third bedroom.'

'Good idea,' said Hilly. 'Ari and I will have to find a flat to rent in London.'

'Do you mind moving? I just thought it would be best to have one of us on the premises of each boutique.'

'I agree. But you will come to London regularly, won't you, Mary?' said Hilly.

'Of course. I think we should promote Sophie to manageress of the Leicester shop. She's efficient and I trust her. We'll also need to employ an assistant to help her. But that will leave me free to float between the two shops and concentrate on the actual running of the business.'

'Presumably we'll need a manager and an assistant for the London boutique,' said Ari.

'Yes. In fact I'm going to interview for two full-time and two part-time staff. Then we'll have back-up if we need it. The higher theft level in London has to be taken into account.'

'Mary, surely we're going to have to more than double production?' said Hilly.

'Well, I've thought about this long and hard. At the

moment we're producing two hundred sweaters a month. What I suggest is that we duplicate each design to sell in London. How do you feel about that?' asked Jenna.

'I think it's the only thing we can do, although it means we'll lose the cachet of every design being a one-off,' said Hilly.

'I don't see how else it can be done without employing another two designers, which at present we can't afford. What do you think, Ari?'

'I agree with you, Mary. We can hardly find the time to design what we need at the moment, let alone doubling our workload. I suggest we see how it goes.'

'Let's try it and see how it works,' said Hilly.

'Then I'd like to propose a toast to Milly of Covent Garden.' Jenna smiled.

The London shop opened on schedule in March 1987. Jenna kept the theme of the boutique the same and was pleasantly surprised at the amount of business they did in the first few months.

In October, Jenna travelled to London for a conference with Hilly. They went out for lunch in Covent Garden.

'We really have to decide where we're going to go from here, whether we want to expand into a chain of Millys all over the country or keep it the size it is now. If we expand much further, the whole concept of Milly will change.'

'I don't know how you feel, Mary, but Ari and I don't want that.'

'I agree. I think the quality of the product which has given us our success will suffer. If we expand much more we would have to think about a small factory. I also find it hard to see the economy growing for ever. I think we should open one more shop in the southwest and leave it at that. I've seen a site in Bath that would be perfect for us. And talking of Ari, I was going to ask you whether we should make him a director. He's been with us a long time and deserves a share of Milly's success.'

'Mary, he'd be thrilled. And it looks as though we're going to be a permanent fixture for the rest of our lives –'

'You're getting married?'

'Yes, but not until next year.'

'Congratulations, Hilly! That's wonderful news.' Jenna ordered a bottle of champagne and toasted Hilly. 'With profits the way they are at present, I think it's time we began to enjoy the fruits of our labours. Cheers!'

Once Jenna had overseen the opening of the boutique in Bath, she put her house on the market and started looking for something a little bigger. She found a rambling farmhouse that she got at a good price because of the restoration work needed. It was in a hamlet a few miles outside Leicester, surrounded by countryside. She employed a firm of builders to set to work on the necessary repairs and within three months she had moved in.

Two months later, Jenna woke up in her delightfully sunny bedroom feeling restless. In the following weeks a feeling of emptiness grew inside her. For the first time since she had moved to Leicester, the past was creeping back into her thoughts. She found herself sitting at her desk and staring into space, remembering Frankie and all the good times they had spent together. Her half-sister! How she wished Frankie could have known before she died. Tears came to her eyes as she remembered the night that Daniel had told her he was her father and the anger she had felt for what he had done. That had faded now, and was slowly being replaced by a deep sadness for what could have been.

Jenna knew something was missing. She had shut out love from her life. She was lonely.

64

'DON'T SOUND SO miserable about it, Mary. You're not going to your own funeral, you know. Just being guest of honour at my dinner party. It is your birthday, Mary.'

'Sorry, Hilly, I've just got in from Bath. I'm a bit tired, that's all. Of course I'll come.'

'Good. See you at eight. It's going to be a very special evening, what with my brother arriving from Canada. I haven't seen him for nearly six years. If you don't fancy him, he's bringing a friend with him. An author or something who's really famous in Canada, so who knows? See you!'

Jenna put the phone down. If there was one thing she hated, it was being placed next to a man she did not know at a dinner party and having to make polite conversation.

However, on this occasion she relented. After all, it was her thirtieth birthday. She left the office early and soaked in a hot bath. She decided to wear her new Nicole Farhi dress.

At six o'clock, Jenna got into her newly acquired Golf and set off on the journey to London.

At a quarter past eight she rang Hilly's doorbell in Fulham.

'Come in, come in, birthday girl.'

Hilly introduced her to Ben, her brother.

'Good to meet you, Mary. Hilly's told me a lot about you.'

'Charlie's opening the champagne in the kitchen,' said Hilly. 'Ah, here he is; Charlie, meet Mary Short.'

The feeling that time had stopped hit Jenna as she stared at the man in front of her. It seemed like a lifetime but it was probably a few seconds before Charlie saved the day. 'Hello, Mary.'

'Hello, Charlie.'

'Right, now that the formalities are over with, let's drink some champagne,' said Hilly.

'Actually, Mary and I have met before.' Charlie stared at her. 'Yes, it was over five years ago but . . . let me see.'

Jenna held her breath.

'I remember. It was Cressida Fitzhugh's sister's twenty-fifth at Nether Longbottom in Gloucestershire. Mary here came with Phyllis Smythe. Isn't that right, Mary?'

'Er, yes.'

'Good. I pride myself on never forgetting a face. Now, another glass for you, Mary?'

Charlie kept up the charade all through dinner and they had a ridiculous conversation about the party in Nether Longbottom.

Jenna asked him what he was doing back in England.

'Well, Mary my dear, the kind and generous British Arts Council saw fit to bring me and my band of happy actors, of which Ben is one, over here to be part of the International Festival at the Nash. Oh, sorry, you would know it as the National Theatre, not being an actor.' He coughed. 'But we in the biz shorten everything to save the dear old actors' voices for their adoring public. 'You know, you remind me of an actress I used to know. She used to have blonde hair and was slightly narrower round the eyes than you are. Nice girl. Very talented, too. Went to Hollywood to make a film and then disappeared off the face of the earth. Pity. I had an inkling she was going to be a very big star. Terrible waste of talent and all that. I often wonder what's become of her.' Charlie stared deep into Jenna's eyes. Then he averted them to look at Hilly. 'Thanks for the very enlightening evening, but I must be on my way to beddy-byes. Night, all!'

And with that he left.

Jenna spent the night in Hilly's spare room tossing and turning. Not just because the inevitable had happened and she had met someone from her past, but because Charlie had stirred something inside her. She lay awake remembering all the time they had spent together years ago. Had she felt like this then? The physical attraction she had experienced for him tonight was very strong. She tried to stop thinking about him. He was probably married with three kids.

She spent the next day in the London shop jumping every time the telephone rang. She couldn't get Charlie out of her mind. In the end, unable to concentrate, she wandered around the piazza in Covent Garden, found a bench and sat down.

She was in love with Charlie. She guessed she always had been. Jenna wondered why she had never seen it before.

Was it too late? She thought he had loved her once, but . . . she walked slowly back to the boutique. She had been so young then, so naïve. It had taken until now for her to grow up and see the truth.

By five o'clock that afternoon she had convinced herself that Charlie had walked out of the door and out of her life for ever.

The thought of the lonely weekend in front of her depressed her even more, so by the time she left the boutique to head for Leicester, she was in a foul mood. To make matters worse, there was a crash on the M1 and she didn't arrive home until half past nine. She climbed wearily out of the car and walked to the front door. It opened before she had time to put the key in the lock.

'You know, you really must be more careful about closing your downstairs windows. Anybody could have got in.'

She looked up at him. 'Oh, Charlie! I thought, well, I thought . . .'

'I know exactly what you thought, my dear, because it's what I thought, too, and that's precisely the reason I'm masquerading as a burglar inside your house. Now do come in. Hope you don't mind but I poured myself a gin and tonic. I've also booked a table at a restaurant the nice rotund girl in the post office recommended.'

They drove the couple of miles to the restaurant and sat down at a table.

'Now, Miss Mary Short. Christ! Where did you dig that

up from, Enid Blyton? Eat up your filet mignon and then we can get down to the really interesting stuff like why you have dyed that beautiful mane of hair, not to mention your eyebrows, the colour of mud.' He eyed her over his forkful of rainbow trout. 'Seems like the knight errant walked back into your life just before it was too late.'

So Jenna told him. It took the rest of the meal, the car journey home, with Charlie driving so she could concentrate, and half a bottle of brandy in front of the fire. She talked of the rape and Jonnie's blackmail attempt and finished with the deaths of Frankie and her mother, and Daniel's revelation. As she spoke, a great wave of sobs overtook her. Charlie took her gently in his arms as she cried.

'Oh, Charlie! All that time I'd spent wishing I had a father, and when I found him, I was so filled with anger for what he had done, I never wanted to see him again. I've lost him for ever now, and we needed each other so badly. He loved Frankie as much as I did.'

Charlie sat silently as he listened to Jenna releasing the pain she had held for so long inside. He knew it could only help her come to terms with her grief.

'I thought that by making a new start I'd be able to forget the past, but you can never escape, can you?' Jenna looked up at him.

Charlie smiled down at her and smoothed the hair out of her eyes. 'No, my angel, you can't escape, but by letting it out the way you just have, you're taking giant steps in the right direction. My poor darling, if only you'd told me some of this before, you know I would have helped.

You've taken too much alone.' He tilted her face up to his. 'Now, Jenna, I'm going to do something that I've wanted to do ever since I saw that little waif crying her heart out over another man more than ten years ago. I'm going to kiss you.'

He kissed her lips, gently at first, then harder. He could barely restrain himself from tearing her clothes off then and there. But he had waited a long, long time for this and he wanted to savour every moment. He picked her up and carried her upstairs.

He undressed her slowly, kissing her as he went, touching the perfect body that had been the centre of his dreams for so many years.

Jenna begged him to enter her before she went insane.

Later, as she lay in Charlie's arms and listened to the birds heralding the dawn, Jenna knew she had at last come home.

65

AFTER A WEEKEND FILLED with passion and happiness, both Jenna and Charlie were dreading the thought of separation.

It was Sunday night and Charlie had to leave first thing in the morning to be at rehearsals in London by nine o'clock.

'My angel, the thought of leaving you fills me with horror.'

'Me too,' sighed Jenna.

'How often do you come down to London for business?'

'Once a week at most.'

'Oh, dear. It's going to be difficult for me to come here in the next few weeks with the opening night at the National so close. On the other hand . . .' Charlie looked down at her, curled up in his arms. He stroked her hair gently. 'You could ask your boss for a transfer to the London office.'

'Charlie, I am my boss!'

'Exactly. I happen to have a delightful mews house that I'm renting from a friend at the National. I could provide the accommodation.'

Jenna turned and looked up at him. 'You're asking me to move to London and come and live with you?'

'I know it's forward of me, having only known you for ten years, but in a nutshell, yes.'

Jenna lay back and thought about his proposition. Businesswise, it would be perfectly easy to run the company from London. And to have Charlie by her side every night would be wonderful. But were they taking this too fast? No, as Charlie said, ten years was a long time and she didn't want to waste another minute.

'Sir, I humbly accept your offer of a roof over my head. I will join you in London as soon as I can.'

'Jenna, oh, darling! You won't regret it, I promise you.' Charlie held her tight.

Jenna put her lips to his. 'I love you, Charlie.'

'And I you, my angel.'

Hilly was confused but delighted when, a week after her dinner party, Jenna announced that she was moving to London to live with Charlie.

'What can I say, Jenna? You don't hang around, do you?'

Jenna knew it was time to tell Hilly the truth, not only about Charlie, but about her real identity. She booked a table at a Chinese restaurant just around the corner from the Covent Garden boutique and ordered Hilly a large gin and tonic.

'Right, I'm going to tell you a story. It sounds bizarre, but I hope you're going to understand. My name isn't Mary Short, it's Jenna Shaw. I used to be an actress. I've appeared in the West End and I went to Hollywood and made a film. I've known Charlie since I was nineteen. We were at drama school together. He directed me in *Angel in Hell*, which he also wrote, several years ago. My hair is not really brown, but blonde.'

Hilly reached for her gin and took a large gulp. 'I *knew* your face looked familiar. Jenna Shaw, oh, my God! Now let me think.' Hilly paused. 'I've got it! Weren't you going to marry some lord? I remember it being splashed all over the papers.'

'Yes.'

'Well, Mary – I mean Jenna, I've got to ask this. How the hell did you end up at a business college in Leicester of all places?'

'As you can imagine, it's a long story and would take an awful lot longer than a lunch hour to explain. Suffice it to say, I became disillusioned with the acting profession. Things had happened to me that were not very pleasant. I wanted to make a completely fresh start.'

'Must have been pretty drastic for you to want to dye that wonderful blonde hair,' Hilly mumbled.

Jenna smiled, grateful that Hilly was not probing too deep.

'So, are you going to revert back to your real name and persona, or stay as the Mary Short we at Milly have come to know and love?'

'At work I'll stick to Mary Short. Our employees might find it a little confusing if I didn't.'

'Agreed. I have to say, Jenna Shaw, that I think I'm

taking this very calmly indeed and you owe me another very large gin and tonic for doing so.'

Jenna moved into Charlie's house a day before his play was to open at the National. He had begged her to come to the first night, but Jenna had declined.

'If you don't mind, Charlie, I'll come on a less conspicuous night.'

'Why are you worried, Jenna my darling? You're a has-been. No one will remember you anyway,' he teased.

He could scarcely believe, after all these years of wanting her, that she wanted him too. Charlie had never been so happy. Jenna was a very different lady to the one he'd known years ago. He had always perceived Jenna as a girl of rare beauty and talent. Now she was a powerful woman who had added a wealth of qualities to her persona.

She took his breath away.

One night Jenna left the office and hailed a taxi. Half an hour later she was sitting in the stalls in the Olivier Theatre. The lights went down and Jenna watched transfixed.

Charlie's talent for playwriting had matured beyond measure. His direction was sympathetic and perfectly judged. As the *Sunday Times* had commented the previous week, he really was one of the biggest talents to emerge in the past thirty years.

Jenna was filled with pride.

He was hers.

They were blissfully happy together. The initial passion that they had experienced did not die, but became stronger as security, understanding and the joy of companionship cemented their bond.

Jenna would leave the mews house in Knightsbridge early in the morning to go to the boutique while Charlie was still asleep. He would call her as soon as he woke, and come to meet her for lunch.

By the time Jenna returned home, Charlie had left for the theatre. She would prepare some supper, have a long bath and wait for the key to turn in the lock. This was the favourite part of their days. They would discuss Milly and how the performance had gone that night.

'Wonderful part for you in it, isn't there?' Charlie commented one night.

'There would have been once, darling. I'm a business woman now, not an actress.'

'Mm. I would say that's a little like your hair. Just look how easy it's been to restore it to its natural colour.'

'I'm happier as I am, Charlie. I . . .'

'I bet you can't sit there and tell me truthfully that when you saw the play, you weren't a little envious of my leading lady.'

'Have I cause to be?'

'No, silly, I didn't mean it like that. I meant, because she was up there on a stage strutting her stuff and you were sitting in the audience.'

Jenna sighed. 'I don't know. All right, I was envious. But I certainly wasn't envious of all the pain that's attached to it.'

Charlie could see Jenna was becoming upset. 'Okay, let's leave it. I just hate to see such a waste of talent, that's all.'

He put his arms round her and squeezed her tight. 'I love you, darling.' He kissed the tip of her nose. 'I thank God every day for bringing us together at long last.'

'Me too,' she said, and followed him with anticipation as he led her up the stairs.

On a sunny June day, they went to watch Hilly and Ari get married. The wedding was in a small village just outside Swindon, where the bride's parents lived. Charlie squeezed Jenna's hand as Ari slipped the ring on Hilly's finger. They stayed overnight in a hotel and drove back to London on Sunday morning, stopping for a pub lunch on the way.

'Jenna, my love.' Charlie put her white wine down on the table in front of her. They were sitting in a pretty garden at the back of the pub and the sun was hot.

'Yes, darling?'

'We have plans to discuss. I've been asked by the National if I'd be interested in writing a play for them. I'd be directing it as well. I've also been approached by Harold Kidd, remember him?'

'Of course I do.'

'Well, he wants to put one of my plays on in the West End. The money is fabulous and I wouldn't have to write anything new but –'

'It doesn't have the cachet of the Nash.'

'Spot on. But, just to complicate things further, the company in Canada want to renew my contract and there's been some talk of turning *Angel in Hell* into a film.'

'Good God, Charlie, there's nothing like being flavour of the month, is there?' Jenna laughed.

'This has all happened quite literally within the space of two days. My head is spinning.'

'What would you like to do, darling? I hope Canada is a no because I couldn't commute from Toronto.'

'Of course it's a no, angel. I was actually quite set on writing this play for the National, but when Harold quoted me some figures and I thought of all the hours I could spend with you instead of burning the midnight oil every night . . .'

'No way, Charlie. Number one, we have plenty of money, and number two, I can't live with the guilt of knowing I denied the world one of Charlie Devereaux's masterpieces.'

'Thank you for that vote of confidence, madam. Of course you're right. When I was living in that bed-sit in Finsbury Park, I used to dream of being asked by the National to write a play. There is one rule, though.'

'What's that?'

'That you swear not to enter the room when I'm writing.'

Jenna looked hurt. 'Why?'

'Because, my love, all literary thoughts will be forgotten for less honourable ones as soon as you walk in.' He leaned over and kissed her.

They wandered back to the car hand in hand and set off along the country lanes towards the M4.

'Reckon you could take a couple of weeks off at the beginning of July?'

Jenna realized that since she had begun Milly, she had

not taken a day's holiday, let alone two weeks. 'I suppose so. Hilly and Ari will be back by then.'

'Good. My play closes on the twenty-first of this month. Before I retreat into purdah and write my next piece of literary history, I intend to take the woman I love on a long-overdue holiday.'

66

AFTER PERUSING the *Sunday Times* travel section and making a number of phone calls, Jenna and Charlie flew to Istanbul.

They stayed at the Hilton in a luxurious suite that overlooked the Bosphorus and spent two days visiting the Blue Mosque, the Topkapi museum and wandering hand in hand round the Grand Bazaar.

Then they flew to Dalaman airport in the south of the country and hired a taxi to take them to Kalkan.

'I've heard that this is meant to be one of the most beautiful spots on the coast,' said Charlie.

Indeed, as the taxi rounded a bend, the picturesque fishing village came into view and the Mediterranean sparkled for as far as the eye could see.

Ayesha's Inn was in the centre of the village. Jenna and Charlie left the taxi driver to bring their cases up the narrow stairs. Ali, the owner of the pension, bid them a warm welcome and invited them up to his rooftop bar for a drink.

'Charlie, just look at the view, isn't it stunning?' Jenna

exclaimed as she stared at the uninterrupted view of the bay.

Ali showed them to their room, one of only seven. It was quite beautiful, with a stone floor, a dark wood-panelled ceiling and a tiny window that looked out onto the cobbled street below.

'I never expected anything like this.'

'Just put your trust in Uncle Charlie, my love. I have a friend who has stayed here. Apparently, our landlord is a little more than he seems.'

They made hot, sweaty love on the comfortable bed. As the boiling sun was sinking slowly over the horizon, they went out to wander through the village. The streets were cobbled, the houses whitewashed and covered with purple bougainvillea. They sat by the harbour drinking beer and watching the beautiful sunset.

'Charlie, this place is enchanting!'

He nodded in agreement.

That evening they went to the waterfront restaurant also owned by Ali. It was packed. Ali seemed to know everyone who arrived and once Charlie and Jenna had finished their meal, Ali invited them to have a drink at the small, crowded bar in the corner.

'Sing for us, Ali,' someone demanded.

'Yes, please,' everyone chorused. So Ali sang.

Jenna's neighbour turned to her and whispered, 'Isn't he wonderful? He used to be the most celebrated singer in the whole of Turkey. Five years ago he gave it up to run this restaurant and the inn.'

Charlie put his arm round Jenna as they listened to

another song. 'Quite a surprising place this, isn't it, darling?'

Jenna looked up at the white, round moon, shining over the bay. 'I think it's perfect, just perfect.'

For the following week, they awoke late and spent hours soaking up the sun. They would return midafternoon for a siesta.

'The sun does something to my libido,' Charlie said as he lay naked on the bed with Jenna entwined around him. He traced the line of her back with his finger.

At seven they would go up to the rooftop bar and watch the sun set over a gin and tonic. Then they would wander down the cobbled streets to Ali's restaurant.

As their last day together approached, Jenna started to feel depressed about returning to the real world. She had arranged to fly straight to Milan; she was looking into the possibility of expanding into Europe and there was an important knitwear show that she wanted to attend. Charlie was going home to start writing his play.

She sat watching the sun set on the last evening. The bar was deserted and Charlie was talking to the boy behind the bar.

He came and sat down beside her. Pavarotti was playing on the sound system. The boy brought an ice bucket with a bottle of champagne over to their table. He poured two glasses and disappeared down the stairs, leaving them alone.

'Cheers!'

'Yes, cheers. To coming back here as soon as possible,' said Jenna.

'You look really miserable, darling.'

'I am.' Jenna's eyes filled with tears.

'Don't cry, sweetheart. What's wrong?'

'It's been so beautiful here. I've been so happy. I want time to stand still.'

'Oh, my darling! We have so much to look forward to. A whole lifetime of holidays like this.'

'Isn't it just perfect here, Charlie?'

'Yes. And as I'm a writer and you're an actress and we both have a sense of time and place, you should know exactly what I'm about to ask you.'

She looked at him and she did know.

'Well, will you?'

'Yes,' she said.

67

MARILYN STIRRED and opened her eyes. She climbed out of the bed, feeling every muscle in her body protest. He'd hit her again last night.

Her hands were shaking. She needed a fix.

He kept it in a cupboard in the sitting-room.

Of course it was locked.

'Bastard!' she screamed, then sank to the floor, beating her fists into the carpet.

Time and again since they had arrived in Paris she had sworn to leave him. But she had no money, no friends, no one that could help her.

Most of the time Jonnie locked the door before he left the apartment. Most of the time she was so stoned she didn't care. In her lucid moments, Marilyn knew that she must get away before he went too far and she ended up dead.

Jonnie was rich now. He was a successful film director.

He was all she had. She needed what he gave her.

She staggered to the window and looked down on the busy Parisian avenue below.

'Oh, God, help me,' she moaned, sinking back to the floor and rocking backwards and forwards.

She knew that no one could help her. Her addiction was destroying her.

One kilometre away from where Marilyn was locked in her apartment, Gerard Langdale was sitting at a pavement café.

He had been in Paris for two months and it was time to move on. It was always the same. Too long in one place and he would start to remember. He had not been back to England since she had deserted him. He had left Langdale Hall in the hands of an agent and the family solicitor and taken off abroad six years ago. Of course he felt guilty for shirking his responsibilities but could not bear the thought of life in England without Jenna. However, he knew he couldn't keep running for ever.

He finished his coffee and wandered along the busy streets to his apartment just off the Boulevard St Michel. The apartment was grand and far too large for him, but it was free. He had borrowed it from a banking friend who had moved to New York and insisted he have it for as long as he wished.

Anyway, tonight was his last night. He wondered where he would go tomorrow. Maybe he'd just get on the next plane going to the Far East. Thailand, Hong Kong, Singapore . . . the actual destination didn't matter. He just needed to keep moving.

Tonight he was escorting Camilla Hamilton to a party. He had bumped into her in Cannes when he had been visiting Bettina and her ever-growing brood. Camilla had become a top model in Paris and had been at the film festival. She had called him a few days ago and asked him to escort her to a party being thrown by a film-director friend of hers.

After a short nap, Gerard showered and dressed. He poured himself his usual gin and tonic and contemplated the evening ahead. He decided he would probably end up getting very drunk. He wished he had said no to Camilla but she had insisted.

Gerard picked up Camilla from her apartment and they took a taxi to the restaurant where the party was taking place.

Everyone was telling Camilla how beautiful she looked, but Gerard couldn't help remembering the girl in the classic pink evening gown who had floated down the stairs towards him . . . soft, gentle and beautifully feminine.

He reached for his drink and followed Camilla to meet another group of 'incredibly interesting people'.

'Jonnie, meet Gerard. Gerard, this is Jonnie Danton, who I'm begging to give me a part in his next film.'

Gerard had heard of Jonnie Danton. The man had made a couple of low-budget second-rate films that had attracted a cult following among the student population of France. Gerard had heard that the films bordered on soft porn, but the man had a high-profile image in the tabloid newspapers. Jonnie Danton was very tall and thin, with long dark hair tied back in a ponytail. He was wearing dirty jeans and a bulky black leather jacket.

''Ello, mate, pleased ter meet yer.' The slurred cockney

sounded strange in a room full of impeccable French accents. He offered Gerard a joint. "Ave a drag, mate. Good stuff. I got a contact in Morocco. Gets me anything I need. 'Ere, try some.'

Gerard shook his head. 'Not my scene, thanks. I think I'll stick to getting drunk if it's all the same to you.'

'Oh, Gerry, you can be so dull on occasions,' Camilla complained, taking a long drag.

Gerard downed his gin and sighed. It was going to be a long night.

By midnight everyone at Gerard's table was either very drunk or very stoned, including Gerard.

Camilla was sitting on Jonnie's knee. She slid her hand inside his leather jacket, pulled out a gun and handed it to Gerard.

'Bet you've not got a gun like this in the collection at Langdale Hall, Gerry darling.'

'Oy, Camilla, give that back!'

'Don't be silly, Jonnie. Tell Gerry what it is.'

'Whatever you do, don't touch the safety catch, mate. It's a Walter PPK. Like the one that James Bond uses. Nice piece of weaponry, innit?'

Gerard handed it back to Jonnie. 'Yes. Not much good for pheasant shooting, though. Why on earth do you need to carry something like that around?'

'You, er, can never be too careful in my line of business.'

'I thought you were a movie director?'

'Yes, among other things.'

'Oh, I see,' said Gerard lamely.

'I tell yer what, mate, for a stuffy English bloke, yer all right.' Jonnie put a conspiratorial arm round Gerard's shoulders. 'Come on, let's get out of 'ere and go back to my place.'

'As long as you drop me off on the way,' drawled Camilla.

'Course. Oy, Marilyn, we're going.'

A tall, very thin coloured girl stood up. She had been sitting at the table silently all evening.

Outside, Jonnie hailed a taxi. The cold air made Gerard realize just how much he'd drunk.

'Bye, darling. Keep in touch.' Camilla kissed him as she got out of the taxi in front of her apartment. Gerard nodded and promptly fell asleep.

'Come on, me old mate, let's get yer out of the taxi and upstairs to me flat.'

Gerard staggered through the door of Jonnie's flat and collapsed on to a large black leather sofa in the sitting room.

'Make us some coffee, will ya, Marilyn? Then piss off to bed and leave us men to it.'

Marilyn went to the kitchen and came back with two steaming cups of coffee. She put the cups on a table and left the room.

'Right.' Jonnie was putting a tape into the video machine. ''Old on ter yer 'ats. 'Ere we go for something that'll really make your eyes water.' He pressed the play button.

A heap of naked writhing bodies appeared on the screen. Gerard sipped his coffee and shuddered.

'I made 'em to earn me a few bob when I left film school. Art, pure art. You'll see me old lady in a minute.'

Gerard didn't want to be here and he certainly didn't want to be watching pornographic videos with Jonnie Danton. He decided to finish his coffee and leave.

'Right, this is me favourite bit coming up now. Not only 'cos it stars Marilyn, but 'cos I managed to make a lot of money out of a blonde bird in it. I got five grand by threatening to send this to the papers. Look, 'ere we go, there's Marilyn.'

Jonnie's eyes were fixed on the screen.

'What did you get five thousand pounds for, Jonnie?'

'Oh, she was a friend of Marilyn's, a real looker, you'll see 'er in a minute. Stroke of luck. I saw 'er picture in the paper 'cos she was gonna marry some knob. Sent 'er a note promising the tapes for five grand. She paid up and I hotfooted it over 'ere to begin my brilliant career. Don't know what became of 'er. Probably married the guy and is now Lady Someone with three kids.' Jonnie grinned. ''Course, I kept the master tape for me little private collection 'cos she looks so 'orny when she screams.' He pointed to the screen. 'See, 'ere she is.'

Gerard saw a naked girl tied by her wrists and ankles to a bed. A man was on top, driving into her. The camera panned to a close-up of the girl. Her eyes were full of terror as she opened her mouth and screamed.

It was Jenna. His Jenna. He didn't understand. Surely she wouldn't have done this of her own free will?

'Jonnie,' Gerard struggled to keep control. 'Is the girl acting?'

'Nah, it's for real. You should 'ave 'eard 'er scream. Marilyn told me she'd done it before but she 'adn't. When she arrived at the studio we 'ad to give 'er something to relax her. She passed out but woke up right at the crucial moment.'

'So you drugged her and raped her, then blackmailed her when she was about to marry?'

'Well, I wouldn't put it quite like that –'

In a split second Gerard had his hands round Jonnie's throat.

'Do you know who I am? Do you?' Gerard dragged him out of his chair on to the floor and knelt above him, squeezing hard, throttling him. 'I'm Lord Langdale, the man that Jenna Shaw was going to marry. You bastard!' Gerard released one of his hands and hit and hit and hit the face below him until it was a mushy pool of blood. He didn't hear Jonnie screaming, he just kept punching until he had no more strength.

Finally he stopped. Jonnie was out cold.

Gerard stood up unsteadily. 'Oh God, oh God, my poor Jenna!' He had to get out of this apartment and find her. Let her know he understood.

He staggered through the door and into the kitchen. He leaned over the sink and threw up. He turned the cold tap on and began to wash the blood off his hands.

A shot rang out behind him. Gerard's legs crumpled and he sank to the floor.

Jonnie stood in the doorway. He turned and saw Marilyn.

'I need a drink. Look what that bastard did to me. I

thought he was gonna kill me. Get me a drink, Marilyn. Now!'

He sat down and put the gun on the kitchen table. Marilyn came back from the sitting room and handed him a large glass of whisky. She sat down at the table and stared at him.

'What we gonna do, Jonnie? He looks as though he's dead. What are we –'

'Shut up, yer stupid bitch! Whose fuckin' fault was this anyway? Yours, that's who! Do you wanna know who that is? It was the fuckin' lord bloke who was gonna marry your mate. If you 'adn't lied to me about 'er then none of this would 'ave 'appened. You fuckin' black whore! It's all your fuckin' fault! Jesus, what are we gonna do?' Jonnie put his face in his hands.

Marilyn reached across the table and picked up the gun. She pointed it straight at his head. He looked up, saw the gun and sneered.

'You wouldn't have the fuckin' guts, love.'

Her finger tightened on the trigger. She saw a flicker of fear in Jonnie's eyes.

'Marilyn, give me that gun!' He stood up and reached across the table.

She fired.

Jonnie fell backwards. Blood dripped down the wall behind him.

Marilyn put the gun on the table. She knew she must leave the apartment quickly. One shot might be ignored, but two were bound to have been heard.

She walked slowly over to Jonnie's body and, with

difficulty, extracted his keys. She went into the sitting room and opened the safe. She took out the heroin and two bundles of French francs.

Marilyn went into the bedroom and put the heroin, money and a few clothes into a holdall. Just as she was about to leave, she realized the video recorder was still playing. She went back into the sitting room, turned the machine off and took the videotape out. Then she hurried out of the flat.

68

CHARLIE PUSHED the front door open and carried his suitcase inside. He was missing Jenna already. They had said goodbye at Istanbul airport as if they would be separated for weeks, not four days.

In some ways it was good that she wasn't here. He had to begin work on the play and she would only distract him. This way, he could have four days of uninterrupted writing.

He was so happy. He had the career he'd dreamed of and the love of his life had said yes to marrying him.

The telephone rang. He went to pick it up.

'Hello,'

'Hello, is Charlie Devereaux there?'

'Yes, speaking.'

'Charlie, it's Bettina here.'

'Good God, how are you?'

'Okay thanks. It's taken me hours to track you down.'

'So it's me you wanted to speak to?'

'Yes. Have you heard about my brother?'

'No.'

'That's incredible, it's been on the front page of all the British newspapers.'

'I've been out of the country for the past two weeks. What's happened?'

'Nobody is really sure. Gerard managed to get involved in a gun battle with a French film director. The director is dead and Gerard is in a coma. I'm calling you at the moment from Paris.'

'Oh no! Bettina, I'm sorry.'

'Thanks, Charlie. I'm afraid the prognosis isn't good. Gerry has a bullet lodged in his spine which they can't get to without causing more damage. We know that if he lives, which is still in the balance, he may never walk again.'

'That's dreadful, Bettina! But how can I help?'

'Well, apparently, when they brought him in he was half-conscious. He kept repeating Jenna's name over and over. By the time my mother and I arrived at the hospital he'd lost consciousness and hasn't regained it since. So I thought that maybe, if I could find Jenna and get her here, she might be able to help. I haven't seen her for years and nobody seems to know where she is. You're a last resort, Charlie. Do you know?'

'Yes, I do, actually.'

'That's wonderful! Where?' He heard the relief in Bettina's voice.

'She's staying at the Hilton in Milan.'

'Charlie, thanks so much. Gerard really loved her so much. Maybe she'll be able to help him.'

'I hope Gerard pulls through.'

'Thanks. Bye, Charlie.'

'Bye, Bettina.'

Charlie sat in the chair in the sitting room for a long time. He had just sent the woman that he loved into her past. He pondered what would have happened if Jenna had not been blackmailed. She would be Lady Langdale with a brood of children by now.

He walked round the corner to the newsagent's and asked for any week-old newspapers they might have. He took the papers home and read the articles on Gerard.

The director was a man by the name of Jonnie Danton.

Jonnie . . . Charlie knew who he was.

All he could do was wait, and hope and pray that he didn't lose her again.

Bettina's face lit up with relief when she saw Jenna walking through Arrivals at Charles de Gaulle airport.

'Thank you so much for coming, Jenna! Ma and I really appreciate it.'

'It was lucky I was so near. It's only just over an hour's flight from Milan.'

'Let's get a taxi. If you don't mind, I think we should go straight to the hospital.'

'Of course. Has there been any change?'

'No, I'm afraid he's still in a coma.'

There was silence as they crossed Paris in the taxi. So much had happened since they had last seen each other. Jenna felt guilty and uncomfortable. However, now was not the time or place to go into the past. The main thing was Gerard and whether her presence would help.

He was lying in a small room by the nurses' station. He

looked so pale and lifeless that Jenna wondered if he'd died and no one had noticed.

'Just sit next to him and talk to him quietly. You never know, hearing your voice may help.'

Bettina left the room and Jenna sat in the chair next to Gerard. She took his cold hand in hers.

'I'm so, so sorry, Gerry. I'm sorry for leaving you and I'm sorry you ever had to meet that Jonnie Danton. I don't know what happened between you. Was it something to do with me?' she whispered.

She looked at his face, the closed eyes, and wished to God he could speak to her. After Bettina had rung her in Milan and told her about Gerard and Danton, she had gone out and bought a *Herald Tribune* and found Jonnie's face staring at her from the front page. Since then, she had gone through hell. It was obvious that no one had any idea what had happened. Gerard must have found out what Jonnie had done to her. She didn't know whether she should tell Bettina her suspicions or not. For the time being, she decided to keep quiet and see how Gerard progressed.

After an hour and a half, she stood up and left the room.

Bettina was sitting in the waiting room just along the corridor. 'Any luck?'

Jenna shook her head.

'Oh, well, it's early days. You've only just arrived. My mother is coming from the hotel to take over. We're trying to do it on a shift basis so someone is with him twenty-four hours a day. I booked you a room at the Plaza Athenée where we're staying.'

'Thank you. Bettina, he looks terrible. What have the doctors said?'

Bettina sighed. 'They don't hold out a great deal of hope. He hasn't woken from the coma in nine days. When they brought him in he was half-conscious. As you know, he gabbled your name and one of the doctors said he talked about a video or something. Anyway, since then he hasn't woken up.'

Jenna's blood ran cold. A video.

'The worst thing is that the press are having a field day. Although he was English, this Jonnie Danton was very well known over here.'

'How's your mother taking it?'

'Badly. Every time we step out of the hospital or hotel we're besieged by reporters. And there's a policeman stationed here at the end of the corridor just in case Gerard wakes up. See him?'

Jenna looked and nodded.

'Apparently, the police have found Gerard's fingerprints all over the gun that shot Danton. But I just can't believe that Gerry is capable of killing anybody. It must have been in self-defence, surely? But for what reason? There's no connection between the two of them. We know Danton had a live-in girlfriend. When they left this party together, she left with them. Camilla Hamilton was also in the cab. She swears this girl, who she thinks was called Marilyn, was with them when she got out. Presumably she was the one who called for an ambulance. She's disappeared now and the police can't trace her.'

Marilyn! The nightmare was returning.

'Are you able to stay for a few days? Both Mother and I would be very grateful. Anything that might help Gerry live is . . .' Bettina bit her lip. 'I'm sorry. I can't tell you how awful all this has been.'

'Of course I'll stay for as long as you want.'

'Oh, Jenna, I'm so scared!' The tears ran down Bettina's face.

The telephone rang and Charlie hurried to pick it up.

'Charlie, it's Jenna.'

'Hello, darling.'

'I'm sorry I haven't rung before. Bettina told me that you gave her my number in Milan. Gerard, Bettina's brother, has been shot and is seriously ill here in hospital. Maybe you've seen it in the papers.'

'Yes, I have. And the fact that it involved Danton.'

'Oh, God! Charlie, I don't know what's happened, but I feel so responsible. I have to stay here and see if I can help. Can you call Hilly and tell her what's happened?'

'Of course. By the way, I didn't mention our relationship. I thought it was better under the circumstances that you told her. Have you told anybody what you think the connection might be?'

'No, I can't. Apparently Gerard mentioned something about a video when he was first brought into the hospital. If I explain what I suspect happened it will give him a motive for killing Danton.'

'Will Gerard live?'

'They don't know. His chances are slim. Poor Gerry! I have to go, darling. I'm taking over from Bettina at his bedside in five minutes. I love you, Charlie.'

'I love you too, darling.'

For the following week, Jenna shared the rota at the hospital with Bettina and her mother. There was little energy for talk of the past. Both sister and mother just seemed grateful that Jenna was there.

Sometimes, Jenna and Bettina would leave the hospital to get some air and have a *café au lait* at one of the nearby cafés, but for the most part, all their waking hours were spent by Gerard's bedside.

There was no improvement.

Another week passed and all three of them started to accept the fact that he might never wake again.

One afternoon Jenna was sitting by his bed reading a book to him. She held his hand because the doctor had said that physical touch was most likely to elicit a response.

She stopped reading to glance up at the wall clock. She had been sitting there for three hours and needed a break. As she extricated her hand she felt the tiniest pressure on it. Jenna replaced her hand and squeezed Gerard's.

There was no response. She decided to sit there for a little longer.

She leaned close and kissed him on the cheek. She tried squeezing his hand again. Nothing. She was tired. Maybe she had imagined it. Her eyes closed.

'Jenna.'
She opened her eyes and looked at him.
'Jenna.'

It was all he could manage, but it was enough. Gerard was alive.

69

'CHARLIE, IT'S ME. Gerard's awake.'

'Oh. That's good news, Jenna. So can you come home?'

'No, not at the moment. A detective has started to sniff around and poor Gerard has only been awake for a few hours. I have to stay in case I . . . well, I want to talk to Gerard. Anyway, how's the writing going?'

'Oh, pretty well, thanks.'

'I'm sure it's good for you not having me around to disturb you.'

'Maybe, but I'd prefer it if you were here.'

'Did you talk to Hilly and explain?'

'Yes, angel. And she says you're not to worry. Everything's under control. I gave her your number at the hotel just in case.'

'Thanks, Charlie. I am sorry about this.'

'Don't worry. Just keep in touch.'

'I will. Bye, darling.'

Charlie put the phone down and felt guilty for not feeling happier that Gerard was still alive.

That night, Jenna, Bettina and Henri ate in the Grill Room at the Plaza Athenée. After the meal, Henri said that she was exhausted and was retiring to bed.

'Do you want to come for a brandy in my room, Jenna? I think the time has come for us to have a chat, now that we know Gerry will live.'

Jenna nodded. They took the lift to Bettina's floor.

Bettina poured them two large brandies and handed one to Jenna.

'I'm terribly concerned, Jenna. I mean, it's wonderful news that Gerard will live, but now the police are going to be on the case with a vengeance. Mother contacted our solicitor in London. He's going to fly out at the end of the week.' Bettina sipped her brandy. 'Jenna, can you tell me why you walked out on Gerard just days before you were about to marry him?'

She had known that in the fullness of time Bettina would ask her. She also knew the relevance it held for Gerard and the police.

'I have to warn you, Bettina, that if I do tell you, it won't make you feel any better about Gerard's position.'

'I had a feeling that there was some connection. Please tell me, Jenna. Then we can decide what to do.'

It took Jenna an hour to tell Bettina the whole story.

'I didn't want to have your family name disgraced, especially after the death of your father. And Danton would have done what he threatened. He was a very evil man.'

'Honestly, Jenna, some of the ghosts in our family closet make your little secret look like child's play. The aristocracy have always behaved appallingly.' Bettina smiled.

'However, you're right. It presents us with one hell of a problem. As I see it, Gerard must have discovered what Danton did to you. Oh, my goodness, Jenna, do you think that Gerry shot him in cold blood?'

'I don't know, Bettina, but I do know that if any judge and jury heard my story, they'd be sceptical about Gerard's innocence.'

Bettina nodded, then shuddered. 'I know how much Gerry loved you. The point is, did he love you enough to kill?'

The question hung in the air, answered by neither of them. Bettina quickly changed the subject. 'Do you still think of Frankie, Jenna? I was in Cannes expecting Benjamin at the time and Freddie didn't tell me until after he was born that she had died. I was devastated when I heard. I know it said in the papers that she had drowned but somehow it didn't ring true. Was that what really happened, Jenna?'

Jenna remembered how close the three of them had been and decided Bettina deserved to know the truth about the circumstances leading up to Frankie's tragic death. Bettina's eyes filled with tears as she listened.

'Oh, Jen, how awful! So no one will ever know whether Frankie drowned accidentally or whether she took her own life.'

'No. It was just such a waste of talent. Frankie had so much to live for. I still miss her dreadfully and I owe her such a lot. She was a wonderful friend.'

'Well, I suppose she'd be pleased to see two of the gang of three united, even if it is under these terrible circumstances. Talking of which, can you stick around for a while longer? I think we're going to have to talk to David, our solicitor, about all this. See what he thinks.' Bettina smiled. 'I suppose that there is a silver lining to this cloud. At least this has meant that you can be reunited with the man you love. Gerard went insane when you left him. And he's certainly going to need you to help him through the next few weeks.'

Jenna thought of Charlie waiting for her in England. But she couldn't tell Bettina. Gerard needed her.

The next morning there was a meeting at the hospital with Gerard's consultant. The news was not good.

'From the tests we've run over the past couple of days, we can be sure of only one thing. The bullet that is lodged in Lord Langdale's spine will prevent him from walking again. He will be permanently paralysed from the waist down.'

Henri burst into tears and Bettina put an arm around her.

'Can't you operate to remove the bullet?' Bettina asked.

'No. The bullet is lodged inside the spinal column, pressing against the aorta, which is the main artery to the heart. We could not reach the bullet without causing further damage that might lead to the loss of Lord Langdale's life.'

'I see.'

'There is also the risk that the bullet will move. As I've said, at present it is pressing against the wall of the aorta. If it moves and pierces the wall, it would lead to massive haemorrhage and subsequent death.'

All three women shuddered. The consultant continued. 'There is an advantage to Lord Langdale's being in a wheelchair. At least it will minimize his degree of movement and keep the bullet stationary.'

'Please, monsieur, are you saying that the bullet will eventually move and cause his death?'

'Yes and no, Lady Roddington. It has not moved since we took the first X-rays three and a half weeks ago, but then your brother has been completely stationary. All I can tell you is that he may have weeks or months. If he's lucky, perhaps even years. I'm sorry. I wish I could be more specific.'

'Thank you for being so honest with us.'

'I would say that Lord Langdale is going to need the support of loved ones to help him recover. When he learns he will not walk again, it will be hard for him to accept. And with the police wanting to interview him . . . ,' the consultant raised his arms, 'this will not aid his progress.'

Bettina sighed. 'I know.'

The three of them left the consultant's office. Bettina suggested she take Henri back to the hotel. 'We don't want Gerry to see you like this, do we, Ma? Jenna, would you sit with Gerard until I return?'

'Of course.' Jenna went along the corridor and into his room.

Since he had woken, he had been heavily sedated. But this morning, his eyes were open and alert. She went to sit in the chair next to him.

'Hello, Jenna.'

'Hello, Gerard. How are you feeling?'

'Awful, but a little better than yesterday.'

'Well, that's a step in the right direction.'

'With you here I have to get better.' He raised his hand towards her and Jenna took it in hers. 'I love you, Jenna.'

She didn't know how to reply.

He beckoned her closer and whispered, 'I know what happened. Why you had to leave me. It was that bast –'

'Sshh, don't upset yourself, Gerry. There'll be plenty of time to talk about it when you're better.'

'I saw that video, that's why I hit him.'

'Gerry, please, we'll talk about this when you're stronger.'

'Okay. When will they let me get out of bed and walk around?'

Jenna's mouth went dry. 'Oh, not for a while. You've only just woken up.'

Gerard seemed content with her answer.

When Bettina got back from the hotel, they sat in the waiting room and had a quick cup of coffee.

'I'm warning you, Gerry asked me when he was going to be able to get out of bed.'

'Oh, dear! I don't know how he'll cope when he knows that he'll never . . .'

A short, heavy-set, middle-aged man was walking towards them.

'*Bonjour, mesdames*. I am Detective Inspector Escoffey. I believe that you are Lord Langdale's sister, Lady Roddington. I am correct?'

'Yes. And this is Jenna Shaw. Friend of the family.'

'And ex-fiancée of Lord Langdale, I believe?'

Bettina looked at Jenna in surprise. The detective had done his homework.

'That's correct,' answered Jenna.

'I will be wanting to speak to both of you in the next few days. And, of course, to Lord Langdale himself. There seems to be a lack of information on the night in question. I hope Lord Langdale will be able to throw some light on the episode. *Au revoir, mesdames.*'

The detective turned and walked along the corridor.

'Thank goodness David arrives tomorrow.' Bettina was pale.

Jenna agreed.

She was just about to turn off the light when the telephone next to her bed rang.

'Hello.'

'Hello, darling. How are you?'

'Fine, Charlie. And you?'

'Okay, thanks. I was just ringing to check when you were thinking of coming home. I miss you, you know.'

'Oh, Charlie, I can't come back just yet. Bettina and Gerard need me.'

'Well, could I fly out for the weekend to see you?'

'Charlie, I haven't told Bettina about us.'

'Why not?'

'Well, under the circumstances, I thought it might upset her.'

'Charming!'

'Please understand, Charlie.'

'All I can understand is that the girl who recently agreed to be my wife is hundreds of miles away from me with her ex-fiancé and wants to keep our relationship a secret.'

'Charlie, you know the circumstances and . . .'

'Jenna, what about *our* future?'

'Please, Gerard has only just regained consciousness. He needs me here at the moment.'

'Are you still in love with him?'

There was a pause. 'Of course not.'

'Then why can't I fly over and see you?'

'No, I . . . under the circumstances I don't think it would be appropriate.'

'Jenna, what is inappropriate about your fiancé flying over to see you?'

'It's hard to explain. I just don't think it would be a good idea, that's all.'

'Then come home. Just for a few days.'

'No, not yet. I can't leave him.'

'Well, if that's the way you feel, so be it. Goodbye, Jenna.'

'Goodbye. I love you . . .' The telephone had gone dead in her hand.

She lay in bed and cried. How could she leave Gerard? She loved Charlie but after what the consultant had said, she couldn't just walk out on him for a second time.

Charlie put down the telephone and cried too. Tears of frustration.

He would give her a little more time, but if she didn't come back soon . . .

Bettina went to meet David Lennox, the family solicitor, at the airport the following day. She had asked Jenna to wait for them at the hotel and sent Henri off to the hospital.

The telephone rang in Jenna's room.

'Jenna, can you come down to the restaurant? David is here and we thought we'd have some lunch and a chat.'

David was a distinguished man with greying hair. He reminded Jenna of Bettina's father.

'It's good to meet you, Miss Shaw. Bettina has been filling me in. Obviously, I'll need to talk to Gerard, but I hear you have some light to throw on the situation.'

They ordered soup followed by omelettes. David studied the wine list and ordered a bottle of Chablis.

'Now, Jenna, would you like to tell me what you know?'

So Jenna told David exactly what she had told Bettina.

'When I spoke to Gerard yesterday, he told me that Danton had showed him the video tape.'

David sighed. 'Well, of course, it does mean Lord Langdale had the perfect motive. Has he told either of you whether he did shoot Danton?'

'No, and to be honest, David, none of us has had the courage to ask.'

'Have the police interviewed him yet?'

Bettina shook her head. 'No. They've asked him a few questions, but he's been so ill that the doctor has kept them at bay. But a Detective Inspector Escoffey is very anxious to interview him.'

'It's good that you called me when you did. I'll speak to

Lord Langdale and we can discuss just what he's going to say to the French police. I also need to discover what they know and how their search for evidence is going. There may not even be a case.'

'Let's hope so,' said Bettina.

'This afternoon I'll go to the hospital and have a word with Gerard. Then I'll sniff around and find out how far the police investigation has got. I'll report back to you this evening.'

After lunch Jenna and Bettina accompanied David to the hospital. While he went to talk to Gerard, Henri took the two of them out for coffee at a nearby café.

'Gerard mentioned that he has been borrowing an apartment off the Boulevard St Michel. He suggested that it might be a good idea if the three of us moved in there. It'll save paying those exorbitant hotel prices and apparently it's large and very comfortable,' said Henri.

'That's an excellent idea. Ma, why don't you and Jenna take a taxi over to see it this afternoon while I sit with Gerard?'

'Yes, that's what Gerry suggested. He gave me the keys and the address.'

Jenna and Henri went to visit the apartment and met Bettina later in the hotel bar.

'How was it?' asked Bettina.

'Very grand and spacious, and it has four bedrooms plus a cleaning lady that comes in three times a week,' replied Henri. 'I suggest we move in as soon as possible.'

'Good. We'll check out of here tomorrow.' Bettina saw David making his way towards them. 'Ma, why don't you go and have a rest before dinner? Jenna and I can talk to David and report back to you later.'

'If you wouldn't mind, Bettina. I do feel awfully tired.'

Henri went off to her room and Bettina ordered a whisky and soda for David and two gin and tonics.

'So, what did you find out?'

'Right, first things first. When I spoke to Gerard, all he could tell me was that he went to Danton's apartment, watched this video tape and had a fight with Danton. Then he says he passed out. He also swears that this black girl, Marilyn, was at the apartment with them. He admits to being very drunk. I told him to say nothing about the video tape until I'd discovered what the police know. I then went to the police station and saw Detective Inspector Escoffey.'

'What do they know, David?'

'Well, obviously the chap was cagey. But it seems that the gun that shot both men was a Walter PPK. There are a number of different fingerprints on the gun but both Danton's and Lord Langdale's have been identified. The gun was found lying on the kitchen table. Apparently, Danton was shot at point-blank range, whereas Lord Langdale was shot in the back from a distance. The good news is that they haven't discovered the video tape. At present they have no motive, and only Gerard's fingerprints on the gun as evidence. But unfortunately, at the end of the day, one man is dead and the man found in the same room as him is living. That might be enough for them to take Gerard in. Escoffey is going to the hospital tomorrow to interview him. I've told Gerard to reiterate the fact that there was definitely a woman in the apartment. Then the police will have to make a concerted effort to find her. It will also give me a little more time to draw up a game plan. I'm going to contact a French lawyer to help me. The legal system over here is different to England. My practice in England has given me the name of a very good lawyer here. Obviously I need to ask you if I can go ahead. I know he won't come cheap.'

'Whatever it takes, David. Please don't spare any expense,' said Bettina. 'Oh, dear, it doesn't look good, does it?'

David shook his head. 'No, but at the moment we'll keep quiet about the video. The police are unaware that there's a connection between Danton and Gerard, namely you, Miss Shaw. Let's just hope this video tape doesn't turn up and the woman does. If the worst comes to the worst, we could plead crime of passion.'

'But that means you're saying that Gerry killed Danton. We don't know that, do we?'

'No, Bettina, of course we don't.' David answered with a confidence he did not feel.

70

'HILLY, IT'S JENNA.'

'Jenna! How are you? Ari and I have been so worried about you. What's going on over there?'

'It's very complicated, Hilly, I'll explain another time. How's the business?'

'Fine, no problems at all. Ari has taken over your responsibilities and we've hired another designer to help me. Is that okay?'

'Of course.'

'Jenna, when will you be coming home?'

'I honestly don't know. I'm sorry to have run out on you like this, but it really can't be helped.'

'Charlie called a few days ago. He asked if I'd heard from you. He said you hadn't rung for at least two weeks. He didn't sound very happy.'

'Thanks for letting me know. I'll give him a call as soon as I can. I'll keep in touch. Take care, and send my love to Ari.'

'I will, Jenna. Bye.'

Jenna put the phone down.

She had been in Paris for almost a month and had not spoken to Charlie in the last two weeks. He didn't know she had moved out of the hotel. She knew she must speak to him, but what could she say? Gerard had taken the news that he would never walk again very hard. He had clung to Jenna for support and she could do nothing but give it to him. Gerard was due out of hospital this afternoon. His consultant had told them that there was little more he could do, and that Gerard might be better off away from the hospital environment.

Jenna sighed. Tomorrow she had to decide what she was going to do. It wasn't fair on Charlie. He deserved better.

The police investigations had uncovered nothing more. Marilyn had gone to ground and since there was only Gerard's word she had been there, David thought the police might have stopped looking.

Gerard's story remained unchanged. He had told David that he had held the gun at the party and that was why his fingerprints were on it. Camilla Hamilton had confirmed this, and the story was backed up by the fact that her fingerprints were on the gun, too.

'Gerard, you may well have handled the gun at the party, but unfortunately, in the eyes of the law, you could also have held the gun at Danton's apartment later when you fired it. A man's dead, you were there, the police want a suspect and that's that, I'm afraid,' said David.

'This Marilyn was there, I swear.'

'I do believe you, Gerard, and the police have found a set of fingerprints on the gun that match up with ones found all over Danton's flat. We presume that this is Marilyn. But that again means nothing. If Marilyn lived there, it's quite possible that she had handled the gun before the night in question. I'm sorry. I understand your anxiety.'

Later, when David had left and Jenna came to sit with him, Gerard grasped her hand.

'They don't believe me, do they, Jenna? Do you?'

'Of course I do.'

'I didn't shoot him, Jenna. I'm sure I didn't.'

'I know, darling. Don't worry. They'll find Marilyn soon and she'll be able to help us.'

Jenna spoke with a conviction she didn't feel.

David had enquired whether it would be possible to take Gerard down to Bettina's house in Cannes, because the consultant thought that the sea air might do him good. Detective Escoffey had shaken his head. 'I am sorry, monsieur, but I would not like Lord Langdale to leave Paris at this present time. You understand, of course?'

So Gerard arrived at the apartment that afternoon accompanied by a male nurse who would stay with him to take care of his day-to-day needs. Fortunately, the lift was large enough to accommodate his wheelchair.

'Welcome home, darling!' Henri kissed her son. Bettina opened champagne to celebrate.

'Here's to your release from hospital!' She raised her glass.

'And here's to me not being incarcerated again in the foreseeable future.' Gerard smiled wryly.

They all knew what he meant.

A week later, Bettina came rushing into Jenna's bedroom.

'Guess what? Freddie's flying out here tomorrow. Ma is going home for a few days and has agreed to look after the kids at Langdale Hall. Oh, Jenna, I can't wait to see him! I've missed him so much.'

Jenna smiled sadly. She knew what it felt like to miss someone. And she still hadn't worked up the courage to ring Charlie.

Freddie arrived the following day on a morning flight from London.

'Jenna, how lovely to see you after all this time! How are you keeping, my dear?'

'Fine, thank you, Freddie.'

'I have a favour to ask you. I'd like to take Bettina out for dinner tonight. Would you be able to stay with Gerard?'

'Of course, Freddie. I think it'll do Bettina the world of good to have an evening out on the town. This has been a terrible strain on her.'

'On all of you. Rum do, rum do.' Freddie scratched his chin.

That evening, when Freddie and Bettina had gone, Jenna and Gerard sat chatting in the sitting room.

'Are you hungry, Gerry?'

'Not particularly. I could murder a gin and tonic, though. I know I shouldn't but surely a small one wouldn't hurt.'

Jenna agreed and went to make them both one.

'Cheers! God, that tastes good! Jenna, I . . . I just

wanted to say how grateful I am for you being here like this. I couldn't have made it through without you.' Gerard stared out of the window. 'You know, sometimes I lie awake trying to piece together that night. I just can't remember any more than I've told the police. But I'm starting to wonder whether . . . whether I did shoot Danton. I wanted to kill him when I saw what he did to you.' Gerard's eyes filled with tears. 'Oh, God! Jenna, I'm frightened.'

She went over and knelt in front of the wheelchair. She took his hands in hers. 'I'm so sorry for causing you this pain. If it hadn't been for me . . .'

He put a finger to her lips. 'My love, none of this is your fault and you must not blame yourself. All I ask is that you don't leave me . . . ever. I couldn't be without you again. Now we can make up for the years we were separated because of that bastard. In a strange way I'm almost happy. This has brought you back to me.'

Gerard lifted her face towards him. He kissed her gently, then with passion. His arms encircled her and held her tight.

'Do you know, the most amazing thing has just happened.' He took her hand and placed it on the bulge in his trousers. 'I can't be as paralysed as they thought.' They both laughed. He kissed each of her fingers in turn. 'Jenna, maybe this is a strange thing to ask at a time like this, but I must ask it. If this situation is resolved and I'm not carted off to jail for the rest of my life, would you consider marrying me? I know I'm in a wheelchair but I love you like no other man ever could. If you would, it would make this whole dreadful business bearable. I need you. Desperately. Will you, Jenna?'

'Yes, of course,' she said. What else could she say?

After the nurse had put Gerard to bed, Jenna went in to kiss him good night. He took one of her hands in his.

'Darling, if we are to be man and wife, will you sleep with me?'

'Of course I will.' Jenna smiled.

'No. I meant now.'

'Well, I, er, don't know. It probably isn't a good idea, Gerry. The consultant emphasized how important it was that you were kept still.'

'Please, darling, just come and lie next to me.'

'All right.'

'Would you take your clothes off, so I can see you? I promise to behave. I'm hardly in a position to rape you, am I?' Gerard chuckled.

Charlie . . . Oh, God! Jenna saw Gerard's eyes pleading with her. Reluctantly she removed her clothes and got into the large bed next to him.

'Hold me, please, darling.'

She put her arms around him and he turned to kiss her.

'Oh, darling, I can never explain how much I missed you and dreamed of you being in my arms.' Gerard took her hand and placed it on his erection. 'See what you do to me. You make me feel like a man again.' He kissed her again and timidly put a hand to her breast and caressed it gently. 'Jenna, no man could ever love you more. Would it be possible to try and make love?'

'Gerry, I really don't think that would be a good idea. The doctor said . . .'

'I know what the doctor said, but what a way to go!' He laughed and stroked her hair. 'I think it would do me a power of good. Please,' he begged her.

There was a pause as she looked at him.

'Okay, but let me do the work.'

Jenna coaxed his half-erect penis until it was ready to enter her. Then she knelt on top of him and eased him inside her. Gently, carefully, she moved up and down until he cried out.

Afterwards he cradled her in his arms. 'Thank you, darling! You don't know how much that meant to me.'

She kissed him. 'Sleep tight, Gerard.'

He was already dozing. 'And you, my love.'

Jenna slipped out of the bed and went back to her room. She sat in a chair and wept. A decision had been taken for her. There was nothing she could do. She pulled out some writing paper and wrote to Charlie. She asked his forgiveness, but told him she had no choice. She was marrying Gerard because he needed her.

She addressed the letter to the mews house and watched the dawn rise over Paris as she said goodbye to the man she truly loved.

At the same time in London, Charlie was packing his suitcase. He had given her almost a month and she hadn't called. He knew why. Jenna was still in love with Gerard. And now she was also filled with guilt over what had happened. There was nothing he could do. Sitting around waiting for her was not going to do any good. If she hadn't even telephoned by now, she wasn't going to come home.

So Charlie sat down and wrote Jenna a letter. He said that he would always love her, but that he could not wait any longer for her to come home. He said he understood about Gerard but couldn't bear to share her with anyone.

The following morning, he called a taxi and had it take him to a hotel where he would stay until he found somewhere else to live.

When Jenna's letter arrived at the mews house, he had moved out.

Charlie's letter arrived at the Plaza Athenée. The hotel sent it on to the address in England that she had given when she checked in.

Both letters lay unopened on the doormat in the mews house.

The following day, David came round to tell them of developments, and to introduce Laurence Dinan, the French lawyer who was helping him.

'Laurence has told me he's quite sure that Gerard will be taken in for questioning sooner or later. He thinks they've been waiting for Gerard's health to improve. It wouldn't look good for an English peer to expire in French police custody.'

Gerard himself seemed to be remarkably calm.

'Now I know I have you, I can face anything,' he would say to Jenna.

Gerard had told Bettina that if things worked out the

way they hoped they would, he would marry Jenna on their return to England.

'I honestly think you're what's keeping him going, Jenna,' Bettina commented one afternoon when Gerard was having a nap.

Gerard had been out of hospital two and a half weeks when the knock on the door that they had all been dreading was heard.

'Maybe it's David.'

'Maybe,' answered Jenna. They both knew that David never arrived at nine o'clock in the morning.

Bettina answered the door. There stood Detective Inspector Escoffey.

'*Bonjour, Mesdames.* Is Lord Langdale at home?'

Bettina nodded.

'Good. I'd like him to accompany me to the *commissariat de police* to see if his time out of hospital has jogged his memory.'

'Are you arresting him?'

The detective shook his head almost disappointedly. 'No, madame, I am not, but I suggest you contact your lawyer, just in case of, should we say, further developments.'

'Couldn't you question him here?' Bettina asked. 'He's still not at all well.'

'I am sorry, Madame, but regulations are in this sort of case that a suspect must be questioned at the *commissariat*.'

'Oh. Well, it'll take a while to get him ready.'

'I can wait, Madame.'

While Jenna woke Gerard, Bettina called David, who

said he'd be over as soon as he could. Then they sat in silence with Detective Inspector Escoffey until Gerard was wheeled into the sitting room by the nurse.

'How long will you be?' asked Bettina.

'All being well, we should be able to return Lord Langdale this evening.'

Bettina and Jenna kissed Gerard and watched as he was wheeled out of the room by a gendarme.

'Oh, God! Poor Gerry!' Bettina burst into tears as soon as the door was closed.

David arrived ten minutes later.

'Don't panic, ladies. It's pretty much what we expected. It may be that they'll question him, then release him. I'm going down to the *commissariat* with Laurence to see what's happening. I'll phone you as soon as I know anything.'

Jenna and Bettina waited in the apartment. The clock on the mantelpiece ticked slowly through the hours. At six o'clock that evening, the telephone had still not rung.

'I'm going to make myself the stiffest gin I've ever had. Want one?'

Jenna nodded and Bettina handed her a glass. 'I just daren't think what's happening. And what effect it's having on Gerry. He doesn't deserve this, Jenna. I keep going over and over things in my head. I just don't know what to think. The way that Gerry loves you . . . I keep wondering whether he did shoot Danton.'

'Don't say that, Bettina! I just wish we could find Marilyn.'

'David still thinks she's in the country.'

The telephone rang. 'I'll answer it.' Bettina picked up

the receiver. 'Hello, David. They have? Oh, God! Yes, all right, thanks for calling. We'll see you later.' She put the phone down and sank in to a chair.

'They've charged Gerard with the murder of Jonnie Danton.'

David finally arrived at the apartment at ten o'clock.

'David, what's happening?' Bettina's face was as white as a sheet and her hands shook.

'First things first, Bettina. Make me a cup of strong black coffee and I'll tell you what I know.'

The coffee was made and both women sat and listened to what David had to tell them.

'I was allowed to see Gerard before I left. He's fine. He sends his love and told me to tell you both not to worry. As I told you earlier on the telephone, they have charged him formally.'

'What with?'

'First-degree murder, I'm afraid.'

'Dear God,' whispered Bettina.

'However, there is some good news. They are prepared to let him out on bail, due to his fragile condition. They don't want a death on their hands. He won't be allowed to leave Paris, and the bail will be very high, but we're appearing in court tomorrow. Laurence is ninety-nine per cent certain that the judge will grant it.'

'So he should be home tomorrow?'

'If you're able to raise the bail money. I reckon it could be as much as two hundred thousand pounds, maybe more.'

Bettina whistled. 'I'll get straight on to Freddie and

tell him to call our bank. I'm sure we'll be able to sort something out. We have to.'

'Good. Also tomorrow, a date will be set for Gerard's court appearance.'

'That'll be months away, won't it?' said Jenna.

'No. Probably more likely a matter of weeks. I've discussed things with Gerard and Laurence and we think the best plea to go for is self-defence.'

'But surely that means you're accepting that Gerry did kill Danton?' Bettina looked indignant.

'What you must remember is that I'm representing a client who is unable to give the police a reasonable explanation about the night concerned. His fingerprints have been found on the murder weapon and a high-profile man is dead. If there were only the two of them in the apartment, it's unlikely the judge will believe that Danton shot himself.'

'Oh, God, if only this Marilyn could be found!' Bettina sighed.

'Quite. I'll have another word with the agency I've contacted. She really does seem to have disappeared.'

'If Gerard pleads self-defence, then what are his chances?'

'Well, Jenna, if we can convince the jury that Danton fired first, pretty good.'

'And if they don't believe he shot Danton in self-defence?'

'Then he'll go down for first-degree murder, I'm afraid. We're hopeful, but the problem with circumstantial evidence is that it's difficult to predict the outcome.'

'But you know the state of Gerry's health and what

the consultant has said. Gerry would die in prison long before his release date.' There were tears of desperation in Bettina's eyes.

'We hope it won't come to that. If we plead self-defence, I have every reason to believe that Gerry will be free.'

'But Gerry may well be innocent!' cried Bettina.

'My dear, I do understand. It's a tragic situation. There's every chance he is innocent. I'm just relying on the fact that this video tape that Jenna told me about does not make an appearance. That would give Gerard the perfect motive.'

'But it's so unfair!'

David nodded. 'I know, Bettina, I know.'

Gerard was granted bail of two hundred and twenty thousand pounds, Freddie having moved heaven and earth to transfer the sum over to Paris. He arrived back at the apartment to be greeted by a crowd of photographers and journalists. The story had broken. David hurried him inside as quickly as he could.

There was an emotional reunion with Bettina and Jenna.

'Thank God you're out of that place, darling!' Bettina hugged him.

'I'm afraid you're going to have that lot camping on the pavement down there for a while. None of you say anything to the press. Understood?' David was peering out of the window at the paparazzi below.

'Of course,' Jenna nodded. She looked at Gerard. He was gaunt and pale. 'Why don't you go and take a nap, darling? You look exhausted. We'll wake you up for supper.'

Once Gerard had been put to bed, the two women questioned David once more.

'Have they set the date for Gerry's first appearance?'

'Yes, it's in three weeks' time. That gives us long enough to pull together some kind of a defence. Obviously, the past two days have been a hell of a strain on Gerard and the coming weeks will be even more so. I'm going to go back to England and see if I can dig anything up on Danton. If we can establish that, as you have indicated, Jenna, he was into illegal dealings, it may help our case. If there are any problems while I'm gone, you have Laurence's number.'

'David, why don't you put me on the stand and let the truth come out?'

'Absolutely not, Jenna. It would open a whole can of worms and, as I've said before, your story gives Gerard a motive. A simple straightforward case of self-defence is our best chance. Trust me, please.'

The two women nodded silently.

71

THERE WAS A WEEK TO GO before Gerard had to appear in court.

Bettina and Jenna had grown used to the journalists and photographers who were camped out on their front doorstep. Every time they left the apartment, flashbulbs would go off in their faces and a barrage of questions would be shouted at them. They always said nothing.

David had flown back to England the day before when a contact in London had called him with some information he had uncovered concerning Danton. His previous trip had uncovered nothing. 'It sounds tenuous, but anything's worth a shot. I'll be back in two or three days,' he had said.

The tension was building with the approaching court appearance. Gerard was being, under the circumstances, remarkably controlled. Jenna looked on with admiration, and guilt, for the way he handled a situation that she felt she had created.

It was nine o'clock in the morning and Jenna had spent an almost sleepless night. She went into the kitchen and made herself a coffee. The smell of it made her feel sick and she had to sit down quickly to counter her dizziness. The stress was affecting her health. She slowly made her way back to her bedroom with the coffee. As she passed the front door, she picked up the post from the mat. There was a letter addressed to her.

She lay on her bed and opened it, noticing the Paris postmark.

'Jenna,
I've got the video tape. Unless you want the police to know why your boyfriend killed Jonnie, come alone to the Piaf Café on the Champs-Elysées at two o'clock, Thursday 21st.
Bring two thousand pounds in cash.'

Jenna's initial reaction was to laugh. First Jonnie, now Marilyn. There was something pathetic about it.

But Gerard's life was at stake.

How many times had she heard David reiterate the importance of the video tape staying hidden? The painstakingly built defence would crash to the floor if the police got their hands on it.

Jenna mulled over her options. Today was the twenty-first. David was somewhere in England and she couldn't talk to him. Laurence? No, he'd insist on coming with her. Gerard? He would be adamant that she should not meet Marilyn or put herself in danger of any kind. Bettina? She was wonderful, but she wouldn't know how to cope with a situation such as this. Charlie? God, how desperately she wanted to pick up the phone and ask for his help and advice! But she could not.

Jenna realized that once more she was alone. The decision rested with her.

Half an hour later, she crept into the deserted sitting room and picked up the phone to her bank in London.

At two o'clock precisely, Jenna walked into the bustling café on the Champs-Elysées. She had slipped out of the apartment building by the service door at the back. She had gone straight to the bank whose address she had been given by her bank manager in London. The money had been waiting for her. Then she had changed cabs three times on the journey to be sure no one was following her. The last thing she needed was a hack reporter tailing her.

Marilyn was sitting in a corner at the back of the café. She wore large sunglasses. She looked emaciated and years older than Jenna knew her to be.

She sat down oppposite Marilyn.

'Hello, Marilyn.'

Marilyn took off her sunglasses. Her eyes seemed hardly to register Jenna's presence.

'Did you bring the money?'

'Did you bring the tape?'

Marilyn nodded. A waitress appeared and Jenna ordered *café au lait* for both of them.

'Well, did you?'

'What?'

'Bring the money?'

'Before I tell you that, I want to ask you a few questions. You were there on the night of the shooting, weren't you, Marilyn?'

'Yes.'

'Then why haven't you come forward and told the police what you know?'

'Don't want to be involved in all that.'

'But you are involved. You were there, for goodness sake. Did you see what happened?'

'Yes.'

'Did you see Gerard shoot Danton?'

Marilyn sighed. 'I was there, wasn't I? I saw everything.'

'So what happened?'

'I can't remember. Just give me the money for that tape.'

Jenna opened her handbag and put an envelope on the table in front of her. She laid both her hands on it.

'All right, Marilyn. Here it is. In cash. Now pass me the video tape.'

Marilyn produced a crumpled plastic carrier bag and put it on the table. Jenna took the bag, opened it and saw the video tape inside. Then she handed the envelope to Marilyn. The girl tore it open and made an attempt to count the notes inside. She seemed satisfied. The waitress arrived with their coffees and Marilyn shoved the money in her coat pocket. She stood up to leave.

'I wouldn't if I were you, Marilyn. It would look very suspicious not to drink your coffee when it's just been ordered. And you never know who may be watching.'

Marilyn sat down again.

'You know the police have been looking for you, don't you?'

'You haven't brought them with you, have you? I'll tell them all about the tape. I'll tell them I saw your boyfriend shoot Jonnie, I . . .'

'No, I haven't, but I suggest that you just answer a few questions if you want things to remain that way. Did you see Gerard shoot Danton?'

There was a pause. 'I can't remember.'

'Do you think it's right for an innocent man to go to prison for a crime he didn't commit?'

'What the fuck do I care?'

'So he didn't do it?'

'Dunno.'

'But you've already told me you were there. The police found a set of fingerprints on the gun that were neither Jonnie's nor Gerard's. Perhaps they were yours.'

'Shut up, Jenna! You don't know nothing. I was the one that was there. If they find me I'll just say that I saw your boyfriend pull the trigger.'

Jenna lost control. 'You selfish bitch! If you do that

and it isn't true, then you're no better than a murderer. Gerard has committed no other crime than loving me and you damn well know it. You're using this pathetic attempt at blackmail to finance your habit and ...' Jenna realized she was shouting and people were staring so she lowered her voice. 'The only reason I've paid you that money is to try and help someone I care for, someone I believe is innocent. Do you know what hell you and your boyfriend subjected me to all those years ago? You lied to me then, Marilyn, and you're lying to me now. You may feel sorry for yourself but what you did almost destroyed me and it's about to destroy someone else. Have you no conscience?'

Jenna stared at the blank face on the other side of the table. It was no good. She was beyond reach. She opened her bag and put some francs on the table to pay for the coffee.

'Well, you've got what you wanted. Go and buy yourself another fix. Indulge yourself as you watch a cripple face imprisonment for something that you started when you tricked me into making that video. That's all I expect of you because you're pathetic, Marilyn. Just one more thing. Take a look in the mirror some time. You won't like what you see.'

Jenna walked from the café without a backward glance. Once outside, she crossed the road and continued along the Champs-Elysées. She slumped down on a bench and tried to collect her thoughts.

Well, she had the tape, that was something. But she

hadn't been able to get through to Marilyn. When she left the apartment her head had been full of heroic intentions. She would talk to Marilyn, reason with her and convince her to give evidence at the trial.

Having met her, Jenna knew that Marilyn was hiding something about that night and she would say anything to protect herself.

Jenna decided not to tell anyone about her meeting. She had the tape and would leave it at that.

She hailed a taxi and set off back to the apartment.

The morning of the hearing arrived. Henri had flown back with David from England. The incident David had gone over to find out about had turned out to be petty burglary when Jonnie was sixteen. Nothing that would be at all useful in this context.

A special minivan with a lift had been hired to take Gerard to the court. They had arranged for it to collect him from the back of their apartment block because of the journalists at the front. Unfortunately, someone had anticipated what they would do and there was a hoard of journalists taking pictures and firing questions as they climbed inside.

It was the same in front of the Palais de Justice. Two porters lifted Gerard's chair up the steps with David, Henri, Bettina and Jenna hurrying after him.

'Dear God, it's like a rugby scrum out there,' Henri commented.

Just before Gerard was wheeled into the court by David,

he beckoned Jenna over to him. He reached for her hand and squeezed it.

'Don't worry, darling. I love you very much. Thank you for being with me.' He kissed her. 'I'm sure that this will be a bit like going to the dentist. Never as bad as you expect and over before you know it.'

He smiled at Jenna and waved as he was pushed along the corridor.

Henri, Jenna and Bettina went into the court a few minutes later and took a seat just behind David, Laurence and Gerard.

The judge appeared and banged his hammer. He announced that the court was now in session.

Everyone spoke French and Jenna understood little of what was being said. She closed her eyes as the voices droned on.

'He didn't do it. I shot Jonnie Danton.'

The familiar English words came through the incomprehensible French. Jenna thought she must have nodded off. She opened her eyes and saw that David had turned to stare at something behind her.

She turned to look too.

Marilyn.

The judge spoke in French to Laurence. 'What did that woman say?'

Laurence turned to the figure at the back of the court. 'Can you repeat what you just said, *madamoiselle*?'

'I said, he's not guilty. I shot Jonnie Danton.'

Laurence repeated the sentence to the judge in French.

An audible gasp went up round the court, then there

was pandemonium as everyone began speaking at the same time.

The judge banged his hammer once more and asked for Laurence to approach the bench. He did so, spoke quietly to the judge, then walked to the back to speak with Marilyn. She nodded and accompanied him forward. The judge stood up and escorted Marilyn, the prosecutor and another woman into his chambers.

Laurence walked back to his desk.

'What's happening?'

Laurence explained to David, who then told Henri, Bettina and Jenna.

'Well, the judge has taken the prosecutor and a lady who speaks both English and French into his chambers to hear what Marilyn has to say. I must admit, this is the most amazing turn of events. It's possible you may be off the hook, my boy.' David smiled at Gerard.

'Thank God! I knew she was there,' he replied softly.

After what seemed like an eternity, but was in fact half an hour, David and Laurence were summoned into the judge's chambers.

Ten minutes later they came out, smiling broadly.

'Marilyn has stated categorically that she shot Danton. She described the incident in detail. They just have to confirm that her prints were the unidentified set found on the gun and all over the flat. I have little doubt that they are. I suggest you ladies go home. Gerard will have to stay here with Laurence and I until they have interviewed and formally charged Marilyn. I'll ring to let you know what has happened. I can't see any reason to think that Gerard won't be a free man by the end of today.'

At five thirty that evening David rang to announce that Marilyn had been formally charged with the murder of Jonnie Danton. He was bringing Gerard home with him immediately.

The champagne flowed and euphoria filled the apartment. David pulled Jenna to one side. 'All right, young lady. Tell me exactly what you did while I was away in England.' His eyes were twinkling.

'I saw Marilyn.'

'I know. She told me. And she asked me to give you a message. She said she took a good look and you were right. She also asked if you would go and see her. You don't have to. Now, tell me all.'

Jenna told him quietly and then went to get the tape that was hidden under her mattress.

'Please, David, take it and destroy it for me. It seems to have haunted me for the past few years.'

'Of course, Jenna. Do you mind if I tell Gerard? After all, he has a lot to thank you for.'

'That's fine, but no one else.' Jenna was beginning to feel very sick. Her vision was becoming blurred and the voices were fading into the distance. Suddenly, everything went black.

Jenna woke in bed. A strange man was staring down at her.

'*Bonjour*, Miss Shaw.' The man had a heavy French accent. 'I am glad you have awoken. My name is

Dr Didier. I would like to ask you a few questions if I may, for you fainted for quite a long time.'

Jenna nodded sleepily. She felt dreadful.

'Do you get many headaches?'

'No.'

'Have you been eating properly recently?'

'Yes, I think so.'

'Are you feeling sick often?'

Jenna nodded. 'Yes.'

'Any particular time of the day?'

'In the morning and sometimes in the afternoon.'

'When was your last period, Miss Shaw?'

Jenna couldn't remember. 'I don't know.'

'Well, many weeks?'

'Yes, I suppose so.'

'Would you mind if I gave you a little examination?'

Jenna shook her head and the doctor took her temperature, felt her pulse, then examined her stomach and said he wanted to take a more intimate look.

Once he had finished, he packed his medical bag and sat on the edge of the bed.

'Miss Shaw, I have reason to believe that you are about five weeks pregnant. Is this possible?'

Jenna thought back over the past few weeks. She hadn't seen Charlie since July. It was now the first week in October. That must mean ... yes, the first time Gerard and she ... It was almost exactly five weeks ago.

'Yes, it is.'

'Congratulations, Miss Shaw. Can I ask Lord Langdale to come and see you? He was most concerned when you collapsed.'

'Of course.' Jenna lay there while the doctor went to find Gerard, trying to take in what the doctor had just told her.

He entered the room, pushed by Bettina.

'How are you, darling? You gave us a scare, fainting like that.'

'I'm okay. I'm sorry I frightened you.'

'The doctor says you have something to tell us.'

'Yes, I'm five weeks pregnant.'

She watched as Gerard's face lit up. He squeezed her hand tight. 'Five weeks. That means ... Oh, Jenna darling, what a gift to be given on a day like this! Are you happy?'

'Of course, Gerry.'

'I think I'm going to cry,' said Bettina. 'I'm so pleased for the two of you.' She hugged them both.

The following day Jenna insisted on going to visit Marilyn. David took her down to the *commissariat de police* and waited while she saw Marilyn.

The girl looked pitiful. She was shaking like a leaf.

'How are you, Marilyn?'

'I need a fix but they won't let me have one.'

David had warned Jenna that Marilyn was likely to be very distressed.

'Thank you for doing what you did, Marilyn. I'm very grateful.'

'I'm sorry, Jenna for what I did to you. I've done bad and I know it.'

'Why did you kill him?'

Marilyn's eyes filled with tears. 'You don't know what he was like. He was a bastard. He beat me and kept me locked up in the apartment. I couldn't leave him 'cos I needed what he gave me. I saw him shoot your boyfriend. Then he started calling me names, terrible names, and saying it was my fault. I knew he was gonna beat me again. Something inside me snapped and I picked up the gun and shot him. He deserved it.'

'I know. He did. Tell me more about what he did to you.'

Jenna listened to Marilyn describe what she had suffered for the past few years.

'Marilyn, listen to me. I'm going to have a word with David, our solicitor. He's outside and I want you to tell him everything you have just told me. I can't believe any jury in the world won't understand why you killed him. I'd be prepared to come and give evidence as well.'

Marilyn's eyes lit up. 'Would you really do that for me, Jenna?'

She nodded. 'And a lot more besides if it can be done.'

'One last thing, Jenna. It doesn't matter very much, but it was me who called the ambulance that night when you tried to top yourself. I found you on the floor and didn't know what to do, so I phoned and ran away.'

'Thank you, Marilyn. You saved my life. And Gerard's. He would have died if he had gone to prison. We'll try and help you.'

Marilyn smiled. 'Thanks, Jenna, and I promise I'll pay back the money I took as soon as I can.'

Jenna talked to David, who then saw Marilyn and returned to the apartment to have a conference with Gerard.

'I'm concerned that Jenna's name is going to be dragged into it once more. She's pregnant and she's been through enough,' said Gerard. 'What if I offered to pay for Marilyn's bail and try and get her into some kind of drug-rehabilitation centre? She surely needs to dry out before she's fit to stand trial. What are the chances of a judge allowing her to do that?'

'Pretty good under the circumstances. It'll save the state having to dry her out. As long as the centre would accept responsibility for her, I would think the judge would agree.'

'Why don't you go back to Marilyn and tell her that I'll pay for everything as long as she keeps Jenna's name out of it?'

'I can certainly try.'

Marilyn was happy to agree. Two days later David appeared in court with her. Gerard put up the bail and Marilyn was allowed to go to a rehabilitation centre where she would stay until her trial.

'Thank you, darling. I know she caused us a lot of trouble, but it wasn't her fault. It was that bastard Danton.'

Gerard looked at Jenna, love shining from his eyes. 'Let's try and forget about the past now. We go back to England tomorrow with a wedding and a baby to look forward to.'

He held Jenna tight in his arms.

Life was good. But he knew how little of it he had left.

72

CHARLIE READ ABOUT Jenna's marriage to Gerard in one of the many papers that ran the story. It had taken place three weeks after they had arrived back from Paris, at the church on the Langdale estate in Yorkshire.

Charlie looked at the picture of the gaunt man in the wheelchair, with Jenna by his side. She looked happy.

He managed to find it in his heart to be glad about that. His suspicions about her feelings for Gerard had been right, although he found it hard to believe that the love Jenna had shown for him when they were together was a sham.

Charlie glanced at the finished manuscript on the desk in front of him. Real life was far crueller than anything he could write in his plays.

'Good morning, darling, how are you feeling today?' Jenna kissed her husband on the cheek and placed his breakfast tray on the bed. When they had arrived at Langdale Hall from Paris, the first thing that Gerard had done was to call in the builders. The study had been converted into a specially fitted bedroom with a bathroom en suite, adapted for handicapped people. The redesigned room had a magnificent view over the parkland beyond, with French doors that opened on to a terrace.

'Wonderful,' said Gerard, stretching. And he meant it. They had been married for three weeks and, so far, every day had been a joy, apart from the pain . . .

'And how are my wife and child doing today?'

'We're both well.'

'You look a little pale this morning. Are you sure you're feeling well?'

'Fine, really, darling. I've just been feeling a little tired recently. It's probably this lump.' Jenna patted her stomach. 'Now, we have to get you up and dressed. The nurse will be in when you've finished your breakfast. We should leave for Harrogate by eleven.'

Gerard was going to the hospital for his monthly visit. His consultant tested him for various things and took X-rays to check that the bullet hadn't moved.

'Henri is coming with us and we'll go and have a spot of lunch in Harrogate while we wait for you.'

They dropped Gerard off at the hospital and went to a nearby restaurant.

'How do you think Gerard is doing, Jenna? He seems to have lost weight recently.'

'He has, Henri. He's eating but the weight just won't stay on him.'

'He seems to spend a lot of time sleeping during the day.'

'Yes. The doctor has upped his dose of painkillers and I think they make him drowsy.'

'Oh, dear, the pain's getting worse, then?'

'Well, Gerry never complains. He's so brave, but yes, I think the pain is increasing.'

'I just wish there was more we could do.' Henri sighed. 'Thank goodness he's got the baby to look forward to.'

Gerard was in the consultant's office, having just completed a gruelling set of tests and X-rays.

'Well, Lord Langdale, I have to tell you that the bullet has moved. Only slightly, but it's not a good sign. Has the pain been getting worse?'

'Yes.'

'Then I really do have to reiterate that you should keep as stationary as possible. Any sudden movement is going to cause you immense pain and could cause the bullet to move further. You also seem to have lost a bit of weight. Are you eating properly?'

'I don't have much of an appetite, but yes, I try to eat three times a day.'

'Fine. I'll give you a vitamin injection before you leave. Apart from the weight loss, your blood pressure is normal and the ECG was stable.'

'May I ask you a slightly embarrassing question, doctor?'

'Yes, of course.'

'You say any sudden movement is dangerous?'

'Yes.'

'Well, how much of a problem is there likely to be if I make love to my wife?'

'I assume she would place herself on top?'

'Yes.'

'Well, it's not really to be recommended, but if you were very, very careful, it should be possible. Which reminds me. The tests from Paris indicate that you are sterile. This might well have been caused by your accident, or may have been the case before. Sterility can be caused by a number of things; emotional trauma, illness or drugs. You will never be able to father children, I'm afraid.'

'But . . . my . . .' Gerard stopped himself. 'So I've been sterile at least since the shooting?'

'Yes. Did the doctor in Paris not mention it to you?'

'No.'

'Well, he may have thought it was better to wait until you'd recovered from the trauma of your, er, accident.'

Back at Langdale Hall, Gerard went immediately for his afternoon nap. He needed to think. So the baby was not his. After hours of fighting with his conscience, he decided to keep quiet about his discovery. He couldn't lose her now.

He pondered who the father might be, then stopped himself.

He loved Jenna.

Without her, what life he had left was worth nothing.

While Gerard napped in the afternoon, Jenna made her daily call to Hilly to keep in touch with what was happening at Milly; then she would go for a walk. The beauty of Langdale Hall and its surroundings always gave her a sense of peace.

She was finding life difficult. Having been used to functioning in a hectic environment, she found the change in her life hard to deal with. She had called Hilly when she arrived back in England to tell her that, at least for the foreseeable future, she would be unable to return to the company. Hilly had been understanding and told Jenna not to worry, everything was under control.

Jenna knew that she should withdraw from the company completely. Being Lady Langdale and looking after a crippled husband gave her no time to run a hectic business. She had decided that after Christmas she would go to London and tell Hilly of her decision.

She had recently visited the farmhouse near Leicester to pick up some of her personal belongings and was thinking of putting it on the market in the spring. It was no use to her now. And it held too many memories of the nights she had spent there with Charlie. She wondered how he was and if he was still in the mews house. She had read the reviews of his new play. It had been another huge success.

She loved him still. If only things had worked out differently . . .

Jenna set off back towards the house. She popped into Gerard's room. He was fast asleep. She went into the library and looked along the shelves for a book to read.

There, sitting between Dickens and Du Maurier, was a copy of *Angel in Hell*. Jenna remembered Bettina buying it after she'd seen the play. She took it off the shelf and went to sit at the desk and opened the book.

There, on the first page, was Charlie's dedication: 'For Jenna, my inspiration'.

Tears came to her eyes. She turned the page and started

to read. Presently the nurse came into the library to tell her Gerard was awake. She rose, leaving the book on the desk, and went to her husband.

Gerard found the play on the desk later that evening. He saw the dedication at the front and began to read.

73

'BETTINA, YOU ARE LOOKING WELL! How was the south of France?'

'Wonderful, just what I needed. How are you, Gerry?' Bettina looked at the thin figure in the wheelchair.

'Oh, I'm fine, Bettina, but . . .' He lowered his voice. 'I'm a little concerned about Jenna.'

'Why? There's nothing wrong with her, is there?'

Gerard shook his head. 'No, but I don't think one or two days away would do her any harm. I've booked three tickets for *Swan Lake* and I was wondering if she could come to London, stay with you and you could all go to Covent Garden together. Jenna has to be in London on Monday anyway for her first visit to the obstetrician and I thought the ballet might cheer her up a bit. It gets lonely for her, stuck up here with just myself and Ma. Would you mind, Bettina?'

'Of course not, Gerry, but what about you?'

'I'll be fine.'

'Well, I'm going to be here until Monday, so I can drive Jenna down.'

'That sounds perfect.'

'Jenna, what did the doctors say when Gerry last went to the hospital?'

The two of them were in the small sitting room on Sunday evening and Bettina looked anxious.

'They seemed satisfied with his progress. Obviously they're still concerned but there's very little they can do to improve the situation.'

'He looks terrible.'

Jenna nodded sadly. 'I know. It breaks my heart to see him. He puts such a good face on everything.'

'I think the fact that he's got you helps him enormously, but the deterioration since last time I saw him is shocking. Has the consultant given you any idea as to . . . oh, dear, as to how long he's got left?'

'They can't be specific. But I gather that they think it's a matter of months.'

'Well,' said Bettina, 'I think we should try and make this Christmas the best Gerry's ever had.'

They sat in silence staring into the fire.

Later that evening, Bettina went to say good night to Gerard. He was not in his room. The nurse told Bettina that he was in the library choosing something to read.

Bettina found Gerard sitting by a roaring fire engrossed in a book. She went and knelt next to him.

'What have you got there, Gerry?'

He looked down at her and smiled. 'I think it's yours, actually.' He showed her the cover.

'Yes, I bought it that night we went to see Jenna in it.'

'You were at drama school with the fellow that wrote it, weren't you?'

'Charlie Devereaux, yes.'

'What was he like?'

'One of the nicest men I've ever met. It was he who told me where I could find Jenna when you were so ill in Paris.'

Gerard nodded casually. 'Oh, really? How interesting. It's a superb piece of writing. I see it's dedicated to Jenna. Fond of her, was he?'

'Extremely. In fact, I think he's been obsessed with her since drama school, but she fell in love with you.'

'I think this scene is absolutely brilliant,' said Gerard. 'It's the part where Christina's real mother has managed to transfer her daughter's affection from the parents who adopted her to herself and then is told she's dying. Do you remember that scene, Bettina?' He stared down at her.

'Of course, Gerry. It's the most powerful scene in the play, but why . . . ?'

'When the mother stands alone on stage thinking how wrong she was to try and steal her daughter's love from the people who had loved her for all those years, and vows to make amends?'

'Yes, Gerry.'

'Good. Let me read it to you.' He started before she could object. 'It goes:

"I know now that I was wrong. That I did love her but my love was obsessive, blind to the feelings of Christina and the people who had loved her before me. My last wish is to give her the freedom to return to those whom she needs. Above all, I wish her to feel no guilt, for she has given herself unselfishly when I asked her to. And now it is her turn!"'

Gerard put the book on his lap. 'Isn't that beautiful, Bettina?'

'Yes, Gerry, it is.'

'Will you put this back on the shelf for me? I hope you don't mind, but I underlined that paragraph, and a couple of others.'

'Of course not. You can keep it if you like, Gerry.'

'No. You put it back on the shelf.'

Bettina did so. She went back and kissed him on his forehead.

Gerard grasped her hands. 'Thank you, sis, for everything. I love you very much, you know.'

'And I love you.'

'Just one other thing. Look after Jenna for me, won't you? She deserves happiness after what she's been through. You'll help her find it, won't you, Bettina?'

'Why, of course, Gerry. I'm sure we'll have a wonderful two days in London.'

Gerard nodded.

'Are you ready to go back to your room?'

'Yes.'

Bettina pushed him out of the library and into his bedroom. 'Now, take good care of yourself and I'll see you at Christmas along with the brood. Jenna will be along shortly. Good night, Gerry darling.'

'Goodbye, sis.'

He watched her as she walked from the room and fumbled in his pocket for a handkerchief.

'Hello, darling, how are you feeling?' Jenna was concerned, having just been told by Bettina that Gerard was acting slightly strangely. She touched his forehead and frowned. 'You're hot.'

'I'm fine, darling, absolutely fine.'

'I don't know whether it's a good idea for me to go to London tomorrow.'

'Oh, you must, darling. I'll be so upset if you don't. I booked those tickets especially for you and they were very expensive. Anyway, it's only one night and you must check that all is well with the baby.'

'Just as long as you promise to phone if there are any problems. I'll be back by Tuesday lunchtime.'

'Don't rush, sweetheart. Enjoy yourself.'

While the nurse lifted Gerard into bed, Jenna went to wash and changed into her nightgown. Then she climbed on to the bed and lay next to him. He put his arm round her and held her close.

The feel of her breast against his chest stirred the never-ending passion he felt for her. He gently traced the contour of her nipples against the silk of the nightgown and felt them respond as they hardened beneath his touch.

He turned her face up to him and kissed her gently, lifting her nightgown to reveal the small perfect female frame with the now noticeable bulge. He put his hand on it. It was new life and it was precious.

'I want to make love with you, Jenna,' he whispered into her sweet-smelling hair.

'Oh, darling, you know the doctor said . . .'

He put a finger to her lips. 'Sh, Jenna, he just said we should be careful.'

Gerard's fingers moved down to her silky mound. He felt her stiffen and he sighed as she took him in her hand and massaged and teased him until he was fully erect. Then she rose above him and put him inside her. She moved slowly. He reached out to touch her breasts and held on to them as she moved a little faster. He could hold it no longer.

'I love you, Jenna,' he cried out.

She lay for a moment on top of him, encased in his arms. Then she rolled over and settled herself in the crook of his arm.

'Oh, Jenna. Thank you for making my life so beautiful.' He kissed her hand. 'Just promise me one thing, darling. If you have any problems, tell Bettina. She loves you too and she'll help, no matter what the situation. Do you promise?'

Jenna heard the serious note in his voice. 'Why, of course darling, but I'll be back on Tuesday.'

'I know, my sweet. I just want you to remember that you can trust her. She takes my place when I'm not there to look after you. All right?'

He tipped her chin up with his fingers and kissed her nose.

'All right. Good night, darling.'

'Good night, my love. Sleep tight.'

'I'll miss you, Gerry.'

'And I you,' he murmured.

Dr Daniels looked faintly puzzled as he studied his notes.

'Is everything all right?' Jenna asked the frowning obstetrician.

'Oh, absolutely, Lady Langdale. I'm just a bit puzzled about something, that's all. Are you sure that you're only three months pregnant?'

'Well, yes, pretty sure. The doctor in Paris told me I was five weeks pregnant so the calculations have been worked out on that.'

'I'm sorry to tell you that the doctor in Paris has made an easy mistake. What I have just examined is an extremely healthy foetus that by my reckoning has under five months before wanting to make an entrance into the world. I'm sorry, Lady Langdale, but that is an eighteen-week old foetus you're carrying. Is that possible?'

'Yes, it's possible. But the doctor in Paris was –'

'It's a small baby, Lady Langdale. It would have been an easy mistake to make. But not now that the foetus is starting to form. This is probably why you've been feeling weary. You're halfway through your pregnancy. It's a good job you came to see me. We need to increase your calcium intake and you should start your antenatal . . .'

The words went in one ear and out the other.

She was having Charlie's baby, not Gerard's.

She thanked Dr Daniels, arranged another appointment, then went out to the reception room where Bettina was waiting for her.

'Everything all right, Jenna?' Bettina saw how pale she looked.

'Absolutely fine. The baby is in good health and so am I.'

'Come on, then. We'll go and have lunch at Harrods, then start on some serious Christmas shopping.'

Charlie's baby. Jenna thought about it at lunch and for the rest of the afternoon.

When they arrived back at Chester Square, Jenna said she felt a little tired and wanted to take a nap before going to the ballet.

She needed time to think.

74

GERARD SIGNED THE DOCUMENT with a flourish and breathed a sigh of relief.

'Well, Gerard, this is most unusual. With Jenna already pregnant, one would assume ... Well, naturally, if it was a girl, then the title would pass as a matter of course to ...'

Gerard held up his hand. 'David, please. My decision is made.'

'You're absolutely sure?'

'Absolutely. Thank you for coming. Now, if you will see yourself out, I would be grateful. Goodbye.'

'Goodbye Gerard. Take care of yourself.'

Gerard watched the puzzled solicitor walk out of the room. He felt better having made his decision. Of course, when the will was read, Jenna was likely to be upset. But he prayed that, as time progressed, she would understand what he had tried to do.

He wheeled himself over to the sideboard in the corner of the library. He uncorked the decanter and poured a measure of brandy into a glass. He threw it back in one.

There was nothing more he could do.

He had tried to organize things the best he could. To enable Jenna to go to the man whose child she was carrying without the restrictions of titles, shame or guilt. It was the least she deserved. He only hoped that the tracks he had laid would be picked up and followed.

He wrote a note for the nurse saying he did not want to be disturbed and pinned it on the bedroom door on his way out. He wheeled himself through the kitchen, out of the large back door and round to the stables.

The horses neighed gently as he passed them, giving each a gentle pat on the nose until he reached the last box.

The elegant black hunter recognized his master immediately. Gerard felt a lump form in his throat as he remembered the first day he had seen Jenna. He had been standing right here, grooming the very same horse now nuzzling into his hand. She had offered him her gloves.

He checked his watch. Half past three. Perfect.

Bob, the old groom who had been with the family since before Gerard was born, was mucking out a stable at the other end of the yard.

'Bob!' he called.

A young man named Stuart who helped Bob look after the horses came round the corner.

'Sorry, sir, Bob's a bit deaf these days. Shall I get him for you?'

'Yes, Stuart, I want to speak to both of you.'

He went to fetch Bob.

'Yes, m'lord, can I help you?'

Gerard took a deep breath. 'I hope so. I want you both to help me get on Sargeant here.'

'But, m'lord, do you think that's such a good idea, what with your health and the like?' Bob asked anxiously.

'Absolutely. I'm not a complete basket case, you know. There's no reason at all why I shouldn't take a gentle walk around the yard.'

Both men looked doubtful. 'If you say so, m'lord.'

'Right. I've thought about how you can help me on to Sargeant. Saddle him up and then take him into the barn where we store the bales of hay. There's a pulley system in there. It should be easy enough to lift me up and then lower me on to Sargeant's back. See what I mean?'

'Er, yes. We'll give it a go, m'lord, but I can't say I'm happy about it. Gawd knows what Lady Langdale will say if she finds out.'

'Well, there's no reason for Lady Langdale to find out, is there?' said Gerard as Bob pushed him towards the stable. 'Bob, you must be able to understand what it's like for me not being able to ride. Being stuck in this thing is most frustrating.'

'All right, m'lord. We'll see what we can do.'

While Stuart saddled Sargeant, Bob tied the pulley rope under Gerard's arms.

'Right. Hold Sargeant still, Stuart, and let's give it a go.'

Bob pulled gently. Gerard was slowly lifted up out of the wheelchair.

'Easy does it, Bob. Lower him now.'

Guided by Stuart, Gerard settled easily into the saddle.

'Brilliant. Good boy, Sargeant,' Gerard stroked his mane. The horse was standing still, held by Stuart. Frissons of pain were running up and down Gerard's back. He said nothing.

'Are you sure you're all right, m'lord?' Bob asked.

'Never better. Now, Stuart, lead Sargeant out into the yard.'

The horse's movements and the fact that his back was unsupported meant the pain was becoming intolerable. Gerard knew it was now or never.

'Right. I feel perfectly comfortable. I'm going to take Sargeant for a walk down to the church.'

'I'll come with you, m'lord. Make sure you don't get into trouble. And it's getting dark,' said Bob.

'No!' Gerard almost shouted the word. 'I'll be fine. Stop treating me like a cripple! Sargeant will look after me, won't you, my beauty?' He stroked the soft, silken mane. 'I'll only be twenty minutes or so. You both wait here to help me down when I get back.' He patted Sargeant's flank and before either of the men could object, he was out of the yard, heading in the direction of the church.

The two grooms shrugged nervously and went back to mucking out the stables.

Gerard walked the horse slowly across the fields in the direction of the church. Once he was out of sight of the stables, he turned Sargeant in the opposite direction and walked off again.

'Whoa, Sargeant.' Gerard pulled gently on the reins and the horse came to a stop.

Gerard looked around at the rolling green landscape. The light was fading fast.

It was time to bow out.

'I love you, Jenna. Please understand what I have done.'

He slapped Sargeant's flank with his whip. 'Giddy-up, boy!'

The horse set off at a canter across the fields.

An hour later Sargeant arrived back at the stables without his master.

75

GERARD WAS BURIED alongside his ancestors in the grounds of the church in which he had married not six weeks previously.

His grief-stricken sister and widow threw roses on to the coffin as it was lowered into the ground.

His mother was not present. She had suffered a stroke a day after hearing of her son's death.

There was a short obituary in *The Times*, recounting the tragic death of the newly married peer, who had taken a fatal fall while riding.

Both Jenna and Bettina were in shock. When they had arrived home from the ballet, Bettina's housekeeper told them that Henri had rung and they were needed at Langdale Hall immediately.

Bettina called her mother and came off the telephone looking white.

'Freddie, I'm afraid you're going to have to drive Jenna and me up to Yorkshire now. It seems Gerry decided to go for a ride on Sargeant. The horse came back, but Gerry's missing.'

They arrived at three in the morning to be told that Gerard had still not been found.

'I don't understand. What in God's name was Gerard thinking about? Why did he get on Sargeant? He knew his condition.' Bettina paced around the room, wringing her hands.

'I don't know, Bettina. Oh, God! I just don't know.' Jenna sat holding Henri's hand.

'The police who are conducting the search interviewed Bob and Stuart. They both swear that he was determined to ride and refused to let them accompany him when he left the yard,' said Freddie.

'If he was riding towards the church, then why haven't they found him yet? If only Bob and Stuart had raised the alarm sooner. God, this is hopeless! They should never have helped Gerry get on that horse.'

'Bettina, you can't blame them. Gerry must have ordered them to help him. And when Sargeant came back alone they immediately went to look for him. When they couldn't find any sign of him they called the police. Come on, now, he has probably just fallen off and is unable to get up because of his legs.'

'Yes, but a fall from Sargeant could well have killed him.'

The police found Gerard as the dawn was breaking. He was lying in a ditch four miles from the church. They brought his body back to the house.

'Why? After all he's suffered? I know he might not have had much longer, but to die like this seems so unfair after the past few months.' Bettina began to cry.

Somehow, they had made it through the next twenty-four hours. Then Henri collapsed in the kitchen and was rushed by ambulance to Harrogate hospital. Jenna and Bettina once again found themselves in an emergency ward.

'Is our family cursed, Jenna? What have we done to deserve all this tragedy?'

'I don't know, Bettina, I really don't.'

Gerard's funeral took place a week later, as soon as they knew Henri was out of danger.

Jenna went numbly through the burial and the gathering at Langdale Hall afterwards.

As the last mourner left, Bettina turned to Jenna. 'Thank God that's over! Only the reading of the will to go through, then we have to concentrate on getting Ma better. They say it never rains but it pours, don't they?'

Jenna nodded silently.

David arrived at eleven thirty the following morning. Bettina, Freddie and Jenna, who, apart from Henri, were apparently the only beneficiaries, filed silently into the library.

'Good morning to you all.' David kissed Jenna and Bettina. 'Now, I'll have to put my official hat on for the next half an hour while I read the will.' David looked concerned. 'I didn't mention this yesterday at the funeral, for obvious reasons, but I saw Gerard on the morning of his death. He telephoned me at my office in Harrogate and asked me to come over immediately to Langdale Hall. The relevance of this may become apparent as I read the will. Right.' David put his glasses on and opened the large vellum envelope. 'First, this will was made out and witnessed by myself and the housekeeper of, I believe, twenty-eight years' standing, on the morning of the twenty-sixth November, the date of Gerard's death. I can also assure you that he was quite specific, clear and adamant in respect of his requests.' David cleared his throat. 'I'll read the will straight through and then we'll go back and clarify any points you don't understand.'

He began and the three of them listened in silence.

Ten minutes later David finished.

No one knew what to say.

Eventually, Bettina spoke. 'Can you explain the part about the title? I don't quite understand that.'

'Gerard has petitioned the Queen for the title to go to you as his only other blood relative. When your eldest son comes of age it will pass to him.'

'What about Jenna's . . . his wife's baby?'

David shook his head. 'Believe me, Bettina, I too queried this. I'm sorry, but the instructions are clear and there is no mention of Jenna's baby.'

Bettina looked aghast. 'But that's crazy! I mean, it's his own child. Surely he would have wanted the title to pass to his son, if the baby is a boy?'

'Quite,' said David.

'And what about Freddie and me inheriting Langdale Hall? Surely Jenna and her child should live here until she, well, until she . . .'

'Yes, it's most odd, but I remember Gerard being quite adamant on that point. He said that under no circumstances did he want Jenna living here. He has, as I read, bequeathed her the house in Chelsea and a healthy allowance, as long as she does not contest the will.'

Bettina turned to a pale Jenna. 'I'm so sorry, darling. I just don't understand. Whatever it says about losing the house and the allowance, I think you should contest the will. Freddie and I will back you all the way, won't we, Freddie?'

'Absolutely, my dear.'

'I would add that you stand a very good chance of winning, Jenna,' said David.

Jenna shook her head slowly. 'No. If that's what Gerard wanted, then that's the way it is. I won't be contesting the will. Now, if you'll excuse me, I think I need some fresh air.'

She stood up and walked to the door. Once the door was closed behind her, she ran down the hall to the bathroom and was violently sick.

'Oh, God,' she moaned as she stood in a cold sweat, propped up against the bathroom wall.

Bettina and Freddie did not understand why Gerard had changed his will, but she did. It had been changed the day that Gerard had died. The day she had been to see the obstetrician. It was possible that Gerard had telephoned the doctor to see that everything was all right with the baby and been told by the obstetrician that she was over four instead of three months pregnant. Gerard had known that it wasn't his baby, so had immediately arranged to have her and the child cut out of his will.

Was that what had made Gerard get on that horse

and ride to his death? Had she provided the final agony?

She went and lay down on the bed she had shared with Gerard and closed her eyes. There was only one thing that was clear in her mind. She must leave immediately. Gerard wanted her out.

As she was packing some of her clothes into a suitcase, there was a knock on the door. 'Come in.'

Bettina entered. She came and sat on the end of the bed.

'How are you feeling, Jenna?'

'A little tired, that's all.'

'Look, please try not to worry about the will. I can't say I understand what was in Gerard's mind when he made this new will, but what I do know is that he loved you to distraction and would do nothing to hurt you.' She paused. 'Jenna, I hate to say this, but Gerry may not have been quite well when he made the will. Whatever, we're going to sort it out. And of course, this is your home for as long as you want it.'

'Thank you, Bettina. Listen, I hope you understand that I need some time alone to think. I'm going to go to the farmhouse in Leicestershire for a while. I need to be by myself.'

'Are you sure that's a good idea, darling? To be alone at a time like this?'

'Really, Bettina, I do need some time. I feel terribly confused.'

'If that's what you want, Jenna. I know how dreadful this must have been for you. We're going to Harrogate to visit Mother at the hospital. Why doesn't Stuart drive you to Leicester in the Bentley?'

'That would be very kind, Bettina.'

'Not kindness, Jenna. You are Lady Langdale. By rights all this, including the Bentley, ought to be yours.' Bettina kissed her. 'You'll come back for Christmas, won't you?'

'I'm not going to make any plans for now, Bettina.'

'Please keep in touch.'

'I will.'

Jenna waved goodbye to Stuart and walked back into the farmhouse. She shivered. The heating had been on for only two hours a day and the whole place needed a warm-through. She went into the sitting room and lit a log fire.

The house was spotless; Mrs Smeeton, the cleaning lady, had come in once a week to dust and hoover.

Jenna took the suitcases upstairs to her bedroom. The wardrobe was half-empty, with most of her business suits still in London.

One of Charlie's sweaters was lying neatly on a shelf. She pulled it out. She could still smell his distinctive aftershave. She closed her eyes and hugged the sweater to her.

All those beautiful times they had spent together. It was only a few months ago, but it felt like a lifetime.

She showered and went downstairs to make a sandwich. She went back into the sitting room and curled up in her favourite chair in front of the now roaring log fire.

Charlie was gone. Gerard was gone.

Only this time she wasn't alone.

She would have her baby.

Jenna spent a quiet weekend at the farmhouse. She ate and slept properly for the first time in weeks.

On Monday morning, she picked up the telephone and dialled Hilly's home number.

'Jenna! They told me when I phoned Langdale Hall you'd gone to the farmhouse. I tried calling all last night and I couldn't get a reply. I was just about to send out a search party.'

'Sorry, Hilly. I had an early night.'

'Are you all right? Bettina's been really worried about you.'

'Yes, I'm fine. I just wanted some time alone, that's all. After the death of Gerard and . . .' Her voice trailed off.

'I understand, Jenna. I really am so sorry.'

'I'm going to come up to London tomorrow. I think we need to discuss a few things. Can I buy you lunch?'

'Sure. It'll be good to see you, stranger.'

'I'll be at the shop at one. See you then.'

'Look forward to it. Bye, Jenna.'

'Bye.'

76

CHARLIE HAD learned of Gerard's death from a television news bulletin. In spite of everything, he felt terribly sorry for Jenna.

He wondered how she was. He couldn't help himself, he still cared. At least the play was keeping him busy. And there were a lot of other things on the boil. His agent had just had confirmation on the offer from Hollywood to write the screenplay of *Angel in Hell*. He was pushing to direct, too. His dream when he was with Jenna was to have her star in it . . . but that wasn't to be.

Hilly had phoned him a couple of times, trying to find out what had happened. He had been unforthcoming and she had taken the hint and left him alone.

He had three weeks until his play at the National closed. Then he would have to make a decision about his future.

'Now, tell me all, Jenna. I've been very patient, leaving you alone and not prying, but I want to know why you and Charlie were together one minute and the next you're flouncing down the aisle with someone else.'

Jenna sighed. 'Hilly. It's a very long story and a painful one, too. Would you mind if . . . ?'

'Okay, okay. I'm just being nosy. Charlie wouldn't say anything, either.'

Jenna wanted to ask Hilly if she'd seen him recently. 'I promise to tell you all one day, but not just now. What I really want to talk about is Milly. You don't know how guilty I've been feeling about leaving you in the lurch.'

'Really, Jenna, as I kept telling you on the phone, you shouldn't have worried. The business almost runs itself. Ari has been dealing with the financial side of things. He enjoys it and seems to be good at it. However, there has been a recent development that we need to discuss. Bloomingdale's in New York have offered us a concession.'

Hilly talked Jenna through the offer. It sounded worth investigating.

'Hilly, the reason I wanted to talk to you is that I see no reason why I can't come back to work immediately. Obviously I'm going to have to be careful and when the baby's born I'll need to take some maternity leave, but . . .'

'Jenna, you're Lady Langdale. I thought you had come to tell me that you were retiring gracefully and planned to live in that mansion in Yorkshire and await the birth of the heir. Surely you don't need to work now?'

'You're right, I don't. But as it happens, Langdale Hall did not come to me, although Gerard left me well provided for. Apart from anything else, I want to work. I'm only thirty-one. I don't think it's quite time for me to be thinking about retirement yet.'

'Jenna, please bear with me. I'm extremely confused. Of course Ari and I would love to see you back. What about when the baby is born?'

'I'll obviously have to take some time off. But there is such a thing as a nanny.'

'Yes, I suppose so.'

'Right. That's settled then. I'm going to live at the farmhouse. I feel comfortable there and I can go into the Leicester office every day just like I used to.'

'Mind you don't work too hard. How long before the baby makes its entrance?'

Jenna had thought about this and decided to stick to her original dates. 'Five months.'

'My God, you're huge, Jenna.'

'Yes.' She smiled. 'Huge.'

When Jenna arrived back home that night, she picked up the telephone and called Bettina.

'I do hope you understand why I want to stay here and go back to work. I feel it's healthier for myself and the baby to keep busy.'

'If that's really what you want, Jenna. I don't want you working too hard, though. We mothers-to-be must take care of ourselves.'

'You're pregnant again?'

'Yes. It was confirmed last week.'

'Oh, congratulations, Bettina!'

'Thank you. And Mother came out of hospital yesterday

so things are gradually getting a little better. Freddie and I are obviously going to stay up here for the time being. He's bringing the brood up tomorrow. Are you sure you're all right, Jenna?'

'Yes, I'm fine.'

'Please take care.'

'I will. Goodbye, Bettina.'

Bettina put down the telephone and went to tell Freddie that Jenna was staying in Leicester.

'Oh, Freddie, she shouldn't be alone at the moment. She must be going through hell. And I feel so helpless. I just don't understand why Gerry did it.' Bettina shook her head as Freddie took her into his arms. 'I just don't understand.'

'Well, darling, he must have had his reasons. His illness had not affected his senses. Gerard still had a very sharp mind.'

Bettina became more confused when she went to visit her obstetrician, Dr Daniels, in London the following day. After he had examined her, he pronounced her fit as a fiddle with no problems at all.

'And how is that delightful sister-in-law of yours? I heard about your brother. I am truly sorry. I hope Lady Langdale isn't taking it too hard.'

'She's being remarkable, considering.'

'I presumed that she didn't come to her last appointment due to the tragic circumstances. However, as she has less than four months to go, I really should see her again as soon as possible. We need to book her into the Lindo wing at St Mary's immediately.'

'I thought Jenna had five months to go. Surely the baby isn't due until the end of May?'

'No, I discussed the situation with Lady Langdale when she came to see me. The Paris doctor made a mistake. The baby is due in mid-April. I'm surprised she didn't tell you. Anyway, can you ask her to ring me to arrange an appointment?'

'Of course, Doctor. Thank you. I'll see you in a month's time.'

Bettina left the Harley Street house and walked down the road to John Lewis. She made her way to the coffee shop. As she sipped her cappuccino she did some calculations. If what Dr Daniels said was true, the baby would have been conceived in July. Jenna did not arrive in Paris until the middle of that month and Gerard did not wake from the coma until the end of it.

Gerard could not possibly be the father of Jenna's child.

Things began to slip into place.

Was it possible that Gerry had found out that the child was not his? Was that what the changing of the will was all about? No, surely Gerard, however upset he had been that the child was not his, would not want publicly to humiliate Jenna? And Jenna knew that the baby could not be his. That was why she was not contesting the will. She understood why it had been changed.

She wondered who the real father was. Who might know? Of course, Hilly, Jenna's business partner. She had spoken to her when Hilly had called Langdale Hall in search of Jenna and Bettina had jotted down her telephone number.

Bettina went to find a telephone box. She dialled Hilly's number, spoke to her briefly and went outside into Oxford Street to hail a taxi.

'Thank you so much for seeing me, Hilly. What would you like to drink?'

They had arranged to meet at a small wine bar near the boutique in Covent Garden. Bettina ordered them both white wine spritzers.

'What did you want to ask me, Bettina? I don't really know if I can help, but I'm concerned about Jenna. She shouldn't be living by herself while she's pregnant and after the shock of losing her husband.'

'Hilly, I know you're a very good friend of Jenna's and I need some help. When did Jenna tell you the baby was due?'

'Why, in May.'

'Mm. Jenna and I share the same obstetrician. I've just been to see him and he tells me the baby is due in April.'

Hilly looked puzzled. 'Why would Jenna tell me that?'

'The doctor who told her she was pregnant in Paris got it wrong. Jenna only found out herself a few weeks ago. I've been doing some calculations and there is no way it can be Gerard's baby.'

'Oh, my God! Then Charlie must be the father.'

There was a pause as Bettina stared at Hilly. 'Are you talking about Charlie Devereaux, the playwright?' Bettina whispered.

'One and the same. I've been trying to figure out what's happened for months. Two days before Jenna went off to Paris, she called me from Milan to tell me that she and Charlie were getting married. Oh, Bettina, they were so in love! To be honest, I couldn't believe it when I heard Jenna was marrying your brother. Are you okay, Bettina? You've gone awfully pale.'

'Sorry, I'm fine.' Bettina took a large gulp of her spritzer. 'Jenna didn't tell me about Charlie. I had no idea. It was Charlie who told me where to find her when I was looking for her. But he didn't say anything to suggest they were engaged.'

'I don't know what on earth has gone on. I spoke to Charlie a couple of times but he won't say a word. I wonder why Jenna didn't tell you,' said Hilly.

'Oh, I know the answer to that. Guilt. Good old Catholic guilt, of which Jenna has always had reams. She felt responsible for Gerard's accident and probably didn't want to upset anyone with the fact she was in love with another man. Very noble, but very foolish.'

'So you're saying Jenna married your brother out of guilt?'

'Something like that. I think she cared about Gerry enormously but . . .' Bettina was starting to remember something – something to do with Charlie that Gerard had mentioned the night before he died. 'Hilly, I have to go back to Yorkshire straight away. Please don't mention any of this to Jenna. I have to check something out.'

'Of course. I won't say a word. Just keep me posted, will you?'

'Yes. Thanks, Hilly. You've helped enormously. I'll call you. Bye.'

Hilly watched bemused as Bettina walked hastily from the wine bar.

Bettina arrived home four hours later and headed straight for the library. On the train journey to Harrogate she had put more of the pieces together.

'The play's the thing,' she muttered to herself as she pulled the slim volume out of the bookcase. Gerard had even asked her to put it on the shelf so she'd know exactly where to find it. She fumbled with the pages until she found the paragraph that Gerard had read to her that night. It had been underlined by his black fountain pen.

She read it to herself once more. '. . . last wish is to give her the freedom to return to those whom she needs. Above all, I wish her to feel no guilt . . . now it is her turn . . .'

Bettina slumped in a chair as tears poured down her cheeks. She cried for the brother whom she had misjudged so dreadfully, and the girl who had loved him enough to sacrifice her own happiness.

Now she understood. Gerard had changed the will to give Jenna the freedom to live her own life with the man whom she loved and who had fathered her child. Without the restrictions of having responsibilities such as Langdale Hall and the title that went with it. Gerard must have known that the child wasn't his. She remembered him asking her about Charlie and asking her to take care of Jenna, to see that she was all right. He had entrusted her future happiness to his sister.

Bettina sat there for a long time, deep in thought, wondering how to reunite Jenna and Charlie. Jenna needed to see for herself what Gerard wanted. Her guilt over Gerard's death would blind her to what he had tried to do.

There must be a way . . .

An hour later Bettina went to seek out Freddie. She poured two large brandies for them and sat him down in a comfortable chair in the small sitting room.

'Right, darling. I'm going to tell you a story. It sounds very strange, but as you will see, it's all true. Then I'm going to tell you how I plan to give it a happy ending . . .'

77

CHARLIE ARRIVED AT THE HOUSE in Chester Square at ten minutes to eight. When Bettina had phoned him three days ago, asking him to come and see her as she needed to talk to him about Jenna, he had wanted to say no. But he couldn't.

As he rang the bell, he berated himself for being so weak. The last thing he needed was this.

The door was opened by a maid.

'Good evening, Mr Devereaux. Please follow me. Lady Roddington is sorry, but she has been slightly delayed. Can I offer you a drink while you're waiting?'

'A gin and tonic would be very civilized, thank you.'

'Very good, sir.'

The maid left Charlie in the comfortable sitting room. A fire was burning in the grate. Charlie sat down in one of the large leather armchairs and picked up a paper.

The maid brought him the gin and tonic as the front doorbell rang again.

Jenna was not looking forward to the evening. She could hardly have refused when Bettina called her and insisted she come to see her at Chester Square. She had said it was urgent, something to do with Gerard. There was a week until Christmas and Milly was in one of its busiest periods. She would hear Bettina out and get straight back in the car and drive to Leicester.

Bettina's maid answered the door. 'Good evening, Lady Langdale. Please follow me. I'm afraid Lady Roddington has been delayed. Can I offer you a drink while you wait?'

'No, thank you.' Jenna followed the maid into the sitting room.

She could see that someone was sitting in the large leather chair reading *The Times*. The back of the chair was facing her and she could only see the top of a head. But that was enough. She knew whom that mop of curly hair belonged to.

He turned round.

The seconds ticked by as they stared at each other.

Finally, Charlie put down his paper and stood up.

'Hello, Jenna.'

'Hello, Charlie.'

'Something tells me that we've been set up.'

'Yes.'

There was another pause.

'Are you having a drink?'

'Well, I wasn't going to, but . . .'

'I'll have another one, too.' He rang the bell and the maid appeared once more.

'Another gin and tonic for me and . . . ?'

'A glass of white wine.'

'Thank you.' The maid left the room.

'Bettina asked you here?'

'Yes, ma'am.' Charlie nodded. 'Ostensibly to talk about you. Seems she thought a personal appearance might be better.'

Jenna sat down in the nearest chair. 'But how did Bettina know about . . .'

'. . . us. Well, I presumed you'd told her, because I didn't.' Charlie shrugged and sat down.

'I didn't tell her, so how on earth did she find out?'

'I haven't spoken to her since . . . Oh, well, it doesn't matter.'

The two of them lapsed into silence as the maid appeared with their drinks. She shuffled nervously. 'Lady Roddington has just called again and she says you're to start dinner without her.'

'Are we, indeed? And did Lady Roddington use telepathy to call you? I can see a telephone and I didn't hear it ring.'

The maid looked embarrassed and made a hasty exit.

Jenna took a sip of her drink. She felt the baby kick. She wondered if it was aware that it was in the presence of its father for the first time.

She felt confused. Why on earth had Bettina planned this? And how had she found out about . . . Hilly! It had to be Hilly. Jenna knew that they had spoken on the telephone a couple of times. But surely Bettina couldn't know about the baby, could she?

'I was sorry to hear of your husband's death.'

Jenna winced at the word 'husband'. After all, Charlie was the man who had once believed he would be that. She could take this no longer. She stood up.

'I'd better go.' She moved towards the door. 'Goodbye, Charlie.'

'Jenna, please!'

She turned round.

'Look, I'm sorry about the letter.'

'What? I didn't receive a letter from you. But I apologize for mine.'

Charlie looked confused. 'You didn't get my letter?'

'No.'

'Well, I didn't get yours, either.'

'Oh. I sent it to the mews house.'

'I'd probably moved out by the time it arrived. I sent yours to the Plaza Athenée.'

'I checked out the day after I spoke to you on the telephone.'

'Did you check in giving our house as your address?'

'Yes.'

Charlie smiled. 'Well, they're probably still sitting there on the mat, keeping each other company. I've still got the keys and the rent is being paid every month just in case you wanted to go back to it. Maybe we should go and read what we said to each other.'

'What did you say?'

'That I was leaving you.'

'So did I.'

'I see.' Charlie sighed. He scratched his chin thoughtfully. 'Well, I thought I'd deserted you and you thought you'd left me. This is almost good enough to be the plot of my next play!' He smiled at her.

'Why exactly did you leave me, Charlie?'

'Oh, that's rich from a woman who's just admitted she did the very same thing.' He chuckled. 'All right. I'll go first. When I spoke to you that night at the hotel, it sounded to me as if you were still very much in love with Gerard. When you didn't ring for three weeks I didn't want to stand in the way of true love and all that, so I wrote to you, packed my things and left.'

Jenna wanted to run into his arms and explain the position she had been placed in and tell him that he was the only man she had ever truly loved. But she couldn't. It was too late for all that now.

'Your turn to explain why you left me. Although you don't have to. Pretty obvious, as you married him a couple of months later.'

The conversation lapsed into silence once more.

'Look, Jenna, I apologize for that last remark. It was unnecessary. Obviously, having just asked you to marry me myself, I was a little peeved when you walked down the aisle with another man.'

'That's all right, Charlie. I deserved it.'

'When is the baby due?'

'May.'

'You look great. Pregnancy suits you.'

The maid entered once more. 'Have sir and madam decided whether or not they're staying for dinner, as I'm afraid it will be spoiled?'

Charlie looked questioningly at Jenna, then nodded. 'As sir has been got here under false pretences and has not eaten since ten o'clock this morning, yes, he will stay. What about madam?'

She shrugged.

'Please stay, Jenna, I'd like you to.'

'Okay.'

What harm could it do?

They followed the maid into the formal dining room. The table was set for two.

'I have a feeling that Bettina has no intention of showing up at all tonight,' said Charlie as he sat down. 'Have you any idea why she has done this, Jenna?'

Jenna did have an idea but she couldn't tell Charlie. 'No.'

'Oh, well. Might as well enjoy the grub now we're here.'

Charlie's brain was ticking. There had to be a reason why Bettina wanted them alone together.

Over dinner they managed to make small talk, the words so different from their feelings.

I love him so much, thought Jenna.

God, she's beautiful! I'll never stop feeling the way I do about her, thought Charlie.

The maid arrived with coffee and two brandies.

'Lady Roddington asked me to give you these with the coffee.' She placed a rectangular brown envelope by the side of both their brandy glasses.

Charlie raised an eyebrow. 'The plot thickens.' He opened the envelope and showed Jenna. 'A copy of *Angel in Hell*.'

'Same here.'

'And a note from Bettina. Shall I read it?'

Jenna nodded.

'It says, "Dear Charlie and Jenna. I hope you have enjoyed my little dinner party. I am sorry I could not attend. However, as an after-dinner entertainment, I thought it might be an idea to brush up on your play-reading skills. Please turn to page sixty-two and read the underlined passage, Jenna of course reading Christina."' Charlie looked up at her. 'What do you think? I mean, we've come this far. I suppose we might as well follow her little game through to the end.'

'All right.' Jenna shrugged. She opened her copy and turned to page sixty-two.

Charlie, being the author, knew exactly which scene they were about to read. This was not a game any more. This was vitally important. Before Jenna had time to glance at the page, he began reading the part of Christina's mother:

MOTHER: What is it, darling?
CHRISTINA: I wanted to ask you something.
MOTHER: Anything, darling, you know that.
Christina crosses left and clasps her hands nervously.
CHRISTINA: Well, now that I've found you, I want . . . I want . . . to ask you who my real father is.

Jenna almost dropped the script on the floor. Charlie pretended not to notice and continued reading.

MOTHER: Oh, darling, I . . .
She pauses and Christina crosses to her.
CHRISTINA: I think every child has a right to know who his . . . real parents are, and after searching for . . .

Jenna's voice trailed off. 'What on earth is Bettina playing at?'

Charlie already knew. 'Let's go on to the next part. What does your note from Bettina say?'

Jenna fumbled for the note inside her envelope.

'It says, "Dear Jenna, could you please turn to page ninety-four and read the lines that Gerard underlined the night before he died? It was his favourite passage from the play and when he read it to me that night, I knew that it was meant for you.

'"I hope you understand.

'"Love, Bettina."'

Jenna turned slowly to the passage. She started reading the words, quietly, hesitantly. Then her voice became louder as she read and understood the words that gave her the freedom to go to the man she loved.

She finished and stared at Charlie.

Then she burst into tears.

Charlie let her cry, dug in his pocket and proffered a handkerchief across the table. Jenna took it and wiped her eyes.

'Why do I constantly seem to find my hanky getting covered in your mascara?' he asked her gently. He stood up and walked round to her. He knelt beside her and took her small hands in his.

'The baby is mine, isn't it, Jenna?'

'Yes.'

'Do you understand what Bettina has tried to do tonight?'

'Yes.'

'Some man, that husband of yours! He must have loved you very much.'

'He did.'

'And you're going to follow his last wishes?'

'Yes.'

'Then I raise my glass and apologize for all the names I've called him in the past few months and thank him for giving you back to me.'

'But Charlie, you see, I felt so guilty when I . . .'

He put a finger to her lips. 'Hush, Jenna. Remember what you just read. "*I do not wish her to feel any guilt.*"' He emphasized each word. 'So, as part of your legacy from your late husband, that word is now officially banned from your vocabulary.'

Charlie pulled her close and kissed her. 'There, that wasn't so bad, was it? You didn't go up in a puff of smoke and get carted off to purgatory by the Devil, did you?'

Jenna smiled at him.

'I love you, Jenna.'

'And I love you, Charlie.'

78

THEY MOVED BACK into the mews house a day later. Charlie found the two letters on the mat and took great pleasure in burning them unopened in the grate in the sitting room.

Jenna was still in a daze.

'I don't know how to thank Bettina for what she's done.'

'You could start by saying you'll marry me and this time doing it. It's obviously what Bettina wants,' Charlie smiled.

'I suggest we have a quiet registry-office ceremony,' said Jenna.

'Absolutely not, my dear. You may have got your degree in marriage ceremonies, but I'm a novice and I intend to do it properly. There's a church I like not far from here in Notting Hill. We'll go and see the priest.' He smiled at her. 'Under the circumstances, we'd better do it as soon as possible. We don't want the little one making an appearance on our wedding day, now do we?'

Jenna shook her head. 'Do you think anyone does a nice range of maternity wedding dresses?'

Charlie kissed her gently on the cheek. 'I know you'll look more beautiful on that day than I've ever seen you.'

Christmas was just four days away. Jenna and Charlie had decided to spend it quietly together in London.

Charlie had called Bettina, who was in London doing some last-minute Christmas shopping. He asked her to meet him at lunchtime the following day before she drove back up to Langdale Hall. Jenna had telephoned Hilly saying she wanted to see her at the shop at noon.

That evening, Charlie took Jenna out to dinner.

'Jenna, my darling. There's something that I must discuss with you.' He looked serious.

'What is it, Charlie?'

'They've asked me to write the screenplay for *Angel in Hell*. If they like the screenplay, they've also agreed that I should be allowed to direct.'

'Who?'

'Warner Brothers. I want you to play Christina.'

'Charlie, that's very sweet of you, but I don't think it mentions anything in the script about Christina being pregnant.'

'Don't be silly, darling. It's going to take me at least six months to write the screenplay. It won't be going into production for at least another year. That will give you enough time to drop our sprog,' he gazed at her stomach proudly, 'and get your strength back. It will all be shot on location in London, so you won't even have to go anywhere near Hollywood if you don't want to.'

Jenna stared at him. 'Don't you think I'm a little too old to play Christina? And no one has heard of me for years. Surely they'll want a well-known name to play the part and . . .'

'Jenna, shut up! I'm the writer and director. That does give me a little control over the casting. And as for looking too old . . . my goodness, you haven't changed a bit since I first found you on that balcony.' He reached across the table for her hand. 'Please say yes, darling. It's what I've dreamed about for years.'

'What about my business?'

'I'm sure there's a way round that.' Charlie's eyes beseeched her. 'I'll be there beside you all the way, my love. You're not alone any more.'

'If you're sure I can do it.'

'I'm positive.'

'Okay.'

'Sweetheart, you've just made me the happiest man in London. I promise to protect you against all those bad memories. I'll have to pop over to Hollywood from time to time to discuss things. You don't have to come with me. You can stay in London. Whatever you want, my angel.'

Jenna looked at him.

'To be with you Charlie, wherever you are.'

Bettina was sitting at a table when Charlie arrived at Langan's Restaurant. She watched him nervously. Charlie sat down at the table.

'Hello, Bettina, Merry Christmas.'

'Merry Christmas, Charlie.'

'I suppose you want to know if your little charade worked.' Charlie's face was grave.

Bettina looked at the tablecloth. 'I'm sorry, Charlie. I just thought that if I could get the two of you together . . .' She sighed. 'Obviously I was wrong.'

'It was a cruel stunt to pull, Bettina. I thought Jenna was going to go into immediate labour when she saw me sitting there.'

'You spoke to her, then? Oh, Charlie, what happened?'

Charlie leisurely studied the wine list. 'Nothing much. We had a drink and something to eat and decided to get married. I don't think we should let you come to the wedding as a punishment for . . .'

'Charlie! You rotter! I thought it had all gone terribly wrong. Oh, I'm so happy!' Tears appeared in Bettina's eyes. 'Thank God!'

He reached across the table and put his hand on hers. 'Thank you, Bettina. Neither Jenna nor I know quite how to repay you for what you did.'

'Don't be silly. I did nothing. Gerry wanted Jenna to be with you, Charlie. I was only carrying out his wishes.'

'He was a good man, Bettina. Neither Jenna nor I will ever forget him.'

'No.' Bettina's eyes filled with sadness. 'Anyway, where is the bride-to-be?'

'She'll be here any minute. She went to see Hilly in Covent Garden at the boutique to discuss a few things first.'

As Charlie said this, he saw Jenna walk through the door with Hilly.

'Hello, darling.' Jenna kissed Charlie. 'Hello, Bettina.' Her eyes smiled her gratitude.

'I believe that you two know each other.' Charlie raised his eyebrows at Hilly and Bettina.

'Er, yes, we have met before. How are you, Hilly?'

'Just fine, Bettina, just fine.'

'Well, make room and let the two partners in crime sit next to each other.'

A waiter appeared with a bottle of champagne. He opened it and poured into four glasses.

'Right. Jenna and I have decided that, as you both seem to be so interested in our lives, you should have a more official footing. We would like you to be godparents.'

'We'd love to be, wouldn't we, Hilly?' said a delighted Bettina.

'I'd be honoured,' said Hilly.

'As I'm sure Jenna has told you, Hilly, she has agreed to star in my forthcoming blockbuster of a film, *Angel in Hell*. I know you'll be losing your business partner and I apologize, but I couldn't bear to see all that talent go to waste.'

'It's all worked out, Charlie. Ari will take over the general running of the company and I'll be promoting my assistant to take Ari's place. Jenna is staying with the company as a non-executive director, so she'll be in on any major decisions.'

'My goodness, there seems to be so much to celebrate,' said Bettina.

Charlie stood up. 'Absolutely. I would like to propose a toast. To you and Hilly, who have so successfully managed to saddle me with such a beautiful wife-to-be. Merry Christmas to you and thank you both so much.'

They raised their glasses, but Charlie continued. 'And also to Jenna, who has made my life hell ever since the day I found her looking like an unloved panda on the terrace of Frankie's flat! Long may she carry on, because . . .' He paused and looked at Jenna. 'I couldn't live without her. To us all!'

They lifted their glasses and drank to the future.

January 1990

Finale

'No one's gonna hurt you,
No one's gonna dare.
Others can desert you,
Not to worry, whistle . . .
I'll be there.'

STEPHEN SONDHEIM,
Sweeney Todd

79

THERE WAS ONE LAST THING Charlie had to do before he finally led the girl he loved to the altar to make her his for ever.

Two weeks before the wedding, he picked up the telephone and dialled the number.

'Jenna, the car's arrived,' shouted Hilly.

'I'll be down in a minute.'

She turned to the mirror and checked her reflection. She looked radiant in the beautiful ivory satin dress that Hilly had made for her. It was Edwardian in style, to match the frock coat that Charlie had insisted on wearing. Hilly had managed to design it so the heavy panels hanging from her waist and gathered in a huge bustle at the back skilfully concealed the bulge of her stomach.

Jenna did not feel guilty about walking down the aisle carrying Charlie's child; in fact, she liked the notion that their baby was going to be present on their special day.

She smiled at the image in the mirror and then brought the lace veil down over her face.

She stood for a second, thinking of all the people she had loved and lost. Frankie, whom she would never forget. Her mother, who had suffered so much, but who had cared in her own way. Matthew, who had been taken tragically young, and Gerard, who had so unselfishly made this day possible.

She remembered the words of that passage from *Angel in Hell*, 'above all, I want her to feel no guilt . . .'

She had suffered enough.

Now it was her turn for happiness.

They made the ten-minute drive to Notting Hill. She stepped out into the crisp January air and walked slowly up the short path to the church, followed by Bettina's four-year-old daughter Rosanna, who was carrying her train. Bettina was waiting for her just inside the entrance.

Freddie was talking to the vicar. It had been decided that he should give her away.

'My, don't you look beautiful!' He kissed her. 'Good luck, my dear. I'll see you later,' and he disappeared into the church.

'Freddie!' she shouted in her best stage whisper, but he had gone. She turned worriedly to Bettina, 'Where's he gone? He's meant to be giving me away.'

'I thought that was my job,' said the familiar voice.

Jenna turned and saw him standing behind her.

'You look absolutely beautiful, Jenna.'

The tears in his eyes mirrored her own.

He walked towards her and held out his arm. 'Shall we go?'

She nodded and put her arm through his.

'All right, Daddy, let's go.'

Daniel Duvall led Jenna proudly down the aisle to give away the daughter he had only just found.

EPILOGUE

From the *Daily Mail*, 26th March 1991

The above picture shows Mr and Mrs Devereaux and daughter (namely Charlie Devereaux, the writer and director, Jenna Shaw, the actress, and Francesca Joyce, their two-year-old) proudly clutching the three Oscars they won when the film *Angel in Hell*, which 'Mr' wrote and directed, and 'Mrs' starred in, swept the board at the ceremony last night. What a boost for Britain to see two of our own talents triumph!

Mr Devereaux has another film to be released in May, again starring his beautiful wife. It is rumoured that, as one of the film world's hottest properties, she was offered ten million dollars to do the new Steiner film, but I hear that they are soon to begin rehearsals for a new play, again starring 'her' and written by 'him'.

Jenna Shaw of course made her debut on the London stage in the original production of *Angel in Hell*, and whenever interviewed has said that her first love (after her husband and daughter, of course) is the stage.

I also hear that they may have tempted Daniel Duvall, who is a great personal friend of the couple, back on to the boards after twenty-five years.

What box office!

We wait with baited breath to hear more . . .

New from *Lucinda Edmonds* in hardback

Hidden Beauty is a gripping tale of forbidden passion, love and revenge. Sweeping across the ghettos of Europe to the super-rich enclaves of New York's Fifth Avenue, it traces the life of Leah Thompson, who rises from nowhere to take the modelling world by storm. But her fateful association with the Delancey family - Miranda, ruthlessly ambitious, and Miles, wild and mysterious - dominates her life, revealing devastating events from her past and shaping her future.

ISBN 0 671 71749 9
£14.99